THE
ACES

By FREDERICK OUGHTON

G. P. PUTNAM'S SONS

NEW YORK

For
*My Mother
and Judith*

Foreword

Research for this book was carried out on many different fronts in several countries. War diaries were discovered and examined, libraries pillaged, official documents read and notable archives visited.

The general aim of this book is twofold: to uncover the personalities of the men called "aces," and to show the reader the actual birth of courage and tenacity in wartime air power, a heritage now shared equally by the air forces of the world.

It has been necessary to quote liberally from many sources, most of them unpublished, but including some of the books mentioned in the Bibliography. Many of the books are out of print and virtually unobtainable. It is felt that some small service is being rendered by bringing these to light.

The word "ace" has been applied somewhat loosely by past writers, but the present author makes a careful selection, maintaining that only very special qualities and equally special combat behavior can combine to qualify a pilot for inclusion in that category.

I wish to extend my cordial thanks to all those who answered technical and historical questions and the many people who expressed a lively interest in this book while it was being written.

One of my most expert advisers, Wing Commander G. Constable Maxwell, M. C., D. F. C., A. F. C., died very suddenly on

December 18, 1959, while this book was being printed. A special debt of gratitude must be paid to his memory. Apart from being a famous fighter pilot of the First World War, he also played a vital part in the life of the Royal Air Force throughout the years, including 1941–45 when he commanded the night-fighter station at Ford, Sussex. Many of the valuable incidental touches which have brought the aces to life for us were drawn from his memories. He was an excellent, good-humored man whom the author will remember with warmth for his unstinting assistance and balanced counsel.

London. 1958–1960   FREDERICK OUGHTON

Contents

1. The Fledglings 11
2. The First Aces 26
3. Boelcke Heads the Wolf Pack 43
4. Richthofen's Flying Circus 51
5. The Laurels of Victory 69
6. The Death of Richthofen 87
7. Holland's Gift to Germany 94
8. The Menace of the Fokker 103
9. The Fortunes of War 116
10. Zeppelins Over London 127
11. A Fighting Chance 139
12. The Enigmatic Irishman 148
13. Love, Edward 155
14. The Year of Heroes 168
15. Death Before Twenty 184
16. The Order of St. George 194

17. The Last Patrol   203
18. Eschwege's Private War   213
19. Balloon Fever   224
20. Captain Willy Coppens   232
21. Bombing By Night   239
22. Alone Over Brussels   253
23. No Pilot Worth His Salt . . .   268
24. The Canadian Ace   283
25. Attack at Dawn   302
26. The Eccentric Russians   315
27. Skyborne Executioners   326
28. American Privateers   334
29. Hellbent for Hades   344
    Bibliography   355
    Appendix   358
    Index   380

Illustrations   *following page* 192

THE ACES

*There shall be wings! If the accomplishment
is not for me, 'tis for some other.*
—LEONARDO DA VINCI *(1452-1519)*

CHAPTER 1

The Fledglings

If the First World War did nothing else, it certainly developed a comradeship among the first aerial combatants, perhaps an understanding of the mentality of others and an entirely new factor which can only be likened to the spirit of the medieval knights. But they were not called knights as they dueled desperately over France and Belgium. They were called the Aces.

No two words could better sum up the first two months of the war than "mass carnage." More than a million members of the Allies were killed before November ended. The rest of the world failed to grasp exactly what was happening in this, the first of the modern conflicts. And all this without the effects of aerial warfare! Few airplanes were seen in the sky in the first months. The war in the mud was bad enough without the effects of light bombs dropped from the clouds.

Authorities on both sides watched with horror the mounting figures of casualties, and out of their horror came the strange belief that the new weapon of the flying machine might easily be a short cut to peace. Both sides believed this, English and German alike, yet neither seemed able to envisage a time when the flying machine would become the most lethal of all weapons. Among the first effects of bombing was a panic in the infantry. Companies of "PBI" (poor bloody infantry) spread out over the countryside on hearing the whirring of engines, believing that death could be sprayed down on them from the very clouds. Then Royal Flying Corps observers noticed that the Germans were getting used to the new hazard with greater facility than the Allies, and, indeed, were actually firing rifles and pistols at our low-flying fighters and bombers.

One of the drawbacks to the new aerial strategy was that pilots were unable to concentrate on bombing and bomb aiming and to control their machines at the same time, with the result that out of 141 raids only three could be said to have had any real effect on the enemy. This lack of coordination became a serious defect in Allied strategy until a new photographic unit was formed consisting of Major W. G. H. Salmond, Lieutenant J. T. C. Moore-Brabazon and Lieutenant C. D. M. Campbell. There was already a great interest in photography and many flying officers bought their own cameras. Unorthodox techniques came into being, and a number of amateurs took into the opening phase of the war all the paraphernalia for processing pictures.

There was a vogue for taking aerial pictures, printing them and arriving back at base with the finished prints ready for examination. This was later discouraged on the grounds that it might prove fatal for a pilot to concentrate too much on photography when he should be flying his machine. When cameras achieved official status, the manufacturer responsible for the equipment was the Thornton-Pickard Manufacturing Company. Their product, a clumsy plate camera, had to be held over the side of the banking aircraft, to which it was fastened with webbing. Among the first successful tests of the Thornton-Pickard camera was one in 1915, when the southern side of La Bassée Canal was photographed. Enlargements showed German emplacements situated at the exact points where the British planned to attack. On this kind of practical demonstration, it was obvious that the camera was going to be of the greatest possible use, but one of the main snags was lack of room in the aircraft itself. New machines had to be built with a rear second cockpit to house both operator and camera.

Aerial warfare was in a primitive stage at this time. Few pilots knew how to give chase, overtake and go into the attack. But in Germany training was becoming stringent. Eight hundred applications for places in the air force were made when forty openings were announced. Cross-country flying was compulsory. On one training flight alone, over a course of 1,000 miles, twenty-six machines started. The route became littered with the wreckage of crashed aircraft, but the German High Command refused to call it off. In that arduous trial some of Germany's best machines were to be seen, including the Luft-Verkehrs-Gesellschaft, a biplane; the Allgemeine Elektrizitäts-Gesellschaft, also a biplane, and the Aviatik. General military opinion has already said that the Germans placed too great an emphasis upon the development of machines and too little upon the men destined to form the nucleus of the air force. But at that time the Dutchman, Anthony Fokker, had not come forward. His entrance into the war drastically altered the entire course of events. His strange story will be told later.

Deeply disappointed over the hit-and-run tactics of its own pilots, the German General Staff issued an order that all pilots would now be supplied with hand grenades and firearms. It was, however, admitted after trials that the effect of pistol bullets upon an object moving at about fifty miles an hour was negligible. Hand grenades, on the other hand, were considered a great discovery, and many of the first Allied air casualties resulted from lucky throws which landed in cockpits to explode and totally destroyed machine and pilot. Many of the Allied pilots felt angry that the Germans were becoming adept at this deadly game. Cricket enthusiasts spread it about that lobbing grenades into German cockpits was as easy as "bowling out a blind man." There were many crazy attempts at flying above the German planes and dropping grenades down on their heads, but the Germans countered this by cultivating new steep-banking tactics.

In Great Britain this primitive, searching way of conducting a totally new kind of war with new weapons was the outcome of the formation of the Royal Flying Corps, constituted by royal warrant on April 13, 1912. Two days after the warrant appeared, an army order was published which outlined the new regulations. On May 13, the Air Battalion was absorbed by the RFC. The first squadrons were formed on a loose and elastic basis. All this was the outcome of a plea for concrete action contained in an official Minute which was circulated in January 1912. Winston Churchill joined others in emphasizing the necessity for early action.

At this time there were in Britain about eleven experienced pilots who became involved in the amorphous RFC. The Royal Navy was able to produce eight fliers. France already had 263 pilots. Other nations had more. It now fell to a committee to force the issue and get work started at the Central Flying School at Upavon Down, Salisbury Plain. Even with a "nursery" well established it was hard to decide which should take training precedence, the pilot or the mechanic. Pilots were expendable, but skilled mechanics were as valuable as diamonds. Fighting one of his early verbal battles, Churchill told the authorities that practically any man who showed any aptitude whatsoever should be admitted for training. Pilots ought to hold commissioned rank, even if they were the sons of grocers.

While the wordy battles dragged on, a subcommittee arrived at the decision that one wing of the RFC should be armed with seven flying squadrons, each squadron to be equipped with twelve aircraft. The commanding officer should have a machine to himself. All other machines should have two pilots with an identical number in the reserve. As a result of this establishment no less than 364 pilots would be needed, about 182 of whom should be commissioned, with the same number of noncommissioned officers.

With the scheme in operation there was a desperate bid to find suitable men. Some commanding officers seemed to believe that the new force was only a junk heap for rejects, the dross of all the rank and file. Those of a vindictive disposition tried to post their enemies to the RFC, thinking that it was some kind of suicide squad where men were polished off quickly and efficiently by the Germans. After continued shufflings and many squabbles, the RFC began to assemble. From it was formed the Naval Wing and the Military Wing. The Naval Wing was based at Eastchurch, where the Naval Flying School operated under the aegis of H.M.S. *Actaeon*. It was an experiment without parallel because naval flying was in less than its infancy. Trials with the new seaplanes had borne some sour fruit, and the records were full of details of crashes and duckings for pilots who wanted to take a chance.

At the Military Wing, on Salisbury Plain, the results looked better. A supplementary wing was set up at Aldershot and men trained as pilots graduated to the Central Flying School, where a subdivision to the Naval or Military wing operated. By this means it was possible to give pilots courses in naval tactics and allied subjects likely to be of use to them later. Pilots intended for the Military Wing were more highly trained and their education included a conditioning for battle flying over France and Belgium.

A new race of aviators began to appear, men capable of instant concentration and action, men with a new fatalistic outlook on life, men who could weld themselves to their machines so that it appeared as if the machine was itself doing the thinking. There was, too, the solitary life of the flying man and his independence in action, for in those days ground-to-aircraft radio was in such an embryonic state that the pilot had to rely upon himself. Tactics, too, required a new mentality. It was all too easy to slip away from a fight. The early squadrons were quickly depleted when it was found that the basic instinct to run was manifest. It took time to instill into the pilots that the airplane was itself a weapon and should be used as such.

Finding the actual training bases was far from easy, placed as they were miles from anywhere, usually in a collection of derelict huts. In these stood a motley collection of aircraft mustered from all parts of the country, some of them already veterans and showing signs of wear and tear in the hands of young pilots. The would-be fliers mustered to take turns in the few dual-control aircraft. It was a lengthy business, involving a lot of hanging about and waiting, and in this period much of the now famous air force slang was born.

Every morning, if the weather was right, one of the dual-control planes was lifted from its resting place in the shed and tugged out onto the turf. Serious deliberation about the direction of the wind and the strength of gusts prevented immediate take-off. Many planes were smashed because of hasty action. Since there was a shortage of dependable aircraft, no risks could be taken. Many of the new recruits found it hard to understand why an airplane must take off straight into the wind. It seemed so much more sensible to take off downwind to gain maximum speed. Some of the early RFC fliers actually tried to do this and went to the hospital or to premature graves. Most of the first training aircraft were Maurice Farman biplanes, called "Longhorns" owing to outriggers fixed to the forward elevators. There was also the "Shorthorn," minus outriggers and considered pretty dangerous for a beginner to fly. At first appearance the Farman biplanes were unbelievably complex, with a tangle of struts and wires into which the would-be aviator had to lower himself. Once inside, he had to try and make sense of the controls before the Renault engine—an eight-cylinder, air-cooled job which could be relied upon in most emergencies— was switched on and revved up. Ticking over, the Renault gave a reassuring sound.

Instructor and pupil sat in the bath-shaped nacelle from which they could signal to the waiting mechanic to pull the wheel chocks away before the great leap into the air. When maximum ground speed was obtained, the Farman could be lifted into the air with a grace not seen in modern aviation. In those days a large amount of human skill was needed to make a perfect take-off. There was an air of the miraculous about the event which few veterans ever forgot.

On the eve of war the British training schools progressed as fast as they could, coping not only with the strange collection of machines at their disposal but also with the oddities of the characters who came from the army and Royal Navy to be made into fliers. Many of these men were about eighteen, just out of school; others were getting on in years, toward twenty-one. To them came the first thrill of reaching a height of 5,000 feet, the maximum ceiling for a training aircraft. To achieve this the air-craft often had to be lightened, so pilot and pupil wore very little, just a jacket, shirt and jeans. Sometimes they left even their boots behind and flew in stocking feet in order to get the best out of the aircraft.

In those days the first indication of the typical air force character and spirit was growing fast. When pupil pilots became philosophical about sudden death in equally sudden crashes, the legend en-larged. They even sang about it:

The young aviator lay dying as 'neath the wreckage he lay;
To the Ak Emmas around him assembled, these last parting
    words did he say:
"Take the cylinder out of my kidney, the connecting rod out of
    my brain,
From the small of my back take the crankshaft, and assemble
    the engine again!"

It was very apt when applied to pupils who had only the vaguest idea how to handle their machines. Some approached the landing strip too fast, bounced off the turf to a hundred feet or so and, if they were astute, gunned their engines to a maximum until the aircraft lifted toward the clouds again. One student did this no less than eight times until his undercarriage was a shattered tangle, but finally managed to make a good crash landing. The system of writing off smashed aircraft was avoided as much as possible, thanks to the efforts of the mechanics. Despite this, the rate of destruction, especially among Americans who later joined the RFC, was alarmingly high. Until administrative matters were clarified, non-English students came under the jurisdiction of their own governments, who were barely engaged in the conflict.

At Hounslow flying training school the Americans were ordered to give a demonstration of aerobatics, but their English instructors refused to fly with them because it was too risky. On another occasion the Americans, determined to make a big impression, took off and started to perform a series of loops. The mainplane of one machine buckled and fell away just at the zenith of a loop and the pilot was killed instantly. Because of this accident the Americans at Hounslow were grounded for one month until the question of administration was arranged and some agreement between the British and American governments reached. As a result, hard feelings existed between Americans and British, and for a time the Americans seemed to believe that the British would kill off more of them than the Kaiser's air force. In his diary one American summed up the muddle in a passage: "But what can you expect when they promote the jackasses on seniority and put men in charge of important technical affairs just because they have spent their lives doing infantry drill in the Philippines and transferred to the aviation section a week ago to get a soft berth and more pay? Why should they worry about their mistakes? They aren't the ones that get killed. An order from the adjutant general can't make a pilot out of a quartermaster."

The later infiltration of Americans caused more than resentment. These men were more adept at crashing aircraft than the British and there was now a growing shortage. American pupils who had done preliminary training in their own country with Curtiss aircraft found it very hard to get used to the Avro and the British conception of battle flying tactics. Boredom increased, but the supply of available training planes did not. With the number of crashes and a shortage of skilled mechanics, there was a growing shortage of dual-control planes. The number of ground classes had to be increased to occupy time.

Men eager to become airborne had to sit on hard benches and accept hours of tedious theoretical instruction about gunnery and other subjects. As more planes became available the flying training schools were once again up in the air. By this time many men were feeling at home in the clouds, though some still suffered from painful bouts of air sickness, especially when they were required to take their machines up to several thousand feet and then let them fall in a long dizzy spin toward the earth before righting them. Some of the new factory-made machines reached an altitude of 10,000 feet or more, but the penalty was a dangerous ice formation on the wings. To many pilots this was the first experience of the real exhilaration of flying, with the sky showing a new blue through the clouds. At this height visibility was easily 100 miles. In such poetic moments, with his machine working to perfection, the pilot still had to keep one eye on reality.

Accidents happened every day, but no student pilot ever got hardened to the sight of death. At one station pilots in training were horrified to see two Avros collide at about 3,000 feet, right over the airfield. Crumbling, they fluttered to earth in a deceptively slow movement, their wings locked while feathers of flame and smoke shot out of the mass. One man escaped with his life but the other pilot was burned to a cinder. Accidents became more plentiful when some trainees were put on the high-speed Spads, "Easy to fly but dangerous as hell," one man observed. The danger of the Spad did not prevent many young pilots from carrying out mock strafing over their own airfields. One man flew a Spad almost at ground level, herding a class of scared gunnery students from one corner of the field to the other, then had his engine stall on him. He managed to pancake in the CO's kitchen garden and was quickly posted to France as proficient. The Spad, opined the authorities, would be an asset over France, so training was intensified. Death was also intensified. Flying over Hertfordshire, a pupil lost control and killed himself in a field at Radlett. He was found embedded in the soil with a broken neck. Nobody could discover exactly what had happened, so the machine was taken back to the workshops, rebuilt and put back in commission.

Many of these rebuilt Spads bore an evil reputation and elaborate excuses to avoid flying them were concocted by students.

The death rate went up and up. Two students were killed instantly when their machines, a Pup and an Avro, collided over Hounslow. The Pup rammed the Avro, ripping out the mid-section, and both planes swept to earth with their pilots dead at the controls. Another student had a horrifying experience before being killed. He was in the second seat when his instructor fell out of the cockpit during aerobatics. As the machine leveled out, the student pulled himself up and tried to stretch across the partition in a wind that tried to tear him loose. He must have been within an inch of touching the control column when the aircraft went into a steep dive and hit a field, killing him instantly. His body was found spread-eagled across the fuselage.

Among the causes of many accidents was the natural tendency on the part of fledgling pilots to show off. It was hard to instill into the new men a feeling for the necessity of iron control at all times, the shunning of what one writer has called "the rubbish of popular applause." A new kind of mentality was needed and it was a long time before the heads of the RFC could even define it. Many men felt that the derring-do of the new service deserved far more acclaim than it got, tucked away as it was from the public gaze on wind-swept airfields and in training camps which often consisted only of some shabby wooden huts purloined from the army. But as training progressed and accidents became more frequent, men began to realize that this was more than a new toy; piloting a plane was serious business. This became even more obvious after the death of Captain Eustace Broke Loraine.

Loraine was the great-grandson of the famous admiral, Sir Philip Broke, commander of H.M.S. *Shannon* which battled outside New York in 1813 and compelled the surrender of the American frigate *Chesapeake*.

Loraine entered the RFC from the Grenadier Guards and quickly qualified as a pilot. He was one of the first to demonstrate the daring deeds which could be carried out in the air, and he was worshiped by the men. He was flying in a fast Nieuport with Staff Sergeant Wilson when he lost control of the machine and nosedived into the earth from a height of only 400 feet.

Two other deaths which made an impact on the men were those

of Captain Patrick Hamilton and Lieutenant A. Wyness-Stuart. They were on a reconnaissance flight in a 100-hp Deperdussin when it spun into the earth at Hitchin, Hertfordshire, killing both men instantly. A few days later Lieutenant E. Hotchkiss and Lieutenant C. A. Bettington were killed when their 80-hp Bristol monoplane crashed near Oxford.

These and similar accidents led to an investigation into and the subsequent banning of the monoplane as an RFC machine. Thus began a new age in aviation, the age of the biplane. Yet even this was no panacea to a danger which must always exist so long as men fly, the danger of human fallibility. Soon after the introduction of the biplane three major accidents occurred in which Lieutenant H. F. Treeby, flying a Farman, Captain C. P. Downer a B.E., and Major G. C. Merrick a Short biplane were killed. It was the authorities who had such great faith in the biplane.

Later, when machines were more plentiful, there still remained the problem of recruiting men to the RFC. It was no use publishing pamphlets and advertisements because these did nothing to give men the real thrill of flying. As a stunt, two young officers, Lieutenant R. Cholmondley and Lieutenant G. I. Carmichael obtained permission to take their machines on a recruiting tour. They decided on Colchester as a likely place, and in July 1913 landed there to invite any candidates to take flights and experience the thrill of flying. Their efforts resulted in a substantial increase in the number of men willing to enlist. Among the first applicants was W. T. J. McCudden, brother of the man who later shot down more than fifty German machines.

These were stirring times. They brought forth the initiative of men like Major C. J. Burke DSO, who transferred to the RFC from the Royal Irish Regiment. When the RFC was formed he commanded No. 2 Squadron at Montrose, Scotland. Burke was a man with little time for paper work. Everything must function, including his men, and when he found that no appropriation could be given to buy factory-made planes, he designed a twin-seater tractor biplane, using parts taken from a Voisin machine and a 60-hp Wolseley engine which had originally belonged to the army, having been presented to one of the regiments by the Duke of Westminster. Burke's handiwork resulted in the creation, almost out of scrap, of a machine which put up a superb performance.

In its later years the same airplane became something of a mascot.

In his diary Burke wrote: "In practice a man cannot always be on the job that will be given him on active service, but he should be trained with that in view, and every other employment must be regarded as temporary and a side issue. Further, though barracks must be kept spotlessly clean, this work must be done by the minimum number of men, in order to swell the numbers of those available for technical work and instruction." To Burke the RFC meant machines flying in the air piloted by men who thought of nothing else but flying.

Some of the first night-flying exercises had been carried out by Burke's squadron in 1912. Men and machines spent a month at Douai in France, studying production methods at the Breguet plant. Several officers decided to fly back to squadron headquarters at Montrose. Lacking navigational aids, some were forced down over England. Lieutenant Longcroft came down at Littlemore and begged a bed for the night at a place which he took to be the local hospital. After a comfortable night he wakened to find that it was the lunatic asylum. Other long-distance night and day flights by No. 2 Squadron about this time included a visit to Knavesmire racecourse where the new heroes of the air were besieged by hundreds of small boys, all demanding to know how they, too, could become pilots. One of the chief difficulties about cross-country flying was that map reading was so difficult. Machines often landed to ask the way and promptly got lost again.

At another Scottish station, Ayr, the atmosphere was not very congenial. This was a school of aerial warfare, and regular displays were put on for visiting brass hats. The CO was Colonel Rees, himself a skilled pilot who enjoyed taking part in the circus. On one occasion he ordered all instructors to fly their Camels in an elaborate display of tactics and aerobatics. This went off very well, and Rees then told his students to take off and follow the same formations. Trying to follow suit, one man was killed.

Also at Ayr a whole series of terrible accidents occurred, including one when Nathan, a pilot, was killed after the wings of his machine broke off at 5,000 feet. The machine came down on the top of a three-story building, destroying the top floor and crashing through into the basement where Nathan's body had to be dug out.

Other accidents at Ayr included the collision of a Camel with a tall chimney, but the pilot lived to fly again. A few days later an aircraft stalled and fell on top of an empty building. This looked so spectacular that the pilot's comrades pleaded with him to climb back into the machine again so that they could take photographs. He was just about in position when the machine began to slip and he went down to the ground with the heavy engine on top of him. His arm was skinned but he was able to start flying again a few days later.

In view of the boredom and the thrills which came to every man in the early days of the Air Battalion and the RFC, it is surprising to note that only ten in every hundred trainee pilots lost their nerve and quit. Apart from those who were temperamentally unsuited to meet all the requirements, two kinds of men existed in the flying schools, according to Captain Charman, an officer who had a lot to do with recruits.

"There are two distinct types of pilots who become successful pilots: the man with the natural aptitude for flying, and the other with the bulldog tenacity of purpose that causes him to stick the flying game out, despite crashes of the worst description; the sort of fellow who always comes out of the aerial debris smiling. They are the keenest pupils, being the first on the aerodrome in the morning and the last to leave at night, and invariably fret about the mess on non-flying days, watching the sky from the windows at frequent intervals for a sign of the rain clearing up. I confess that I would sooner teach the first type, for he takes to the air like the proverbial duck to water, generally getting off on his first solo with only a few hours' dual instruction. . . ."

Charman was the man who taught one of the first aces, Mick Mannock, to fly. Of Mannock he said: "He came to me, at Hendon, in 1916, a raw green Hun (as we call the flying pupils under instruction) from Reading. I do not know, but he seemed not to have the slightest conception of an airplane. To do him justice, there were a few wires which he did not loosen in climbing into the cockpit, but then the machine, a Henri Farman (or Rumpty as they were commonly known), was at all times hard to get into. He finally managed to get into the pupil's seat, and we took off the ground. Mannock, unlike many pupils, instead of jamming the rudder and seizing the joystick in a Herculean grip, looked over the side of the airplane at the earth, which was dropping rapidly away from him, with an expression which betrayed the mildest interest. I liked him immensely from that moment. He made his solo flight with but a few hours' instruction, for he seemed to master the rudiments of flying with his first hour in the air, and from then on threw the machine about as he pleased."

Behind the flying school were the officers. Most came from army regiments, many of them without even having seen an airplane before and with only a vague idea of what they were supposed to be doing. They, and other officers, were immediately put through intensive courses which embraced balloons, observation and general station administration.

While the pilots were being trained, ground staff was assembling under a system of general recruitment. The range of trades was wide, and included fitters, mechanics, electricians, drillers, drivers, cooks, pattern makers, dynamo specialists and even sailmakers, for the fabric of many an aircraft fuselage was by now in dire need of repair.

The development of aerial radio was carried out not by the RFC but by the Royal Engineers, though perfection was a long time coming. As late as the Mons retreat in 1917 no proper means of radio communication existed, but after the disaster the majority of machines were fitted with receivers, thanks to extensive work not only within the military field but at the universities. The first sets were installed in machines of the Naval Wing, and experiments over various distances were carried out by Lieutenant R. Fitzmaurice in conjunction with H.M.S. *Actaeon*. After a great success with the experiments, Fitzmaurice was posted to Farnborough, where he was placed in charge of the *Gamma* airship during army maneuvers. On the "attacking" side, Captain Lefroy was in charge of the *Delta* airship. Both radio sets were very amateurish, built out of odds and ends and regarded as sidelines to the object of the exercise. *Delta*'s engines failed over London, and Captain Lefroy tapped out a desperate SOS, the first to be sent by an airship. He did not for a moment believe that it would be heard, but it was picked up throughout southern England. This was sufficient to demonstrate the advisability of putting the radio at the head of the list of aerial requirements, and from that time on communication by radio was recognized as a vital part of warfare.

In France, traditional home of aviation, it was soon known that every airplane flying in 1914 would be on the way to becoming totally obsolete within the year. In the meantime training on all standard types continued, outpacing British progress. The backbone of training was held by the Blériot monoplane, an adaptation of the machine in which Louis Blériot crossed the Strait of Dover and won the *Daily Mail* £1,000 prize. There, too, a school of would-be aces was becoming apparent. The average age of pilots in training in France in 1914 was twenty. Among pupil-pilots were Pegoud, the man who invented and introduced the aerial loop as a part of aerial strategy, Roland Garros, Gustav Hamel, Graham D. Gilmore, all of whom had become suddenly prominent in aviation circles during 1913, at the time when Blériot's monoplane demonstrated its capacity for hard work and endurance. Standard training had to be carried out in these planes, each of which was equipped with an 80-hp Gnome rotary engine, giving a top speed of 66 mph. Handling of the Blériot was said to be easier than the British planes because the French model possessed wing warping, not ailerons. Also, the mainplane was strengthened with wooden spars and there was an open fuselage behind the nacelle, later called the cockpit. Voisin and Farman biplanes were also in regular use in France.

By August 1914 the hard core of military minds and military opinion believed that aircraft could be very useful, but not as fighting instruments, only as toys of psychological warfare. They frightened the enemy as they zoomed down out of the skies and this was deemed to be their sole use. As far as France was concerned, said the older school of strategists, the airplane was useful if it had a noisy engine and could fly low over the enemy heads, encouraging a retreat, harrying them and becoming a nuisance. Of course, if it were possible to drop a small bomb or two, so much the better, but a loud engine counted for so much more than actual destruction.

Defying this point of view, French flying schools pressed on with the training of combat pilots. The system differed from the British pattern, where an effort was not being made to form a *corps élite* of fliers. Encouraged by the offer of something unique in warfare, many French gentlemen joined private flying schools, where they took lessons in handling planes before joining what amounted to the nucleus of the French air force. Here they merged with the professional pilots and ground crews at Pau, eight miles from Paris, where four main camps and a maintenance section comprised the station headquarters. Each section was named after an aviation pioneer. Pau was famous for its thoroughness in training pilots to service their own machines, a wise precaution as it turned out, for many pilots later had to make forced landings behind the German lines and some were able to take off before being captured, thanks to an ability to remedy a minor defect. After gaining proficiency and passing a series of examinations, graduated pilots were sent to Chartres, the cathedral town, where Maurice Farman biplanes were used to impart advanced knowledge. After the period at Chartres, the aviator was passed in the grade of *pilote aviateur,* remaining there pending a posting to a squadron in the field.

Surprisingly, the Germans placed greater store in the Uhlan cavalry units than in the use of airplanes in warfare. In 1910 a flying school was opened at Doberitz, west of Berlin, and in 1911 two more schools were established, one at Metz and the other at Merseburg. Two years later, in 1913, the German Air Service was enlarged to embrace five Luftschiffe *Bataillonen.* Each of these contained four companies of balloon and airship technicians and four battalions of flying-machine personnel. Controlling these were two bodies, the *Inspektion der Luftschiffetruppe* and *Inspektion der Fliegertruppe.* One of the most incredible administrative blunders occurred when the ultimate authority was vested in the Commander of Railways and Transport. In charge of the field was a Chief of Field Aviation Service on the General Headquarters Staff. Each army then received a staff officer, *Stabsoffizier der Flieger,* who was responsible for all individual operations within that army. Teaching units were set up within the commands, including Flieger-Ersatz-Abteilung Nr. 7 (FEA7), Cologne. It was to become one of the most famous centers, for Manfred Freiherr von Richthofen, the "Red Baron," trained there as an observer.

The pick of the nations' young men were now airborne in the newly discovered kingdom of the sky, where the broad blue acres stretched out in glorious immensity—an open invitation to fly and to fight.

CHAPTER

2

The First Aces

World War I was a Prussian war, organized with Prussian thoroughness, with a set of predetermined intentions and a goal of total victory. Those who want to gild the noxious lily and claim that there was something "sporting" about it are misguided. Apart from the famous Christmas Day incident, when German and Allied soldiers fraternized between the trenches, the only sporting instinct was to be found in the air, and even that was a deadly sport with a blood-spattered code all its own, the trophy being the wreckage of shot-down aircraft and young men maimed or destroyed.

Out of it came the brave legends, stories of courage and daring which stemmed from times when pilots were forced into the wide corners of the skies in an attempt to save their own lives, the hungry flames belching out of blazing engines and licking at their chests and faces. The legends kept on growing. Richthofen, for instance, was almost a god, and both the British and Germans idolized him beyond reason. He was supposed to be unsurpassable as a combat pilot and over the years has become an international hero loaded with laurel wreaths and eulogies. Between the wars the French air force organized a parade to honor his memory.

In Germany itself the superman legend was revived in newspapers and radio programs. But Richthofen was perhaps no greater than the others.

One of the early aces hid his identity behind the title, "The Mad Major," but he was, in fact, Captain A. A. B. Thomson of No. 16 Squadron. Tall and with a spare figure which looked undernourished, this man was stationed at La Gorgue airfield, not far from Lestrem, in 1915. In that same year the legend of the Mad Major, inventor of strafing, came into being when a lone machine was seen to leave La Gorgue on independent dawn sorties to strafe the German front line. The origin of the title came about when nearby Allied troops saw Thomson trying out strafing strategy, skimming along only a few feet from the ground, popping away with a revolver and other armament.

Thomson waged a one-man war. He was a scholarly man who kept to himself, rarely explaining his motives or even discussing the progress of the war. When first he formulated the idea of the ground-level harrying of infantry, he did not mention it to anybody else, but obtained permission to take his machine over certain parts of the German sector. Permission was given by his superiors, who were under the impression that he wanted to carry out routine reconnaissance. It was not until later that his hair-raising habit of flying at very low levels was noticed and reported and he was asked to desist. He agreed, but next day went and did exactly the same thing again. Called to account for his actions, he said: "My machine was out of control. It wouldn't rise at all. I'm awfully sorry, gentlemen." This satisfied his officers until he was found doing the same thing again, this time during an organized raid. His technique was breath-taking. From above, it looked as though he would crash at any moment, but he never did.

The Germans had ample if uncomfortable opportunity to study Thomson's methods, but failed to do so. Some authorities believe that if the Germans had adopted the idea of strafing, the 1918 retreat of the Allied armies would have been a total disaster, leading to victory for the Germans. Bunched together as they plowed through the impeding mud, Allied soldiers would have made an ideal target for fast low-flying machines.

Thomson had all the cool bravery of the typical ace. His dawn missions were carried out without any assistance or support what-

soever. His machine, a BE2, was always serviced the previous
night and left in position. Thomson himself had a few drinks in
the mess and chatted about unwarlike subjects with other pilots
before turning in. He found a room of his own in a ruined house
and brought to No. 16 Squadron several boxes of books which
he was now reading slowly and thoroughly. His favorite subject
was mythology; this perhaps provided him with the philosophy
which took him so stoically through the war.

The arena of the First World War is often described as being
gray and desolate, but there were long periods of wonderful
weather when the blinding sunshine was both a hindrance and a
help to pilots. For those who specialized in long dives before
dropping light-caliber bombs on the German artillery, the sun was
an ally. It also provided a cover for escape, and the fast-thinking
pilot could always fly straight into its rays, probably dazzling himself in the process but at least being sure that ground gunners would
not be able to take accurate aim at his machine.

Thomson enjoyed the summer months after the long weeks of
winter when clothing was perpetually damp and the soil stuck to
one's boots, making walking an intolerable job as compared with
flying. His gait was that of a thinking man. Those who saw him
moving toward his machine saw a long thin figure holding an
open book, trying to finish the page before climbing into the cockpit. The waiting mechanic saluted and helped him up, taking the
book and later returning it to Thomson's private library.

"Good morning to you, sir," the mechanic saluted him.

"Morning. It's not too bad. . . ." Thomson ran an eye over the
BE2, then surveyed the short length of airfield bordered with other
machines. He squirmed down into the narrow seat, tucking his
cushion under him. He was a man who liked his comfort, even if he
did have to skim through the jaws of death within the next hour. He
leaned out. "I say, was she patched up yesterday?"

They said that Thomson could convert a complete aircraft into
a total sieve within ten minutes, given that amount of flying time
over the German lines. Service crews spent hours pasting patches
over all the bullet holes, wondering how Thomson remained alive.
His instrument panel had to be replaced now and then after German
bullets smashed the delicate dials, and it was not uncommon for
him to return home with shreds of torn fuselage flapping like

triumphant banners. He never seemed to take much notice of danger. His only concern was the engine itself, and it was believed that the Mad Major could pilot an engine alone over the earth, given the chance and somewhere to sit on it.

The engine stuttered and he lifted his arm to signal his intention to take off. He taxied his plane over the rough turf until it was in position, nose pointing into the wind. A few early risers gathered to watch. Then suddenly he was off, lifting the BE2 almost prematurely as though unable to wait for that moment when he would be able to look down on the airfield.

For all his quixotic behavior, Thomson was a man of fixed habits. He always circled briefly around the airfield, dipping his wings in salute before heading for the German lines. Asked why he did this, he once replied: "Just to let my mechanic know I am all right." His patriotism was well disguised.

The Mad Major's machine seldom attained a cruising height of more than 2,000 feet on these strafing missions. One day, as he was making his climb, he noticed an enemy Albatros following him, shaking its wings in a derisive gesture. Although Thomson had a sense of humor, he took his flying very seriously. He completed a turn, still watching the Albatros as it approached from a quarter of a mile away. The wings waggled again. Was this an invitation to fight or was the pilot having a private joke? Thomson did not know, but he felt angry at being tailed. He prided himself on being able to outpace enemy planes on these early-morning sorties when the skies were clear and sparkling.

In a sky which showed no cloud he banked so that the rising sun was immediately behind him. As he expected, the Albatros flew straight into the blinding golden beams just below him. Thomson throttled back, reducing his air speed so that he almost floated as he waited for the German to make up his mind. Suddenly he reached forward and advanced the throttle until the engine raced, then leaned back to brace himself against the seat support. The BE2 began to fall in a steep dive. After 500 feet of heart-pounding descent he was nearly on the Albatros. He could see the pilot in the cockpit and smiled gently, picturing the panic which must be forming in that Germanic mind. He would be expecting a savage burst of gunfire. His fists would be tightening on the control column, quickly working out a banking movement which would take him out of range.

At 300 feet Thomson leveled out and almost skidded past the Albatros, waving gaily. He kept his eye on the German and was surprised to see him waving an infuriated fist. The Germans' certainly lacked humor. They could not take a joke. The fellow was probably sweating, wondering what was to come next.

In those days there was a certain code of ethics in the air, but the Albatros pilot did not seem to know that. For ten minutes he tried every kind of trick to get the better of Thomson, but the Englishman countered skillfully, risking the strength of the BE2 in sharp turns, climbs and dives which could have ripped the mainplane off.

The Albatros now began to drop to a lower altitude, followed by an irate Thomson who, by this time, had had enough of this time-wasting play. If the Albatros had been sent to distract him from the main purpose of his mission, he was going to be unlucky.

The initiative now fell into Thomson's hands. By a series of low dives above the Albatros, he forced the German down to ground level until the two planes were literally playing hide and seek at 150 mph over the battlefield itself. Unversed in this kind of flying, the German narrowly missed thin clumps of shell-shattered trees while the more versatile Thomson did some quick lifts, hopping over the tops and catching up with the Albatros.

Like two maddened gadflies, the Albatros and the BE2 missed crashing a dozen times in this duel for supremacy, while German troops kept up a running rifle fire at Thomson.

At this time Thomson was flying a machine which had very inadequate armament. True, he had a gun of sorts, but this situation did not call for the use of it. In any case, he felt so disdainful of the German that he would not shoot him. The German was obviously very young—perhaps twenty-one or so—and did not guess how much the autocratic Thomson objected to being diverted so early in the morning. But if the Albatros was heading for its own base, this might be a good chance to go in and shoot up any parked machines.

With the seconds flashing by, Thomson kept one eye on the sparsely wooded ground which came and went. He could not see a sign of any German airfield, only the occasional field kitchen where queues of German soldiers waited for their breakfast. Hearing the roar of the approaching aircraft, they scattered, some snatching up rifles to shoot at the pursuing Thomson.

The Albatros was only a matter of yards ahead when the pilot kicked the controls and lifted it in a mad loop. Thomson did not meet the temptation to follow, guessing that he would only receive a burst of bullets in his back. Instead, he banked a little farther on and caught the Albatros napping as it returned to a low level again.

They were now over a piece of open terrain, a place of close-cropped fields. Snapping up the chance, Thomson wedged his feet against the control stick and rummaged in his belt for a revolver which he always kept loaded for emergencies. He had never used it before, except once when he brandished it in the face of advancing German troops after being shot down behind enemy lines.

The Albatros still tried to evade him, but he deliberately kept to the agricultural area, a place which had miraculously escaped shelling and the sickening ravages of trench warfare. Thomson shoved his stick forward a fraction and leveled out until he was flying immediately over the German at a height of less than twenty feet. Edging down, he showed that he had every intention of locking his wheels in the top of the Albatros unless the German landed.

It was a fantastic way to fight a duel, but the Albatros finally took the hint, made a short approach to an open space and bumped to a standstill. Quickly turning, Thomson flew closer and closer, holding his engine in rein, until he was on a level above the Albatros. The pilot was standing there, waiting for the next move. He was very young, indeed; Thomson could see that when the pilot peeled off his helmet. Yes, very young . . . and very frightened.

Thomson debated whether to take a pot shot with his revolver and try to fire the grounded Albatros, but there was a danger that he might hit the German by accident. It was important to do this thing right, he thought, swinging the stick around to bring his machine into a third circuit of the area.

The German was still there, swiveling his head to watch the antics of the Englishman. Time was now running out. If Thomson spent many more minutes here he might easily run out of fuel or stall and have to make a crash landing. It would certainly be a wry meeting between the duelists. No, he could not afford to waste any more time!

Sending the BE2 into one last skittering run at a height which swept him within feet of the Albatros pilot, he gaily waved a salute and then set about gaining altitude. His fuel level was so low that he had to return home and postpone the strafing mission.

He landed perfectly and taxied into the dispersal area where his mechanic sat waiting for him. Thomson switched off the engine and watched the propeller blade make its last sweep. It was less than an hour since he had left this same spot. Looking around at the peace of it, he climbed out, regretting losing his temper with the Albatros. The entire incident would look pretty childish in the official report which he must file. But that was war, a combination of silliness and seriousness. It was not quite as clear cut as people liked to make out.

"You'll need a new machine in the morning, sir."

Thomson halted and looked back to where the mechanic was examining the BE2. For the first time he noticed that it was possible to see right through the holes. Large areas of fabric had been ripped away where German ground fire had caught him during the chase. He had noticed nothing at the time, though.

"You couldn't have been in the air more than another five minutes," the mechanic observed, dip-stick in hand. "Juice nearly gone."

This was not unusual. Many pilots left the return to base until the last possible moment, landing on the last drop of fuel. Some of the more daring ones left no margin at all and managed to glide the last quarter of a mile in a long gradual descent. Others came down short of base and arrived home on foot, grinning at their good luck. One, who walked back from behind the German lines, was reprimanded for crashing his machine. Asked to submit an official report, he wrote: "Sir, While flying my BE2C I got into the backwash of a sparrow. My machine got out of control, spun, and crashed. The pilot is doing well." The author of this cheeky piece of reportage was the monocled Captain Gordon Bell, one of the First World War's perfectionists. On one occasion when he had engaged a German and come off much the worse for wear, his machine would not fly any way except upside down and it was piloted in this fashion for a long distance until the nonchalant Bell

nearly passed out from the rush of blood to his brain. In a period
when he was staving off faintness, the machine slithered down
into a clump of trees, still in the reverse position. Bell recovered
very quickly when he felt the branches against his face. Fixing his
monocle, he climbed out of the wreckage to find a British army
officer standing below, watching him with the keenest interest.

"I say, have you crashed or something?"

Bell hesitated, then put one foot on a stout limb and began to
get down.

"No, you damned fool, I always land like this."

Bell had an impediment of speech which made him somewhat
self-conscious, but under combat conditions he showed no hesita-
tion in dashing into the middle of a dogfight regardless of his own
safety, especially when the lives of others were at stake and he
could act as a diversion, drawing the attackers away. He dueled
for hours over the French and Belgian battlefields, knocking down
as many as six enemy machines in one day and returning to base
in time to eat a large dinner. He was later killed on a test flight, but
at the height of the war spent days searching for Max Immelmann,
the German inventor of the "Immelmann turn," which became
standard practice. But Bell was always unlucky. It was said that
Immelmann had no great wish to meet a man willing to fly through
his own cockpit merely for the sake of marking up another victory.
It was true: Bell would turn his own machine inside out to gain
an advantage.

Immelmann himself had a very peculiar mentality. At the
beginning of the war he went out on patrols flying in the center
of the pack, from which favored position he directed the attack.
Later, though, he flew alone and unguarded over the British lines,
inviting Allied pilots to come up and fight. In the spring of 1916
he entered one of his dogfights with Captain O'Hara Wood, an
Australian formerly famous as a professional tennis player.

Wood was carrying Ira Jones as observer-gunner. Their briefing
had been short and to the point. The Intelligence department was
growing very concerned about the activities of Fokker aircraft
around Lille. With the Dutchman Anthony Fokker on the German
side there was a definite danger that the Germans might after
all win the war in the air. The briefing officer pointed this out to
Wood and Jones. "We can't afford to lose the aerial war. It would

mean a loss of prestige and the Germans would press in on the attack. Now, we have word that Max Immelmann is flying with a Fokker squadron near Lille. If you go out on your reconnaissance near Lille—round here"—his pointer swept the map in a small circle—"there is a chance that you might get a crack at Immelmann. Good hunting. . . ."

Wood and Jones took off a few minutes later in a freshly serviced BE2C, aware that an encounter with the German ace would mean a fight to the death. The Germans were lauding Immelmann to the exclusion of other pilots. He had shot down seven Allied planes, seemingly with uncanny ease, but he was still an unknown quantity as far as tactics were concerned.

Cramped in the rear cockpit of the BE2C, Ira Jones checked the heavy Lewis gun. The machine had four separate gun mountings, and the observer-gunner had to lift the Lewis out of one and into the other whenever the enemy plane moved into a new quarter. The Germans were known to tempt the gunner into making fruitless moves and, while he was busy lifting the gun, to shoot him in the back. When this occurred the life of the British machine was very short. Traveling at about a hundred miles an hour, it was hard for the pilot to turn and see what was happening. The Germans were able to sneak in from behind and rake the machine with gunfire. Death followed a pattern.

As he steadied the Lewis gun Ira Jones was uncomfortably aware of the hazards of this mission. He knew, too, that the Lewis gun was one of the clumsiest weapons to handle in the restricted space of the BE2C cockpit. He leaned forward to exchange a few words with Wood, but could not make himself heard above the whistle of the wind.

They were now high over Lille. Both men looked downward when Jones noticed a German machine coming up behind them at a great rate. He signaled Wood, who banked the machine to enable Jones to sight the Lewis gun. He fired one short burst, but it went wide and the German fell into a deliberate spin, coming up under the unprotected belly of the British machine like a fast mosquito, firing fast. Most of the rounds missed, but some of them did tear through the fabric.

Sweating, Ira Jones waited for Wood to move the BE2C around so that he could encourage the skillful German to come down in a steady dive. In that position he ought to be able to get in some firing and perhaps plant a lucky shot in the engine.

"A bright thought occurred," Jones said later. "I would hold the gun in my arms, lean over the cockpit and fire down at him. I did, but unfortunately I had not allowed for the sudden and sharp vibration of the gun and the rush of air, and a cold sweat ran down my back as the gun jerked itself out of my grasp and fell earthward."

They were now completely at the mercy of the attacker, recognized as a fast-moving, well-armed Fokker. Jones believed that it was only a matter of seconds before they would be shot down in flames. It was a gloomy way to die and he felt damnably guilty over the loss of the Lewis gun. He cursed the moment when he had that "bright idea" to lift it out of its mounting. He had not been flying very long and it did not look as though he would be flying much longer. Trying to apologize to Wood, he leaned forward until he could crane and look into the pilot's grim face.

The Fokker was readying for a final run across their path, and they prepared to meet their end. At that moment a near miracle happened. The German ran out of ammunition and retreated, leaving them alone in the sky. The rest of the reconnaissance was carried out with Jones "shivering in the cockpit, getting colder and colder, and wondering whether a court-martial would soon end my visions of a flying career."

But there was no court-martial and Wood smoothed the matter over in his report. Some time later they met again and Wood said: "By the way, I didn't tell you at the time, but that day over Lille we were up against somebody rather important. I recognized his plane and his tactics."

"Who was it?" asked Jones, mystified.

"Max Immelmann himself," was the answer.

Few people ever understood the mentality and true personality of Max Franz Immelmann. He qualified as a pilot in 1913, one of the first to be plunged into the essentially hazardous business of finding out for himself the methods of air fighting. From the first he demonstrated a rare daring and imagination; rare, that is, for the German air force where teamwork, not individuality, was assumed to be the keynote to victory. In his entire career Immelmann shot down only sixteen planes, yet his reputation remains to this day for reasons which become more and more obvious as we study his life.

Others, like Richthofen, Udet and Voss, were afflicted with all the class-consciousness of the Uhlan officer. Shortly after arriving at the front, to commence air operations, they formed a *corps élite* which gave birth to the highly selective idea of the fighting "circus" with a restricted membership, a brotherhood of blood and death which flew to a shrill symphony sung by the wind in the strut wires. The persistent legend that Immelmann was one of the greatest pilots is partly accounted for by a humanity which he shared with Boelcke, but in the air he, unlike Boelcke, could be devilish, a slayer and a murderer who flew with glory in his heart. His low score of kills is best accounted for by virtue of the fact that he was a poor shot. He was a bad marksman, but as a pilot in supreme control of his machine he was superb.

Max Immelmann was the first ace of the First World War. Seizing the opportunity offered by the fast Fokker aircraft, he tested the early machines with a thoroughness which often brought him close to death, racing the 80-hp Gnome engine at 70 mph at an altitude of 6,000 feet for more than two hours at a time before idling it to test its staying power. When we recall that such hazardous tests were carried out over the front, it certainly shows how cool-headed this man was. He could easily run into enemy packs on patrol and they would have had no compunction about shooting him down in flames. The Fokker I in which he made the tests was unarmed, presenting a sitting target for the most amateurish Allied pilot. All Immelmann had to rely upon was the speed of the machine which, at that time, was superior to anything used by the Allies.

From the first, Immelmann worked alone, regarding the Fokker aircraft as his own pet interest. Satisfied at last with its fine performance, he had it armed and rehearsed the maneuver to become known as the "Immelmann turn." Taking advantage of the sun, the Fokker would dive down and pull up under the enemy machine and, in Immelmann's own graphic words, "sew the opposing airman in a shroud of bullets." It was Fokker himself who first noticed the courage of Allied airmen in wriggling out of this deadly predicament. Immelmann then introduced a method of evasion at high speeds. If the attack was unsuccessful, the enemy made a steep climbing turn, half-rolling at the zenith and coming down on his opponent as before. In time all pilots, Allied and German, began using these tactics and they were accepted as standard textbook practice.

Immelmann's machine, a famous one, was the first to incorporate Fokker's gun-firing mechanism, but on April 8, 1916, the Allies captured a Fokker which force-landed, and were able to examine the prized arrangement of synchronization of armament and propeller—hitherto a deep mystery—which had accounted for many deaths. The British passed the equipment over to a Rumanian called Constantinesco, who eventually brought out a gun-firing mechanism which, unlike the Fokker, did not rely upon a purely mechanical arrangement, but used instead the principle of hydraulic pressure.

Shortly after Immelmann arrived at Douai to join Boelcke's group, there occurred an incident which enhanced his reputation in Boelcke's eyes. It was written by Boelcke himself.

"Early on the morning of 1.8.15—it was Sunday—the clouds hung so low that the officer on duty telephoned it was no use going out to the airfield. So I was lying quite happily in bed when Fischer woke me and said there was an Englishman about. I jumped out and ran to the window. But as the Englishman was making for the front and as I had no chance of catching him, I crawled back under my bedclothes, cursing. I had hardly got warm once more before Fischer rushed in a second time; the Englishman was coming back again. Well, if the fellow is so impudent, I thought, I'll get up quick and have a go at him. So all unwashed, with my nightshirt still on, but no puttees, I shoved along to the airfield on my motor bike and came just in time to see those chaps— there was not one but four of them—amusing themselves by dropping bombs on our airfield. I jumped into my machine and took off. But as the Englishmen flew home as soon as they had dropped their bombs and had very fast machines, I did not manage to get within range of them. I turned back sadly.

"When I got over the airfield again—I could scarcely believe my eyes—there were another five machines that had come to pay us a visit with their bombs. So I went for the nearest, a monoplane. I got to grips with him nicely and peppered him well, but when I was close enough up to think that the next shot must send him crashing—Lord, my gun jammed! Oh, I was wild. I tried to remove the jam up there, and used so much force in my rage that the obstructing cartridge broke in half. So there was nothing for it but to land and get a fresh supply of ammunition.

"As I went down I saw our other monoplane coming up and felt pleased that those English machines would at least get their tails twisted by it. While I was loading with new cartridges down below, I saw Lieutenant Immelmann attack an Englishman in grand style and send him bolting. I climbed up again quickly to help Immelmann against the others. But they cleared off again as soon as they saw me arrive on the scene the second time, and I only had disappointment for my trouble. Meanwhile Immelmann had forced his Englishman to land; he put a bullet through his elbow, so he had to come down as quickly as he could.

"Immelmann was extraordinarily lucky over the whole business; I only gave him his first lesson on a Fokker three days before, i.e., I went up with him in his machine and let him help handle the controls. The day before he did his first solo and had great difficulty in pulling off his landing. He had never flown against the enemy in a Fokker and had never fired his machine gun before— and then he had the luck to catch a defenseless biplane over our airfield, because the Englishman had left his observer at home to save weight for his bombs. All the same, Immelmann did his job beautifully, and I congratulate him sincerely on his success. But I am really annoyed at my own bad luck; it was the first time in four weeks that I got an opponent bang in front of my gun, and then it must go and jam!"

Immelmann came to possess an almost puckish daring which was often frowned upon by his superiors, but their disapproval did not put him off. In 1914, when most German aircraft were undeniably better than the French or British, he borrowed a Rumpler Taube plane and flew a long mission to Paris, where he circled low to drop a note. But there was something more than foolhardiness about this man, whose temperament later changed. Only a few days later a Taube returned to Paris to drop a series of four-pound bombs on the outskirts of the city. It was a frightening demonstration that the Germans knew the meaning of air power and intended exploiting it.

Immelmann the man was now coming to the notice of others

concerned with strengthening Germany's air power. Sometimes they felt at a loss to understand this small pilot, who always asked so many questions and yet kept them at a distance. But for his growing prowess as a pilot he might have been posted elsewhere because he was so bearish and temperamental. After the Paris incident he became very sharp-mannered, demanding everything from others but seldom extending warmth to anyone for fear they might take advantage of him. Others saw in him a man of action who was also a deep schemer. He made a point of cultivating anybody who could be useful to him, including Anthony Fokker. The rest—even the powerful Boelcke, who enjoyed tremendous prestige—were of no interest to him. He often went to Berlin, where he had meetings with Fokker to discuss the improvement of synchronized guns. Immelmann was then operationally flying a Fokker E-3, a very light aircraft designed primarily for reconnaissance purposes but specially armed with twin air-cooled Spandau guns. On Immelmann's suggestion, Boelcke had just gone over to the Fokker E-3 and found it very satisfactory. After one meeting with the Dutch genius, Immelmann returned to the front with a new E-2 and put it straight into combat. Soon after this he was awarded the *Pour le Mérite* for outstanding bravery. Boelcke also received the decoration. At that time it was known as the "blue Max," after its origin by Frederick the Great, who would speak only French.

The high decoration went to two men with conflicting personalities: Immelmann, cool, frigid, ambitious, and Boelcke, warm, humorous, good at human relationships. Yet both qualified.

Oswald Boelcke, man of power and infinite humanity, son of a schoolteacher, always considered himself one of the people. Before the war he trained as an engineer, but graduated to flying very quickly. Throughout the war, despite his high position, he retained an understanding of his men and became a frequent visitor to German military hospitals, where he met Allied pilots whom he had shot down. He brought them gifts, anything they wanted, and stayed for hours, talking about the war and flying. Small wonder that such a man as this did not get on very well with Immelmann, who shot down anything in his path with RFC markings on it and always fought to kill. Boelcke did not like the job of slaying other aviators, with whom he felt strong kinship and harmony. Immelmann and Boelcke were known as heroes to the German public. After that the likeness ended.

But time was to bring them together in a common purpose. In 1916, German Intelligence detected an elaborate plan to bomb the huge Krupp works at Essen. The raid, it was rumored, was being organized by the French, but certain other nations were involved. The German High Command ordered Immelmann and Boelcke to an airfield not far from Essen, charging them and their echelons with the aerial defense of Krupp.

Imbued with an affection for the two outstanding aces of Germany, Fokker produced a new machine especially for Immelmann. This fast monoplane carried three guns that sprayed 1,800 bullets a minute through the propeller, and Fokker was justly proud of it. He set up a demonstration in which he himself was the pilot, but onlookers were scared out of their wits when he skimmed low along the tarmac to spray a setup of targets at the far end. Something went wrong with the synchronization and he nearly shot away most of his own propeller. He later found that sixteen bullets had passed right through the actual blade, and part of the propeller assembly could be knocked off with the fist. Fokker was shocked to realize that Immelmann himself might have been flying this same machine. He did not want the death of a famous pilot on his hands. He would rather die himself than have that happen. He made the necessary adjustments, had a new propeller fitted, tested it, and then notified Immelmann that the machine could be used the next day. Immelmann was delighted with the tests. After landing, he stroked the fuselage like a horseman petting his mount, complimenting Fokker on the excellent functioning of the triple guns. With such armament as this nothing could escape.

Only six days later, when Immelmann was at the controls of this machine, the rocker arm of the engine came loose and swung up in a deadly arc, wreaking noisy and massive damage, slashing through some of the engine supports until the Gnome engine was hanging literally on a single steel thread. Immelmann controlled his natural panic and set about taking the machine down toward the inhospitable earth. After a few hundred feet of shaky descent, the remains of the engine began to shudder and shake, and it looked as though the front section of the machine would break away.

At 500 feet he held the controls with his feet and tried to pull

on the control column until the Fokker flattened out. He finally
got the machine under control and landed within an inch of a deep
ditch. The heavy waterlogged soil helped to brake the wheels.

Climbing out of the cockpit, he tramped away in search of a
telephone and calmly called Anthony Fokker to report that the
new armament and engine did not quite combine to make a very
reliable plane. No, of course he was not angry. He was very happy,
he told his friend, but he thought that Fokker and his assistants
should come out and examine the wreck before something happened to it. After this incident Fokker was discouraged from designing individual machines for the top pilots.

While Immelmann willingly let himself become involved in the
displays organized by Fokker and his technicians, Oswald Boelcke
was quietly flying the only kind of war he knew. He went out on
daily sorties and general operations, trying to tempt British planes
to engage in combat over the German lines because he did not
want to waste fuel by flying to meet them over their sector. To his
consternation, soon after receiving the *Pour le Mérite,* he was forbidden to do any more flying. He received the order on May 21,
1916. Two days before, Boelcke had shot down his sixteenth
machine. Instead of remaining an active pilot, he was now posted
to the Eastern sector as a VIP, there to instruct the Turks, Austrians
and Bulgarians in flying. It was a tedious, time-wasting experience
for a man of his caliber and he eventually rebelled, insisting that he
be returned to active service on a war front. Realizing that a dis-
contented man was no use to them as a technical emissary, the
High Command reluctantly agreed, and Boelcke was returned to
duty with a request—nobody ever gave Boelcke a direct order—
that he organize a special combat squadron. Soon after starting
this he greeted a promising young recruit by the name of Manfred
von Richthofen.

Boelcke was an extraordinary man in many ways. He was greater
in stature than Immelmann, greater even than the celebrated
French, British and American fliers. After his death, when his
body lay in state at Cambrai, British machines passed overhead,
parachuting wreaths with such messages as this attached: "To the
memory of Captain Boelcke, our brave and chivalrous foe. From
the British Royal Flying Corps."

Another message read: "To the officers of the German Flying

Corps in service on this front; we hope you will find this wreath, but are sorry it is so late in coming. The weather prevented us from sending it earlier. We mourn with his relatives and friends. . . . (Signed) F. Seaman Green., Lt."

And from the young Manfred von Richthofen, soon to be labeled "The Red Baron," we may learn in bare detail the cause of Boelcke's death, in a letter written to his mother on November 3, 1916.

Boelcke Combat Squadron.

Liebe Mamma:

Unfortunately I missed the train to Boelcke's funeral, to which I was detailed as representative of the squadron. Now I can only visit you at the beginning of the month. Boelcke's death came about in the following manner:

Boelcke, some men of our squadron, and myself were engaged in a battle with British planes. Suddenly I saw how Boelcke, while attacking the enemy, was rammed by one of our fliers, to whom, poor fellow, nothing else happened. I followed him immediately. But then one of his wings broke away and he crashed down. His head was smashed by the impact: death was instantaneous.

During the funeral services and in the procession, I carried a pillow displaying his decorations. The funeral was like that of a reigning prince.

In the last six weeks we have had, of our twelve pilots, six dead and one wounded, while two have suffered a complete nervous collapse. Yesterday I brought down my seventh shortly after I had accounted for my sixth. The ill luck of all the others has not yet affected my nerves.

Manfred

CHAPTER

3

Boelcke Heads the Wolf Pack

The growing combat tradition and the incentive to fight by invitation stemmed directly from men like Oswald Boelcke, and many British pilots soon came to recognize his deadly trademark in the skies over France. Boelcke was also known to them as a distinctive, vivid personality, especially among those who had been shot down and taken prisoner only to escape and return to the British lines. They reported that Boelcke had entertained them in his own mess, granting them as much freedom as he possibly could under the circumstances. It was this same freedom which went by the board when Boelcke lost many of his "guests" after they calmly walked away and headed for their own lines, their stomachs full of solid German food, their feelings toward Boelcke very cordial indeed!

In the air things were slightly different. Granted *carte blanche* by the High Command to pick his own pilots for the formation of a new fighting force which would utilize the best in aircraft design, Boelcke found Richthofen, Bohme, Max Müller and many others who were to serve under the official banner labeled Royal Prussian Jagdstaffel No. 2. There never was any Royal Prussian Jagdstaffel No. 1., and Boelcke's formation was, to all intents and purposes, the first of the hand-picked circuses, every member of which was an ace in his own right.

For a long time Boelcke chafed at the necessity of remaining on the ground, but he was eventually allowed to fly and teach his fledglings how to use their wings. He generally went out very early in the morning on one lone sortie, returning in time for breakfast. Sitting around the big table in the mess, his pilots did not need to question him about the sort of hunting he had had. If his chin bore traces of blackness from the fire of his guns, they knew he had been fighting the enemy. Boelcke never wasted his ammunition. His grimy chin attested to the fact that he had scored another victory. And it happened morning after morning.

One of Boelcke's more ardent enemies was Captain G. L. Cruikshank, leader of No. 70 Squadron, which was armed with Sopwiths. Possessor of a colorful war background, Cruikshank once flew spies right behind the German lines, going to the risky length of actually landing his machine and waiting while his passengers sorted out their luggage before calmly taking off under the noses of the Germans. But those days were over now. The war had become more personal. Cruikshank had been in the bloodbath of the front for some time before he came in contact with Boelcke in several skirmishes. He fastened onto the idea that he was the man appointed to shoot the German out of the sky once and for all.

The main difficulty was that few of the German pilots ever ventured very far over the British lines, least of all Boelcke. Their tactics were to remain somewhere over the front, tempting fate. As soon as a British machine appeared likely to give chase, they scurried back toward their own airfields, enticing the British into a deadly trap. Over many German fields an umbrella of armed fighters flew for short periods, keeping watch for the returning decoy and the quarry. Some time before his death Boelcke said that these were unfair tactics, and he tried to talk his eager young pilots out of using them. All aerial combat should be as fair as circumstances allowed, he said, but this was a tall order for a group of men intent upon making their first kills and gathering some of the glory which was fast accruing to Immelmann and others. Already he and his kind were becoming known as the older generation, older by two months' experience, but in age leaving nothing much to choose one way or the other.

Cruikshank wasted gallons of gas looking for Boelcke, but he never felt quite sure about the tactics of his sworn enemy. How, he asked himself, could he recognize the German if he came across him? It was known that his Fokker looked the same as all the rest and showed no insignia of rank. It was not long before Cruikshank began to realize that he must trust to luck, that firm ally of all war pilots. And it came at last.

On this morning he took off at a quarter to six with a strong sun shining down on him. His machine was a well-tuned Sopwith, fast but no faster than the Fokker. It was a morning like any other, perhaps a little warmer, he thought, circling over the British trenches, watching ground operations and avoiding the spasmodic bursts of fire from bored German gunners. Then came a last-minute order, asking Cruikshank to remain over his own base. As he idled, coasting about and wondering, six other Sopwiths came up to join him. It seemed that his personal patrol was to become a sortie against any suitable targets, including some nearby ammunition dumps and a convoy said to be moving a few miles away.

With one skilled hand nursing his control stick, Cruikshank mulled over the possibilities of meeting Boelcke. The chances were thin. Boelcke would not take on seven Sopwiths all at once. The others were in position now. With a sigh of resignation he gave a signal and the arrowhead formation took shape.

Every pilot felt invigorated by the anticipated flight, and most of these young men looked upon the exercise as a way of working up an appetite for breakfast in about an hour.

They were approaching the German lines when Cruikshank suddenly sighted a similar number of planes, each bearing the distinctive Gothic emblem of the enemy. Throttling back to conserve fuel for the time being, he signaled his followers that they were about to run into a German pack. At this stage he certainly did not dream that the great Boelcke himself was less than a mile away, out for an early-morning flight with his youngsters. He and Cruikshank certainly had something in common that day; they were veterans in charge of the inexperienced.

The Germans began to split up, skillfully peeling off to match themselves against the British marauders. Believing that he could get the feel of the situation by flying immediately above the scene, Cruikshank climbed and was still climbing before making a searching dive through the growing melee in the hope of picking off some of the Germans. He then noticed that the German leader was tailing him and gaining. The Fokker certainly could move, out-stripping the Sopwith and yet conserving power.

Cruikshank saw that the rest had now cleared away from the aerial arena and several fights were going on in the distance. He hoped that his men were sticking to the faster Germans, saving their ammunition for the golden chances. The Sopwith had certain disadvantages, including a limitation of armament, and many a rash pilot had found himself suddenly and fatally disarmed in the heat of battle.

They were over Havrincourt Wood when Boelcke came down in a brilliantly executed sharp-angled sweep, firing an experimental burst which did not, however, come anywhere near Cruikshank's Sopwith. The Englishman immediately banked to bring Boelcke into his sights. Sensing what might happen, Boelcke whipped the Fokker away, and Cruikshank's first burst in the duel went wide.

The odds were even. Both sides had tried to launch a killing blow but failed. Now was the time for more sophisticated tactics. Boelcke was tired of this shilly-shallying. He had not reckoned on meeting the English this morning. Had Cruikshank turned away and flown toward his own lines, Boelcke would undoubtedly have done the same. But Cruikshank now ripped toward him in a series of drops from the top cover of low-lying cloud. Boelcke watched until he came within range, then thumbed his trigger while Cruik-shank was steadying his plane. Under the stutter of the guns the tip of the Sopwith's wing broke away. The machine went on fly-ing, but obviously not answering to the controls very well.

Cruikshank settled down in the cockpit, hunching over the ring sunsight and gingerly moving the stick until the Fokker came into view again. He was about to fire a string of bullets point-blank at Boelcke—whose technique he now recognized—when the German beat him to it and fired first. Captain Cruikshank was beaten by less than one second!

Boelcke's first bullets tore into the Sopwith's delicate engine, then spattered into the cockpit and passed along the smooth fuselage, finally smashing through the tail. It was brilliant, cal-culated shooting of the first order. We do not know if Cruikshank was still alive when his machine started to break up, but within a few seconds it showered the area surrounding Havrincourt Wood with blazing fragments.

Cruikshank, hunter of Boelcke, was defeated in his first encounter with the man he had sworn to kill.

Oswald Boelcke, now well on the way to scoring forty victories before death claimed him, flew home for breakfast, a sadness gnawing at his heart. As he sat down with other members of the patrol, who were chatting about the encounter, he alone was the silent member. He had killed a man, another one, and he wondered how he could go on and still face another day.

The weather closed in and Boelcke was pinned to the ground, trying to contend with the young pilots who urged him to let them fly under these difficult conditions. He knew that it would be as good as signing their death warrants and refused to sanction their requests. He tried to pass the time lecturing them on strategy and the vulnerable points of British planes, but he knew that their attention was wandering. They were not listening to what he was saying. They could only learn from experience and time was short. At last, on September 19, 1916, he agreed to lead them on a reconnaissance mission.

Idling his engine on the verge of the tarmac, he watched the Fokkers skimming away to bank around the field and await his arrival in the air. When they were all airborne, he was able to open his throttle to roaring pitch. A few minutes later he was at the head of his eager pack.

They flew more than twenty minutes before sighting anything. Boelcke was not in the mood to fight against the sullen background of those rain-saturated skies. He enjoyed the sunshine, in the golden light of which the wretched business of killing was done. The sun was also an ally. When the sky was as leaden as this, and the clouds formed up in a high mass, it was hard to escape the pursuer. But the sun was different. It was his friend. He could drop down its blinding rays and be on top of the British before they could wake up.

Over Quéant they flew straight into a full squadron of FE's, obviously on their way back to base. With his usual thoroughness Boelcke waited for his men to take up their prearranged positions, then led the attack, flying immediately over the FE's and spraying them with hundreds of bullets. Completing his run, he banked, conscious that his young men were already attacking. In his lectures he told them to wait a little longer, but they were headstrong, disregarding the possibilities of an ambush, a trap.

Before he could turn back he was overtaken by a sleek Morane which came screaming after him. It was moving too fast to engage in an orthodox fight, so he gained speed and kept up a running fight. Only when the Morane broke up and began to fall in flames was he free to return. He was just in time to see one of his Fokkers artfully forcing an FE down near Delville Wood. There was every sign that the FE's engine was on its last gasp. Boelcke flew lower and lower until he saw the machine land. The pilot climbed out and helped the obviously wounded observer down to the ground. Satisfied, he pulled his stick back and climbed, circling, waving the victor away.

With only a shattered squadron left, the FE's fled home as fast as they could, harried by the Fokkers until the last minute when they reached their own base. In their report the FE pilots said that they had been beaten up by "the toughest lot of Huns" they ever met.

Checking the casualties, Boelcke found that Winand Graffe and Reimann had been killed in the foray. Two of his most promising fighter pilots were no more. He could ask for replacements, but those men had shown great promise and were regarded as future leaders. Investigating, Boelcke discovered that Reimann's death was due to poor skill as a pilot in a tight corner. He had allowed a Morane to collide with him. It was something which had almost happened to Boelcke many times, and he had impressed upon his pilots the need for quick thinking in such emergencies. Reimann had evidently not learned to think and act quickly. The penalty was swift and irrevocable—death.

British irritation over the activities of Boelcke's group manifested itself when six Martinsydes were sent to bomb the German field. It was a short sharp raid, and the Germans could not get off the ground because of bombs exploding along the runway. In their bunkers and slit trenches, Boelcke's pupils angrily vowed revenge, but Boelcke assured them that bombing could be expected all the time now that the British were getting heavier planes over from England.

Two days later, persuaded by appeals from pilots, Boelcke

agreed to head the pack in a foraging raid. Immediately after take-off they met six Martinsydes and the fight took place right over the German airfield. And a grim, bloody fight it turned out to be, with Boelcke picking his first victim and chasing him higher and higher in a series of straining climbs. At last he fired point-blank at the Englishman, Lieutenant S. Dendrino, and then turned away, satisfied that another enemy pilot and plane were now permanently out of action.

He was banking in preparation for a fast dive straight into the fight below, when he took in the peculiar sight of the same Martinsyde still airborne and flying. By all the rules it should have been hurtling in flames through the air to bury itself in the earth, but there it was, still flying as though nothing had happened.

He went in for a closer look, but the machine only took evasive action. Following it, one thumb resting lightly on his gun trigger in case these were new battle tactics, he waited. But there was not a sign of fight from the Martinsyde.

Boelcke made another wide sweep, returning again, puzzled. There must be a solution to all this. Had the English invented a pilotless plane? Or was it a trap, an elaborate setup to dispose of him once and for all? He did not know, but felt that such thoughts were far-fetched.

The Martinsyde continued on course, then went into a third circuit of Boelcke's airfield. He flew under it for a time, then suddenly put a few rounds into the belly. Nothing happened. No answering fire. Not a sign of life. It was uncanny.

He decided to risk a closer inspection. Getting to within fifty feet, he now saw the slumped form of the pilot lying across the controls. The incredible truth was that a dead man sat at the controls. In his first burst of gunfire Boelcke had caught him square in the back and his body had fallen forward against the stick, keeping the plane on course.

Swooping to the fight below, Boelcke now gave full chase to one of the Martinsydes, seeing it off with spasmodic bursts of fire. Turning again, he saw that the fracas had subsided, so he went back to scout for the last time before landing and came across the Martinsyde still making its circuits with a dead man in the cockpit. Preparing to land, Boelcke dipped his wings as a salute to the solitary vanquished pilot flying up there alone through the now silent skies.

Boelcke's bout of strange incidents had a sequel. During October he and his pilots encountered several British groups. Their bag was five in one day, and during one fight Boelcke went in pursuit of an FE. As soon as he was in range he managed to get a salvo right into the Englishman's control panel. The FE began to spin away at a crazy angle, then suddenly dipped sharply. Boelcke noticed a sacklike object hurtling out of the rear cockpit. He began to divide his attention between the doomed plane and the falling shape. Only in the last few moments did he see that it was the observer, apparently thrown out of his seat when the pilot was killed and lost control. It was the sort of sight he never forgot.

After Boelcke's death on October 28, 1916, Jagdstaffel No. 2 was taken over by Lieutenant Kirmaier, who himself was destined to be killed within a month. In recognition of the former commanding officer's prowess in the air and for the mark which he left on the Allied air forces, the High Command rechristened the group Boelcke Jagdstaffel. That November, Boelcke's pupils, who felt the loss keenly, shot down 21 British planes, often in the bloodiest combat imaginable, without quarter given on either side. Many British pilots talked about the way the Germans were fighting like mad dogs. It was no longer a gentleman's war.

Many of the new kills were made by Richthofen, the young man with the firm jaw and the avowed intention to sweep all British planes out of the sky. To him aerial combat had a similarity to his favorite prewar pastime of hunting the wild pig.

Later the same year, at the beginning of one of the worst winters of the war, Richthofen, now battle-imbued and with a spirit which made many of his contemporaries seem like mere babes in arms, was transferred from the Boelcke Jagdstaffel and placed in command of Jagdstaffel No. 11. It was not very long before Richthofen's new squadron was waging a fiery competitive war with the Boelcke Jagdstaffel. The victor, declared Richthofen, would be the squadron which shot down the most British planes.

But what took the wind out of the German sails was the arrival in France of something new in fighting machines, the Bristol fighter and the SE5. During May the Boelcke Jagdstaffel downed only five British machines. It was a sickening drop from the former victory peak. Even Richthofen was forced to adopt new aggressive tactics.

Richthofen's Flying Circus

The "circus," the foregathering of those German pilots who scorned death, banding together to work toward the common end of winning the war in the air by use of breath-taking and original methods, now came into its own. The groundwork had already been done by Boelcke and Immelmann, but it was Richthofen who perfected this lethal devise.

Now, also, was the time when German propagandists were in need of Wagnerian heroes to present to the disillusioned public. The war was going badly, and the bravery of the young pilots gave the propagandists a chance to boost morale on the civilian front. One of the first setbacks to the deliberate building up of this trait of heroism was the death of Immelmann. He was killed in a crash on July 18, 1916, surrounded by what Anthony Fokker called a "mystery."

Fokker was in a very worried state when he heard about Immelmann's death. They had been comrades for a long time, mainly because the pilot was the man responsible for talking the authorities into adopting many of Fokker's inventions, including the synchronized gun which played havoc among the Allied air forces.

"Immelmann's plane suddenly fell to the ground as he was flying near the German front lines," Fokker wrote later. "It was first given out that his Fokker fighter had failed in mid-air. This explanation naturally did not satisfy me, and I insisted on examining the remains of the wreck, and establishing the facts of his death.

"What I saw convinced me and others that the fuselage had been shot in two by shrapnel fire. The control wires were cut as by shrapnel, severed ends bent in, not stretched as they would have been in an ordinary crash. The tail of the fuselage was found a considerable distance from the plane itself. As he was flying over the German lines there was a strong opinion in the air force that his comparatively unknown monoplane type—which somewhat resembled a Morane-Solnier—had been mistaken for a French plane."

Trying to dispel the cloud of doubt which now cloaked his reputation, Fokker had meetings with members of the High Command and in the end succeeded in exonerating himself and his planes from all blame, but only unofficially. It was many years before the German public heard what happened to Immelmann. Fokker had a good point when he told the High Command that ground gunners were not sufficiently well acquainted with the new German planes to identify them all at sight. As a result, diagrams and silhouettes of the shapes were distributed throughout the front.

Boelcke and Immelmann did not die as a result of combat with the enemy. They died because of misjudgment, Boelcke owing to the action of one of his own pupils, and Immelmann because the German gunners did not recognize him. These two facts are a reflection upon the high reputation of both men.

Richthofen was now reaching new peaks against the British machines. Out of the running skirmish was evolved the savage dogfight, with a high death toll on both sides. Many planes collided in mid-air, and at one time the crashes equaled those shot down in action.

Richthofen's technique was to improve enormously. They started saying that he flew with his brains, not with the "innocent courage" of other pilots mentioned by Fokker. Richthofen, the Red Baron, so called because he had his plane painted scarlet to make it easily recognizable by enemy and friend alike, flew with a kind of mathematical certainty. He always moved fast, attacking before the others, and scoring his most telling blows while his companions were still jockeying for position.

On taking command of the Boelcke Jagdstaffel he instituted a series of daily meetings to discuss tactics, insisting that his men adopt the new methods even if they did not care for them. Twelve days after his first conference there came an opportunity of putting his opinions and orders to the test. It led to one of the massive air battles of the war, with a total of eighty German machines in the sky against only forty British machines. That day, November 9, 1916, more than one hundred fliers were airborne at the same time.

The incident came shortly after the Battle of the Somme, ending four months of death-or-glory fighting. The weather was bright, visibility was excellent, and Richthofen, exultant because of the chance of combat, predicted a good day's sport. All he wanted was the weather report. As soon as it came he paraded his pilots on the tarmac and gave them their instructions.

After fifteen minutes' flying, Richthofen himself sighted the British force of sixteen heavy bombers over Vraucourt. At this moment Richthofen had only six machines in the air, but glancing to the left and right of him he saw the dazzling blue of the sky filling up with reinforcements from other bases.

Richthofen's killers were waiting to strike. Below them, serene on their deathly mission, hummed the British bombers, unaware that they were being watched. Had the British paused to think, it would have seemed much too simple, flying straight to the vulnerable point called Vraucourt and being able to drop bombs without once being molested. The whole operation had been discovered by spies, and the High Command spent days working out a plan to wipe out the entire task force.

The British objective was Vraucourt, important to the Germans, and the site of an operational headquarters for the army. It also had a sugar factory which was working at full pressure to keep up with the demand. The factory itself was worth bombing. The High Command decided that Richthofen was the only officer commanding a squadron who could play the role of executioner, and he was sent for and ordered to prepare a plan of attack. With his customary precision Richthofen worked out his strategy in collaboration with his pilots, and he now put the plan into operation. His attacking force was the Boelcke Jagdstaffel armed with Albatroses. Richthofen took the lead at the apex of the V-formation, and began the long dive toward the bombers. His air-speed indicator began to push around the dial until it reached 100 mph. He held on to this until the last moment, when he would need even greater momentum and velocity.

While the German ace was giving an example to his pilots, fourteen British escort machines of Nos. 11 and 60 Squadrons went into a powerful interception dive from an opposite quarter of the bright sky. Their leader recognized the Red Baron, and now planned to head him off and stage a diversion. It was going to be a long shot because it was not known how the Germans would react.

The clash was one of the momentous sights of the First World War. The two V-formations began to converge on one another, arrowing through miles of clear sky, the wind tearing at their wings, the wires giving out their agonized song.

Within the bombers there was plenty of hurried activity as the gunners scrambled into firing position in case the escorting fighters missed out in their mission to head off the Germans. Bomber pilots struggled to see what was about to happen. What they saw made them all feel very vulnerable, naked. The two fast-moving formations were now plunging down toward the bombers to a fugue of dully roaring engines.

Bomber pilots always have had the thankless job of trying to get through the harrying screen of fighters, but this was one of the first occasions when the British realized how inadequately armed they were. All they could do was keep to course and fly on toward Vraucourt.

Hundreds of feet above, Richthofen's machine set the pace for the rest. He was now in the steepest part of his vertical dive, looking down at the earth and approaching the bombers at more than 115 mph. Fists tight about the control column, he crouched down, one eye on the flickering agitation of his instruments, his brain still much cooler than the air outside. To try and pull out of this suicidal dive would mean death. It would tear the wings off the machine, plummeting the fuselage down in a funeral pyre.

Behind him, sprouting out in two directions, were the rest of the diving fighters, their pilots no doubt wondering when he would stop diving and start in on the attack. The bombers grew closer in Richthofen's sights, but he still held his fire. At this angle he was unable to send a single burst. He would be below them before he could throttle back and bring his machine up again.

Still howling in at another angle were the British machines, diving in the same head-swirling style as the Red Baron. The point at which they would bisect and engage the Germans would be several hundred feet below the bombers. It would be nemesis for many at this pace.

As the first German raiders flashed into range, the gunners in the bombers swung their barrels around, but the range was so extreme that it was practically impossible to hit anything. The first fighters, still led by Richthofen, banked steeply so that they could get a good view of the bellies of the bombers. Then they curved away at fantastic angles to reach the bombers again within seconds. The gunners could only shoot wildly, throwing out a haphazard curtain of steel death through which the German fighters came hurtling unscathed.

Leading his Albatroses in a *Kurvenkampf,* a whirlwind tactic which took the Germans right in on the tails of the pursuing British machines which had just arrived, Richthofen made a quick survey of the area. Over there, to his right, the cousin of the great Immelmann was spurting away after two bombers which were divided from the formation. Immelmann passed over the lumbering bombers at more than 100 mph, pursued by two machines of No. 11 Squadron, piloted by Captain Dewey and Lieutenant Harrow-Bunn. Although they were practically onto Immelmann, Richthofen could see that his countryman still had a fighting chance of getting out of an ugly situation.

A slight twist, only a flick of the ailerons, and Immelmann was on the deserted bombers a second time, firing in one long stream of bullets, pouring living lead straight into their long clumsy bodies.

Believing that he might be able to help with the downing of the second bomber—still airborne while the first spun down in flames—Richthofen altered course and thundered toward the bigger target. It grew larger and larger in his sights and he was about to shoot when the Lewis gunner, Lieutenant J. G. Cameron, fired at the scarlet machine with a stream of tracers. In that moment Richthofen was nearer to death than he had been for weeks. Angry, he flew at full speed over the bomber, and then sliced back to fight a private duel with the plucky Cameron.

Within seconds Cameron was dead, killed by a blasting fusillade from Richthofen's deadly armament. Satisfied that the machine was now at his mercy, Richthofen swung away to get a long view of it. He started to fire, putting several disastrous rounds into the engine, then turning his gun on the wires and spars which held it together. In his murderous mood he was determined to smash it to pieces in the sky.

Sitting in the cockpit, Lieutenant G. F. Knight did not realize that his persistent attacker was the Red Baron himself. He felt confident that he could outwit the German pilot right up to the moment of Cameron's death, but when that happened he knew that he was at the mercy of the enemy. After the second attack, Knight tested the controls, finding them loose in his hands. He was about to raise himself from his seat to see what was happening when he felt the bomber dip under him. It went into a dive which became faster despite his efforts to make the controls respond.

Still tagging along, intent upon making a kill, Richthofen held his fire until he felt quite sure that the bomber would never fly again. In one circuit he noticed with apprehension that the bombs were still in their racks. The plane was nosing toward Vraucourt with a load of death. If the pilot was still alive he might have the courage to try and drop his load on the target from a low level, blowing up the greater part of the town and himself included in one huge explosion. Richthofen pictured the devastation.

But he need not have worried about it. Knight had already considered releasing the bombs, but he could not reach the levers because they were covered by Cameron's slumped body. There was not a chance of getting at the release mechanism in the time available. Resigned, Knight sat in the pilot's seat, wondering how the crash would come and whether he would be killed. Without any control over the dead plane, he could do nothing except wait. He was too low to bale out.

Circling a few hundred feet above, Richthofen watched the bomber hit some trees and topple over in a field. A man climbed out of the debris, shook himself and then surrendered to a group of German army officers who arrived on the scene a few moments later. The bombs did not go off.

Seventy-two British bombs were dropped on Vraucourt that day despite German opposition, but few of them did serious damage. Richthofen's campaign, risky though it might have been, saved the town.

Landing, the German ace rushed into the town to see for himself exactly what the damage amounted to. Nondescript, his features covered with the grimy fumes of backfire from his guns, his clothes besmirched with oil which had leaked and blown back from his overheated engine, he looked quite unlike the usual Richthofen. In Vraucourt he was introduced to a man whose name he did not quite catch, but who was obviously somebody of importance. The ace clicked his heels, accepted the thanks of grateful staff officers, and hurried away to inspect the carcasses of downed bombers.

Only later did he discover that the VIP to whom he had been introduced was His Royal Highness the Grand Duke of Saxe-Coburg Gotha. Two days later he was called to the headquarters of His Highness and decorated for his part in the Vraucourt incident.

In the following November the Red Baron scored his greatest victory by killing Major Hawkes, VC and holder of many decorations. The encounter has been called a "battle of eagles." It took place over the battle lines between Bapaume and Albert, with thousands of soldiers of both sides watching in breathless silence. Here is Richthofen's own description of it.

"I must confess that it was a matter of great pride to me to learn that the Englishman I shot down on November 23, 1916, was the English equivalent of our great Immelmann. Of course, I did not know who he was during the fight, but I did know from the masterly manner in which he handled his plane and the pluck with which he flew, that he was a wonderful fellow.

"It was fine weather when I flew away from our airfield that day. I was in the best of spirits and keen for the hunt. Flying at an altitude of about ten thousand feet, I observed three English planes. I saw that they saw me, and from their maneuvers I gathered that our hopes for the day's fun were mutual. They were hunting bent, the same as I. I was spoiling for a fight, and they impressed me much the same. They were above me, but I accepted the challenge. Being underneath and in no position to attack, I had to wait till the fellow dived on me. It was not long to wait. Soon he started down in a steep gliding dive, trying to catch me from behind.

"He opens fire with his machine gun. Five shots rip out, and I change my course quickly by a sharp turn to the left. He follows and the mad circle starts. He is trying to get behind me, and I am trying to get behind him. Round and round we go in circles, like two madmen playing ring-o'-roses almost two miles above the earth. Both our motors are speeded to the utmost; still neither seems to gain on the other. We are exactly opposite each other on the circumference of the circle, and in this position neither one of us can train our single forward-shooting machine guns on the other.

"First, we would go twenty times around to the right, and then swing into another circle going around twenty times to the left. We continued the mad race, neither gaining an advantage. I knew at once that I was dealing with no beginner, because he didn't appear to dream of trying to break off the fight and get out of the circling. His plane was excellent for maneuvering and speed, but my machine gave me an advantage by being able to climb better and faster. This enabled me at last to break the circle and maneuver into a position behind and above him.

"But in the circling fight, both of us had lost height. We must have come down at least six thousand feet, as now we were little more than three thousand feet above the ground. The wind was in my favor. Throughout the fight, at the same time that we kept getting lower the wind was gradually drifting us back across the German lines. I saw that now we were even behind the German lines in front of Bapaume, and my opponent must have noticed that it was time for him to back out of the fight, because he was getting farther into my territory.

"But he was a plucky devil. With me behind and above him, he even turned and waved his arm at me, as though to say, *"Wie gehts?"* We went into circles again—fast and furious and as small as we could drive them. Sometimes I estimated the diameter of the circles at between eighty and a hundred yards. But always I kept above him and at times I could look down almost vertically into his cockpit and watch every movement of his head. If it had not been for his helmet and goggles, I could have seen what sort of face he had.

"He was a fine sportsman, but I knew that in time my close presence behind and above him would be too much for him, particularly as all the time we were getting lower and lower and farther behind my lines. We were getting so close to the ground that he would soon have to decide whether he would land behind our lines or would break the circle and try to get back to his own side.

"Apparently the idea of landing and surrender never occurred to this sportsman, because suddenly he revealed his plans to escape by going into several loops and other maneuvers of equal folly. As he came out of them, heading for his own lines, my first bullets began whistling around his ears, for up to now, with the exception of his opening shots, neither one of us had been able to range on the other.

"The battle is now close to the ground. He is not a hundred yards above the earth. Our speed is terrific. He starts back for his front. He knows my gun barrel is trained on him. He starts to zigzag, making sudden darts right and left, right and left, confusing my aim and making it difficult to train my gun on him. But the moment is coming. I am fifty yards behind him. My machine gun is firing incessantly. We are hardly fifty yards above the ground—just skimming it.

"Now I am within thirty yards of him. He must fall. The gun pours out its stream of lead. Then it jams. Then it reopens fire. That jam almost saved his life. One bullet goes home. He is struck through the back of the head. His plane jumps and crashes down. It strikes the ground just as I swoop over. His machine gun rammed itself into the earth, and now it decorates the entrance over my door. He was a brave man, a sportsman and a fighter."

And some time later the victory-flushed pilot who was worshiped by all Germany wrote this letter to his mother.

Squadron Boelcke
November 25, 1916

Liebe Mamma,

Accept my most sincere congratulations for your birthday. I trust this will be your last birthday in wartime.

My eleventh Englishman was Major Hawkes, twenty-six years old and commander of an English squadron. According to prisoners' accounts, he was the English Boelcke.

He gave me the hardest fight I have experienced so far, until I finally succeeded in getting him down. . . . Unhappily, we lost our commander three days ago, and eight days ago a plane of our squadron was brought down.

Manfred

Richthofen felt that in shooting Hawkes out of the sky he had at last avenged Boelcke. He wanted to savor the glory of it. For days after the duel, specially detailed salvage squads brought back souvenirs of fuselage fabric, bits of the engine, all torn from the wreck of Hawkes's plane. The gun, a special prize, was taken by Richthofen to his mother's home at Schweidnitz and fastened over the door. His mother was outraged and had an argument with him about it, but it stayed there for many years, a reminder of the glory that was once Richthofen, German ace.

In the following year, 1917, Richthofen was honored to receive not only the *Pour le Mérite* but also the Austrian War Cross from Francis Joseph. Almost overnight he became to the German nation the epitome of the legendary Teutonic Knight, riding the skies astride a charger. It was the kind of Wagnerian myth the Germans wanted and had to have in order to maintain their faith in a war which had already stripped their larders and taken a tremendous toll of their young manhood. One man, Richthofen, became the stimulus to go on and on. Richthofen himself soon became embarrassed by the amount of attention forced upon him, and he was self-conscious when he realized that the eyes of the nation were fixed on him as he flew and fought. His mailbag was full of letters from adoring women, many proposing immediate marriage or the offer of rapturous intimacy.

In this period he entered into a pen friendship with a woman, who still remains unknown. He was infatuated, although they never met. Her handwriting was known to the unit postal orderly, and his batman had elaborate instructions to keep an eye open for the letters. Involved measures were taken to ensure that Richthofen received her letters as soon as they arrived. As soon as he landed after flying against the English, his batman met him with a new package which he would open there and then, ignoring the congratulations of his pilots as they passed on their way to mess. Richthofen, the knight of the air with the grime of battle on his face, would stand motionless, drinking in the words, living in imagination a thousand miles away. Who was she, this unknown woman? Had he ever met her? It was doubtful; he seldom went away for very long leaves, and most of them were spent with his mother or close friends. The woman never was found.

When the air war became even more intense, he began to experiment with different forms of camouflage. He had the machines of his pilots painted with irregular patterns of brown and green, on the assumption that if they were spotted from above, it would be very hard to distinguish them against the earth below. This worked very well, though he himself stuck to his own scarlet plane, deliberately flaunting and advertising his presence in the now dangerous skies. All the leader planes, flown by senior pilots, were marked in some distinctive way so that Richthofen could see them throughout action.

When Richthofen finally joined Jagdstaffel No. 11 he celebrated his promotion by going out on a sortie on January 23. His official report is terse and to the point.

Requesting Acknowledgment of My 17th Victory
Date: Jan. 23, 1917
Time: 4:10 P.M.
Place: Above trenches southwest of Lens.
Plane: No details, as plane dropped on the enemy's side.

About 4:10 P.M., together with seven of my planes, I attacked an enemy squadron west of Lens. The plane I had singled out caught fire after I had discharged 150 shots into it from a distance of 50 yards.

The plane fell burning.

The occupant of the plane fell out of it at a height of 500 yards.

Immediately after it crashed, I could see a heavy black smoke cloud rising. The plane burned for some time with frequent flares of flame.

(Signed) Baron von Richthofen

Behind those lines stands terrible tragedy. The British pilot, cruelly slain by the experienced Red Baron, was John Hay, so new to flying over the trenches that no official record existed of his presence in the air that day.

Hay had joined No. 40 Squadron a few days before. On January 23 he took off from the airfield west of Lens at about three o'clock with a group of squadron machines. His airplane was an FE8 with a forward-firing Lewis gun. He was ordered to escort two photographic reconnaissance planes on a routine patrol over the German front, the idea being to obtain a plan of the trench layout in preparation for a future attack by the British infantry. The camera planes were slow movers and seemed to take a long time getting into position. Hay was not well versed in this kind of operation, but he was young and eager, and he welcomed the chance of acquiring this kind of vital experience.

He was flying along at a moderate speed, keeping the camera machines under observation, when Richthofen's five killers suddenly swept down in his path. In an instant Hay's supporters, single-seater fighters, took up the challenge and tried to fire back at the Germans. Hay followed, making sure that the camera planes were well on their way toward the appointed area, then returned to the fight. It was like a baby trying to fight a giant.

Richthofen's bullets crashed into Hay's machine in a single hail of destruction, creating havoc in the delicate engine, slashing into the fuselage like a shower of daggers. Hay's plane fell toward the earth, dropping headlong under its own fiercely accelerating momentum. At about a thousand feet a shape came hurtling out.

Canadian soldiers rushed to the spot, but all they could do was recover what was left of John Hay. He was buried two miles southeast of Aix Moulette, and the place was marked for the War Graves Commission: R.30, a.92.

British camera planes were becoming a nuisance to the Germans and Richthofen's pilots were charged with hunting them down as quickly as possible. Richthofen himself did not care for the job because it was time-wasting in his estimation, and he preferred to fly on his usual combat duties. Attempting to shift the responsibility to other squadrons, he was summarily ordered by the High Command to carry out his orders.

The day after shooting Hay out of the sky, the Red Baron's machines were ordered to fly in wolf-pack fashion and scour every inch of the vicinity. Pilots had orders to shoot on sight. Richthofen's temper began to boil. All this was a waste of time when they could be out, engaging the enemy properly.

That day Captain O. Grieg, pilot, and Second Lieutenant J. E. MacLenan, in charge of the camera, of No. 25 Squadron RFC, were flying west of Vimy Ridge on a delicate task. They were taking a series of mosaic pictures which, when placed together and rephotographed, would provide a comprehensive portrait of this part of the front. Grieg was trying to keep the machine on an even keel at a certain speed while MacLenan operated the camera.

The two men were escorted by three fighters, who were also in charge of a second photographic plane. The escort flew at some distance from the other two. As it turned out, they were too far away to be of any great assistance when action suddenly flared up.

British photographic planes were incapable of any great degree of speed with their pusher-type propellers and 160-hp Beardmore engines. The armament was a pair of Lewis guns, one moving in a forward position, the other firing at the rear area. Observers often complained that it was impossible to shoot at planes which attacked downward and backward, but there was no sign of any changes being made so that they could protect themselves more efficiently.

The day MacLenan and Grieg were attacked, Richthofen was flying the latest B.U. Albatros, a splendid piece of well-designed mechanism considered to be the very latest in lethal instruments. It had a 200-hp Mercedes engine and two synchronized guns which fired through the propeller. In the cockpit of the Albatros the Red Baron had every advantage because he was able to climb three times faster than anything the British could put into the sky.

MacLenan continued their straight-line run, taking photographs, when the Richthofen squadron came thundering down in a surprise attack. MacLenan was adjusting the focus of his camera as Richthofen's guns beat out the first savage tattoo of death. The next thing Grieg knew, his legs were a mess of bloody ribbons and the cockpit scarlet with his blood. Dazed, he tried to lift himself up, but was paralyzed from shock. From the knees down he could feel nothing and his feet dangled uselessly, inches away from the controls he wanted so badly to reach. By pulling himself sideways he did at last manage to get his shaking hands on the joystick and pulled the machine out of its downward glide. He was still trying to steady it when Richthofen shot across with another burst of ferocious fire. Several rounds hit the gas and oil tanks, shattering feed pipes and releasing the pressure. Caught up in the holocaust, MacLenan left his camera and stood up, reaching for the Lewis gun. He was seconds too late. Richthofen was flying where he could not be touched by British bullets. Seconds later he was back in one slashing upward swing, guns blazing at such close quarters that the British plane did not stand a chance. Both Englishmen shook their fists in rage.

Grieg was in a bad way, blinded by the blood which kept gushing up into his face. He was so weak that he expected to die at any moment. Nobody could expect to escape Richthofen's clutches.

Still not satisfied, Richthofen came on them again, ignoring the angry stutter of MacLenan's gun. How long could these English airmen hang on under such an onslaught from the Albatros? The Red Baron was expecting the plane to go down, but it was still there, chugging along through the sky, losing altitude all the time.

By making a head-on run directly toward the FE2 he hoped to finish it off, but he suddenly received a shower of hot lead which splattered into and fractured his mainplane. This was almost Richthofen's last moment of combat. Only his instinctive movement took him out of range of the Lewis gun. Trying to correct the Albatros's erratic movements, he soon discovered that the controls were badly affected. He had to force-land about a quarter of a mile away from where a sick and wounded Grieg fought to bring his shattered FE2 onto an open stretch.

While Richthofen was still wondering how he had misjudged his distance and lost his first major battle in what now seemed to be a stupid amateurish fashion, Grieg and MacLenan were painfully pulling themselves out of the wreckage. They had a few minutes left before the approaching German soldiers reached them. MacLenan slipped his hands under Grieg's armpits and dragged him away to safety. When the Germans were almost on them, MacLenan ran back to the FE2, grabbed a flare pistol and stood back to fire a single shot into the pilot's cockpit. There was an explosion and the FE2, soaked in gas and oil from broken fuel lines, started blazing.

The Englishmen were escorted to a twenty-month sojourn in a prison camp, but they would have given a lot for a sight of Richthofen's report of the incident.

Requesting Acknowledgment of My 18th Victory
Date: Jan. 24, 1917

Time: 12:15 P.M.
Place: West of Vimy.
Type of Plane: FE2. No. 6937.
Fixed Motor No. 748.
Occupants: Captain Grieg and Lieutenant MacLenan.

Accompanied by Sergeant Howe, I attacked about 12:15 P.M. the commanding plane of an enemy formation. After a long fight, I forced my adversary to land near Vimy.

The occupants burned the plane after landing.

I myself had to land, as one wing had been cracked when I was at an altitude of 900 feet. I was flying an Albatros D.111.

According to the English occupants, my red-painted plane was not unknown to them, as on being asked who brought them down, they answered "le petit rouge."

Two machine guns have been seized by my staff. The plane is not worth being removed, as it was completely burned.

(Signed) Freiherr v. Richthofen

The courage of Grieg and MacLenan made a deep impression upon Richthofen. He was in danger of considering himself indomitable. The fight sobered him up. He did not mind giving credit where it was due, but the idea had never occurred to him that he himself might some day be the pilot who was corkscrewed into the hard earth in a blazing wreck, or thrown out of his burning cockpit to live the last moments of life in a horrifying vortex of sensation from which there was no escape. In a letter to his mother he hinted that he was viewing war in a different light.

With the Eleventh Combat Squadron
January 27, 1917

Liebe Mamma,

I am certain you wonder at my silence. So much has happened in the meantime that I do not know where to start. I have been appointed commander of the Eleventh Combat Squadron stationed at Douai.

I left the Boelcke squadron only very reluctantly. But no matter how hard I resisted I had to go. The Eleventh Squadron has been in existence as long as my former one, but so far it has no enemy to its credit and the way they do things here is not very edifying. I have twelve officers under my command.

Luck has been with me. On my first time up with my new command, I brought down my seventeenth, and on the following day, number eighteen.

As I settled down with the latter, one of my wings broke at an altitude of 900 feet, and it was nothing short of a miracle that I reached the ground without a mishap.

On the same day the Boelcke squadron lost three planes, among them dear little Immelmann—a thousand pities. It is quite possible that they met with a similar incident. Unhappily, there is no chance of leave, and I would have liked to show you my *Pour le Mérite*.

Manfred

This letter certainly has a more somber tone than the others. Richthofen was now aware that war was serious. He was seeing too many ugly sights, coming to daily grips with the enemy in bitterly cold weather, which made flying doubly dangerous. Many of his missions were against the slow-moving photographic planes, for the early order of the High Command to sweep the skies clear of the menace still held and he had to obey it, no matter how tempting the other prizes might be. He learned to think more deeply and was able to put his conclusions about enemy tactics into print for the benefit of other German pilots. In one report to the commander of the Sixth Army Forces, he said:

"The adversary often slips downward over one wing or lets himself fall like a dead leaf in order to shake off an attack. In order to stick to one adversary, one must on no account follow his tactics, as one has no control over the machine when falling like a dead leaf.

"Should the adversary, however, attempt to evade attack by such tricks, one must dash down (Sturzflug) without losing sight of the enemy plane.

"When falling like a dead leaf, or intentionally falling wing over wing, the best pilot loses control of his machine for a second or two, therefore it is a maneuver to be avoided.

"Looping the loop is worse than worthless in air fighting. Each loop is a great mistake. If one has approached an adversary too close, a loop only offers a big advantage to the adversary. Change of speed should be relied on to maintain the position desired, and this is best effected by giving more or less gas.

"The best method of flying against the enemy is as follows: The officer commanding the group, no matter how large, should fly lowest, and should keep all machines under observation by turning and curving.

"No machine should be allowed either to advance or to keep back. More or less, the whole squadron should advance curving.

"Flying straight on above the front is dangerous, as even machines of the same type of plane develop different speeds. Surprises can be avoided only when flying in close order. The commanding officer is responsible that neither he nor any of his pilots are surprised by the enemy. If he cannot see to that, he is no good as a leader."

Richthofen believed that the RFC had its faults. "The English single-seater pilots always fly in squad formation when on pursuit work," he wrote. "Reconnoitering and artillery fire is also now carried on by squads of two-seater machines, sometimes containing as many as twenty machines. Many English airmen try to win advantages by flying tricks while engaged in fighting but, as a rule, it is just these reckless and useless stunts that lead them to their deaths.

"When flying in large squads, the English planes keep close together in order to be able to come to one another's assistance at any given moment. When attacked, they maintain even closer formation. When an English plane which has fallen behind is attacked, the first planes of the enemy formation make left and right turns and hurry to its assistance. After the rest of the formation has passed them, they close up the rear as the last planes."

Richthofen was one of the few men flying in the German air force who bothered to make detailed notes on the actions in which he was involved. Here is an extract from his logbook about a fight which he had with the English, coming off rather the worse for wear.

"I watched whether one of the Englishmen would take leave of his colleagues, and soon I saw that one of them was stupid enough to do this. I could reach him, and I said to myself, 'That man is lost!'

"I started after him, and when I got near, he started shooting prematurely, which showed he was nervous, so I said, 'Go on shooting, you won't hit me.' He shot with a kind of ammunition that ignites (tracer bullets containing a phosphorus mixture that leaves a trail of smoke behind and shows the gunner where his bullets are going. These fiery bullets are deadly to fuel tanks).

"At that moment I think I laughed aloud, but soon I got my

lesson. When within 300 feet of the Englishman, I got ready for firing, aimed, and gave a few trial shots. The machine guns were in order. In my mind's eye I saw my enemy dropping.

"My excitement was gone. In such a position one thinks quite calmly and collectedly and weighs the probabilities of hitting and being hit. Altogether, the fight itself is the least exciting part of the business, as a rule. He who gets excited in fighting is sure to make mistakes. He will never get his enemy down. Calmness is, after all, a matter of habit.

"At any rate, in this case, I did not make a mistake. I approached within fifty yards of my man. I fired some well-aimed shots and thought that I was bound to be successful. That was my idea. But suddenly I heard a tremendous bang when I had fired scarcely ten cartridges, and something hit my machine.

"It became clear to me that I had been hit, or, rather, my machine had been hit. At the same time I noticed a fearful stench of gas, and I saw that my motor was running low. The Englishman noticed it too, for he started shooting with redoubled energy, while I had to stop.

"I went right down. Instinctively, I switched off the engine. I left in the air a thin white cloud of gas. I knew its meaning from previous experience with my enemies. Its appearance is the first sign of a coming explosion. I was at an altitude of 9,000 feet and had to travel a long distance to get down. By the kindness of Providence, my engine stopped running.

"I have no idea with what rapidity I went downward. At any rate, the speed was so great that I could not put my head out of the machine without being pressed back by the rush of air.

"Soon I had lost sight of the enemy plane . . . I had fallen to an altitude of perhaps 1,000 feet, and had to look out for a landing. These are serious occasions. I found a meadow. It was not very large, but it would just suffice if I used due caution. Besides, it was very favorably situated on the high road near Henin-Lietard. There I meant to land, and I did, without accident.

"My machine had been hit a number of times. The shot that caused me to give up the fight had gone through both the fuel tanks. I had not a drop left. My engine had also been damaged by bullets."

5

The Laurels of Victory

Something about Richthofen's personality suggested that his fanaticism was growing. He started to kill for the sake of killing, and was known to shoot helpless grounded men as they struggled out of the cockpits of their burning machines. He fought like a madman, but maintained the cool manner of the professional executioner, and only when he killed did his face break into smiles. The rest of the time he was withdrawn. Although he was never very articulate, he did maintain an iron discipline among his men, setting an example and expecting them to emulate him. He was now coming to have a morbid curiosity about death, brooding over and sometimes talking about the kills he had made, the kills he would make. He was always passing a photograph around. It showed a terribly mutilated body, the remains of a pilot. On the back of it was written: "Sir, I witnessed on March 17, 1917, your air fight and took this photograph which I send to you with hearty congratulations because you seldom have occasion to see your prey. *Vivat sequens!* (Here's to the next!) With fraternal greetings, Baron von Riezenstein, Colonel and Commander of the 87th Reserve Infantry Regiment." Richthofen seemed to love this wretched picture to an unhealthy degree.

69

The victim portrayed was, in fact, Lieutenant A. E. Boultbee, who was found in the reserve-line trenches near Oppy. Richthofen celebrated later the same day by shooting down two more Britishers, Second Lieutenant G. M. Watt and the observer, Sergeant F. A. Howlett. They were flying as artillery spotters on March 17, and most of that afternoon was spent avoiding German artillery fire at a height of about 2,500 feet. It was nerve-wracking, flying at this altitude, because the plane was an antiquated BE with a cumbersome radio transmitter for sending messages back to the British artillery, a pair of Lewis guns and two 20-pound bombs for use in emergencies. It was a wonder the plane got off the ground at all under this load.

Richthofen had been scouting for prey throughout the late morning and early afternoon. The slow-moving BE looked a likely target. Waiting until the spotter plane was in the best position, he started his dive from a high altitude. As the speed increased, his machine seemed to become welded to his body while his mind was concentrated on the task of destruction. He was a veteran at this kind of strategy, and the possible dangers in subjecting his plane to such strains never worried him.

The British BE was more than a sluggish speck now. It was taking shape as a target. When he was close enough he let them have a warning shot, and came up seconds later at an angle and started the fight.

Watt and Howlett were startled to hear the shriek of the attacking plane, but as it came down at them out of the sky they both recognized the scarlet trademark of Richthofen. Watt tried to throw the creaking BE out of the path of the high-powered enemy. Both planes were now playing hide and seek at 100 mph, Howlett firing the Lewis gun every time Richthofen came within range, but it looked—and it was—quite hopeless. The British plane was snared between German artillery fire from the ground and the antics of the Red Baron, who was now teasing and taunting them.

On the ground English troops stared up at the incredible sight. The BE was less than 1,000 feet above their heads, swinging about like a pendulum to avoid Richthofen's mad-bull charges. No BE could be expected to withstand such strains as those created by Watt's desperate piloting.

Without any warning, the BE broke up in mid-air just as

Richthofen was starting another run. It was a terrible sight as the jumble of spars, fabric and engine crumpled and parted, falling down toward the hushed trenches.

Richthofen flew straight home to write this report:

Requesting Acknowledgment of My 28th Victory
Date: March 17, 1917
Time: 5 P.M.
Place: Above trenches west of Vimy.
Plane: BE two-seater. No details as plane landed between lines.
I had been watching an enemy infantry flier for some time. Several of my attacks were directed upon him from above, especially as my adversary did not accept fight and was protected from above by other machines.

Consequently, I went down to 2,000 feet and attacked from below my adversary, who was flying at 2,700 feet.

After a short fight, my opponent's plane lost both wings and fell. The machine crashed into no man's land and was fired upon by our infantry.

(Signed) Baron von Richthofen

It was not a fair fight and the Red Baron later admitted that he felt disgusted by German artillery, which fired at the dead aircraft as it lay on the ground, obviously out of action for good.

Day after day Richthofen took his younger pilots out on scouting forays to fight in a private war of their own. The insistence of the High Command upon wiping out all British photographic planes died a natural death, and Richthofen was now planning to get more of his new, inexperienced pilots well blooded and imbued with combat courage while the war was still in full swing. By March 26, 1917, his own score was thirty-one and he was proud of his collection of miniature silver cups which he had made and inscribed to commemorate his run of victories.

In one month the airborne Allies did very badly indeed. That April no less than 151 machines were missing over no man's land. Despite the entrance of the United States into the war that same month, Germany stubbornly retained an undoubted and undisputed superiority in air power, and British and American losses began to climb to alarming numbers. The skies were swept daily by the powerful Albatros and Halberstadt machines, better in all respects than their British counterparts. They could climb faster, were easier to handle and in battle were the dream of any pilot.

Under such conditions the Allies could only look around for new fighting methods. They would have to depend upon their brains, not the machines. Among the new tactics was the game of "ring-o'-roses" in which the aim was to circle round and round the enemy until you were on his tail and flying slightly above him. Another of the new gambits was the power dive. If British planes could do nothing else, they could dive at an alarming rate. While the Albatros and Halberstadt might be able to follow at greater speeds, it was possible for the Allied machines to pull out of a dive at about 500 feet and then start the long job of hopping over the treetops in the general direction of home. If an Allied pilot was sufficiently cunning, he might be able to induce the German to follow him in the fast dive. Many German planes nose-dived into the earth as a result.

Then, also in April 1917—the "bloody April" created by the German stand following the retreat to the Hindenburg Line—Richthofen and his brother Lothar, who was also flying with No. 11 Jagdstaffel, entered a violent fight, one of the longest, which terminated in the Red Baron's thirty-second victory.

This is how he himself described it:

"The second of April, 1917, was a very warm day for my Jagdstaffel. From my quarters I could clearly hear the drum fire, which was again particularly violent. I was still in bed when my orderly rushed into the room and exclaimed, 'Sir, the English are here!'

"Sleepy as I was, I looked out of the window, and there were my dear friends circling over the airfield. I jumped out of bed and into my clothes in a hurry. My red bird had been pulled out of the hangars and was ready to go. My mechanics knew that I would probably not allow such a favorable moment to go by unused. Everything was ready. I snatched up my furs and went up.

"I was last to start. My comrades had started earlier and were much nearer to the enemy. I feared that my prey would escape me and that I should have to look on from a distance while the others were still fighting.

"Suddenly, one of the impertinent Englishmen tried to drop down upon me. I allowed him to approach me quite near, and then we started a merry quadrille. Sometimes my opponent flew on his back and sometimes he did other tricks. He was flying a two-seater fighter. I realized very soon that I was his master and that he could not escape me.

"During an interval in the fighting, I assured myself that we were alone. It followed that the victory would belong to him who was calmest, who shot best, and who had the clearest brain in a moment of danger.

"Soon I had got him beneath me without having seriously hurt him with my gun. We were at least two kilometers from the front. I thought he intended to land, but there I had made a mistake. Suddenly, when he was only a few yards above the ground, I noticed how he once more went off on a straight course. He tried to escape me. That was too bad.

"I attacked him again, and to do so I had to go so low that I was afraid of touching the roofs of the houses in the village beneath me. The Englishman defended himself up to the last moment. At the very end I felt that my engine had been hit. Still I did not let go. He had to fall. He flew at full speed right into a block of houses.

"There is little left to be said. This was once more a case of splendid daring. The man had defended himself to the last. However, in my opinion, he showed, after all, more stupid foolhardiness than courage. It was again one of the cases where one must differentiate between energy and idiocy. He had to come down in any case, but he paid for his stupidity with his life.

"I was delighted with the performance of my red machine, and returned to the field. My comrades were still in the air, and they were surprised when we met at breakfast and I told them that I had scored my thirty-second machine."

Richthofen's official report gives a few more details.

Requesting Acknowledgment of My 32nd Victory
Date: April 2, 1917
Time: 8:35 A.M.
Place: Farbus (village).
Type of Plane: BE two-seater. No. 5841, Motor P.D. 1345/80.
Occupants: Both killed. Name of one Lieutenant Powell. Other occupant had no documents of identification.
    I attacked an enemy artillery flier.

After a long fight, I managed to force the adversary onto the ground, but without being able to put him out of control.

The strong and gusty wind had driven the enemy plane over our lines. My adversary tried to escape by jumping over trees and other objects. Then I forced him to land in the village of Farbus, where the machine was smashed against a block of houses.

The observer kept on shooting until the machine touched the ground.

(Signed) Baron von Richthofen

Later the same day Richthofen asked his brother Lothar to take a car and drive to Farbus to examine the wreck of the British plane, but just before Lothar started, Richthofen decided to go with him after all. The two men reached Farbus and found the wreck. Richthofen carefully avoided looking at the two scarlet smears, practically all that was left of the plane's crew, but took several photographs as souvenirs. Describing the visit, Lothar wrote: "It was a sad sight which we saw. Half of the machine was hanging from a roof, and the other half was on the ground. After inspecting the remnants, we went home. The soldiers around the place had in the meantime recognized my brother and cheered us madly."

It was an eventful day. In the afternoon, on Richthofen's return with Lothar to the airfield, Lieutenant Werner Voss, a friend and rival of the Red Baron, came to congratulate him on his mounting victories. While they were discussing the war, the weather took a turn for the worse, with gusts of snow sweeping across the airfield. The two aces, daredevils and always ready for something new, agreed to fly together to Voss's airfield. Lothar decided to accompany them, but in his own machine. Voss and Richthofen flew in the Red Baron's machine, barely cool from the day's hunting, and they ascended to a level higher than the banks of cloud. What started out as a casual piece of fooling around was to grow into one of the most vivid examples of Richthofen's character.

They were flying toward Arras when, in Richthofen's words, "Suddenly we saw an English air patrol approaching from the other side. Immediately the thought occurred to me, 'Now comes number thirty-three.' Although there were nine Englishmen, and although they were on their own territory, they preferred to avoid battle. I began to think that it might be better for me to repaint my machine. Nevertheless, we caught up with them. The important thing in airplanes is that they should be speedy.

"I was nearest to the enemy and attacked the man at the rear of the formation. To my great delight, I noticed that he accepted battle, and my pleasure increased when I discovered that his comrades deserted him, so I had once more a single fight.

"It was a fight similar to the one I had had several hours earlier. My opponent did not make matters easy for me. He knew the fight business, and it was particularly awkward for me that he was a good shot. To my great regret, that became quite clear to me.

"A favorable wind came to my aid, and it drove both of us over the German lines. My opponent discovered that the matter was not as simple as he had imagined. So he plunged and disappeared in a cloud. He had nearly saved himself.

"I plunged after him and dropped out of the cloud, and as luck would have it, found myself quite close behind him. I fired and he fired, without any tangible result. At last I hit him. I noticed a ribbon of white vapor. He would have to land, for his engine had stopped.

"But he was a stubborn fellow. He would not recognize that he was bound to lose the game. If he continued shooting, I could kill him, for meanwhile we had dropped to an altitude of about nine hundred feet.

"However, the Englishman continued to defend himself by shooting at me exactly as his countryman had done in the morning. He fought on until he landed.

"When he reached the ground, I flew over him at about thirty feet in order to ascertain whether I had killed him or not, and what did the rascal do? He leveled his machine gun and shot holes into my machine.

"Afterward Voss told me that if that had happened to him, he would have shot the aviator on the ground. As a matter of fact, I ought to have done so, for he had not surrendered. He was one of the few fortunate fellows who escaped with their lives. I felt very merry as I flew home to celebrate the downing of my thirty-third plane."

This is just a fragment of a controversy which went on long

after the war, for in his official report, given below, Richthofen claims to have killed one of the aviators on the ground.

Requesting Acknowledgment of My 33rd Victory
Date: April 2, 1917
Time: 11:15 A.M.
Place: Givenchy.
Plane: English Sopwith two-seater. Clerget Blin motor, type 2, without number.
Occupants: Sergeant Dunn and Lieutenant Warren.

Together with Lieutenants Voss and Lothar von Richthofen I attacked an enemy squadron of eight Sopwiths above a closed cover of clouds on the enemy's side of the lines.

The plane I had singled out was driven away from its formation and tried to escape me by hiding in the clouds after I had put holes in its fuel tanks.

Below the clouds I immediately attacked him again, thereby forcing him to land 300 yards east of Givenchy. But my adversary would not surrender, and even as his machine was on the ground, kept shooting at me, thereby hitting my machine very severely when I was only five yards off the ground.

Consequently, I once more attacked him already on the ground and killed one of the occupants.

(Signed) Baron von Richthofen

A footnote which throws fuel on the controversy is added by Lieutenant Peter Warren. After the war he said that his observer, Sergeant R. Dunn, died shortly after the plane was forced down. This was a result of receiving a bullet in the stomach. Warren claimed that Dunn was shot when the Sopwith was 12,000 feet up in the air, not on the ground.

"Richthofen dived down out of the sun and took Dunn by surprise," said Warren. "The first notice I had of the attack was when I heard Dunn from his seat behind me shout something at me, and at the same time a spray of bullets went over my shoulder from behind and splintered the dashboard almost in front of my face. I kicked over the rudder and dived instantly, and just got a glance of the red machine passing under me to the rear. I did not know it was Richthofen. I looked back over my shoulder, and Dunn was not in sight. I did not know whether he had been thrown out of the plane in my quick dive or was lying dead at the bottom of his cockpit."

After the battle and chase Warren managed to land the Sopwith. "I managed to flatten out somehow in the landing and piled up with an awful crash. As I hit the ground, the red machine swooped over me, but I don't remember him firing on me when I was on the ground."

Of course, Warren was in a dazed, shocked condition, and it may be that he did not hear Richthofen's fire if the German ace did shoot at him. Even so, this does not tally with Richthofen's remarks about the English pilot turning the Lewis gun on him after the landing.

"I looked into what was left of the observer's cockpit," Warren continues, "and saw poor old Dunn crumpled up on the bottom. He was quite heavy, and I had some difficulty in lifting him out. He was unconscious. I laid him on the ground and tore open his coat. He had been plugged through the stomach, apparently from the back. I lifted him and spoke to him. 'I think I'm done,' he mumbled and then became unconscious. German infantrymen rushed out from dugouts nearby; some of them brought a stretcher."

Dunn received medical attention, but six hours later a doctor told Warren that the observer was dead. "Dunn was a stout fellow," Warren says. But the mystery of whether Richthofen had performed a cowardly act in shooting grounded Allied airmen has never been solved.

Richthofen continued to garland himself with the laurels of victory. On April 5, 1917, he filed two more reports requesting acknowledgment of his thirty-fifth and thirty-sixth victories. Both were hard, strenuous fights, one at Lembras, southwest of Douai, the other over Quincy. Worried about Richthofen's continued dominance in the air, the British decided to stage a massive raid on Douai in an effort to cripple the notorious Jagdstaffel No. 11. But German intelligence was well aware of the British plan to wipe out Richthofen's base and machines. Given the chance to evacuate, Richthofen decided to stay where he was, and, only a few hours before the raiders were due, sat down to dinner with his senior pilots. By the time they reached the coffee-and-cigars stage the rest were jittery, but the Red Baron was quite calm, demonstrating some of the new fighter tactics of the English. His particular interest was the Sopwith, and he had been working out the best blind spots from which to attack. He ran on, citing his latest conquests, smiling slightly at the tense faces all around him. Then, as though on a cue, he paused when the telephone bell tinkled. Somebody picked up the phone, listened and put it down again. "The English bombers are on their way."

Richthofen picked up a bottle and some glasses. "Come, gentlemen."

They went into the deep shelter and, according to Richthofen himself, "we were particularly merry."

Flying through the black sky, thirty-six young English bomber pilots were trying to find the Douai field, but Richthofen did not think much of Allied navigation. For himself, he said, he thought that it would be simple to find Douai. It was surrounded on all sides by major roads and other landmarks.

Richthofen refilled the glasses of his guests and cracked jokes. He wondered if there would be a chance of getting out of the shelter and up into the hazardous sky to fight the invaders. It was no good taking off at present; the British had not yet arrived. He finished his drink and helped himself to another.

Eventually, bored with waiting, he went up to ground level and stood there, listening and waiting. Total silence except . . . yes, there was a low humming sound!

". . . Suddenly we noticed that one low-flying plane had shut off his motor," Richthofen recalled. "So he was coming lower. Lieutenant Wolff, who was standing beside me, said, 'Now we are for it.' "

Richthofen snatched up two carbines, threw one to Wolff, and they began blazing away in the direction of the oncoming plane. "We could not see him. Still, the noise of our shooting was a sedative to our nerves."

Then, quite suddenly and on a prearranged signal, the entire airfield was ringed by searchlights. The German anti-aircraft batteries had made their plans hours before the raid.

"Suddenly the searchlights reveal him in their glare. A shout rises all over the airfield. 'There he is.' Shots ring out from all sides.

"Our friend was sitting in one of those prehistoric English crates, and we could clearly recognize the type. He was half a mile from us, but was flying straight toward us."

Richthofen and his officers stood their ground, curious to see what kind of tactics the raider would adopt. The engine was not running, the propeller was motionless. At less than a quarter of a mile the pilot switched on his engine with a roar.

Phosphorus bombs rained down and the outlines of the hangars showed up. A couple of bombs fell at the back of the workshops, smashing in the walls, creating tremendous damage. Receiving the signal while they were circling above, the other seventeen British planes went in with a cacophony of engines that deafened those who waited on the ground. Twenty-pound bombs fell everywhere, in the hangars, which were now blazing fiercely, on the fuel dumps and in the administration offices.

For this first twenty-minute pattern bombing raid the British used superannuated FE's, machines which sometimes fell to pieces if handled roughly. That night they took more punishment than any pilot would have believed possible, weaving and dodging anti-aircraft fire which followed them almost at zero altitude. Dropping the bombs was hard physical work, for the observer had to sit well back in the forward cockpit, his fists wrapped around the lever until the last moment when the end of the dive was reached. As soon as the bombs left the aircraft the pilot pulled back the stick and the FE strained to reach the clouds, shuddering ominously and hinting that this might be the last moment of life. By miracle, every single plane returned to Izel le Hameau for another load of bombs.

At Douai the panic was considerable and even Richthofen was seen to be acting the part of fireman. Some old French water pumps arrived in time to put a stop to the fire spreading in various quarters, but the damage already done was massive.

On the second raid a couple of phosphorus bombs hit two hangars, creating havoc. Watching for the signal, the rest of the British bombers, drawn from No. 100 Squadron, swept down and planted their bombs in a pattern, causing even more destruction. From the air it looked like hell.

Realizing that they were at the point of no return, Richthofen ordered his men into the shelters. They stood there, drinking, and listening to the new salvo of explosions. Richthofen shrugged in reply to the questions fired at him by the pilots. They could do nothing now. The British had scored, there was no doubt about it. More than a ton of high explosive had thundered down in the last hour. The hangars and many machines had been severely damaged. Most of the machines would have to be written off. It might take hours to quell the fires now that they had caught hold of the fuel dumps. Richthofen, now moody and angry that he had been unable to get off the ground and fight it out with No. 100 Squadron, returned to his bottle, ignoring the worried expressions of those around him.

No. 100 Squadron got off lightly. They lost one plane, piloted by Second Lieutenant A. R. M. Richards with Second Class Air Mechanic E. W. Barnes as crew. Richards caught a burst of machine-gun bullets in the FE's engine and had to land near Douai. Both men were taken prisoner and interned.

This was one of the first major blows struck by the British, and the bombing raid resulted in the temporary crippling of Richthofen and Jagdstaffel No. 11. The Red Baron's circus was not in the air.

The raid occurred on April 5, but the original order to No. 100 Squadron read: "No. 100 Squadron will bomb Douai aerodrome on the night of April 5-6 if the weather is suitable." It meant that a second raid might be organized if conditions were right.

During the sixth of April, Richthofen worked hard to get his base into working shape again. The chaos was terrible, and he had to send out to Douai for additional laborers to patch up the runway, which was so pitted with craters that it would be impossible to try and take off under these conditions. Believing that the British might return for another crack at Douai, the Red Baron sent out for machine guns and tripods on which to mount them. Soon the airfield was ringed with armament, a series of lines of gun barrels, arrayed there like the teeth of a dragon.

That night the British did return. "We all rushed to our machine guns," said Richthofen. "Some of the men who were known to be good shots had also been given machine guns. All the rest were provided with carbines. The whole squadron was armed to the teeth to give a warm reception to our kindly visitors."

The first British FE swept down to 150 feet and tore across the airfield toward the barracks. He was picking up speed when the first searchlight flickered on and picked up the shape of the machine. Blazing away with carbines, revolvers and machine guns, the Germans tried to get a bead on the FE's engine, but he was moving so fast that it was impossible. He flew straight over Richthofen's head, shaking the nerve of the German ace by his audacity. Barely had Richthofen climbed out of his shelter again when thirteen British bombers came down out of the night sky, dropping TNT high-explosive bombs directly on the remnants of the hangars and again setting fire to the ammunition and fuel dumps. This time, however, they did not head for home as soon as the damage was done. They had a new target, the anti-aircraft and searchlight nests on the perimeter of the airfield. It was a secondary carnage, terrible to see, as the FE's came thundering down the beams, pulling out at the last possible moment, and shooting as fast as they could, down the beam, killing the crew and sometimes dropping the last bomb to make sure that destruction was complete.

Again, only one plane was lost, this time piloted by Second Lieutenant L. Butler with Second Class Air Mechanic B. Robb as observer. No. 100 Squadron later heard that the two men had been taken prisoner.

Richthofen was now beyond the point of being amused. To be precise, he was in a rage! On April 7 he managed to take to the air.

Requesting Acknowledgment of My 37th Victory
Date: April 7, 1917
Time: 5:45 P.M.
Place: Mercatel, other side of our lines.
Plane: Nieuport one-seater, English, details not available.

Together with four of my officers, I attacked an enemy squad of six Nieuport machines south of Arras and behind the enemy lines. The plane I had singled out tried to escape six times by various tricks and maneuvers.

When he was doing this for the seventh time, I managed to hit him, whereupon his engine began to smoke and burn, and the plane itself went down headfirst, twisting and twisting.

At first I thought it might be another maneuver, but then I saw the plane plunge, without catching itself, to the ground near Mercatel.

(Signed) Baron von Richthofen

Next day Richthofen shot down another plane, his thirty-eighth. In that fight was Lieutenant Heagerty, presumed killed by the German ace, but in fact he survived.

"The German scouts were higher than we were, and they dived down on us from out the sun," said Heagerty. "They seemed to drop down in all directions, pumping lead as they came. Cantle

[Lieutenant Heath-Cantle] was working the aft Lewis, and I heard him let out at a good blast at someone at the back of us. At the same time, a spray of lead whipped past my head, and several bullets tore through the woodwork beside me. I kicked over the rudder just in time to see the red plane passing below. He swerved at the same time, and round and round we went, each trying to get on the other's tail. I believe his Albatros was a little speedier than mine, but at that the Sop [Sopwith] was a stout bus.

"With six or seven planes all mixed up and diving around, it took almost all my attention to avoid collisions, but I managed to rip out several bursts from the forward-firing Vickers. . . . Cantle's gun was rattling away, when suddenly he ceased firing, and at the same time the pressure on the joystick was suddenly released. It was useless. My controls had been shot away. They must have gone in the same burst that killed Cantle.

"From a glide, we went into a dive. All the way down the red machine, or some machine, kept right at the back of me, ripping burst after burst of machine-gun bullets into the plane from the rear.

"I remember seeing the windshield in front of my face fly away in small pieces, and then the propeller stopped. Our speed was terrific. There was no chance to choose a landing place. I could only hope to get her out of that dive. I recall putting my weight on one foot on the rudder and seeing one wing tip swing toward the ground, which was coming up at a fearful rate. That was my last recollection. I thought it was all over. I must have fainted then, because I don't remember the crash. . . ."

After being unconscious more than twelve hours, Heagerty woke up in a German dugout with a German soldier attending to his fractured jaw and pouring brandy down his throat. He was taken to a dressing station where a German doctor sewed up a split eyelid without benefit of anesthetics. "He did a mighty good job on it, too, although I cursed him and yelled murder at the time. . . . The doctor was an old fellow, and he sewed away as if he were darning a sock while three of his assistants sat on me."

Next day a scarlet plane ripped across the German front line with a message which told the authorities that Heagerty was wounded and had been taken prisoner and that Heath-Cantle was dead. The pilot of the plane was Baron von Richthofen. He did the same thing again on April 13, 1917, after shooting down his forty-first enemy. His luck was becoming phenomenal. He destroyed three Allied planes one day, seeming to play with death in his flaunting strategy. He boasted that the British were too slow. Sitting behind twin Spandau guns, he could shoot anything out of the sky, given an Albatros machine and just enough gas to get there and back.

In one day his Jagdstaffel of six planes downed thirteen Allied aircraft. To celebrate the High Command's commendation, he put his machines in the air next day and fought several duels. The score was advanced by eight more kills, and Richthofen himself was responsible for one of these. By April 14 the Red Baron was able to mark up his forty-fourth triumph. Incredibly, the year was still 1917. He had a long way to go yet. Two days later, on April 16, he was asking for confirmation of his forty-fifth victim, a BE two-seater which came down between Bailleul and Cavrelle. It was his fifteenth that month.

Between sorties he wrote and told his mother that he had been invited to have lunch with the Kaiser. He also intended to go pheasant shooting. It was difficult to get away from the press of operations, though, and he stayed where he was for the time being. The war in the air had taken an encouraging turn for the Germans. In a period of one week, twenty-six enemy planes were shot down and Richthofen's Jagdstaffel was responsible for the high average of twenty-three. The High Command reckoned that the Red Baron and his group were doing seven times more work than the rest of the German air force put together.

As a combat pilot Richthofen was without peer. Seemingly invincible, he often flew only two days of the week, but was able to return to his base consistently and make claims which were always substantiated. His fighting methods were deadlier than they had ever been. One of the men to encounter Richthofen at the peak of the Red Baron's career was Second Lieutenant F. J. Kirkham of No. 13 Squadron. His pilot was Lieutenant Follet, and they were spotting for the artillery.

"I was watching the ground for the arrival of our shells when a burst of machine-gun fire came to my ear directly behind me. I turned quickly and stood up to man the rear gun. I was too late.

The red Albatros had continued its dive downward just in back of our tail and was way out of range.

"He must have been doing 150 miles an hour. He was away in the flash of an eye. I saw two others swing by, so I knew that at least three of them had dived on us from above and behind. They had taken us quite by surprise."

They were about 1,000 feet from the ground when Kirkham managed to lean forward to see what his pilot was doing.

"Poor old Follet had crumpled up and fallen forward on the stick. I couldn't see his face, but I knew that some of that first burst had hit him. His body on the stick sent the plane down in a steep dive. He must have rolled off it, however, because we seemed to straighten out once or twice."

Before Kirkham could do anything Richthofen was on them again, hovering over the tail and firing all the time.

"We were going down at a frightful rate. There was a dual-control stick in my seat which I might have rigged and pulled her out of the dive, but that would have meant turning my back to the Hun scout's machine gun, and I should have got it the same as Follet. I thought everything was over but the finale, so I just stuck to the rear gun and fired away at him in the hope that I might get him also. Apparently not a chance. I emptied the entire drum without effect. The red scout stuck close on the tail, and his two machines were pumping lead all the time.

"I had a number of bullet splashes on my face and hands. The sleeves and shoulders of my flying jacket had several dozen holes through them and then one bullet hit the barrel of the machine gun right under my nose. I remember looking over my shoulder, and the ground didn't seem over ten feet away. I closed my eyes and said good night. I had seen it happen before.

"But luck was with me. The plane hit a clump of small trees in the German big-gun positions. I woke up while German gunners were cutting me out of the wreckage. The first thing I heard was Follet's voice: 'God, we're on fire!' he shouted weakly.

"I think he must have been unconscious and raving. The tanks had split wide open and gasoline was over us and everything, but no fire started, although the radio key had not been switched off."

The Germans carried both men through a hail of British artillery fire to a dressing station somewhere near Vitry, but Follet died five minutes after arrival. They removed Follet's gold ring and gave it to Kirkham to look after. Kirkham was later asked to write a message to Follet's mother. He did so, asking her to break the news to Follet's widow. The message was dropped over the British trenches the next day. Kirkham himself was taken to Richthofen's headquarters at Douai, but the Red Baron was away on a mission and they never met. At Douai airfield the staff was very polite and went to some pains to make Kirkham as comfortable as possible.

One of the more bizarre aspects of the Richthofen story is that his father, then in residence at Douai airfield, was to be found scanning the skies with a telescope every day. Whenever Manfred and Lothar were in the air, the old man hopped up and down with excitement, hoping that his sons would fight a major battle within range of his telescope. The day that Manfred bagged his fiftieth victim, his parent lamented that the fight took place far beyond Douai. In the Vickers two-seater was Sergeant G. Stead, married only eight days before in his native Manchester. He was nineteen years old and this was his first major flying mission.

Richthofen's report read as follows.

Requesting Acknowledgment of My 50th Victory
Date: April 29, 1917
Time: 4:55 P.M.
Place: S.W. of Inchy, Hill 90, near Pariville, this side of line.
Plane: Vickers two-seater. No details. Burning in first line.
Occupants: Capt. G. Stead and unknown.
   Together with five of my officers I attacked an enemy squad of five Vickers.
   After a long curve flight, during which the adversary defended himself admirably, I managed to put myself behind him.
   After 300 shots, the enemy plane caught fire.
   The plane burned to pieces in the air, and the occupants fell out.

(Signed) Manfred von Richthofen

That same day Richthofen attacked an artillery spotter plane and shot it out of the sky. The pilot's identity was never discovered because the BE tumbled to the ground, burning, and was battered to nothing by crossfire between the lines during the battle of Arleux. Richthofen was cruising around later, looking for trouble, when a fast Nieuport, one of the new machines supplied to No. 40

Squadron, picked on him as a victim. The pilot, Captain F. L. Barwell, deliberately singled out the red plane because he thought he stood a chance of ridding the wartime skies of their biggest menace. Richthofen saw Barwell coming from above, waited until the Nieuport was almost on him, then swerved violently and let the enemy go by at top speed. Eastward, over Lens, Barwell somehow managed to get mixed up with Richthofen's own machines and for a few moments actually flew in the center of them with the Red Baron on his tail all the time.

Tired of having to tag along, Richthofen began to fire bursts from his twin Spandau guns, making Barwell bank and swing to and fro in the misapprehension that he was being fired on. It was a trick Richthofen often used and it had the effect of making the enemy unsure of himself. The banking motion also lost the Nieuport some speed and the German was able to fly a straight course and get a little closer in preparation for the kill. It was the moment Richthofen had been waiting for. He lowered his sights and concentrated on firing a few rounds into the petrol feed pipes which were clearly visible. He watched the holes spread over the fuselage, then saw a stream of vapor come shooting out. The Nieuport was enveloped in a scarlet spread of flames as it began to fall.

That night Baron von Richthofen received a message from the Kaiser congratulating him on his prowess.

CHAPTER 6

The Death of Richthofen

While Richthofen was on leave he went pheasant shooting at Freiburg, had a long meeting with Hindenburg and received a message that his brother Lothar was dangerously ill in the hospital after being shot down. He was not completely taken aback or even surprised at the news. Lothar was a rabid killer and lacked a sense of science—the sort of man who would take a machine gun to kill a herd of elephants.

When Manfred was on leave after his fifty-second victory, Lothar was placed in command of No. 11 Jagdstaffel. Picking a fight with an infantry spotter plane, Lothar selected the wrong man and found himself pursued instead of filling the role of pursuer. Try as he would, he failed to shake off the Englishman, who was shooting at him all the time. He force-landed, found that he was badly wounded in the legs, and passed out. The incident did not detract from Lothar's popular appeal, for he was the man who shot down the British ace, Captain Albert Ball. That, at least, was the story, but it was not substantiated.

Ball was flying a slow triplane and got mixed up in a fight from which he never emerged. He was a man with the special qualities of Lothar and Manfred von Richthofen. Ball was engagingly young but he possessed that killer streak which maintained a stubborn superiority over other pilots. But unlike the Richthofens, he often flew alone, hoping to pick up the trail of a Jagdstaffel and single out a victim. Once he found something to fire at, Ball never gave up until the enemy lay on the ground, a smoldering ruin. His tactics were rather similar to those of Manfred von Richthofen, and he was an expert in the art of getting behind a victim without being noticed. On several occasions he was seen to approach to within twenty feet and remain there until the moment when he could look through his gun sights and press the hair trigger.

Albert Ball often flew with the Germans, his favorite gambit being to find a V-formation flaunting their Gothic crosses and then tag along, firing now and then to announce his presence. In reality he was challenging any or all of them to fight. The first one out was his man. Ball perished in the fight which led to Lothar von Richthofen making his forced landing, but there is no certainty that Lothar was actually responsible.

Manfred von Richthofen cut his leave short on hearing that Allied superiority was on the upsurge. New British planes now arriving in quantity at the front included the DH4 two-seater fighter-bombers, Bristols, the SE5 single-seater fighter.

On June 14 the Red Baron was back at the front to hear about the tactics of the new planes. Their first asset was speed. They could nearly equal the German Albatros, he heard, and the German High Command even at this moment was planning to reorganize the air force to combat this new threat to their superiority. The entire system of the Jagdstaffel was to be enlarged in scope and size. The new idea was to make up fighting squadrons, or *Jagdgeschwader,* each consisting of four staffels. The operational number of machines would be in the region of forty-eight. But most important was the High Command idea not to allow the new groups to stagnate in one area as Jagdstaffel No. 11 had remained throughout its early service at Douai. They were to be mobile and able to move at short notice.

By July 1917, Richthofen was marking up his fifty-seventh victory, but in that month he suffered the sharpest setback of his career. He came up against Flight Commander A. E. Woodbridge and Pilot Captain D. C. Cunnell of No. 20 Squadron.

"Our job was offensive patrolling," said Woodbridge. "In other

words, we were supposed to go out and light into any enemy planes
we could find. We knew the Albatroses and Halberstadts could fly
rings round us and shoot hell out of us from that blind spot under
our tails."

Six British FE2's set out on the patrol over an area which
featured Comines, Warneton and Frelinghein. They were found by
eight German machines, and the fight started immediately.

"Cunnell handled the old FE for all she was worth, banking her
from one side to the other, ducking dives from above and missing
head-on collisions by bare margins of feet," said Woodbridge. "The
air was full of whizzing machines, and the noise from the full-out
motors and the crackling machine guns was more than deafening.
The Jerries showed more spirit than usual. They went at it hammer and tongs. This enabled us to fire from the closest range and
was really to our advantage. Cunnell and I fired into four of the
Albatroses from as close as thirty yards, and I saw my tracers go
right into their bodies. Those four went down, and fortunately some
of our flight saw them tumble, because we were given credit for
them. Some of them were on fire—just balls of flame and smoke,
you know—a nasty sight to see, but there was no time to think
about it at the moment.

"Two of them came at us head-on, and I think the first one was
Richthofen. I recall there wasn't a thing on that machine that
wasn't red, and gosh, how he could fly!

"I opened fire with the front Lewis, and so did Cunnell with the
side gun. Cunnell held the FE on her course, and so did the pilot
of the all-red scout. Gad! With our combined speeds, we must have
been approaching each other at somewhere around 250 miles an
hour.

"Thank God, my Lewis didn't jam. I kept a steady stream of
lead pouring into the nose of that machine. He was firing also. I
could see my tracers splashing along the barrels of his Spandaus
and I knew the pilot was sitting right behind them. His lead came
whistling past my head and ripping holes in the bathtub.

"Then something happened. We could hardly have been twenty
yards apart when the Albatros pointed her nose down suddenly
and passed under us. Cunnell banked and turned. We saw the all-
red plane slip into a spin. It turned over and over and round and
round. It was no maneuver. He was completely out of control. His

motor was going full on, so I figured I had at least wounded him. As his head was the only part of him that wasn't protected from my fire by his motor, I thought that was where he was hit.

"But I didn't see him crash—Gad, no—too busy for that."

It was a long time before Woodridge knew for certain that he had wounded Richthofen. After landing, Richthofen was taken by ambulance to the hospital at Courtrai, where it was discovered that a British bullet had laid bare part of his scalp. It fell to skilled surgeons to examine the wound in the head of a man who had brought down fifty-seven Allied planes. The wound gave the German doctors a lot of trouble. First, the flesh would not heal; and then, when it did show signs of knitting together it was found necessary to reopen it in order to facilitate the removal of several splinters of bone which had worked to the surface. On landing, he had stumbled out of the Albatros cockpit and fallen headfirst into a thorn bush. Attending to the greater injury, the doctors had shaved away most of his hair and the points of the thorns were left in his scalp. But instead of coming to the surface they remained in position, creating intense irritation. In great pain and subject to violent headaches, the result of the near-fracture of the skull, Richthofen stood it as best he could. The nights were made hideous by bombing raids and the days were a torture while surgeons tried to keep the gaping wound clean and healthy.

On leaving hospital he was raised to the rank of captain commanding five Jagdstaffeln. It was a tremendous responsibility for a man who had been an invalid and could even now benefit from recuperative leave, but Richthofen shouldered his burden and prepared to go into battle again. His pilots were full of conjecture whether the wound had affected him, and indeed it sometimes seemed to. For ten days Richthofen did not fight or score a victory. In itself, this was very unusual, but on August 26, 1917, he did bring down one Spad piloted by Second Lieutenant C. P. Williams, No. 19 Squadron. In a letter to his mother Richthofen admitted that he felt ill immediately after his fight. All the same, Williams was his fifty-ninth victory. On September 2 he requested confirmation of his sixtieth, followed the next day by a report of a fight with a Sopwith single-seater.

Christmas of 1917 Richthofen spent at a number of parties given by German society women, and in January he went to Brest-

Litovsk to witness the final downfall of the Russians. But the inactivity bored him despite the presence of Lothar, with whom he went hunting in the forest of Bialowicza. He was not a political man and the haggling of the Germans with the Russians failed to hold his interest. He returned to the front after fighting to get permission, and was soon back in action. His sixty-fourth victory was over Second Lieutenant L. C. F. Clutterbuck and Second Lieutenant H. J. Sparks, MC, flying a Bristol fighter of No. 62 Squadron. In the hospital, having his wounds treated by the Germans, Sparks one day received a visitor who courteously bowed to him and handed him a box of cigars—with the compliments of Baron von Richthofen.

Manfred von Richthofen's last victim, his eightieth, was Second Lieutenant D. E. Lewis. On April 20, 1918, along with twelve other planes, Lewis took off for an offensive patrol. The clouds were low and it was decided to fly above them owing to the proximity of German artillery. Four miles over the German front line the group ran into fifteen German triplanes. Lewis was in the middle of a fight, when he banked his machine to find himself facing the famous scarlet Albatros. Lewis was flying a Sopwith Camel, and he immediately tried to get out of Richthofen's line of fire. For a moment he was actually in position to shoot the Red Baron down without imperiling himself, but Richthofen was quicker on the trigger and set fire to Lewis's reserve fuel tank.

Lewis hit the ground at sixty miles an hour, but he was unhurt, aside from a few burns, and was about to make a run for it away from a party of approaching German soldiers, when Richthofen's plane came down to within a few feet. Wondering whether he was about to be shot at, Lewis stared up at the red shape. Richthofen flew past, waving at his latest victim and apparently enjoying himself.

Next day, April 21, Captain Roy Brown, a Canadian serving in the RFC (No. 209 Squadron), headed a formation of three flights of five planes each, which took off from Bertangles. The three flights flew in three individual V-formations, hoping for combat. Every pilot in the air had fought against the Richthofen circus regularly in past weeks. At one stage parts of No. 209 Squadron encountered the Red Baron's machines twice a day and acquitted themselves nobly.

Looking down, Brown could make out two lumbering photographic planes of No. 3 Australian Squadron flying at 7,000 feet and making for the German lines near Hamel, a small village. Heading east and covering the Australians, Brown kept his eyes on the sky ahead until he and his machines were over Hamel. There they were plunged into a fight with four Fokkers, who were intent upon shooting down the photographic planes. Brown himself was about two miles above the engagement, and on seeing more German planes, including Albatroses, arriving, he gave the signal to his waiting Sopwith Camels to start their dive into the fight.

The fight, lasting about ten minutes, consisted of thirty machines which kept weaving in and out of one another's track, almost scraping noses, flying upside down, banking and shrieking down in short dives. Somewhere in the middle of it a newcomer, Lieutenant May, tried to get away. He had orders not to get involved in any fights, but this was harder than it looked. Pursued by Richthofen, he stood very little chance. May went down in a dive in the belief that he might be able to shake off the German ace, but it was hopeless.

Moving in from 1,000 feet, Brown tried to come alongside Richthofen but failed. As he was dropping behind, Brown made one last effort to spray the Red Baron's plane. Some of the bullets battered home . . . and the scarlet plane started its last dive to earth. And at that point, near Sailly-le-Sec, a miserable group of ruins once a prosperous French village, Manfred Richthofen made his last landing.

The machine was dragged to safety by Australian gunners, one of whom went into no man's land with a rope, the end of which was lashed around the ruined airplane. Hauling hard, they eventually pulled it into their sector and examined it. Sitting in the cockpit, as though still in control of the machine, was a figure, bolt upright. Even the hardened gunners paused when they saw that blood had gushed from the open mouth. It was not a pleasant sight.

Swallowing their doubts, the gunners searched the body, leaning over the cockpit. Papers were found and handed down.

"Christ, it's Richthofen! It's the bloody Baron!"

The body of Richthofen was buried at a cemetery near Bertangles and a photograph of the ceremony was taken. Next day a

British machine flew over Richthofen's base at Cappy and dropped a print of the picture together with the message:

TO THE GERMAN FLYING CORPS

Rittmeister Baron Manfred von Richthofen was killed in aerial combat on April 21, 1918. He was buried with full military honors.

From the British Royal Air Force

On November 19, 1925, the body was exhumed and taken by train to Berlin, where it lay in state for two days before burial. It was the last interment of the greatest aerial fighter of the war.

CHAPTER 7

Holland's Gift to Germany

Without Anthony Fokker, the Dutchman who once said that pilots could be as "temperamental as prima donnas," particularly about their machine guns, the war against Germany could have been shortened by as much as a year.

He was a boy who did badly at school. One of the reasons for his headstrong nature was an early youth spent running wild in Java, where his father was a coffee planter. The colonial idyl was broken when his parents returned to Holland to live at Haarlem, in the bulb-growing country. Anthony could not settle down to school, and never did reconcile book learning with life. The only subjects he liked were connected with what he called manual training— woodwork, mechanics, anything calling for the use of tools. His attic workshop was covered with railway lines and small loco- motives that ran on springs. Tired of having to wind them up all the time, he planned to tap the electric cable which ran past the attic window. His parents caught him just in time, but this did not put him off. His first real experiments were with the electrification of doorknobs and the near electrocution of his cousin. After that he tried to make some miniature gas-combustion engines, but without much success, so he turned to toying with a Bunsen burner.

94

This had to stop when his father complained about mounting gas bills. Trying to get around the difficulty, the boy burrowed under the floor boards until he located the neighbor's gas main. He made a T-connection and plugged in with a lead pipe. The connection was faulty and he nearly gassed himself. But he did get the gas he wanted and it was many years before he admitted what he had done.

Another project was the building of a canoe in the attic. When it was finished he showed it to the family. Impressed by his son's ingenuity, Fokker senior sent the craft to a paintshop to have it made ready for the water. When all is said and done, Anthony Fokker, *enfant terrible,* genius of wartime Germany and the force behind such aces as Immelmann and Richthofen, was only a typical boy.

Because he was such a poor scholar, Anthony rigged up a device which fitted underneath the lid of his desk. It enabled him to fix a series of circular crib sheets suitable for all subjects. By such means as this he was able to pass his examinations. When he eventually left school, he showed his teachers how he had managed to get through the scholastic trials.

During his period at school, particularly toward the end, Anthony was often ordered to go home. His teachers considered him an infernal nuisance. One of his friends was another "dunce," Fritz Cremer, whose father was known to Fokker senior. Cremer owned an automobile. In the Haarlem of 1908 this vehicle was so rare as to be a curiosity. Naturally, Anthony was agog for a ride in it, and was soon talking Fritz into teaching him how to drive. After that it was but a short step to thrusting his hands under the cowl and into the engine. One of the annoying things about the auto, he thought, were the tires, which were always puncturing or going flat through wear on the uneven roads. It puzzled Anthony that nobody had yet invented a punctureproof tire which would never go down after being inflated. It did not take long before he decided to invent one himself.

It is safe to assume that Anthony Fokker lived about half a century ahead of the times. Between 1957 and 1958 manufacturers were making a big fuss about a new driving innovation, the punctureproof tire.

Anthony began by experimenting on his own bicycle because he could not readily get hold of the Cremer automobile. The first tests were made at night on the worst roads in Haarlem. Anthony believed loss of sleep to be unimportant compared with the chance that his invention might be pirated if anybody saw it, therefore he worked when the world was asleep. When he reached the end of his own small savings he talked his father into sinking some hard cash into the idea. "Since that night I have done lots of selling in disposing of millions of dollars' worth of airplanes, but my father was the hardest prospect," he said. In the end the father agreed to go into partnership with his eager young son, and Anthony immediately made arrangements to get a two weeks' leave from school in order to be able to work on the tire. This was only a beginning. He entered into another partnership, this time with Fritz Cremer. The fathers of the boys got together and pooled some of their resources. It took over a year and a large sum of money before the tire was anywhere near perfection. In the initial tests it often fell apart, but as time went on Anthony made more and more tires which traveled more and more miles without disintegrating.

The Cremer car was used for some of the tests. In less than a year it was fit for the junk yard. Cremer senior then decided to buy another one. Only a few days later the old car stopped. It was a Peugeot, one of the first in Holland, and the mechanics of it had always fascinated Anthony. Helped by Cremer, he took the cowl off and had a good look at the engine. He found a mechanic who was supposed to know about such advanced matters, and they discovered that the fault lay in the gears. Anthony gave the mechanic all available funds and packed him off to the Peugeot factory near Paris to buy a new set of gears. Time went on and still no word came from the mechanic. Anthony was impatient. He wanted to fix the car and go on with testing the tire. He found a scrapped Peugeot in a junk yard near Haarlem, took out the gears and as many spare parts as he could detach, and carted his prizes back to Cremer. The car had to be stripped down again, but this time Anthony also ripped out the back seats, making a space for spare parts and other odds and ends. He had not done anything quite so ambitious as this before, but managed to grind the valves and time the magneto.

Tests on the punctureproof tire were carried out on a sixteen-mile stretch of road alongside the railroad between Haarlem and

Amsterdam. The rebuilt Peugeot shot along at forty-five miles an hour through the black night. Miraculously, the boys never met any of the horse-drawn carts which thronged the same road by day. The experiments were becoming more successful now. While Cremer drove the car up and down the road, Anthony relaxed in the place where the seats had been, his feet on the wooden boxes of spare parts, a blissful smile on his sharp features. There was every chance of making a success of the tire.

Fokker senior was worried about the way in which the invention had seized hold of his son, driving all thoughts of a formal education out of his head. Trying to hurry things up, he found a lawyer who specialized in the registration of patents, and this man carried out appropriate action to protect Fokker's interests in all the principal European countries, undertaking a search of records before final clearance when the invention could be put on the market. The expense was large, but Fokker senior paid up without protest, hoping that this would clinch matters, bringing back his investment with interest and sending Anthony off to school. It did neither. They found that a French firm already had a punctureproof tire on the market.

Anthony was naturally disappointed, but an aerial show which he saw at Brussels a few months later took his mind off the setback he had suffered. Going home, he told his father all about the Latham airplane, one of the highlights at Brussels. Wilbur Wright's visit to the Continent was past history, but Anthony knew about his work in detail. Blériot was also prominent in his mind. Unlike many other boys, he did not write to all the pioneers, asking technical questions. He posed the questions in his own mind and then went upstairs into the untidy attic to make his own models out of paper and wood and discover the answers. Up there, with the muted sounds of the street outside as accompaniment to his thoughts, he made an airplane with swept-back wings. He was still young and had not had any contact with people in aviation, yet this is how he described his model:

"I finally came to the conclusion that a sweepback wing with a pronounced dihedral, combined with a high center of gravity, would give me an airplane of perfect stability. When I actually had found an airplane which was inherently stable, I decided that it was not necessary to warp the wings as the Wrights and others had done before Glenn Curtiss invented the ailerons.

"For that reason my first monoplane was built two years later along my own lines, without ailerons. It had a high center of gravity and V-shaped sweepback wings and practically perfect stability."

Without receiving further help from his parents—in fact, after the fiasco of the tire they nearly disowned him—he decided to build a man-carrying kite that would take him over the nearest patch of water, from which position he would be able to work in a practical fashion, solving the problems of control and using the air currents. He was about to start building his first kite when the Dutch government introduced a scheme of one year's compulsory military service for boys of Anthony's age. Flabbergasted that any government should try to hinder his progress, he malingered without shame, telling the doctors that he had bad feet. Psychiatrists interviewed him without making headway, and he had to be sent to a hospital ward on a diet of rice and water which, they thought, would bring him to his senses, but he got around it by smuggling in some bread, jam, cakes and sausage. His larder was the underside of his bed, where he suspended the packages out of sight of the doctors.

One weekend he got out of this detestable place and went to Amsterdam. Jumping off a streetcar, he sprained his ankle and then offered a civilian doctor one hundred guilders if he would declare him unfit for military service. Three days later he was home, discharged, with his soldier's pay of forty-nine cents in his pocket. His father was furious with him, demanding that he agree to enter the University of Delft, where he could settle down to study for a professional career. But his own mind was far too occupied with problems of flight even to take notice of his parent's offer of 2,400 guilders a year if he went to Delft. In the end they had to compromise. Anthony would study engineering—in a practical sense, he stipulated—at the technical school at Bingen, on the Rhine.

He had not been at Bingen more than a few days when he happened to hear about a school for motorcar engineers at Zalbach, near Mainz. Knowing that his father was interested in cars, he wrote home, saying that he had decided against Bingen and was going to a better place at Zalbach. He had not been there more

than a few hours when he discovered that they had an airplane engine which was supposed to form part of the study course. The
engineer in charge told him that there was a long-standing plan to
build an airframe around the engine so that pupils could learn how
to fly. Questioning the man, Anthony came to the conclusion that
he knew nothing about aeronautics, yet ten years later he was to
give him a job in one of the wartime Fokker factories.

He again wrote to his father, this time asking for the loan of
one thousand marks, the deposit required by the school against
possible breakage of the machine by students. Receiving the money
from a now outraged parent, he enrolled for the aviation course
only to discover that he was the only student. Appeasing his father,
he kept up a constant stream of letters home, saying that he was
making superb progress in aviation among some of the best fliers
in the world. In fact, his tutor was Hugo Buchner, a man fated
to crash many planes during his career. He traded shamelessly on
the fact that he came from the famous Johannisthal flying school
near Berlin, but never produced a license issued by the controlling
body, the Fédération Aeronautique Internationale. But then, nobody ever asked to see it, so he was safe. From the beginning
Anthony viewed him with suspicion, believing that the man was
actually afraid to fly.

Anthony Fokker's first experiments were conducted with the
school's four-cylinder air-cooled motorcar engine which had been
"converted" into an airplane engine, but it developed no power at
all, and most of the time was spent running it up, then stripping
it down again before going through precisely the same routine.
Perhaps the only thing he ever learned from this useless piece of
equipment was the working of an engine. All the time Anthony
was tinkering with the thing, Hugo Buchner was trying to put
on a show of eagerness to start flying. As soon as the first airplane was ready he took his student out to a field near Wiesbaden.
He was to be first off the ground, of course, but they soon discovered that the machine was far too heavy and could only run up
and down the field. At one end was a steep slope down which the
"grass cutter," as they called it, frequently ran and had to be
hauled up again.

It might be thought that Fokker was now losing interest in aviation when the very school where he was supposed to be learning all

about flying could not find even one serviceable machine to put up in the air. This was not the case; he was more eager than ever, and talked one of his fellow students into buying a 50-hp water-cooled Argus engine. This young man was just as ardent as Fokker to become airborne, so the Dutchman did not have to do much talking before his wish came true and the engine was being un-crated at the school. Fokker himself did much of the carpentry on the airframe which eventually enclosed the Argus engine, and dur-ing trials both young men were overjoyed to find that the machine could actually fly for short distances.

Now in a very uncomfortable position and faced with an airplane which *could* fly, Buchner, the tutor, surreptitiously took it out and gave himself secret lessons before trying to show off in front of his students. Fokker stumbled on the sight when he noticed the Ger-man taxiing the machine round and round the field, trying to man-age its 45-foot wingspan. The biplane had to clock up a speed of fifty miles an hour before it could rise and Buchner was evidently scared of it. At one demonstration, given before the students, he ran it across the grass at full tilt, forgot to throttle back to get it into the air, and ran straight into a ditch. There was a cloud of summer dust. When it subsided, all the students could do was pull a disheveled Buchner out of a tangle of wires and wood and spars. It was the end of Hugo Buchner. Next day he packed his bags and left. Fokker was glad to see the last of him, but was de-pressed to realize that the school was having financial difficulties. There were rumors that it might shortly close down.

Fokker now became friendly with a German army Oberleutnant, Von Daum, who said that he was willing to put some money into aviation experiments if Fokker could raise a little capital as a guarantee of good intentions. After an acrimonious discussion with the director, Fokker managed to get a rebate of 500 marks deposit made by his father when first he entered the school. Fokker senior received a letter from the director, complaining about his son's conduct, but he did not take any action. He knew how Anthony regarded all teachers and saw no future in having a row with the school director. A few days later he received a request for a loan of one thousand marks from Anthony, who explained that he had just gone into partnership with Daum, and needed the money to start a business. The money went into the design of a new plane for which Daum bought the engine while Fokker spent his total capital of 1,500 marks on a tubular steel airframe.

They worked together in a Zeppelin hangar at Baden-Baden while the airships were away on trials. Their first specimen had sweepback wings, following the wood-and-paper models which Fokker made at home in the attic. At the last moment Fokker discovered that he had failed to take into account some ground-steering gear. The plane would have to be pushed out onto the landing ground and pointed into the wind before it could take off. This occurred to him only after the machine ran amuck . . . "like a headless chicken," he said.

In December 1910 Fokker gave the machine a trial, and it flew successfully. After sweating over trying to get the recalcitrant engine started, he went flying without any protective clothing and consequently caught a cold which developed into pneumonia. Recuperating from an illness that nearly cost him his life, he was shaken to read a telegram from Daum. It said that there had been a slight accident. He himself was a little shaken up and the machine was in need of repairs. Fokker was angry about it. He never had trusted Daum as a pilot, and knew that he had taken advantage of his absence to fly. Reaching Baden-Baden, Fokker found that the German had lost his nerve during take-off and run the machine up a tree. Working day and night, still feeling the aftereffects of pneumonia, Fokker rebuilt the machine and applied for his flying license. When he received it, after tests which seemed to him to be elementary, it bore the number 88. He was flying every day, making quite long flights of twenty minutes' duration at about 300 feet, and in general feeling "like the monarch of all I surveyed." Visitors to Wiesbaden airfield often asked when Anthony Fokker would be coming to fly. Unrecognized in his dirty overalls and oil-smudged face, he told them that the aviator would be along shortly. For imparting this information he received plenty of tips which he passed on to his own mechanic.

For some time Fokker, who was not the easiest person in the world to get on with, had been having arguments with his partner, Daum. The German yearned to fly, perhaps out of motives of vanity, but always had to stand back and let Fokker get all the limelight. Fokker at last said that he might use the machine. After several satisfactory circuits, one day Daum lost his nerve and crashed the plane. He said he did not want to see another machine. He was sick of them, and sick of Fokker, too.

Snapping up the chance, Fokker offered him 1,200 marks for his share in the business and left Daum to get some treatment for his gloomy anti-aviation mentality. Daum was to be the last of Fokker's partners. From that time on, the Dutchman made up his mind to be responsible only to himself. To keep his independence he had to send frequent letters to his father, asking for more money. For a time he was pestered by get-rich-quick promoters, who thought that the flying machine was something for the fairground. Casting about for something to do, Fokker was invited to fly in honor of Queen Wilhelmina's birthday. Reaching Amsterdam, where the airfield was supposed to be, he was shown a patch of marsh and bog from which it would be practically impossible to start a plane. Yet he did manage to start after all, but nearly lost his life when the wheels caught in the mud. He flew over Amsterdam at about 300 feet, waggling his wings in triumph to a goggling crowd below. That day, he said, was perfect for everything—except flying.

He moved on to Haarlem to give another display, and his pessimistic parents were in the crowd to see him break his neck. He flew brilliantly, and on landing was met by his overjoyed father, who saw in the machine a very worthwhile return for his frequent investments. So overcome was Fokker senior that he took off his watch, a family heirloom, and gave it to Anthony.

Soon after his return to Mainz, where he was making new experiments, Fokker received an invitation to go and work at the famous Johannisthal airfield. Before he was ready to start, his school friend, Fritz Cremer, turned up and the two young men were able to laugh at their early work on the punctureproof tire. In later years Cremer became very closely associated with Anthony Fokker, being appointed postwar agent for Fokker aircraft in the United States.

Arriving at Johannisthal, Fokker was greeted by raucous laughter as he unpacked his swept-back-wing machine for a test flight. They had never seen anything like this before. On the other hand, they had never before met anybody like Fokker.

8

The Menace of the Fokker

What the German aviators thought of the thin, wiry, forceful young Dutchman, who arrived at Johannisthal airfield with every intention of becoming a force in aviation, we do not know. From their actions it is obvious that they believed it possible to squash him in a matter of days. What actually happened was quite the reverse; he squashed them.

What was the position of aviation about this time? The Wright brothers were back in America, disillusioned after their continental journey to raise funds and interest in the Flyer. In France airplanes were circling Paris every weekend. There was nothing very positive about flying machines and to the man in the street they were at best an engaging toy. To the journalist they were something to write a humorous column about. Very few people believed that these dangerous, noisy structures of wood and wire could ever play a tremendous role in world history.

To the Germans, Johannisthal was something of a circus, a place to visit weekends in hopes of seeing machines crash. A clique of dashing young pilots were making a good thing out of it, charging admission fees and giving rides in the dangerous-looking machines. Among the crowds a sprinkling of German army officers could be seen, many of them interested in flying, others who just wanted to become involved in the gay milieu of the airfield.

The man who invited Fokker to come and fly at Johannisthal turned out to be an agent of the Dixie Engine Company. He was little more than a traveling salesman, aiming to sell some of his products to the Dutchman. Fokker only found this out later, but nevertheless stayed where he was, determined to make a success of it.

Practically all the Johannisthal pilots flew for the benefit of the weekend crowds on a profit-sharing agreement, those who were airborne reaping the biggest rewards with extra pay for hazardous stunts. Nobody actually minded Fokker coming in on it, but his strangely shaped machine was an unknown quantity and might become one of the attractions of the place, bringing him higher rewards than the rest. A German, Willy Rosenstein, headed the aviators and set the tone of the reception committee by guffawing at the sight of Fokker's creation. Rosenstein arrogantly said that the machine would not even fly. Without bothering to reply, Fokker housed it in a hangar belonging to the Dixie Engine Company, serviced the engine and, helped by one of the innumerable free-lance mechanics, prepared to take the air.

On the day when he was supposed to fly, the engine kept stalling for no reason at all. It would not even run long enough for him to taxi out of the hangar and take off. Angry and desperate, for he was losing money all the time he was stuck to the ground, he stripped the engine down and found a strange white deposit in the carburetor. It was sugar, perhaps poured into the fuel tank by the purse-conscious Rosenstein.

When the Fokker machine did fly, it eclipsed all the others. In every sense of the word, Anthony Fokker had arrived. He became the top money-maker at Johannisthal and the first attraction. Yet throughout his success, which mounted every time he flew, he never once copied the other pilots. He seldom wore the dashing flying jackets, the painted helmets, and could not be bothered to put the usual white scarf around his neck. All he wanted was to sell the design of the plane to any country with enough interest to take it up. He was intensely disappointed when the Dutch government ordered its first planes from the Henri Farman company in France. He had pinned his hopes on getting that bit of business and making enough profit to carry on with his exhibition flying for the time being.

Fokker was never a nationalist nor was he politically minded, but he did believe that his own government should have patronized a native son's designs since the machine had been well proved at Johannisthal.

Believing that business must materialize sooner or later, he set up a manufacturing company, the Fokker-Aeroplanbau, employing about thirty technicians and engineers, but very few of them were highly qualified in this new industry, and he had to watch over every little detail. When his factory was in full production he was visited by prominent army officers. They said they were interested in his ideas but could not hold out any hopes of placing orders at the moment. Then quite suddenly he received an order for two machines at 10,000 marks. It was the biggest day in his life. Overjoyed, he invested as much capital as he could in staging demonstrations of the machine, once risking everything, including his life, in looping the loop, a trick then believed to be extremely dangerous. At a first try he nearly died from fear, but later repetitions convinced him that it was much easier than it looked. Furthermore, it impressed potential buyers.

Looking about for the means to continue his business and encourage young bloods to enroll for training at a flying school he started, Fokker decided to enter the airplane trials which were to be held in Russia. This was 1912. Aviation was growing everywhere, and more than thirteen competitors from several different countries were heading for Russia. Soon after he got there, Fokker discovered that the trials were to be very demanding. A machine must climb to 3,000 feet in twelve minutes and then curve at terrible breakneck angles. There was a definite time limit on all entrants and the bouts were organized on a knockout basis. In the next week Fokker did more flying than he had ever done in his life before, competing against the best French pilots and designers and even the famous Igor Sikorsky, who was trying to win a prize for his newly organized factory. Feeling dispirited, he knew that he could not go on any longer. He left his machine in Russia and went back to Germany. Soon after reaching Johannisthal he heard that he had been awarded third place. The financial reward was poor and nothing much came of it. All he had was the 10,000 marks for the two planes.

He hesitated to approach his father for more loans. The last loan was not yet paid off. Once again he had to fall back on exhibition flying despite the time lost in moving about from one airfield to another. True, he could have taken the easier course. Albatros and Rumpler, both large concerns and just now expanding, approached him with tempting contracts, but he had to refuse. He wanted his freedom and independence. The company negotiators went back to report that Fokker could not hold out much longer. He barely had enough to feed himself. When he closed down his tiny company, he would come running.

Fokker did not lose heart. One of the gloomiest barriers to real progress was this lack of ready cash, but past experience with partners stopped him from looking around for somebody to share the load. Debts were piling up all the time, but he still had some credit left. He was at rock bottom when a group of businessmen invited him to meet them at one of Berlin's biggest banks. In the next hour the whole course of his life was changed. The men explained that they felt aviation was going to be of the greatest military and civil importance to Germany in the future. They were practically sure that the navy and the army would soon be in need of machines, dozens of them at a time. Would Herr Fokker be interested in a position as head of a new aircraft company at a starting salary of 12,000 marks a year?

He went back to his small factory and started ordering engines, raw materials, expanding and making promises to people he hardly knew. This was what he had been waiting for, but it turned out to be bigger than his dreams, bigger than anything! He personally authorized all the accounts, believing that the new company would eventually meet them when all the formalities were over. Only when he was thoroughly enmeshed in a financial web which he himself did not clearly understand did he hear that the new company would not be formed unless the navy and the army actually offered the contracts.

The discussion at the Berlin bank had been of an exploratory nature, but they did not tell him so. There was no question of floating a huge business empire on the off chance that they would be able to recover their outlay later. When he inquired about the capital currently available he was told that only 20,000 marks was to be had. It was not enough to meet all the outstanding bills. In a panic, he went to see various heads of the forces and tried to sell them on the idea that now was the time to order airplanes. They were only half convinced and said they would think it over. When they did come back to him, he had to confess that most of their preliminary expenditure would have to be spent settling outstanding accounts and developing prototypes. But it was hopeless, useless. Nobody swallowed his bait. He was nothing more than a mad Dutchman who did not know the first thing about money.

Fokker was forced to call a meeting of the bankers and plead for a release from the contract which he had so foolishly signed. He must have his freedom. They told him that he could go if he paid them 4,000 marks. He scraped it up somehow, canceled the purchase of a car ordered at a time when he believed that everything was going to be all right, and once again sat down to write to his father for a loan. Fokker senior had by now poured more than 100,000 marks into his son's business ventures without any return for the investment. Within a few days Anthony received a point-blank refusal from his father: "Now I have had enough. You have never shown me any books. You have never shown me any real statements. I am not going to believe any more promises."

Angry that his own father should no longer have any faith in him, he turned to his uncle, Edouard Fokker. After prolonged argument he received the sum of 20,000 marks. Edouard had his reward years later when the still-grateful Anthony made him president and chairman of the Dutch company. Even now, though, he was still in need of money and managed to wheedle out of his father the allowance of 2,400 guilders a year, which was promised if he entered Delft University. Before Fokker senior's death in 1925, Anthony had paid back every penny he ever borrowed and into the bargain declined to accept his share in his father's will.

It was only comparatively late in life that Anthony Fokker realized how poor a businessman he was: it was the war that made his fortune. Had it not come along in 1914 he might have gone on and on, trying to establish himself and always failing despite his flair for aircraft design.

By 1912 a Captain Geertz, one of the strange and nebulous figures of European history about whom the truth has never been uncovered, was trying to obtain official sanction to remove the aviation section of the German army signal corps and develop it as an individual fighting force. It was due only to Geertz that Fokker received the majority of vital contracts at the outbreak of war.

Fokker was among the first aviator-designers to have army pupils sent to him for flying lessons, most of them very stiff and precise Prussian officers who believed in the divine right of the Prussian caste system. A few days after the first batch arrived, twenty more came to Johannisthal, and within two weeks every wildcat pilot on the field had a full list of would-be pilots. This naturally created some confusion because there was no proper airfield control. Pilots and teachers took off and landed very much how and when they thought best. When the toll of crashes and deaths rose alarmingly, the authorities stepped in and insisted that a control be arranged. The turnover in would-be pilots still rose, especially when the tutor obtained permission from the army to grade the officers as fit or unfit. Fokker was to see some of his finest planes so badly handled by clumsy learners that he evolved his own system of telephoning the army headquarters and arranging for the immediate recall of the worst of the brood before they killed themselves and the onlookers.

One of the strangest incidents in Fokker's life occurred at this time. A Captain Felix Schultz came to him as a pupil and claimed that he was actually a spy for the British government. He said that he already knew enough about Fokker's work to be able to go to London with blueprints and plans of the latest machines. Fokker could see no reason why he should be disbelieved, but he did not guess that the British already knew quite a lot about Anthony Fokker and his airplanes, a few models of which were to be found in London. There had been some talk of "adopting" Fokker and bringing him over to work in England, but the financial estimates were large enough to deter the champions of the idea in Parliament. Fokker found a way of putting Schultz off by saying that he would like him to act as his agent in England. From London the faithful Schultz, who was willing to spy for any side that paid him and very often for both sides at once, sent valuable prints of British seaplanes and other machines to Fokker. When this dual-sided gentleman came back to Johannisthal, he immediately attached himself to another aviator who had more or less copied Fokker's latest design. Inspecting the machine, Fokker did not believe it to be so well built and warned Schultz against flying it. He was standing on the edge of the field, watching the spy putting the machine through its paces, when it went into a steep dive and crashed into some trees. Schultz's career had come to a quick end.

There was a growing opinion among the Johannisthal aviators that the German government was about to equip the army with fast machines. Sure enough, an official announcement was made, and as the government did not have an aviation expert of any kind it was decided to hold tests to decide which was the best plane, the winner to receive a contract to build army machines. A second reason for the test was that none of the existing types had yet shown any endurance qualities. In those days long flights were very rare. Fokker had carried out a number, but they passed unnoticed in an atmosphere of showmanship which demanded stunts rather than long-distance flights.

The government laid down a course of 250 miles, the airplane to be carried by motor vehicle to each town and flown there. Scoring would be done on a points system. Ten units would receive an award of 45,000 marks, a fortune to the impoverished Fokker. As soon as the first announcements were published, he went to see the principals of Mercedes-Daimler and talked them into building a truck which would accommodate a complete aircraft. The plane itself was elementary in construction, with wings which folded down and were secured for flight by a turnbuckle. Strut wires and other stress points could be fixed in a matter of seconds.

When he started out on the 250-mile course, the truck scooting along the narrow roads like a mad thing, Fokker rode along with the conviction that he was going to win this competition and make a fortune. Almost before he realized it, they were at the last point and he was flying to the satisfaction of the adjudicators. Other competitors were still strung out over the course, struggling to put their machines together or take them apart.

Having won against stiff competition, Fokker soon came to be regarded as a leading force in military aviation, and he moved his headquarters to a more important airfield, Schwerin, Mecklenburg, 200 miles north of Berlin, in the Baltic coastal region. This was to become the official army flying school. Hangars and living quarters were erected, the ground leveled off, surrounding trees chopped down. 1914 was not very far away, but as an apolitical person Fokker did not appreciate the reason for Germany's hurry in preparing a flying school. One writer has said that Fokker's head was too close to the drawing board to see the gathering war clouds. His first students included the Graf von Bismarck, grandson of Bismarck. After several lessons, his famous pupil took such a liking to the experience of flying that he bought his own plane from Fokker. Other students did the same. Fokker was now becoming moderately wealthy, but he was spending his money at a fearful rate. He had to because, for many reasons, it was not easy to start a factory at Schwerin. Despite this, and because the outlook for the next three years looked bright, he went to Haarlem and called a conference of relatives, including his sorely tried father. His uncle, Edouard, and Cremer were also present. Together they formed a company with a declared capital of 300,000 marks.

At Schwerin once more, he sketched out the expansion plans which would enable him to build twelve planes at a time. One of the chief advantages of holding army contracts was the financial arrangement which gave him some working capital while the machines were still on the drawing board. He was able to claim one-third of the total sum in advance, another third when the work was half finished, the final third being paid when the planes were handed over. Apart from such orders as these he also built machines for private use and attempted to meet Germany's naval demands for seaplanes, using the blueprints which had been sent from London by Schultz.

In the midst of all this prosperity he discovered that he was again running short of capital, and had to appeal to his investors for another 100,000 marks to tide him over. Reluctantly getting down to some paper work, which he abhorred, he wrote to tell his family that the future was very bright if they could see their way clear to letting him have additional working capital. Beyond all doubt, the army and the navy would go on ordering machines. In a day of unskilled pilots, the mortality rate was high for aircraft. Once a Fokker was thoroughly smashed up, it was almost impossible to patch it up again. He ended with the observation that if the 100,000 marks was not forthcoming, he might have to close down at Schwerin and either come home or return to exhibition flying at Johannisthal. Receiving the capital—there is no trace of the furor which his letter must have created at Haarlem—he took on extra staff, bringing his labor force up to 150, and sought better raw materials, including the wood and support cables which played a vital role in all Fokker machines, the paint which reinforced the fuselage fabric. He believed that he would be able to show a clear profit of 40,000 marks by the end of 1914.

When war broke out in the summer of 1914 no one was more surprised than Anthony Fokker. He was not so much concerned with the conflict itself and the fierce drive against France which started on August 4, as with the future of his factory and expansion plans which he was just then putting into operation.

No blame whatsoever can be attached to Fokker for throwing in his lot with the Germans. When he was flying at Johannisthal the British had every chance to secure his genius, but they preferred to let it go by. Apart from one brief parliamentary discussion which was ruled by purse strings, not ethics, Fokker never came to the notice of the House of Commons until it was too late. When the war started he was only twenty-four years of age, a talented young man trying to stand on his own two feet after many spirited attempts to gain independence. He had no means of guessing that the planes he built might easily be used to strafe his own roads in Holland in a war about which he knew nothing until it exploded under his nose.

The German government's first action was to confiscate all Fokker's machines for its own use. He was about to dispute their claim, when he met a naval officer who thought that the machines might be of use to the navy. An argument was going on about the terms of the appropriation. Fokker was asked if he would let the German navy use the machines. He said that he could not give any sanctions one way or the other. He would sell to the highest bidder, taking the purchase price as compensation. When this became known, he had no peace at Schwerin. The place swarmed with officers, poking at the machinery, inspecting half-finished planes, making wild bids. Fokker cleverly let the prices rise. Most of the time, he was to be found in his office, keeping a note of the bids but refusing them all for the time being. He was hoping to make a fortune and get away to Haarlem as fast as he could, but he quickly changed his mind when the German government ordered that everything in the factory be confiscated and shared out equally. He was pacified on receiving a note that he would be paid, and when he did receive an accounting felt astonished to find that the prices they would pay were far in excess of those run up during the bidding by the army and navy.

There was no question of running away to Haarlem after this. Germany needed Fokker, though he did not necessarily need Germany. He was retained to train pilots, and he started off by pointing out that the airplane was a fighting machine, not necessarily something from which only scouting could be done. All this sounded somewhat revolutionary to the early pilots, but in time his theories caught on to form the basis of the training manual.

He was now engaged to build twenty-four single-seaters for the signal corps. On the crest of this wave of prosperity, he wrote to tell his father, uncle and other investors that he was not in a position to find a German bank to underwrite any financial setbacks. He was giving them the chance to get out if they wanted to. The war would last less than three months, he said. Of course, if they remained in control, he would probably be able to offer them a 30-million-mark profit. They accepted an offer of payment with interest and before he knew it Fokker was alone in Germany and one of its biggest assets.

He became interested in the design of the Caudron, a French twin-engined bomber seen to be carrying an outsize machine gun. The German artillery shot one down, and he was called in to examine it. He came to the conclusion that the big gun which it mounted so prominently was a mere showpiece. All the same, the Caudron did give him certain ideas about armament. Such aerial combat as did take place in the early months of the war was done by pilots shooting at one another with revolvers and rifles. Mounting quick-firing guns on airplanes seemed impractical. When reconnaissance pilots started dueling with rifles, Fokker reconsidered the question, remembered the Caudron, and wrote a report to the German High Command. Other nations had already produced machine guns mounted on the side of the cockpit, and German losses were mounting. Fighting in the air was regarded as being something of a sport, though Fokker foresaw a time when death would enter the arena. Germany, the country which had placed her trust in him, must be the first to have the most lethal instruments. After that day, when he suddenly discovered that war was a serious affair, Fokker planes took on a new look. "A sinister-looking craft," wrote A. J. Install, adjutant of a British squadron, "in the air rather like a large mosquito removed from a collector's setting board, and suspended from an invisible thread."

Fokker wrote: "The synchronized machine gun with which weapon Richthofen, Boelcke, Immelmann, Udet, Fonck, Guynemer, Nungesser, Bishop, MacCudden, Ball, Lufberry, Rickenbacker and Landis became such glamorous figures during the World War, was an inevitable device. Necessity is the mother of invention, and the necessity for the synchronized machine gun became increasingly imperative."

There was a sadness in Fokker's heart as he realized that no sooner had man discovered how to use the air for his own leisure and enjoyment than he must start using it as a battleground.

"They fought in the high blue sky like knightly champions of the muddy armies locked in deadly combat far below. It was only when death called, leveling them to the common fate, that these heroic youths came hurtling down, each plane a bloody, flaming pennon, bent for destruction. That was not a pretty sight to watch, and it is even sadder to contemplate when all the trumped-up fervor has gone out of the spectacle," he wrote.

We can see that he was a man of peace, but this did not stop him from inventing, in the autumn of 1915, one of the deadliest war weapons ever produced, the synchronized machine gun which maintained German air superiority for a full year.

The effect of the debut of Fokker's fighting machines, which became supreme in October 1915, may be judged from this letter written by Rothesay Stuart Wortley, a flying officer of the RFC:

"The appearance of the Fokker monoplane . . . was soon to put a very different complexion upon the state of affairs. At first our pilots were not much impressed by this new apparition. They had been far more concerned with 'Two-tails,' a frightful-looking contraption with a double fuselage, which forged its way through the air like some ungainly troll.

"But there were two outstanding features about the new machine. First it was difficult to spot. A thin black line with a blob in the middle, very like a cormorant on the wing, was all that could be seen. Secondly, it was fitted with an 'interrupter gear,' by means of which the machine gun could be made to fire directly ahead in the line of flight, the bullets passing between the propeller blades, and the trigger automatically stopped when the blades came opposite the barrel of the gun. This was a development of the first importance."

In his letter Wortley went on to say that as soon as the German pilots obtained a better working knowledge of the Fokker, the sky became a very dangerous place.

"As the months slipped by the list of our casualties grew. Artillery observation machines were shot down in full view of our men in the trenches, while long-distance bombers frequently failed to return from patrol. The Fokkers were gaining a complete ascendancy over our machines. They had a superior performance both in climb and speed over our Vickers fighters and the remainder of our first batch of 'Scouts.' The tactics of the pilots seldom varied. They would climb to a height of about 10,000 feet whence they would swoop, hawklike, upon our machines as they passed below them, firing continuously as they dived. They could dive at and pass their opponents, continuing straight onwards and downwards until well out of range; then they would climb again at their leisure to repeat the process later on. The Fokkers hunted in pairs, sometimes even three of them would fly together for mutual protection. . . .

". . . [the] advent of the Fokkers brought about the first serious consideration of aerial tactics. How best to tackle the Fokker with all its advantages in speed and climb? Whether, when dived on from above, to fly straight on, risk being hit, and trust to the observer's expertness in gunnery to bring the enemy down; or to 'turn in' under the enemy to avoid his field of fire, but in so doing to deprive one's own observer of his chance of destroying an enemy machine? The bravest of the brave advocated the former theory; but in the end this method proved too expensive; and maneuvering for position became the accepted rule."

During the time about which Wortley wrote, the air war was moving faster than the Allies. One day in December there were forty-six dogfights over the trenches. The frequency was becoming the rule, not the exception. The skies belonged to Germany, thanks to Anthony Fokker and the young pilots, and they were destined to remain so for many long weary months.

Duncan Grinnell-Milne, MC, DFC, a notable British pilot, also had impressions of the new phase of winged warfare ushered in by the Fokker fighters.

"The Germans had brought out a new fighting craft: a Fokker monoplane with a rotary engine. It was very fast, very maneuverable, with a gun firing through the propeller by means of a mechanism captured, it was said, from the French. For these good reasons the machine was proving almost certain death to our BE's, particularly when it was flown by a German pilot named Immelmann. Very vaguely, it was being rumored that this young officer (who had already brought down the incredible number of six machines) had invented a new method of turning. As a matter of fact, I believe he never did any such thing, but he certainly had a remarkably clever way of throwing his machine around so as to appear suddenly, almost sitting on his enemy's tail, with his machine gun banging away through the propeller. The 'Immelmann turn' it was beginning to be called, and it opened up a new set of problems in aerial fighting. . . .

". . . The Fokker announced the first phase of a new era. . . . To bring down an enemy machine at any time required luck, persistence, a fast airplane, and a well-aimed machine gun; but to bring down the Fokker or even to defend oneself successfully against it required something much more. It required from the scientist a better war machine. But with or without such a machine it demanded from the pilot a skill in swift maneuverability that went far beyond the aerobatics put up by even the most famous stunt pilots of the past.

"Sometimes we would talk far into the night, waiting hopefully for the fine morning when we might start practicing these new ideas that were to guard us against the menace of the Fokker."

CHAPTER 9

The Fortunes of War

Fokker believed that such armament as French planes possessed up to 1915 was quite inadequate for real combat fighting. He was not alone in his work to invent a gun which could be fired without interfering with the handling of the machine. Other nations had tried and failed. At best, he reasoned, gun, plane and pilot should act as one, but pilots were attempting to divide their function with the result that many lost control and crashed.

Progress was not made by the Germans until the French ace, Roland Garros, was shot down behind the lines. It was then discovered that he had used a machine gun placed directly in front of the cockpit, firing directly through a propeller fitted with steel wedges to deflect the bullets. Fokker observed: "Nevertheless, crude though it was, it had worked. Garros had shot down a number of unsuspecting German pilots before he was captured."

Fokker was called to Berlin to inspect Garros' gun and machine. Up to that moment he had never handled a gun in his life, but within forty-eight hours, working day and night, he adapted a Parabellum gun, an air-cooled weapon issued to the German infantry, and solved the problem of how to fire hundreds of rounds of bullets through a revolving propeller blade which made 2,400 revolutions per minute. He explains that he based his reasoning on the boyhood memory of throwing stones through windmill sails and remarking upon how seldom they ever hit the sails. Instead of going about it the obvious way and making the pilot do all the work, he used the propeller itself as a motive force, and within two days was able to show how a synchronized machine gun could fire 600 rounds a minute through the propeller area without once touching it. In his own words, here is how he evolved the prototype:

"For a temporary device, I attached a small knob to the propeller which struck a cam as it revolved. This cam was hooked up with the hammer of the machine gun, which automatically loaded itself. Thus, as I slowly revolved the propeller, I found that the gun shot between the blades. During the night I found out the basic operation, and began next morning to perfect the device. One blade was enough to strike the cam, because the gun could shoot only 600 times a minute while the blades passed a given point 2,400 times a minute. To the cam was fastened a simple knee lever, which operated a rod, held back by a spring. In order that the pilot could control the shooting, a piece of the rod which struck the hammer was hinged to hit or miss as the operator required. That was the entire device." Fokker adds that he had ". . . an immense feeling of pride to invent something which I knew would have a fundamental effect on strategy in the air, once it was adapted for combat work."

After announcing to the High Command that he would demonstrate his new method of gun firing, he towed his own plane to Schwerin airfield, and there showed a gathering of staff officers how the invention worked. Dubious at first, they were quite convinced after he flew over the airfield and strafed a series of targets. Indeed, he scared most of the high-ranking officers, perhaps deliberately, because their doubt annoyed him. They told him that they would be finally convinced if he shot down an enemy plane with the gun. He had no choice but to allow himself to be taken to the field headquarters of General von Heeringen, near Laon. Members of the general's staff were frankly dubious, so Fokker was again passed on, this time to the Crown Prince, a young man to whom he took an instant liking but who, nevertheless, ordered that he be disguised as a German pilot and sent into the air with the new gun to shoot down an Allied plane.

For several days an uncertain Fokker pilot patrolled the front, looking for a target, a victim of his own misgivings. He had every faith in the gun, but could not regard himself as a fighter pilot. At 2,400 feet he was too busy thinking about technical matters to keep an eye on the territory below, and only when the French artillery opened fire on him did he realize where he was and what he was supposed to be doing. All this happened after only a little more than a year of war. The chances of picking a fight with an enemy plane were remote because air activity was widely scattered. Fokker said that a berth in the air corps was supposed to be much safer than one in the trenches.

He went on patrolling without much luck, and transferred himself to Douai airfield. One week after arrival, when he was high over the area, he saw a Farman two-seater biplane emerge from a cloud below. He began to dive on it. This was the chance to demonstrate the gun, the chance he had been waiting for. He moved his sights about, swinging the machine to left and right to make sure that the Farman was dead in the sights. He wanted to fire first at the tank and feed pipes; then, when the plane was burning, he would follow it down, still shooting.

"Suddenly," he admits, "I decided that the whole job could go to hell. It was too much like 'cold meat' to suit me. I had no stomach for the whole business, nor any wish to kill Frenchmen for Germans. Let them do their own killing! Returning quickly to Douai, I informed the commander . . . that I was through flying over the front. After a brief argument, it was agreed that a regular German pilot should take up the plane. Lieutenant Oswald Boelcke, later to be the first German ace, was assigned to the job. . . ."

A few days after Fokker returned to Berlin he received news that Boelcke had shot down an Allied plane after only three flights. The success of the Fokker gun mechanism was no longer in the balance. On October 11, 1915, while all German planes were being armed in this fashion, Immelmann shot down his fourth plane, a BE2C of No. 16 Squadron, which was on photographic reconnaissance over Lille. Others quickly followed and it became evident that the Germans were holding a whip hand as far as the air was concerned. Until a German plane made a forced landing in heavy fog at a French airport, not one of the Allied nations even guessed why they were losing the war in the air. When the captured machine was examined, the reason became clear. Without proper security measures, Fokker's secret invention appeared in newspapers and magazines. The British government was embarrassed to hear that pilots were calling themselves "Fokker fodder." Awkward questions were asked once more about Anthony Fokker . . . but there were no replies.

With the success of his gun yet another feather in his cap, Fokker returned to Schwerin to organize the expansion of his factory. He spent a lot of government money, putting up new blocks of buildings, taking over old ones and converting them, arranging for a run-down piano factory to take a new lease on life, manufacturing the mechanism for the synchronized gun. By the end of the war 1,800 men were employed by the Dutchman. About 4,300 Fokker airplanes were built during the war. In other parts of the country they were constructed under license by various concerns. The end-of-war production total was in the region of 7,600. Fokker personally worked out a method of prefabrication which stepped up production. In eighteen months the labor force increased from 160 to 1,500, and at the head of it all was a Dutchman still in his twenties, a man who not only designed and test-flew airplanes as they came off the assembly lines, but also traveled to Berlin to negotiate contracts, obtain commissions and meet special orders. When the work became more specialized and greater than he could handle alone, he appointed Wilhelm Horter to look after management, Reinhold Platz as boss of the experimental department, and Heinrich Luebbe to look after the armament division. Fokker's interests in Austria were watched over by Wilhelm Seekatz. Bernard de Waal was later taken on as a test pilot and he also ran the flying school at Schwerin.

Soon after, the military authorities decided to accelerate the graduation of pilots. Fokker himself blamed the failure of this scheme on "quantity production" when twenty-two training planes crashed in less than one year. They approached Fokker and asked him to devote part of his plant to the production of seaplanes for naval use. This meant that he had to leave the flying school and factory and go to Travemunde, where he knew of a seaplane factory at which the German navy was trying to train seaplane pilots. Fokker's idea was to buy it and, after the war, convert it into a commercial proposition.

Seeking to secure some assets against a time when peace must surely come, he met Hugo Junkers and bought a half share in the latter's business for 3 million marks. He later had a row with Junkers and bought himself out of the contract for 1,500,000 marks. He was still paying heavily for experience, but it did not stop him buying a major interest in the firm which was then building Gnome and Le Rhone rotary engines. He spent 4 million marks on this venture. Right up to the end of the war it was one of the wealthiest industrial undertakings in the whole of Germany.

Early in 1916, when wind, gales and rain made operational flying almost impossible, the RFC strategists began to think very seriously about the massacre wrought by Fokker machines. On January 14 an order was put out which stated that the British were working on a plane which would make a better match for the Fokker. In the meantime, however, it was deemed advisable for all reconnaissance planes to work with an escort of at least three other fighting machines flying in close formation. If a single plane became detached from the formation for any reason, the reconnaissance must be discontinued immediately.

The plane referred to in the order as being under development was actually two different planes, the FE2B and the de Havilland Scout (DH2), both believed to be the answer to the Fokker.

The FE2B had the advantage of a fine engine, the 120-hp Beardmore, and an unusually wide cockpit from which it was possible to watch all parts of the sky without difficulty. The Fokker specialized in the fast attack, and Allied pilots constantly complained that they were cramped. The FE2B, originally designed and built by Geoffrey de Havilland, was believed to be the answer to the surprise attack. After passing out of use as a day fighter it became a night bomber over France.

Geoffrey de Havilland's other machine, upon which the experts pinned their faith in the present crisis, was the DH2, a single-seater powered with a 100-hp Monosoupape rotary engine. It could reach a speed of about eighty-six miles an hour at 6,500 feet, could climb to 10,000 in twenty-five minutes, and operated at a maximum ceiling of 14,000 feet.

Both the FE2B and the DH2, handled by fledgling pilots, entered the skies over the battlefields to acquit themselves in masterly fashion. The British were holding a winning hand. All they had to do was learn how to deal the cards. It had taken a year, but when it came it was worth waiting for.

Losing face, Anthony Fokker was chagrined to find that his machines were now being replaced by the Albatros and Halberstadt. His day was nearly over, but like all men with a pioneering instinct he refused to acknowledge it. It scarcely seemed possible that he was no longer wanted after his dedicated service in the cause of German aviation.

One of the major needs of the German air force was greater power. Most engines were somewhat limited. Up to 1916 the Germans were seriously hampered, but when the 160-hp water-cooled Mercedes made its appearance German war fortunes showed an improvement. Another singular achievement was the 185-hp BMW, in Fokker's opinion superior at very high altitudes to the British Rolls-Royce and the Spanish Hispano-Suiza. These perfections were, however, far away. In the meantime the German pilots had to be satisfied with the 80-hp Gnome, which ate up fuel and was bedeviled by all kinds of ailments, including frequent flooding of the engine with gas if the ignition was switched off without throttling back.

Among other drawbacks was a speed of only 70 mph and a ceiling of 6,000 feet, with a flying duration of two hours. Above certain speeds some of the early Fokkers were apt to crumple and have their wings torn off, especially during power dives. Despite all these drawbacks, the Fokker remained a better machine than, say, the Farman, which it could outpace. The British BC2E's were snails in comparison, while the French Morane-Solnier two-seater, although nearly as fast as the Fokker, was no match in fast-moving combat.

When Fokker heard that the French had introduced a 110-hp Le Rhone Nieuport which was being matched against the German 80-hp Gnome, he rushed back to his drawing board at Schwerin, intent upon outpacing the development. In a short time he produced the Fokker triplane, one of the best aircraft of its time, and the one in which Voss, leader of a Richthofen *Staffel,* brought down twenty-two Allied planes in three weeks. In comparison, the French Spad was faster and so was the English Sopwith Camel, but neither was quite as quick to handle as the Fokker triplane. Fokker later introduced the first of his "personalized" monoplanes, this one powered with a 160-hp Le Rhone engine with triple machine guns, and gave it to Immelmann. By this time he was a frequent visitor to the Boelcke-Richthofen-Immelmann headquarters and they were all good friends. He was regarded as the man who could give them the tools with which to do the job.

Here is an eyewitness report of what it felt like to be matched against the early Fokker machines. It was written by an anonymous airman.

"We got into a dogfight this morning with the new brand of Fokkers and they certainly were good. They had big red stripes on the fuselage diagonally, so they must be Richthofen's old circus. There were five of us and we ran into five Fokkers at 15,000 feet. We both started climbing, of course. And they outclimbed us. We climbed up to 25,000 feet and we couldn't get any higher. We were practically stalled and these Fokkers went right over our heads and got between us and the lines. They didn't want to dogfight but tried picking off our rear men. Inglis and Cal were getting a pretty good thrill when we turned back and caught one Hun napping. He half-rolled slowly and we got on his tail. Gosh, it's unpleasant fighting at that altitude. The slightest movement exhausts you, your engine has no pep and splutters; it's hard to keep a decent formation, and you lose five hundred feet on a turn.

"The other Huns came in from above and it didn't take us long to fight down to 12,000 feet. We put up the best fight of our lives but these Huns were just too good for us. Cal got shot in his radiator and went down and Webster had his tail plane shot to bits and his elevator control shot away. He managed to land with his stabilizer but cracked up. I don't know what would have happened if some Dolphins from 84 [Squadron] hadn't come up and the Huns beat it."

And the sensation of dueling against a Fokker went like this:

"I got to circling with one Hun, just he and I, and it didn't take me long to find out that I wasn't going to climb above this one. He began to gain on me and then he did something I've never heard of before. He was circling with me and he'd pull around and point his nose at me and open fire and just hang there on his prop and follow me around with his tracer. All I could do was to keep on turning the best I could. If I'd straightened out he'd have had me cold as he already had his sights on me. If I tried to hang on my prop that way, I'd have gone right into a spin. But this fellow just hung right there and sprayed me with lead like he had a hose. They have speeded up guns, too. All I could do was watch his tracer and kick my rudder from one side to the other to throw his aim off. This war isn't what it used to be. . . . The new Fokkers are giving us hell. . . .

"These new Fokkers can dive as fast as we can. First you must turn, bank ninety degrees and keep turning. They can't keep their sights on you. Watch the sun for direction. Now there's one on your right—shoot at him. Don't try to hit him—just spray him— for if you try to hold your sight on him you'll have to fly straight and give the others a crack at you. But you put the wind up him anyway and he turns. Quick, turn in the opposite direction. He's out of it for a moment. Now there's another one near you. Try it on him—it works! Turn again, you are between them and the line. Now go for it, engine full on, nose down.

"Two of them are still after you—tracer getting near again. Pull up, zoom and sideslip and if necessary turn and spray them again. Now make another dive for home and repeat when necessary. If your wings don't fall off and you are gaining on them, pull up a little. Ah, there's Archie [anti-aircraft fire], that means they are behind you—woof—that one was close—you now have another gray hair—they've been watching you—better zigzag a bit. You can laugh at Archie, he's a joke compared to machine guns. You dodge him carefully and roll in derision as you cross the lines and hasten home for tea—that is if you know where it is. That is discretion—many a man has gotten out of a fight only to lose to the others who have nothing to do but shoot him down at leisure."

Toward the middle of 1916 Fokker finally ended his experiments with the six-cylinder water-cooled 120-hp Mercedes. The resultant machine was the D-I, a biplane and the first German fighter to use a water-cooled engine. It was the fastest machine at the front for a long time. As a result, Albatros produced the D-II with a Mercedes 160-hp engine, the same engine as had been used in observation planes. Fokker was beaten in the D-II's tests, but before he could start work on something new, Albatros came out with the D-V. However, it did badly on test and had to be withdrawn. When Fokker tried to interest the German government in backing experiments to improve the D-I, he was put off. Disappointed, he realized that he was being "cunningly jockeyed into the ruck of mediocre manufacturers after making a flying start to supply the Germans with their first fighting airplanes." It was a sickening thought, and he could see no way out of it. The truth of the matter was that the Germans wanted him to become a subject of the Kaiser, an act which he had steadfastly resisted when approached several times in the last two years. While still trying to get out of the dilemma so that he could regard himself as a neutral Dutchman, he was granted a contract for 400 training machines. He was on the point of celebrating when he was told that the training planes would not be Fokkers. They were to be built under a license granted by the General Electric Company of Germany. He gave orders for the work to start, his mind only half devoted to the task. He absorbed his energies by designing an entirely new machine while his departmental heads went on with the government's training-plane order.

The new machine created some surprise with its upper wing, which stood close to the fuselage—"like a parasol," explained the designer. The lower wing "was narrower and of lesser span." The fuselage was fabric over welded steel frame. When the prototype was first flown, with Fokker himself at the controls, he found that it had "both speed and climb, and went through all the combat maneuvers like greased lightning." The reception given to the new machine by the committee which gathered at Schwerin for the occasion was one of "chilled silence." They thought that the basic welded construction was quite all right for bridges, but for fighting aircraft it looked impossible. Fokker again put it through its paces, nearly turning it inside out in the process, but still there was very small interest in the new machine.

Fokker was greatly puzzled about it until he realized that his mail was being censored. The Germans were actually suspicious of him! He stopped all communication with his family in Holland, and curtailed his social activities. Only after the war did he hear that the British Intelligence Service in Holland had been trying to reach him with a £2 million offer if he would return to his native country. Discovering this, the German Secret Service chiefs concluded that he must be negotiating for an escape. Coupled with his refusal to become a German subject, it looked most suspicious. They made it their business to watch their erratic genius day and night. They made one final effort and again he refused. He was then told that he would get no more contracts. They believed that they could starve him into submission, but he countered their ultimatum by announcing that when the current order was finished he would sell his Schwerin factory and go home to Haarlem.

The Germans then refused him permission to leave the country on any pretext whatsoever. He knew far too much. Some time later he received a letter from the War Office which told him that he was now a naturalized German subject and as such registered in the German army reserve.

Anthony Fokker, prisoner of Germany, the country which had reaped enormous benefit from his brain power and drive, was in an untenable position. No longer could he count on the freedom to return to Holland. If he closed down his factory he could be called up and posted to an infantry battalion in the trenches. He buckled down under the burden, and months later entered a competition with a new machine, flying against such high-powered companies as Rumpler, Pfalz and Aviatik, and winning. When he received an order for four hundred new machines, he deliberately quoted a price which would bring him the sum of ten million marks. He also granted a manufacturing license to Albatros to build the new machine. This contract brought into use more Fokkers than ever before.

German air power was almost supreme. The young Richthofen was now in command of his own "circus." Every pilot at the front voiced a distinct preference for a Fokker machine, and the factory was besieged with orders. Richthofen's disciplined pilots refused to fly any other—the only time they flaunted authority—and thirty D-8's were needed quickly. They got them and again the war skies thundered to the roar of engines and flashed to the sight of the Fokker warbirds as they moved through the skies toward the kill.

When the war looked as if it might soon reach an end, Fokker was among the first to notice a lessening demand for planes, a weakening in the great flow of orders and special contracts which had issued from government offices for more than three years. He did not, however, diminish his own efforts. The experiments with new guns, new planes, went on because he did not think that he would be hindered in any way by the Allies once peace came. It was already obvious that Germany, the country to which he had given his talents, was the vanquished nation. His consolation lay in the fact that his machines had received bloody advertisement in action, and the Richthofen Circus had shown beyond all doubt that the Fokker was the best plane of its kind. Waiting for peace, he had to devise a way of keeping more than 6,000 pairs of hands busy. Morale among his workers was low, interest flagging, but he was a man who somehow maintained cohesion and, incredibly, the continued production of planes which would never be flown in war.

The Allies' Armistice agreement was couched in disappointing terms. Under the provisions of Article IV, all aircraft which had been used for war purposes were to be reduced to scrap. This sent Fokker into a temper, coupled with the fear that his work would be lost forever. Cheating the victors of their triumph, he did a fantastic thing in persuading pilots and technicians to hide more than 220 airplanes and over 400 engines throughout Germany. Even this scheme fizzled out. After a number of abortive attempts at starting up again as a manufacturing industrialist, Anthony Fokker made his way to the United States and there achieved something like his old eminence, but this time in the airlines business.

In his way, this man played just as great and important a part in the First World War as any general, strategist or diplomat. In fact, he did more than most of them: He worked with his hands, and the results today form part of the symphony of the skies.

CHAPTER **10**

Zeppelins Over London

The young men who cheerfully labeled themselves "Fokker fodder" in the bad year of 1915 averaged only twenty-one years. In the autumn, German victory claims were, for once, more accurate than usual, and about 75 per cent of the triumphs went to the new highly mobile German squadrons, which could be moved hundreds of miles along the front in a matter of hours. When that mobility was destroyed by something over which neither side had any control, the weather, the "circus" idea came into being.

The Allies had to face a new merciless slaughter carried out by some of the most skilled members of the German air corps. The Germans scattered circuses at new bases situated along the Western front and saw to it that a high efficiency was maintained. On the Eastern front the Germans became busier than ever, constructing a huge airplane base at Libau and putting up a Zeppelin hangar to house the craft, which were prefabricated in Germany and brought overland for assembly and testing. Libau now became Hindenburg's most able support as he floundered through the marshes toward the Russian lowlands and a famous battle.

On September 11 a flock of deadly-looking Zeppelins toppled bombs on choked railway centers at Vilijka, east of Vilna. A few savage duels between fighting aircraft took place, but there was no sign of the tempo evident on the Western front. Fourteen days later, not far from Friedrichstadt, a brisk fight started in which a German pilot shot down a Russian machine. On September 30 two more Russian planes were shot down in flames. The Germans were now bringing the war in the air into a new sector and utilizing the Zeppelin.

"During last night," Berlin reported on October 13 and 15, "one of our airships bombarded the fortified town of Dvinsk, which is full of troops, with a good number of bombs." A later communiqué said that the railway station at Minsk had been raided by the Zeppelins. "Five heavy explosions took place, and a great fire was observed."

The Germans did not get away without encountering some resistance. Russian planes flew against them with total disregard for personal safety. In June the Germans lost 53 planes, in July 43, in August 89, and in September 79. The Russians shot down a number of enemy pilots, including Werner von Beaulieu, heroic winner of the second prize at the 1914 Prince Henry Circuit Competition. The ranks of the aces were thinning out. Otto Stiefvater and Lieutenant Pappe died at Johannisthal while testing a new machine. Lieutenant von Hiddessen, the first German to drop war bombs on Paris, was behind barbed wire in a French prison camp, his Iron Cross tucked away in his pocket as a relic of the past. Another German ace, Werner Landmann, was in a Russian camp, where he complained of being foully treated by Russians "who are not gentlemen."

German technical faith in the Zeppelin as the ideal weapon became hard-pressed in 1915, the year when it was thoroughly tried and tested under combat conditions. In the air it became the obvious target, even for the new fledgling pilots. It was not even risky to fly straight over the top of the great craft, pumping holes in the envelope with a Lewis gun. Sometimes, however, the Zeppelins managed to destroy themselves. The Z 18, biggest and costliest member of the Zeppelin fleet, exploded shortly after being housed in the new hangar at Tondern, Schleswig, on November 17 at eight o'clock in the morning. At first the Germans tried to blame it on an act of sabotage, but a court of inquiry announced that the real cause was a cigar end which had been dropped on the top of Z 18

while she was being topped up with gas. The Z 18 was the apple
of the High Command's eye. Before destruction she made only
one major testing trip, over the Isle of Sylt, and was the first to be
coated with a new type of paint which, while camouflaging her,
also created difficulties for ground gunners. The explosion which
led to her total destruction consisted of a single brilliant flash. It
lifted the roof right off the new hangar and blew the walls out in
a dramatic holocaust. All surrounding buildings were flattened and
eleven men injured or killed. Precautions were taken to guard
against the news leaking out, but the New York newspapers were
featuring it less than a week later in the face of wordy denials by
the Germans.

For a time the Zeppelin became a psychological weapon, but
when it was decided to utilize it as an expensive bomber against
London and other cities, the monstrous weapon altered its complexion, bringing a new reality into the conflict.

Here is the experience, unique in itself, of a Zeppelin commander who was ordered to bomb London. His name was Commander Mathy and he held the senior command. In the misty mild
dawn of September 9, 1915, four Zeppelins made a return to Evere
landing field, near Brussels. All were in bad shape, shattered in
parts by British artillery fire, but returning after the efficient dis-
charge of their orders. September 8 was a bad night for London.
Mathy was happy that he had not lost one Zeppelin in this, the
most daring raid of the entire war. However, the small, tubby man
with fair close-cropped hair did not show any satisfaction. He
carried himself with a naval bearing because he once held command of a destroyer and most of his life had been spent at sea.
Zeppelins always fascinated him and he managed to get a transfer
to the air service on the strength of his seamanship record. He
knew what death was, but he did not fear it because he was totally
devoid of superstition, even the traditional naval ones. The raid
from which he was now returning had been his hundredth and he
had known some terrible moments in the last six hours, but he kept
up a stoic calm.

"My instructions," wrote Mathy, "were to attack certain points
to the south of the City of London, such as railway stations,
bridges, industrial establishments; strict orders to do everything
possible to avoid hitting St. Paul's and other churches, museums,

the Palace, Westminster Abbey, Parliament, and, of course, residential districts."

Keeping an eye on the ground crews who energetically hauled his Zeppelin to earth while doctors stood by to attend to the wounded, Mathy's mind went back to the start of the operation when he sat in a leather chair in the well-furnished gondola, headquarters of the bombing fleet. There were other chairs and shaded lamps in the light of which he had known some sublime moments, sailing through the heavens.

He called in his first officer and asked for a note of the position of the other Zeppelins. His flagship was in advance, but not too far ahead as to be completely out of sight. He looked through the steel-framed windows, remarking on the splendor of the sun as it sank down toward a horizon bounded by the iron-colored North Sea. It was peaceful up here, the engines little more than a distant humming, but he knew that every member of his crew was active, watching their dials, checking the air screws which had been known to break away from the spindles and rip into a delicate envelope containing thousands of cubic feet of gas.

Mathy prohibited drinking during bombing operations. A Spartan by nature, he never made any allowances for hot meals; his crew had to carry their own provisions.

There was still enough light left to spot the Essex coastline as they slipped across at a fair height. He could distinguish the mud flats and sent a radio message to his three followers to note their position. Down there, like a sea-locked speck, stood the island in the Thames estuary which was the marker for the beginning of a journey that had been planned to follow London's river right into the heart of the capital.

Mathy asked for a reduction of speed, waiting for the others to catch up. They emerged out of gray skies, almost nuzzling each other like affectionate beasts. Mathy signaled them to spread out in the prearranged formation.

"Below us it was rapidly getting dark, but it was still light up where we were. On one side or the other was a Zeppelin, in gray war paint, like that of my craft, visible in the waning light against the clear sky, gliding majestically through the air. A low, mistlike fog hung over the line where England lay. Stars came out and it grew colder."

He was about to pull on his greatcoat when he heard the first officer's cry: *"Klar zum Werfen"* (clear for action). Leaning on the rail, staring down through the shatterproof glass, he saw some activity down below, red glares which could only be one thing, gunfire. In a matter of seconds he had the monster's nose pointing upward, making the decks tilt steeply. Reaching a higher altitude, he called for more speed. Although the Zeppelin was the most silent of all weapons used by the Germans, British artillery observers trained themselves to such an acute listening pitch that they could detect the approach of a Zeppelin at anything up to 10,000 feet on a calm, windless night.

Gunners aboard all four Zeppelins gathered about their weapons in groups. Mathy had to move to one side to make room for the bomb aimer, a young man whom he did not know very well but whose judgment could be trusted. Every man aboard his Zeppelin was hand-picked and specially trained. He could not stand bunglers. Asking the aimer whether he was ready, he received a curt nod.

Coming up immediately ahead of them was the scattered glow of the target, London. It seemed to spread out for miles. They could hardly miss this, but Mathy wanted to be quite meticulous about keeping to his orders. He was no hot-blooded young murderer. The High Command had given him a definite list of targets. It was his job to find those targets.

"I saw the reflected glow in the sky thirty-seven miles away shortly before ten o'clock," he wrote in his personal log, conscious of the bomb aimer, still waiting and probably wondering when he would get the order to release the load.

They were over the silvery Thames now, a British feature which could never be camouflaged.

"I headed for the glow of London in the sky, and then a point on the Thames to get my bearings for my objective attacks." He blotted the last sentence and shut the log. There would be more to write later.

By this time searchlight batteries were throwing out probing fingers, running across the layers of smudgy cloud. At first it looked impossible, but soon a crisscross pattern was made and the Zeppelins were trapped in the middle of it.

Mathy was too old a hand to panic when the white shafts first invaded his cabin. He waited for the thud of artillery and the sound of shells exploding in the near vicinity before instructing his bomb aimer to start releasing the first missiles. Of that moment he wrote: "It is a beautiful, impressive, but fleeting picture seen from above, the grayish outlines of the Zeppelins gliding through the wavering ribbons of light and shrapnel cloudlets which hang thick. . . . Our eyes and minds are concentrated on our work, for at any moment we may be plunged below, a shapeless mass of wreckage and human bodies shattered beyond recognition."

The load of bombs which could be carried by four massive Zeppelins was enough to convert parts of London into a fiery inferno. The night was to be ripped apart before the raid ended and the Zeppelins were able to head for the coastline. Half an hour after midnight Mathy radioed the signal: "Place, North Hinder Lightship. London attacked."

The British death toll was twenty, with eighty-six injured. Mathy wrote: "Balfour said London was not a fortified city, and that its defenses against aerial attacks were poor. We know, however, there are several forts and batteries around the city and outside, and had he stood by my side and looked into those flashing guns, all over, he wouldn't say London was not a militarily defended city, and perhaps not think so poorly of its aerial defense."

There were no textbook tactics to guide pilots who wanted to have a crack at the Zeppelins. The first men who tried to bring down the craft returned to say that it was like a gnat stinging an elephant . . . except that this particular elephant carried enough venom to strike back in the shape of devastating streams of machine-gun bullets fired from all sides of the gondolas. It was sheer suicide to attack from underneath, shooting at the steering mechanism, because German gunners were both deadly and accurate in their firing. There was the problem of swinging a fast plane up around the swollen bulk of the Zeppelin. A few pilots lost their lives as a result of running full tilt into the gaseous envelopes. Their sacrifices accomplished nothing, thanks to the ingenious German design of using several different gas envelopes. Puncture one only, and it meant nothing. The Zeppelin could still get home safely. Allied pilots found that the best strategy was to make several runs over or alongside the Zeppelin, firing all the time. Even then, there was no guarantee that the Zeppelin could be downed.

On May 17 at 3:15 A.M., the massive LZ 39 was separated from the other three craft with which she had been bombing Ramsgate. She drifted slowly and majestically along the coast, near Dunkirk.

The naval air unit at Dunkirk had long been in a state of gloomy boredom. Hours of patrol over a featureless sea, on the off chance of finding traces of enemy submarines, together with the uncertainty of ever getting into a fighting war, made most of the men lethargic. News of the sighting of LZ 39 seemed to be just another occurrence until Squadron Commander Spenser D. A. Grey and Flight Sublieutenant R. A. J. Warneford decided to fly out and pick a fight with her. With them went Flight Commander A. W. Bigsworth. Until now it had always been assumed that the only way to destroy the Zeppelin was by gunfire, but Warneford, for one, was eager to try bombing, placing as many twenty-pound bombs on the upper surface as possible. Today, the day of the hunt for LZ 39, was as good a time as any to test bombing theories.

Bigsworth was first over LZ 39. He was flying at 10,200 feet. The Zeppelin was 200 feet below him. As a traditionalist, Bigsworth took what he considered to be the only course open to him. When he was flying at such a level as to be quite incapable of missing the target, he quickly let loose four twenty-pound bombs. They swung down, almost idly, while he held the same height and speed, risking his life from the possible backwhip of the explosion. Then, by a quirk of the wind or faulty deflection on Bigsworth's part, he noticed the Zeppelin moving slightly off course. The bombs looked as if they were missing the target completely. He was about to touch his gun trigger when all the bombs burst near the box tail of the Zeppelin. Thwarted, he saw wisps of thick black smoke coming up from the point of impact. He knew that he had failed, but did not realize that the entire Zeppelin, with its shuddering gasbag, was in a chaotic state. In the gondola the crew could not even see the attacker, though they could hear the whine of the engine. They could do nothing about him because they were too busy trying to deal with the harassing guns manned by Warneford and Grey. They started strafing early to let Bigsworth get into position overhead. The first sprays of fire went wide, not even touching the Zeppelin or gondola. When they saw Bigsworth dropping his bombs, they expended more ammunition, firing at a frantic rate into the gondola where they could clearly make out members of the crew.

In LZ 39 dead men were thrown aside by those still living, and replacement gunners jumped into position behind their weapons, thrusting them around with their hips, trying to pump tracers into the attackers. The barrels of the guns heated to such a degree that they were reduced to firing in short bursts. Wounded men toppled helplessly from one side of the battered gondola to the other, leaving trails of blood as they clasped agonized hands to their wounds, crying out for help—help they could not obtain at this dire moment. Very few of the bombing Zeppelins ever carried a doctor. The LZ 39 barely reached home at Evere. With only a skeleton crew of unwounded men trying to recover from the terrible onslaught of the three British planes, it was practically impossible to make the proper landing. As the Zeppelin bumped down to earth, ground crews rushed up to manhandle the clumsy leviathan into the sheds. A small corps of medical officers boarded the gondola, sorting out the dead and hospitalizing the wounded. It was a horrible, ghastly scene. The LZ 39 had flown through a special kind of hell.

After several British coastal towns, outer London and the East Coast suffered further raids which terrorized the population, the RFC and its echelons decided to make a strenuous attempt to wipe out the Zeppelin base at Evere. Coincidentally, this was planned to take place on the same day as the bombing attack on the LZ 39. It was a decision that had to be made quickly. The finest pilots were selected. Although Flight Sublieutenant Warneford could show a great deal of experience in dealing with the Zeppelin menace, he was left alone for some reason, hence his freedom of action when the rest were away on the Evere job.

About to return to base after the early attack, Warneford, now flying alone, suddenly spotted the LZ 37, sister ship to the one he had just helped cripple. She was over Ostend, flying almost casually through the clear sky, but obviously with her crew on the alert.

Warneford's Morane seemed slow and sluggish as he tried to estimate the distance between them. Opening his throttle until the engine screamed, he found that he was not gaining on the Zeppelin as fast as he wanted. Not until Bruges was spread out below did he come within range. Gunners aboard the LZ 37 started their usual fusillade, forcing him up to 11,000 feet, beyond their sights.

Warneford was in a poor position. He was still carrying the regulation load of six twenty-pound bombs that helped reduce his speed and curb any rapid gain in height. It was not exactly propitious for fighting a gun duel with the Zeppelin and he thought he might lose. He was very much alone up there, turning the possibilities over in his mind. Making quick decisions at 11,000 feet in an open cockpit, with all France and most of Belgium below him, was far from easy. The air battered against his face and even the thick goggles were poor protection.

The nose of the Morane tilted downward as Warneford made his decision, bracing himself against the incredibly strong gravity pull and the pull of the skimming machine when it gathered nerve-shattering velocity. It was in itself a bomb. If he made a mistake, an error of judgment, and collided with the Zeppelin, it would mean the end of him and the end of the Zeppelin. He certainly did not want to kill himself in this style, spectacular though it might look. Warneford liked life; he wanted to go on living.

The shape of the Zeppelin was more distinct now that he was through an altitude of 10,000 feet. Making a great muscular effort, he managed to get his hand down to where the bomb levers were located. One hand on the joystick, the other on the bomb-release mechanism, he counted the seconds. He was petrified by the on-rush of air and only by the strongest will power did he manage to control the plane.

He was 150 feet over the Zeppelin's broad upper surface when he shoved the bomb levers, letting the missiles go in one continuous string.

The explosion came in a mammoth roar and the Zeppelin started falling, cloaked in a sheath of fire. The explosive force rushed up, worrying the air and grabbing hold of the Morane to tip it upside down. Warneford nearly lost consciousness, a victim of his own vengeance against the Germans. Dazed, shaking his head and trying to breathe in some air free of the stink of cordite, he suddenly realized that his machine was in a vertical nose dive. If he did not level out, it would plow into houses or a field. He had to do something within the next few seconds or die.

The will to survive nearly cost him his consciousness as he

began gently to ease back the joystick. The Morane's entire sub-
stance whined and shrieked in almost human pain, then fell into
an even keel, jolting the pilot out of the nightmare.

Warneford leaned over the side of the cockpit to see what was
happening. It was a breath-taking scene. The Zeppelin's ruins
covered a wide area of ground. Parts of it were still spitting fire,
and plumes of varicolored smoke eddied up as pockets of gas
ignited. The bulk of its heavier parts fell on top of a nunnery.
Only one member of the crew got away with his life. He was
projected out of the falling wreckage like a bullet, plummeting
through the nunnery roof. Pieces of machinery fell on two of the
sisters and killed them.

Circling over the scene for a time, Warneford felt dazed at the
result of his one-man war against something the Germans considered to be invincible. At last he gunned the Morane's engine
and began to head for home. Minutes later he knew that he might
never see his airfield again. The Morane's engine was not pulling
as well as it usually did. It kept stuttering in a sickly fashion. He
cautiously opened the throttle, demanding more power. The engine
coughed, so he checked the dials. Oil pressure was good. Other
details were more or less correct. It was dusk when his eyes went
back to the fuel-pressure gauge. The needle kept on jumping up
and down, whereas it was usually as steady as a rock.

He now knew that he must land while time remained. Spurts of
gas were probably being jetted out through a broken fuel pipe.
Let one of them touch the hottest parts of the engine and the
Morane would blow up without warning. Not only that; he was
losing precious gas which could get him home. Was this fit retribu-
tion for victory?

With its engine dead, the propeller idle, the Morane came
winging down like a bat from the heights of the sky, skimming over
some village rooftops until it reached the rear of the enemy front
line. If the artillery gunners heard the swish of wings above
their heads that night, they did not fire. The Morane was past them
before they knew it. Some gunners may have dismissed it as unimportant. By night the war between men gives out some strange
sounds.

Warneford reckoned on being lucky enough to land in an open
field, but at 200 feet he could not see anything. It was pitch black,

but he felt sure that he was over open country. The Morane was still gliding nicely; he put it down neatly and got out. As he climbed from the cockpit, he scanned a skyline which was almost nonexistent. No trees. Not a sound. Total silence except for the rumble of gunfire miles away.

He waited a few minutes, prepared to blow the Morane up if German troops came looking for him, then began to explore the fuel lines by touch. He could not risk using a flashlight or matches. One carelessly placed match could send the plane up in smoke; this he might have to do on purpose if anybody came to investigate the source of the odd swishing sound over the trenches less than ten minutes before.

The palm of his hand found the fracture, a crack big enough to cause real trouble if he tried to fly with it in that condition. He hunted out some rags and other materials, and began to bind it up. There was still a very definite risk that the fuel level would be too low to allow further flying time, but he just had to take that risk.

At last, after much fumbling, it was as ready as he could make it. Already the fuel was soaking through the tightly wrapped cloth on the pipe, but it could not be helped.

Then came the moment when he must start the Morane's roaring engine in the stillness of the night. He would have to be fast and expeditious if he was to avoid having Germans shoot at him as soon as he was up in the air.

The propeller jerked around once and stopped. Heart in mouth, Warneford tried again. There was the small explosion of the ignition system and it held. Fumes from the exhaust strengthened and he knew that he could take off now. He held the engine at maximum throttle less than thirty seconds, then sent the Morane careening through the black shroud of night that enfolded the land. When he was moving at a speed as great as he could hope for with a broken fuel pipe, he lifted the machine into the air, conscious of the tremendous release of nervous tension within himself. In the air he stood a good chance of getting away with it. Let them shoot as much as they wanted to now.

Five hundred feet. . . .

Six hundred feet. . . .

Seven . . . eight . . . nine. . . .

At 1,000 feet he trimmed the plane and flew on a level line.

He reckoned the time he had spent behind the German lines with the liability of a crippled plane on his hands. Exactly thirty-five minutes.

Flying west, he ran into thick vaporous mist and fog. Resigned to the worst, he edged the plane down, noticing that his fuel tank was almost empty. Half standing, he looked over the side, through the wet mist, trying to find the ground. It could be 500 feet, it could be 200. At any moment he might crash. He throttled back and let the Morane down a few more feet without seeing any sign. Then, so suddenly that he was nearly caught unaware, it was there. He made a neat landing and ran in search of help. Some French people told him that he was at Cap Gris-Nez.

Warneford, the first man to send a German Zeppelin to total destruction in the air, was killed only ten days later. He was flight-testing a Henri Farman machine, showing off its finer points to an American passenger, when it crumpled and fell in pieces over Buc airfield, six miles from Paris. However, for his exploit in bringing down the Zeppelin, he was posthumously awarded the Victoria Cross.

Warneford's adventure and those of other Allied pilots had a telling effect on the Germans. All Zeppelin airfields in Belgium were abandoned some months later and the High Command came to the conclusion that a Zeppelin war was an expensive war. They hoped to achieve better results with Gotha long-range bombers.

CHAPTER **11**

A Fighting Chance

It was not until 1916 that British aviators began to have any significant effect on the German air force. When the war entered its new phase it was enough to demoralize the remnants of the German air circuses. Boelcke, Immelmann and Richthofen were no longer a force. In the air a new type of fighter pilot appeared, generally very young, somewhat inexperienced and lacking the boldness of the first aces in whose fine tradition he was flying.

Here are extracts from the diary of a captured German army officer. They express feelings common to many about that time.

"The French aviators fly about 600 feet above our lines, while none of ours put in an appearance. We cannot fire on them without immediately attracting heavy artillery. We have, therefore, to remain in our trenches, where it is as hot as ever, dying of thirst and waiting to be killed or buried by shells. . . ."

"The French use nothing but heavy guns, and have been bombarding us all day, their fire control being beyond reproach as the result of the action of their aviators. The French aviators are masters of the air. . . ."

"The value of our aviators is so small that even far behind the lines they are not masters of the field. Generally our aviators are far from being as good as the French or English and consequently we dare not move a step outside our leaf-covered shelters. Enemy aviators keep circling around the wood we are in and signaling our presence. Whether we like it or not, it is evident from this point of view that we are inferior. We are told that Germany is holding her own in the air, but it is no use telling us that, and that is why we have these enormous losses. There is absolutely no one to drive away these parasites that give us no respite from dawn till night. The moral effect on us all is as bad as it can be. Final success, however, depends on the coordination of all available arms, and that is what is wanting here. The situation is the more astonishing because of the large number of French airplanes we bring down. . . ."

"Enemy aviators flying at one hundred meters took part in the fighting with machine guns. Some of our men were wounded in the head by bullets from above. . . ."

German morale had to be bolstered. In March it was decided to combine in one huge fighting force all the air and anti-aircraft sections. In command was a young man, General von Hoeppner, a protégé of Hindenburg.

As a follow-up, the Kaiser gave orders for an intensive propaganda campaign. Lavish claims became the order of the day. Among the first was a statement that a German seaplane squadron attacked and sank part of the British fleet off the Flanders coast. This was disbelieved from the start. Everyone knew that the German seaplanes lacked the fighting power to sink anything bigger than a canoe. Embarrassed over their blunder, the propagandists put out a string of other claims. They said that Regent Street, London, was in total ruins after a mass bombing raid, that a south London ammunition factory had been destroyed, that the Piccadilly underground station had to be closed following bombing attacks. Then, to crown everything, they said that a four-funneled cruiser and three warships had been attacked in the Humber, killing sixty seamen and injuring many more. A Grimsby military barracks was bombed and four hundred soldiers killed outright. Thameshaven benzene tanks had been hit and were still burning.

Outrageous claims such as these made Germany a laughingstock throughout the world, and she was soon forced to return to the business of fighting a war with weapons instead of lies.

Although time was obviously against them, the Germans now began to develop new airplanes, most of them based more or less directly on the old tested types; the tractor biplane, the low-powered triplane and the enclosed monoplane and biplane. The new tendency was to cut down the wide wingspan and return to the original birdlike proportions. The intensive design and construction program which went into action far behind the lines quickly became more impressive than anything ever accomplished by the Allied powers. The Fokker, for instance, was still very much favored and the plane of the moment, though the new modified machine showed a straighter mainplane and a hexagonal fuselage which was drawn out to a knife edge in the tail assembly. It was powered by an Obererursel monosoupape engine and Garuda propeller. Winter operations were carried out by the Roland biplane with a fuselage which equaled the space between the mainplanes, the top one of which was attached to the upper longerons and the bottom planes secured to the lower longerons. The observer-gunner was placed directly behind the pilot, tandem style, and observation carried out through a series of small windows. The Roland biplane was powered by a 160-hp Mercedes and could climb to 1,500 feet in four minutes, 3,000 in eight minutes, and 6,000 in twenty-two minutes. In the range of bombers, the Halberstadt was still in commission with a fuselage devoid of all cross-bracing, but just as strong as its predecessor. It was driven by the 120-hp Argus engine. The Albatros machines, famous since the downfall of Anthony Fokker from his position at the head of German designers, was also a firm feature of the war in the air, harassing the Allies with the greatest success. It was driven by a water-cooled engine in a fuselage built along the lines of the *monocoque* type.

While the construction of the new aircraft was being organized, the Zeppelin menace was diminishing, though in its day the industry which surrounded this clumsy weapon was sufficiently impressive.

Until the LZ 77 took the air practically all Zeppelins followed a symmetrical shape, but the new ones had a great forward bulk and a tapering stern. As far as accommodation was concerned, two gondolas were provided, in one of which was situated the engine line-up together with the engine-room staff and some of the general ratings. This gave onto a main cabin where the bomb aimers, pilots and other key personnel were stationed with the commander.

The communications department was placed in the same compartment as the bomb load. From this a vertical ladder led up through the Zeppelin to the gun platforms. The ladder ran between two of the twenty gas-containing envelopes.

The LZ 77 and her sister ships each had five engines developing 180 to 200 hp, with six vertical cylinders of 160 by 170, water-cooled, weighing 448 kilograms and consuming 230 grams of fuel per horsepower, and 2,500 grams of oil per hour per motor. The engine was developed by Maybach in collaboration with Daimler of Mercedes.

In its heyday the construction of the Zeppelin went ahead with all the vigor which later characterized the German aircraft industry. By the summer of 1916 forty Zeppelins were in commission, most of them being used to patrol the Baltic and North Sea.

As far as training was concerned, pilots were sent to a special school near Leipzig. There were actually two schools, one for artillery officers who were to become responsible for army co-operation, and one for naval officers who were to enter sea-patrol work.

Leipzig was the major Zeppelin center, for it also had the Chemnitz factory making hydrogen for the craft, and the massive Zeiss factory which turned out all the fittings. The area was dotted with aerial lighthouses, standing as it did on three routes crossing Germany and in constant use.

Yet even with such a high degree of organization as this, and a construction program costing millions of marks, the Zeppelin was already losing its power and being relegated to patrol duties. The propaganda program, which placed the Zeppelin at the head of the invasion of England, tailed off to be replaced by a number of spasmodic airplane and seaplane raids. These took place throughout 1916, but were a waste of time. Twelve people were killed and forty-one injured.

German propaganda was now beginning to concentrate on the battlefield itself. Claims were made that no German losses had been sustained, though the French and English lost twenty-one machines, five shot down from the ground, thirteen in aerial fights, and three by forced landings on the German side. In April 1916, the war in the air took on a deadlier note. Combat was bitter, and there was a greater inclination to fight in groups of squadrons instead of singly. That month, according to the Germans, the Allied powers lost twenty-six machines, ten being shot down by German artillery fire. German losses amounted to twenty-two, fourteen in aerial fights, four which never returned to their airfields, and four shot down by artillery. November was one of the worst months of 1916. Ninety-four Allied machines came down out of the chill sky.

1916 was the bloody prelude to what the Allies had decided to do, but the twelve months' waiting time had an air of doom and desperation about them. In England there were long delays and stupid muddles in aircraft production. Britain suddenly found herself in a position where she had neither men nor machines while the Germans were organizing the transition from Zeppelins to seaplanes and airplanes for bombing missions with an almost uncanny, well-oiled ease.

In British air schools the average age of the student pilot was between nineteen and twenty-one. The RFC was regarded by the other services as a school for suicide. In the months of the Somme battle, during the heavy winter of 1916-1917, Britain lost 867 airmen, hardly a good incentive for recruiting new pilots. New plans were desperately needed and eventually resuscitated from an idea originated by Trenchard. They called for the formation of 106 field squadrons with a further 95 in reserve, including two night fighter squadrons which would also carry out reconnaissance as required. The Trenchard plan, endorsed by Douglas Haig, was ambitious enough to arrive at a moment when it was practically impossible to carry it out. In the resultant search for men, the army was asked to organize a call for volunteers. The appeal ended as an early-morning announcement by sergeant majors, most of whom regarded this as an invitation to reach heaven more quickly than was usual, even in the infantry. It was not exactly an impassioned appeal to the spirit of adventure, but it did produce several hundred young men who were seconded to the RFC for selection and aptitude tests. In time they were augmented by a number of Canadians and Americans, all volunteers, who had done their initial training in the United States, on airfields in Texas. It was the beginning of a new air force for Britain, and only the time required for training these men stood between Germany and Britain and the struggle for power.

Belonging to the RFC had a certain distinction, as Cecil Day Lewis has said in his book, *Sagittarius Rising*.

"The RFC attracted the adventurous spirits, the devil-may-care young bloods of England, the fast livers, the furious drivers—men who were not happy unless they were taking risks. This invested the Corps with a certain style (not always admirable). We had the sense of being the last word in warfare, the advance guard of wars to come, and felt, I suppose, that we could afford to be a little extravagant. Certainly our pay gave us the opportunity to be so in one sense. It was good because our work was skilled and hazardous. But, looking back now, I feel we had many compensations. . . ."

Feelings began to run high among Canadians, Americans and British. For some time transatlantic pilots training near London were forbidden to enter the city. One Canadian wrote: "Here we are stationed within the city limits, the tube station is right at the entrance to the field and yet we are forbidden to go down to the center of town. In other words, we are confined to our quarters as if we were under arrest. . . ."

This was supposed to be necessary and in the public interest because pilots from overseas had been whooping it up at some of the hotels, and, in general, behaving wildly. The authorities maintained—quite rightly—that training was all-important, and efforts were made to keep as many pupils in the air as possible.

"We are going to the front," one outraged aviator wrote, "and get killed off like flies. Two or three get killed in England every week. Yet these great moguls are so afraid that we will have a little fun before we go West that they have forbidden us to come to London to see a show or join our friends and try to forget for a little while what is going to happen to us. It's an outrage. They think we are so much dirt. . . . I'm an American and I'm proud of it but I'm damned if I can take any pride in the boobs that are running the flying corps. For instance how can we fly when our necks are being choked off by these 1865 collars?"

At the front, however, things were a little more intense than the desire to have a good time in London or change collars. A new machine, the Bristol two-seater, with its 250-hp Rolls-Royce engine, was becoming available to the RFC. In performance it showed a combination of the best qualities of a reconnaissance plane, yet it was able to fly like a fast single-seater fighter. Apart from the synchronized Vickers machine gun, it was also armed with two machine guns for use by the observer.

Six of the new Bristols were hurriedly ferried across to No. 48 Squadron. One of the men who had long dreamt of having a new kind of machine to fly against the Germans was Captain Leefe Robinson, VC. As soon as the Bristols arrived, he called a meeting with the other pilots, and together they decided to take the new planes up for a trial flight as soon as they were checked and serviced next day. It should be mentioned that Robinson disregarded certain important questions about the performance and handling of the Bristol, and never admitted how little he knew about the machine. All he wanted was to get it into the air and learn from his own experience.

Early next day, with a clear sky above them as they climbed into the cockpits of the six new machines, the British pilots prepared for the mass take-off. They all felt justifiably thrilled with the Bristol. It looked a good hunting, fighting machine, even on the ground, and the layout of the instrument panel and the armament showed that it ought to live up to their expectations.

At 1,000 feet Robinson signaled them to take up their positions in a broad arrowhead formation. The sustained roar of the powerful Rolls-Royce engines reverberated through the air, reached the cluster of mechanics gathered far below, who were estimating how the pilots would fare with the new weapons. General opinion was that the Bristols looked "bloody good."

Leefe Robinson was flying at the head of the formation. He did not attempt to put the Bristol through its paces at this stage. A practical-minded man apart from his impetuosity, he never bothered with the mock warfare, the shadow-boxing which other pilots practiced as a warm-up for the real thing. He had won his VC in a welter of blood, barely getting away with his life.

Fifteen hundred feet. Satisfied with the Bristol's performance, he twisted around in his seat to watch the rest of them, spread out across the sky. He signaled them to close up a trifle so that they came within easy eye range.

They were now over the German lines, but Robinson was not greatly worried. It was a quiet morning and he doubted very much if any of the German patrol planes would be airborne at this time of day. He was still flying along smoothly, and thinking about turning back, when suddenly he spotted the five black specks high above him. He waggled his wing tips to attract the attention of his own pilots. By this time a risen sun was shining down on them. Even as he passed the signal, the specks gathered together like flies basking in the golden beams. It was hard to see exactly what they were doing. He was dazzled by the effusion of light.

Staring upward, blinking into the sun until his eyes watered, Robinson suddenly realized that the flies were German planes, all watching for a sign of his intentions. Who was to be the aggressor and who the prey? At this stage, neither side knew. Robinson himself had serious doubts about starting anything. He was in the worse position. His intimate knowledge of aerial tactics made him realize that there was no time left to get away from the danger. Within five minutes he and the others would be in the center of one of the whirlwind battles which periodically broke out over the trenches.

The position was bad for the English. There was no time to change it now. Although the Bristol was said to be a superb machine, Robinson could not hope to outpace the Germans in a dash for home. They had the first advantage because of the bright sun.

The Germans were on their way down now, moving fast, each marking a Bristol. There was no sign of gunfire. They were too far away to start shooting, Robinson estimated.

But any moment now. . . .

He swung his machine around in a wide semicircle, and the others followed suit. By this time every man had noted the presence of the Germans and every man's thumb was on his trigger, ready to shoot hell out of them if the chance came.

Right up to the last moment Robinson believed that they had a fighting chance, but in that last minute they were beaten.

The German Albatros had the advantage of tremendous speed at the end of a dive. They were moving at 120 miles an hour or more, and started shooting straight at the Bristols.

Robinson, staring along the mainplane of his own machine, was startled into sick horror as a row of bullet holes appeared, tearing through the fabric like small knives.

While he was trying to check the German advance, a bullet spattered into his engine and he heard it begin to falter. It was the end. While the other Bristols tried to quell the Germans, Robinson quietly took his machine down behind the German lines. He landed safely and was taken prisoner. It was the end of his war.

This was also the end of a disastrous test flight which had started in high spirits. Three Bristols plunged to earth in flames, and only two out of the six managed to get home at all. The German attackers numbered five.

The German pilot responsible for the ignoble rout of the new Bristols was Richthofen. Questioned later by a neutral journalist in a Berlin hotel about the qualities of the Bristol fighter, he scoffed, saying that it would have only a negligible effect on the war in the air. He was, of course, estimating it in the light of his own brilliant abilities. Younger pilots accepted too readily his abrupt dismissal of the new Bristols, for they were quickly shot down by Bristol pilots who took the trouble to familiarize themselves with the machine.

But it was now 1917, the year of new strategy and new pilots.

12

The Enigmatic Irishman

Edward Mannock was a quiet-mannered, smoldering Irishman who came of a poor family. His body developed on top of a pair of thin, twiglike legs, and throughout his life he wore a lugubrious expression which was totally misleading. Mannock grew up with an intimate knowledge of the army. Born on May 24, 1887, he never really knew his father, nor did he ever speak about him, except in the most superficial fashion.

His father was an enigma, never quite understood, a mixture of rollicking good humor and sullen tempers. When his first period of army service was drawing to an end, he took his family to Newbridge, Dublin, but later returned to England and settled at Highgate, London. Mad-mannered and restive, he finally re-enlisted in the army and was posted to India where his children grew up.

Mannock, the future ace, was a quiet, reserved, gawky boy, not at all quarrelsome, always thoughtful. He read book after book, any book, and gradually suffered an impairment of vision. Even when he became totally blind, he did not whimper or cry. He always sat quietly, believing that he would soon be able to see properly. The blindness dragged on, month after month, and in the end he was able to make out dark objects in the house and the swaying trees that surrounded the hill station. Two months later he was completely blind again, and the trouble came and went for the rest of his life, including his time as an RFC pilot.

One of the remarkable sides to Mannock, the boy, was his hatred of killing for the sake of killing. He could never join other lads in the slaughter of a bird or animal. Even when he went poaching fish as a schoolboy at Canterbury, he made a special point of going to Confession as soon as possible afterward to atone for his "sins."

The Mannocks—two boys, three girls, the mother and unpredictable father—sailed for South Africa soon after the start of the Boer War, returning later to Britain and the base at Shorncliffe, then on to Canterbury Cavalry Depot where Edward was sent off to school.

Quite suddenly, without giving any reason or even leaving a note behind him, Mannock senior packed his bags and left. Nothing more was heard of him until he unexpectedly turned up at Buckingham Palace to receive his dead son's decorations from King George V.

Edward's life was hard as granite. He had to stand by and watch his mother trying to make shift with any work she could get, for the lowest wages, supplemented with pennies earned by the elder children. Most of the time the family barely got by.

At the age of twelve Edward attended St. Thomas's School, but was soon forced to leave and look for work because of the family's poverty. He made half a crown a week, carrying sacks for a greengrocer ten hours a day. This nearly crippled him, so he became a lather boy in a barbershop. He made five shillings a week at this, slopping soap on the chins of hard-swearing customers. In the process he completed his worldly education. Sickened by the behavior and crude sentiments of his rough customers, he talked his brother Patrick into putting in a word for him as a clerk at the firm where Patrick worked. He was hoping to become an engineer with them, but it seemed a long arduous climb. He did get a place, though, and when his health worsened, he was transferred to the Wellingborough branch of the same company as a linesman, climbing telegraph poles.

One of his hobbies was the comradeship of the Church Lads Brigade. He played cricket and other games, then entered the Home Counties (Territorial) RAMC Company, Canterbury, not because he was at all bloodthirsty but merely for the sake of having something to do.

By this time he was finding new books to read and his mind was becoming livelier than ever. He told some friends: "I'm going to become a successful engineer, tea planter, or rancher. I feel it is the duty of every man to try and raise himself to whatever heights his ideals take him, whether they be spiritual or worldly. It only requires the determination to try."

It was this refinement of his father's spirit which took him to Turkey aboard a tramp steamer in the belief that something would turn up. Over there he talked himself into a job with an English telephone company at Constantinople. Within six months he was made district inspector, stationed at Istanbul. If he had trouble with his eyes, he did not mention the fact to anybody.

When the war started, and the Germans talked Turkey into joining their side, Mannock wrote a letter home: "Things very very serious here. War in the air. Great anti-British feeling displayed by the people. Things at famine prices. The company is not paying wages. Banks closed. Credit stopped. Everyone starving. Cannot grumble. I had a bloater last Monday."

Because of the tense international situation, and Turkey's feelings toward Britain, he was made a prisoner of war and managed to get only one letter, a Christmas greeting, through to his friends in England. On February 19, 1915, an inquiry made through official channels by his friends brought this reply: "Sir, The Embassy is in receipt of your inquiry of January 11th and in reply takes pleasure in informing you that Mr. Edward Mannock is still in Constantinople and in good health."

The depressing truth behind these few severe lines was that Mannock had been forced to work for the telephone company, which had now fallen into enemy hands. He tried to escape many times and was severely punished for being so rash. Thrown into a cell, he tried to eat the bread and water, but vomited and felt ill. He lost weight, broke out in septic sores.

Miss Florence Minter, also a prisoner at the same time, wrote the following about Mannock:

"I see that his comrades invariably spoke of him as a 'sport.' That he was always, and in the dark days of our internment and during that bad time when we were under arrest coming home, he was always cheerful and helpful, and kept the men 'British' all through; he was our philosopher, friend and guide."

At last the Turks decided to repatriate Mannock if only for the reason that he was a physical wreck, apparently good for nothing. In this condition he would only be a liability to the Allied powers. He looked so insignificant and broken that the Turks did not believe he would make a soldier. They despised him for his "soft" approach to life.

On the way home, still under arrest along with many more British nationals, Mannock again suffered a pain in his left eye. It gave him hours of agony. He needed proper medical attention, but it was not available.

As soon as he landed he went to report to his original RAMC Territorial company and was posted to Ashford, Kent. Given an immediate rank of sergeant, he was then sent to the transport section of the 3/2nd Home Counties Field Ambulance Company. One of his friends wrote: "To all his intimates he was known as 'Jerry.' He was what is vaguely called a 'character'—one of those vivid and colorful personalities that make an impression wherever they are found. His career was extraordinarily varied. He joined the transport section of a field ambulance—the 3/2nd Home Counties, commanded by Major Chittenden.

"I was a sergeant in the 3/3rd unit, and we 'lay' next to each other at dear, muddy, rat-haunted Halton Park Camp West in 1915 —a winter which changed Lord Rothschild's stately park into a slimy mass of chalky mud, dreary beyond conception.

"Jerry was a member of a combined sergeant's mess that had roughly 100 members. It was he who suggested a weekly debate, and this gradually became transformed into a mock Parliament. He was the 'Hon. Member for Newmarket,' a delicate compliment to his knowledge of horses, and he engaged us in many an active debate on socialism.

"Alas, how many of the good fellows who made speeches and tinkered with the affairs of the nation are lying in hastily made graves in all parts of the world! And now Jerry. The flashing, original, lovable comrade of those transitory days is gone too. When the transport personnel of the RAMC of the Field Ambulance became part of the ASC, Jerry decided to make a change."

What made Mannock change his tactics and transform himself

from a good-humored, speech-making Irishman, plodding along through the war in the medical corps, into a fighting machine, intent upon killing as many Germans as possible? Perhaps the explanation lies in a speech which he made to the mock Parliament. He said: "We are fighting for the freedom of civilization. We must fight to the last man! We must kill every enemy."

Soon after this, and no doubt after a lot of thought, he suddenly applied for a transfer and told the CO that he could not and would not help the wounded enemy. Remaining in an ambulance unit was a waste of time as far as he was concerned. He wanted to be sent to the Royal Engineers. On April 1, 1916, he wrote: "I intend to become a Tunneling Officer and blow the bastards up. The higher they go and the more pieces that come down, the happier I shall be."

In training as a sapper he discovered that he lacked a textbook mind. He could not begin to understand the large number of orders which came his way, and developed an uneasy feeling that he was being cheated out of something, namely, the excitement of war. He remained good-humored, though it was sometimes a strain under the dull training routine. Then, one day when he could stand it no longer at Fenny Stratford camp, he demanded to see the adjutant. He wanted to be transferred to the RFC.

"For one thing," wrote his adjutant, "I thought he was too old —he was over thirty at the time—to adapt himself to the newest arm in warfare and the strange business of flying, especially as the prevailing opinion was that only young men were suitable for the job. Still, the novelty and excitement of flying must have appealed irresistibly to his adventurous spirit, and despite all opposition and the disadvantage of his age, he stuck grimly to his decision and eventually realized his ambition."

Mannock's first obstacle was his vision, still as bad as ever it was. The RFC medical order said: "An air pilot must have 100 per cent eyesight." He approached the examination with a great show of confidence and faced the doctor.

"Are your eyes good, Mannock?"

"Of course!" he exclaimed.

In August 1916, Second Lieutenant Mannock was officially transferred to the RFC. In his personal diary he wrote: "When the Adjutant sent for me today and informed me of my transfer to the RFC I could have kissed him, though he has the most repulsive mug of any man that I have ever met. Yes! I could have kissed it; such was my unbounded delight. Now for the Boche. I am going to strive to become a scout pilot like Ball. Watch me. I wonder what Fate has in store. . . ."

He was sent to Reading No. 1 School of Military Aeronautics and worked his way through such subjects as map reading, rigging, mechanics, the theory of flight, machine gunnery and bombing. They called him "Mick," and most of them envied his almost fierce application to the job. It was different for him now. As a soldier he felt dull and stupid when it came to learning how to burrow through mud, but he was sprouting wings and the world was a wonderful place, war or no war.

He passed and went to Hendon, but the place was choked with airmen in training, and he barely managed to find a space to qualify. He received the Aero Club's Certificate No. 3895, after a stiff test. On December 5 he passed on to No. 19 Training Squadron at Hounslow, and on February 1, 1917, was commissioned flying officer attached to Hythe Gunnery School. After fourteen days there they sent him to Joyce Green Reserve Squadron where he realized that he was just beginning to learn something about flying.

Captain J. B. McCudden, another British ace, was also at Joyce Green, employed there as an instructor. "I reported to the Wing at Maidstone," McCudden wrote, "and was told to make my headquarters at Joyce Green for the time being. I was allotted a Bristol Scout for my work, but as it was not yet ready, I used a DH2, which I 'spun' regularly to the great consternation of the pupils there, who regarded the machine as a super death trap, not knowing that in its day it was one of the best machines in the RFC. . . . The machines we are using here are principally the DH2s, Avros and Vickers fighters, which were very good for training pilots preparatory to their flying De Havilland 2s and FE8s."

McCudden and Mannock became great friends and were almost brotherly in their affection for one another. Mannock's other friend was Captain Meredith Thomas, who shared quarters with him.

"I first met Micky in February 1917 when he came along from Hythe to No. 10 Reserve Squadron at Joyce Green to fly DH2s and FE8s. We shared a room and he told me many interesting stories of his prewar life; it appeared to have been a hard one," Thomas related. At this time Mannock was a staunch teetotaler and a fairly regular churchgoer, although during chats he professed to have no particular religion.

"One particular incident regarding his flying training I well remember. That was his first solo flight on a DH2, when he was told, as all were told in those days, 'Don't turn below 2,000; if you do, you will spin and kill yourself.'

"Micky proved this wrong early one Sunday morning in March, when he accidentally got into a spin at about 1,000 feet over the munition factory—then just across the creek on the edge of the airfield—and came out extremely near the ground and the munition factory, and landed successfully in a small field which was too small to fly out from. He was accused of spinning intentionally, and after a rather unpleasant scene in the mess and later in the CO's office, was threatened with being turned down.

"We were great friends at Joyce Green and had many both amusing and serious talks when waiting in the cold on a fuel drum—at one period for a whole three weeks—for a flight, but I cannot recall anything definite beyond our mutual disgust because of the manner in which the staff threatened the pupils, many of whom had seen pretty severe war service before transferring or being seconded to the RFC, while the Staff had seen very very little, and in some cases, none.

"My first impression of Micky was: he was very reserved, inclined to strong temper, but very patient and somewhat difficult to arouse. On short acquaintance he became a very good conversationalist and was fond of discussions or arguments. He was prepared to be generous to everyone in thought and deed, but had strong likes and dislikes. He was inclined to be almost too serious-minded."

By the end of March he was a completely qualified pilot. He was eventually sent to No. 40 Squadron where he played his part in the war. The instrument on which he played his bloody concerto over the battlefields was a Nieuport Scout. From the very start he felt at one with it.

13

Love, Edward

"1.4.17. Just a year today I received my commission, and a year to the day earlier I was released from a Turkish prison. Strange how this date recurs. Let's hope that a year hence the war finishes, and I return for a spell to merrie England.

"Well! Landed at Boulogne. Saw the MLO and discovered that I was to be away to St. Omer the following day at 3:45 P.M. Rested and fed at the Hotel Maurice. Quite a nice place as continental hotels go. Wisher, Tyler, and two more strangers (RFC) kept us company. Rotten weather. Rain. I'm not prepossessed with the charm of La Belle France yet.

"2.4.17. Breakfasted on coffee and omelettes. The Eternal Omelette. By the way, they are good. Left at 4 P.M. Quite punctual.

"Arrived at St. Omer at 8:30 P.M. feeling very fed up and tired. Rotten journey at 2 mph. After portering luggage and practicing my execrable French, reported to No. 1 AD. Orders to put up for the night on our own. Proceeded by tender and devious ways to Hotel de France. Horrible place—*déjeuner* worse—and filled with subalterns of all sorts, sizes and descriptions. No room for me—so to Hotel de Commerce. Small, cold room. Candles and damp sheets, ugh!

155

"3.4.17. Rose at eight. The eternal coffee and omelette. Really the hens must be on war work. Tried to find the office again and subsequently managed to do so. Instructions to proceed to airfield. Met Lemon, Dunlop, and Kimball on the way. Was catechized and placed in the School—on Bristol Scouts. Censored lots of letters. No flying. Billeted at YMCA in St. Omer."

Mannock went to No. 40 Squadron in great confidence, though some of the things he saw while in transit made a horrifying impression on his mind, and he knew that war was not all swings and merry-go-rounds. He was told that he would be sent on offensive patrols and bomber escort, both duties carrying the highest mortality rate in the combined air forces. His CO was Major Dallas, a bouncy Australian, who regarded the war as one long joke. He once took a pair of flying boots on a lone trip, and dropped them on a German airfield together with a note: *Ground officers—for the use of.* Banking over the enemy airfield, hiding in low cloud, he then descended to see if the boots had been found. A few Germans were clustered around them, reading the sardonic message. Dallas drew a bead on the gathering and fired, then fled for his life.

Mannock's mess mates were like Dallas, and included such distinguished names as Mulholland, Barwell, Blaxland, McElroy, Ellis, Todd, De Burgh, Bond, Keen and Gregory, practically all of them either decorated or recognized as aces after their deaths in combat.

It was an entirely new atmosphere for Mannock. All his previous experience had been acquired as a solitary man, but he had, of course, made one or two friends at various squadrons during his training period. At No. 40 Squadron he was suddenly thrown into the melee of the mess atmosphere and on his first entrance there invited to occupy the chair of an officer who had been shot down that same morning. He accepted, trying not to worry too much about false premonitions. The mess was in a more sober mood than usual. The battle of Arras stood somberly in the offing, and preparations for this conflict were costly in human lives. Thirty-one officers and seven other ranks appeared that day on the list of missing men. And this was only a softening-up of the Germans! He was shown reports of the day's activities. What he read made him realize that he was going to become embroiled in the real war at last. They said that the battle of Arras was only a prelude to the larger and more important fight by the French against the Germans at Chemin des Dames. As it happened, the latter was a fiasco and did not benefit the Allies.

These are the reports which Mannock read the evening of the day he joined the squadron.

"Reconnaissance was carried out by all Brigades and 9th Wing, and 700 photographs were taken. Artillery cooperation—123 targets were dealt with by artillery with airplane observation, many OK's were obtained, and much ammunition exploded. *Hostile Aircraft:* As a result of the offensive patrols and bombing raids, hostile machines were kept well east of the lines. Thirty-one officers and seven other ranks were missing and two officers wounded. Some thirty enemy machines were accounted for, and fifteen of these were definitely ascertained to have been destroyed. The following summaries taken from the RFC *Communiqués* are typical of the day's combats:

"1. Second Lieutenant Smart and Second Lieutenant Hampson, No. 20 Squadron, while on a bombing raid attacked three hostile aircraft. The pilot of one of the hostile machines was shot and the machine broke in the air and fell. The second machine was driven down in a spinning nose dive, while the third, after having been attacked, dived vertically.

"2. A formation of No. 54 Squadron while acting as escort was attacked by a fast hostile scout. The enemy pilot appeared to be very good and maneuvered with great skill. Finally, however, he was enticed to attack one of our machines from behind, whereupon Lieutenant Stewart dived on the hostile machine and destroyed it.

"3. Second Lieutenant Vinson and Second Lieutenant Gwilt, No. 15 Squadron, were taking photographs over Bullecourt when they were attacked by six Albatros scouts. Unfortunately both machine guns fell out of the BE, and it was forced to land near Lagincourt, as one hostile machine pursued and continued firing at it. The pilot and observer jumped out and got into shell holes. The enemy artillery opened fire on our machine, but just before it was hit by an 8-inch shell, Second Lieutenant Vinson managed to obtain the exposed [photographic] plates of the Hindenburg Line and Bullecourt.

"4. An offensive patrol of Sopwith Scouts of No. 66 Squadron

shot the observer in a hostile machine and he was seen to fall from
the airplane. They drove off three hostile aircraft which were interfering with our artillery machines.

"Bombs were dropped on airfields, railways, billets, and
dumps by all brigades. Two 112-lb. bombs were dropped on a train
on the Menin-Wervicq line from a height of 500 feet. One burst
immediately in front of the train and destroyed the permanent way.
The train stopped and was attacked by machine-gun fire from the
air by an officer of No. 6 Squadron, who was slightly wounded by
gunfire from the ground.

"Bombing was also undertaken by the 9th Wing. One raid
against Valenciennes was made by DH4's of No. 55 Squadron, at
a height of 11,500 feet. From this height two bombs were observed
to fall on the station, two near the engine depot and the remainder
on and around the objective. On the return journey the De Havil-
lands were pursued by hostile fighters which, however, they were
able to outdistance owing to their superior speed."

This was just one day's activity on one part of the front, Mannock reflected. It looked very promising.

The flight commander, Captain Todd, remarked that Mannock
was ". . . like a highly strung pedigree horse at the starting post.
I let him have his head, but at first he was unable to shoot down
any Huns and his efforts were disappointing." In fact, Mannock
was far from happy with the Nieuport machine they wanted him to
use. It seemed heavy and clumsy on the controls, and it took several weeks before he could get used to it, but at last he wrote in
a letter home that he felt "almost at home in it." He flew up to the
front line at Béthune and was fascinated by the sight of the gun
flashes and to note the *chevaux-de-frise* of trenches. Soon afterward
he went up on his first offensive flights, but nothing very much
happened for a time. A few days later he wrote:

"14.4.17. Another OP this morning with Brown leading. Kept
formation grandly. Brown tried to lose me but failed. Observed
fires in Lens. Saw two formations of hostile aircraft very far away.
They won't wait. Went over again twice. Passed over Lens, Avion,
Annay, La Bassée, Vimy and Arras. Nothing doing at all. Brown
forced to land (engine trouble) at Isbergues, fortunately for him
we were not over the enemy's lines when it happened. He's OK.

"15.5.57. Very bad weather. High wind and clouds. Got three

letters today. First correspondence to be received in France by me. Heavy bombardment from the direction of La Bassée. Advanced again today in the region of Vimy and Avion. Rumor that we have lost Lens."

On April 19 he wrote to his mother:

Dear Mum,

I haven't heard from you in reply to my last letter (2nd), so I suppose that it has gone astray. I wrote you from Boulogne, as I hadn't time to send you a line from the other side, before being packed off to France. You will see from the address above that we are prohibited from giving the name of the place at which we are stationed, but I can say that we are in the actual thick of it, and I go across the lines every day (sometimes three times) when the weather is not actually prohibitive.

The battlefields wear an awful aspect as viewed from above— covered with shell holes and craters, which remind me of photographs of what the earth looked like at the very beginning of things. It's extraordinary how anything can live through such a bombardment. Just like a plum pudding with ten times too many currants and raisins mixed. I fly a machine on my own, and I can tell you it's very lonely being up in the clouds all by one's self, with the anti-aircraft shells coughing and barking all around one, and big guns on the ground flashing and spitting continuously. I've been over the German towns, but the Huns clear off almost invariably when they spot us coming.

I hope Norah is getting along all right. Presumably she is still at the same place. Personally I think she ought to get on to aircraft work as soon as possible. Shells and other kindred things will be played out soon. I am writing to Paddy regularly, and hope also that you are hearing from him to your advantage. It is the only way I could arrange to let you have something occasionally.

Now I don't want you to send me anything along, as there is plenty of everything here—tobacco, food, music, sports (when the weather is bad), but no girls, so don't waste what little cash you have in needless expense. I'm all right here.

There are lots of interesting things I should like to tell you, but the censor forbids, so I'll leave it to your imagination.

In the meantime . . . get ready for my leave, as I promise calling at the first opportunity.

Love,

Edward

An hour after writing that letter he shook hands with death. He was due to carry out some firing and diving exercises in his Nieuport, and when he came down from a thousand feet he let his machine gather speed before testing his guns over the dummy target area. He was in the middle of the first few rounds when he heard a loud snapping sound. Before he could pull out of the dive he saw the right bottom wing smash to bits and fall away from the body of the machine. Using strength and a still-crude skill, he somehow managed to land, but the plane piled up. One of the riggers scrambled forward to see if he could drag Mannock out of the wreckage, and was amazed to find him strolling away in another direction. They met and Mannock looked very strict and stern, telling him off for fitting defective wing struts. It was the Irishman's idea of a joke. Everybody knew that the fault lay more with the French manfacturers than with the well-trained and efficient RFC riggers.

"One day," said Sergeant Bovvett, the NCO in charge of rigging on Mannock's flight, "he returned from a job and his plane had been set alight by tracers which he managed to extinguish by diving; calling the armorer over he demanded more tracers than usual in future. 'I'll give the bastards what for,' he said. *And he did*. He was a man with plenty of nerve. When he became Flight Commander, he fixed a pair of silk stockings on his struts for streamers —where he got them from we don't know—more nerve, I suppose!"

For all this show of "nerve," Mannock was not entirely insensitive to the hazards of the job that was now occupying all his time. On March 20 he was over the lines when his engine cut out three times. He flew on, his heart in his mouth. "Now I can understand what a nervous strain flying is. However cool a man might be, there must always be more or less of a tension on the nerves under such trying conditions," he wrote. "When it is considered that seven out of ten forced landings are practically write-offs and fifty per cent are cases where the pilot is injured, one can quite understand the strain of the whole business." He knew even more strain when he got lost in the dark, thirty miles away from his airfield. He managed to get home all right, but admitted that he was scared to death by the experience.

By this time he had been made leader of his flight. In the air he set a difficult example, especially when it came to the younger pilots. On the ground he lectured them, telling them not to try and fly home at the first sign of trouble. He would lead them into all the trouble they could handle, he explained, and teach them how to fight. Next day a pilot did attempt to turn away from the flight as it arrowed toward the German lines. Mannock whipped around and fired ten tracer bullets over the coward's head. While he was banking to see what was happening ahead, he realized that some of his pilots were warding off an attack about to be made by German machines. With one eye on the would-be deserter, the other on the enemy, he fought brilliantly, bringing down two of the enemy within ten minutes.

After a squadron move from Aire to Auchel, he was detailed to act as escort to a photographic reconnaissance over Douai, home of the German aces. His diary reads:

"We were attacked from above over Douai. I tried my gun before going over the German lines, only to find that it was jammed, so I went over with a revolver only. A Hun in a beautiful yellow and green bus attacked me from behind. I could hear his machine gun cracking away. I wheeled round on him and howled like a dervish (although of course he could not hear me) whereat he made off toward old Parry and attacked him, with me following, for the moral effect! Another one (a brown-speckled one) attacked a Sopwith and Keen blew the pilot to pieces and the Hun went spinning down from 12,000 feet to earth. Unfortunately the Sopwith had been hit, and went down too, and there was I, a passenger, absolutely helpless not having a gun, an easy prey to any of them, and they hadn't the grit to close. Eventually they broke away, and then their Archie [anti-aircraft] gunners got on the job and we had a hell of a time. At times I wondered if I had a tail-plane or not, they came so near. We came back over the Arras with two vacant chairs at the Sopwith Squadron mess! What is the good of it all?

"A week ago, the Germans posted a notice up in their trenches which read:

" 'For God's sake give your pilots a rest.'

"We sent three BEs along at once and machine-gunned the trench where the notice was. Such is war. . . ."

What was Edward Mannock really like about this time? Older than the rest, he was certainly more mature than the majority, but he was beginning to get a bit edgy, telling juniors off for trivial faults, sometimes shouting at nothing at all. He was considered to be a human curiosity because he chose to keep his background dark. Sometimes, though, he spoke about his adventures in Turkey, but it took a lot to get him to converse very freely. Here is what another pilot, De Burgh, wrote about him:

"Mannock was an extraordinary character, and a very forceful one. Although I knew him for less than a month, and that thirteen years ago, his personality is as clear to me now as if we had only parted the other day.

"We had two things in common, he and I, so that I came to know him well (though I doubt if any man saw much beneath the surface of him)—we were both Irishmen, and we both dearly loved an argument.

"He was the only man in the mess who would talk beneath the surface. Many was the time that we would argue fiercely on some highly controversial subject such as politics, socialism or religion— he usually won the argument, though heaven knows what his views really were.

"As a curious contrast to the warfare of the tongue, Mannock was very keen on boxing, and as I had done a good deal, we often used to blow off steam by having a set-to in the mess. In fact, it used to be a stock event, if the evening was livening up, for Mannock and me to have a round or two—and he nearly always said, 'Let's hit out,' and we used to have a good slog at one another. I think, on the whole, that I used to get more than I gave, as he had the height of me, and a slightly longer reach; but I had him at footwork.

"As far as I know, there were only two things which would rattle him, and he would always rise to them, if drawn: the first was his very bitter hatred of the Germans, and the second was 'Society' women. The former has been amply confirmed by others. The latter caused us all no small amount of amusement—it was only necessary to leave a copy of one of the weekly papers open showing 'The beautiful Lady . . . who is organizing a charity concert in aid of . . . etc.' for Mannock to go off the deep end for about half an hour . . . he surely had the power of words!

"I often wonder how, and where, he would have fitted into a peacetime world.

"I gather that in prewar days he had led a pretty wandering life in the Near East. What he would have made of the postwar chaos, heaven knows, for he was undeniably a dreamer and idealist, though what those dreams were, I doubt if anyone knew.

"Had he lived, he would have made a marvelous politician; he had all the Celtic fire to move multitudes. And what a leader of a lost cause!"

By May 1917 Mannock was suffering from a serious attack of nervous trouble which seemed beyond his personal control. While the German propagandists were building up their heroes, regardless of actual integrity, the British made only scant mention of the personalities who had to fly out and meet the Richthofen and Boelcke squadrons. Mannock believed this to be a good thing. He liked the near-anonymity of it all. There was nothing of the god about him and to be surrounded by what he considered to be the sickly aura of hero worship suggested to him something of the society set which he abhorred.

During that damp month of May he overcame his nerves because flying conditions were good and he wanted to get into the air. He used to go off on his own, looking for trouble, and often managing to find it. On May 13 he arranged to carry out an early-morning patrol with Glin, a friend of his. They took off at about quarter to five, rising with the dawn into a sky heavy with thick cloud. They were just approaching their agreed patrol height when Glin zoomed alongside, signaling that he was not too keen on the weather conditions. They would be better off if they turned back and had breakfast. This could not be a very fruitful patrol, because the Germans might not be flying at all. Mannock half agreed, but did not want to go home. Mechanics had serviced the machines, ground crews had filled the tanks. It seemed a pity to waste the efforts of so many men. He made a hand signal to the waiting Glin. He would not go home just yet, but Glin was free to do as he wished. Glin seemed to hesitate a moment, then waved farewell, leaving Mannock to his own devices.

Some time later Mannock was flying over the Lens-Arras area, dodging in and out of the cumulus cloud banks, wondering whether the Germans were going to come up for a bit of early-morning sport, the terrible death-dealing sport which both sides played all the time. He came gliding out of the clouds and went straight into a torrential rainstorm which drenched him within a few minutes. He was soon so wet that he no longer cared about keeping dry. The bottom of the cockpit was awash. Every time he banked, even slightly, there was a rush of water from one side to the other. It sloshed about over his feet, chilling his toes. A fight in this water-logged condition could lead to trouble, he knew, but he went on searching for Germans. There was no sign of a plane, and he was about to turn and go home for breakfast when an ominous sound told him something in his engine was broken. Before he could reach out for the controls, the engine coughed again, then stopped. He was high enough to have plenty of time to try and rectify the matter. He juggled with the stubborn throttle, wondering how long this was going to last. He was about to try and land behind German lines when the engine picked up and responded to his touch.

He was banking for a new bearing when he caught up with three triplanes, all of them from British squadrons. Trying to get rid of the cold water in his cockpit, he looped round and round the formation, letting the shower of water cascade over him. Leaving the triplanes after saluting them, he scooted through the skies until he could see the ground. He was trying to plot a course for home when German artillery started banging away at him. Cramming the map into a sleeve at the side of the cockpit, he went into a zigzag, noticing the course of the acrid black cordite puffs on his tail. They were not shooting very well this morning, perhaps because of the weather. The rain had stopped and he estimated that the night crews were still on duty and therefore tired of sitting about in the mud. He took one more chance, sweeping in close, almost at ground level where he knew they could not get at him. His engine was running sweetly now, but he did not want to take too many chances. As he pulled the stick back, feeling the machine rise under him, he could see the faces and helmets of the Germans and resisted a temptation to turn around and give them a dose of their sort of hell. They might be more alert next time, holding their rifles at the ready. One well-placed bullet could put an engine out of commission. He did not want to wind up as a burning corpse near a German artillery nest. He was always frightened of fire, from the first day he flew, and told friends that he preferred to shoot himself rather than go down in a burning plane.

He was back in the mess by six-thirty, eating his bacon and eggs and saying very little about his one-man patrol.

Mannock's reputation was a strange, incongruous one. While he was friendly with most of the other pilots, this did not stop them spreading some scandal about him. His nerves, they alleged, were shaky. Fighter and scout pilots were not supposed to suffer from this complaint, and most of those who did so managed to cover up any tendency, especially when in the presence of senior officers. Mannock, however, did not try to cover anything up. He cheerfully told people that he often felt scared while flying in combat. It did not go down very well, especially among the veterans.

Captain G. L. Lloyd, Mannock's CO at No. 40 Squadron, wrote: "He was not actually called 'yellow,' but many secret murmurings of an unsavory nature reached my ears. I was told that he had been in the squadron two months, and that he had shot down one single Hun out of control, and that he showed signs of being overcareful during engagements. He was further accused of being continually in the air practicing aerial gunnery as a pretense of keenness. In other words, the innuendo was that he was suffering from 'cold feet.' "

When Lloyd had a few words with him about it, Mannock said: "Of course, I've been very frightened against my will—nervous reaction. I have now conquered this physical defect, and having conquered myself, I will now conquer the Hun. Air fighting is a science. I have been studying it, and I have not been unduly worried about getting Huns at the expense of being reckless. I want to master the tactics first. The present baldheaded tactics should be replaced by well-thought-out ones. I cannot see any reason why we should not sweep the Hun right out of the sky."

Lloyd was satisfied that he was telling the truth and tried to kill the scandal which was being tossed about in the mess. It did not seem fair that Mannock, who was serious about the war, should be the victim of such gossip.

Mannock now assumed a different personality, that of a ruthless killing machine, a man with an unremitting grudge against the Germans. It is possible he thought that Lloyd might regrade him and stop him from flying. Pilots who could not make the grade were being sent back to England where they were remustered and posted to infantry units at the front. With distaste, Mannock remembered his days in the Royal Engineers and RAMC. He could not stand any of that again. Some idea of the new mentality which made him one of our most daring pilots may be obtained from the following entry in his personal log:

"2.6.17. A beautiful morning, with more than a handful of cold wind blowing from the northwest. Am standing by to escort Sopwiths over lines on photography. No sign of them yet, thank God.

"Had several exciting moments since writing the last notes. Led the patrol yesterday (five machines) and had a scrap. Emptied a full drum of rounds into a big colored two-seater Hun from about 25 yards. Must have riddled the bus, but nothing untoward happened. She put her nose down and went straight. 'Melbourne' Bassett got hit in the leg in this scrap. Made a good show by flying all the way back to the field and landing, and this with a shattered leg! It was just bad luck that this shot was the only one on the machine.

"I tried my hand on a balloon northeast of La Bassée just after the above scrap. Fired about 25 rounds of Buckingham, but couldn't set the darned thing alight. In the meantime clouds of Archie all round me, but managed to zigzag away. Later was Archied by our people at 7,000 feet. Felt very mad.

"MacKenzie came back from leave on the 1st and was promptly ordered to Home Establishment again. Lucky dog! . . . I had almost forgotten to record the visit of the GOC Army on the 28th last. He came specially to congratulate us on the success of the last balloon stunt. He was very pleased indeed, and advised us to shoot at the observers as well as the balloons. He shook hands with the ' 'eroes.' Our CO was very pleased, I imagine."

In June, however, he had a recurrence of the nervous trouble. Life moved very fast, and he was shaken when forced into a fight with five German machines, all controlled by crack enemy pilots. It happened north of Douai. Only twenty-four hours after that encounter, from which he barely escaped with his life, he nearly crashed his plane while landing. Like most pilots, he was in the habit of pushing his flying goggles up on his forehead just before landing, so that he could see better and make sure of bringing the machine in on an even keel. This time a piece of grit flew up from the ground and went straight into his right eye, nearly blinding him. He was landing at about 120 mph and only just managed to get down safely. He went at once to see the MO, who said that the foreign body seemed to be lodged quite deeply in the membrane of the eye. Mannock insisted that something be done right away. The MO gave him an injection of cocaine and dislodged the grit. "My eye feels like a bell tent," Mannock commented painfully.

It was not only such incidents and accidents as these but also the chaffing of his fellow pilots, who liked to pull his leg, that played up the nervous tension. At last, late in June, he wrote: "Feeling nervy and ill during the last week. Afraid I am breaking up. . . . Captain Keen very decent. Let me off flying for today. I think I'll take a book and wander into the woods this afternoon—although it rather threatens rain. Oh, for a fortnight in the country at home!"

A few days later he was granted leave. The only salient feature of it was a surprise visit to Hanworth to inspect some new machines. A few days earlier somebody introduced him to a sporting baronet. To an acquaintance at Hanworth he said that it was a pity such people as baronets mattered merely because they had handles to their names.

Less than a month later he had a historic encounter with a German machine, and described it in a letter to a friend:

". . . I was interrupted in this letter to get out after a Hun. That was yesterday morning at 9:50 A.M. At 10:20 A.M. I was lucky enough to get a big two-seater Hun down in our own lines. I shot the pilot in three places and wounded the observer in the side. The machine was smashed to pieces and a little black-and-tan dog which was with the observer (a captain) was also killed. The observer escaped death, although the machine fell about 9,000 feet. The pilot was horribly mutilated."

A day or two later he had the chance of examining the wreckage on the ground, but it was a nightmare journey and, like many other aces, he felt sickened to see the war in the trenches at such close quarters. "The journey to the trenches was rather nauseating—dead men's legs sticking through the sides with puttees and boots still on—bits of bones and skulls with the hair peeling off, and tons of equipment and clothing lying about. This sort of thing, together with the strong graveyard stench and the dead and mangled body of the pilot (an NCO) combined to upset me for days."

Mannock was now averaging one German per day. By way of recognition he was awarded the Military Cross in August 1917, and then promoted to the rank of captain. He still believed that his part in the war had yet to be fought.

14

The Year of Heroes

Mannock had now sustained so many blows that he knew the strain on his nerves to be almost more than he could stand. He had to acknowledge that his early and youthful ideal of the non-Germanic superman did not exist, could not exist, under such conditions as these. After flying three or four missions each day, every week, he knew the effect of this kind of living. The effort of taking off from his airfield more than twenty times a week was too much for even his strong reserves of energy and he was beginning to lack the primitive savagery which had taken him through so much of the war in the air. Apart from the muscular drag from which he now suffered, there was the terrible lack of sleep to contend with. He found himself feeling drowsy in the thin coldness of the upper air, and had to shake himself awake. He knew that attack could easily come when he was caught nodding over the controls. If it happened like that, he would not stand a chance. Members of all the crack German squadrons used high speeds to make their kills. Mannock had watched too many Allied planes going down in a plume of flame to want the same thing to happen to him. His long-standing fear of being "sizzled" was intensified when he dwelt on the horror of being trapped in a blazing machine which was plummeting into the mud and sludge. As a man of many phases, he finally did manage to pull himself together. On July 28, 1917—the "year of heroes," as it has been called by one author—he scored a new victory which made a big impression on his mind. His own report best describes what happened.

"Hostile machine observed at 3:10 P.M. crossing our lines south of Thelus.

"E.A. attempted to attack our balloon west of that point and descended to low altitudes for that purpose. Nieuport engaged E.A. at approximately 1,000 feet over Neuville St. Vaast and fired 70 rounds during the course of a close combat. The hostile aircraft was observed to be hit, a glow of fire appearing in the nacelle, and glided down under reasonably capable control south and east of Petit Vimy, landing downwind and turning over on touching the ground. Prisoner: Lieut. von Bartrap, sustained fracture of left arm and flesh wounds in right arm and leg, and was taken to hospital immediately on landing. Machine was in very good condition, although upside down, but was unfortunately affected by eventual hostile gunfire."

A few weeks later—weeks of hard, violent fighting in which he was nearly shot down several times—he had another momentous encounter, and in his log described it thus:

"5.9.17. The end of a fairly hard day. Went over to Petit Vimy and Thelus in a sidecar this morning in an endeavor to pick up some relics of the last victims, downed yesterday afternoon in flames. Regret that nothing remained of the machine. I met this unfortunate DFW at about 10,000 over Avion coming southwest, and I was traveling southeast. I couldn't recognize the black crosses readily (he was about 300 yards away and about 500 feet above me), so I turned my tail toward him and went in the same direction, thinking that if he were British he wouldn't take any notice of me, and if a Hun I felt sure he would put his nose down and have a shot (thinking I hadn't seen him). The ruse worked beautifully. His nose went (pointing at me), and I immediately whipped around, dived and zoomed up behind him, before you could say 'knife.' He tried to turn, but he was much too slow for the Nieuport. I got in about 50 rounds in short bursts while on the turn and he went down in flames, pieces of wing and tail, etc., dropping away from the wreck. It was a horrible sight and made me feel sick. He fell down in our lines and I followed to the ground, although I didn't land. The boys gave me a great ovation.

"The same evening I got another one down east of Lens, confirmed by the A.A. people. Captain Keen had previously engaged it but broke off combat in order to renew the ammunition drum. I got quite close up and let him have a full drum, and he went nose-down east. Owing to the haze, I couldn't see him crash.

"Prior to that at 9:40 A.M. I had a beautiful running fight with another two-seater at 17,000 feet, from Bruay to east of Lens. This one got away, notwithstanding the fact that I fired nearly 300 rounds at close range. I saw the observer's head and arm lying over the side of the machine—he was dead, apparently—but the pilot seemed to be all right. He deserved to get away really, as he must have been a brave Hun. This fight was watched from the Advance Landing ground by the mechanics and caused great excitement. Anyhow, two in one day is not bad work, and I was today congratulated by the Colonel.

"Had a scrap this evening with six Hun scouts east of Lens, but had to retire early owing to gun trouble.

"This is the first gun trouble I've had for months.

"The CO bet me tonight ten to one . . . I don't bring down a two-seater tomorrow (if fine) on this side of the lines. I've taken him on, so I am going all out tomorrow to win my bet."

He got his two-seater and won his bet, but the sequel distressed him. It came in the shape of a note received when he was on leave in England.

To The British Flying Corps,

The 4th of September I lost my friend Fritz Frech. He fell between Vimy and Lievin. His respectable and unlucky parents beg you to give any news of his fate. Is he dead? At what place found he his last rest? Please to throw several letters, that we may found one.

Thanking before,
His Friend,

K.L.

PS: If it is possible, send a letter to the parents, Mr. Frech, Königsberg 1, Pr. Vord Vorstadt 48/52.

Reading this plea, Mannock felt sickened by the war which seemed to create so much suffering. He immediately wrote to the parents, making special arrangements for the delivery of the letter. He himself often flew over the German lines with replies to notes from the Germans, notifying them of deaths, burials or imprisonments. When all is considered, there were similarities between Oswald Boelcke and Edward Mannock.

Now in his mid-thirties, Mannock's vigorous ability was at its height, but his combat duties were somewhat curtailed when he was seconded to duties which involved the training of young pilots newly arrived at the front. He was ready to complain about the tediousness of the work when he was awarded a bar to his Military Cross with a citation which read:

"October 14. He has destroyed several hostile machines and driven others down out of control. On one occasion he attacked a formation of five enemy aircraft singlehanded and shot one down out of control. On another occasion while engaged with an enemy machine, he was attacked by two others, one of which he forced to the ground. He has consistently shown great courage and initiative."

This marked the end of a chapter of his life, and he knew that sooner or later he would be sent on leave, his second since being posted to the front. Before it came, he was flying on January 1, 1918, when he happened to find a German two-seater. Unable to resist the bait, he went in to close with it. It was one of the shortest, sharpest and most decisive fights of his life, and the enemy exploded before his eyes. He could not make out what had happened to the pilot or observer in the tumult of the explosion as the fuel tanks erupted in a scarlet violence all their own. This was the twentieth time he had shot down a German machine, and he went on leave the next day to the sound of cheers of assembled mechanics and fellow pilots.

At home everybody knew how tired he was, and a gentle conspiracy sprang into being to keep him at home for a time. Despite his often angry endeavors to return to the front, he was detained in England for three months, resting and trying to curb his tongue when meeting the inevitable society lionizers. A month after leaving France, he was sent to the Wireless Experiment Establishment at Biggin Hill, but from the start he hated the atmosphere, the quietness of it all, and he longed to escape. When his outbursts became so loud that they could not very well be ignored, he was posted to No. 74 Training Squadron, London Colney, Hertford-shire. He arrived there wearing a threatening expression, but was quickly pacified on hearing that No. 74 Squadron would be going to France in February. His posting to the squadron was organized with a minimum of red tape; otherwise, as he himself threatened General Henderson, he would go straight back to France without official permission. He told Henderson that he would fly back, not follow the overland route, stealing a plane for the purpose if he had to. The authorities could do what they liked about it. Hender-son was the one who capitulated and arranged for him to be sent to London Colney.

While with this squadron Mannock spent hours lecturing young pilots, giving them hints on the handling of the SE5, a machine about which he knew practically everything there was to know. He was able to talk the more imaginative fledglings out of the idea that they were mere "Fokker fodder."

By March 1 No. 74 Training Squadron was reorganized, be-coming known as No. 74 Fighter Squadron, under the command of Major A. S. Dore, DSO, Mannock was promoted to flight commander of "A" Flight.

Over in France things were happening quickly. Before Mannock really had a chance to realize that he was in the thick of things once more, he was flying every day, engaging in some of the quick-est aerial fights he had ever known. He had the double task of seeing that the newly qualified fighter pilots were sufficiently astute to act on their own responsibility and, for his own part, lifting his personal score, now standing at more than forty, even higher. The following extract from the diary of Lieutenant Ira Jones, him-self an ace, will perhaps explain why Mannock was often short-tempered and intolerant when it came to the faults of others. Mannock was living faster than any other man at the front, both mentally and physically, and it was engagements such as this which made his temperament sometimes smolder, sometimes burst into violent flame. "Mick" was Edward Mannock.

"28.5.18. The CO saved Giles' life today. Giles very carelessly allowed a black Albatros to pounce on him while he was con-centrating on the destruction of a silver-gray two-seater. Giles had his leg pulled unmercifully; we declare he was decoyed. Pilots hate admitting that they have been taken in as a sucker!

"Clements tells me that Mick saved his life tonight, too. Mick and Clements went up for a bit of fun after tea. They each got what they wanted. . . . Clements spotted a large formation of Huns obviously making a beeline for them. Clements put on full throttle . . . to catch up to Mick, who as usual was wasting no time in getting at his enemy. Mick had seen the Hun formation all the time . . . he turned west quickly and dived, the Huns following and firing. Mick saved Clements by losing height directly beneath them and so drawing them on to him, while Clements got clear. Clements says it was a rotten sight to see one SE being attacked by such a bunch, and that had it been anyone except Mick, he would have been anxious about his safety. (We all believe that no Hun will ever shoot down Mick.) One Pfalz followed him very closely, and suddenly Mick went down apparently out of control; on his back —spinning—and doing everything imaginable from 8,000 feet to 4,000 feet. At 5,000 feet, the Hun, completely fooled, flattened out to watch the crash. Mick then decided he had had enough, and flattened out too and made for our lines, diving hard. . . .

"29.5.18. Mick took Clements and me up at 7 P.M. . . . Mick spotted about a dozen Huns coming from the direction of Roubaix; we were then over Lille. As we had not too much time for a fight, having already been up for over an hour, he decided to go straight at them, as we had a slight advantage of height. The Huns, who were Albatros scouts, were of the stout variety, and they accepted our head-on challenge. Both Mick and the Hun leader opened fire at one another, as they approached from about 300 yards range, but nothing happened. This burst of fire was the signal for a glorious dogfight—as fine and as frightening a dogfight as I've ever been in. Friend and foe fired at and whistled past one another at a tornado pace . . . I have never been so frightened in my life. Of late I have been able to keep very cool during the actual fight, but tonight I became so flustered that occasionally I fired at my own pals in an effort not to miss a chance—thank God, my shooting was erratic. How terrible it would have been if I had, say, shot Mick down! The thought gives me the very creeps. . . . Mick sent two slate-blue Albatroses down out of control, and Clements crashed his first Hun. He is very bucked about it. It is wonderful how cheered a pilot becomes after he shoots down his first machine; his morale increases by at least 100 per cent. This is why

Mick gives Huns away—to raise the morale of the beginner. . . ."

Analyzing tactics between combats, Mannock often wondered whether the extended course, which most of his pilots had taken at Ayr Fighting School prior to their transfer to France, was having effect. He believed there was far too much idiocy and clumsiness manifesting itself. There were also times when he had rows with Caldwell, the CO of No. 74 Squadron who replaced Dore. Before leaving for France Dore told him that he might not be going to France at all.

"Surely you don't mean to say you would rather stay at home on a staff job than be commanding this fighting squadron in France!" Mannock exclaimed.

"But I am going to be promoted," Dore said.

Mannock yelled: "What! That's worse than ever."

As it happened, Dore did stay at home, and Major Keith Caldwell, a New Zealander, was appointed the new CO. He called all airplanes "grids," had obtained his fighting experience with men like Albert Ball, VC, believed in *esprit de corps,* and decried the cult of the individualist which, he believed, was what led to the downfall of the German air force. Adjusting his own personality to that of Caldwell, Mannock found that he had to alter his attitude to the war itself, and immediately got down to the not inconsiderable job of merging with the other pilots, instead of being *the* Mannock. He never pretended that it was simple. Part of his private objection to Caldwell's dogmatic creed was carefully covered by bouts of jokes and leg-pulling. The New Zealander retaliated with grim humor about the way Mannock would "sizzle" when he was finally shot down. Mannock certainly did not relish the prospect, but nevertheless allowed Caldwell his bit of fun. He still had the same old black fear of being lapped by flames as his machine fell to pieces. It was one of the few things which he could hardly bring himself to face. In France on his second tour of duty, he seemed to pay much more attention to the fire hazards while he also subjugated his long-standing hatred of the Germans, though when news came of Richthofen's death he would not join in toasting the Red Baron's memory. He walked out of the mess in disgust. The only Germans he ever admired for their skill as pilots were Boelcke and Werner Voss.

The daily fight in the air had now become so commonplace that

Mannock frequently forgot or omitted to report exactly what had happened after he returned from his sorties. For this reason, reports of his most memorable actions must come from others, including Van Ira, a South African member of No. 74 Squadron. Mannock was leading his fighters into battle and presently Van Ira witnessed a terrible sight.

"I saw a dogfight going on between a number of machines east of Merville at about 14,000 feet, so I went along to join in the fun, although I was at a lower altitude. As I was climbing toward the scrap, I suddenly saw a machine falling away from the whirling mob and come tumbling down in my direction. I awaited its approach with a considerable amount of anxiety, as I suspected a ruse, and that he was going to attack me. However, as he approached my level, the Pfalz, which was highly colored with a black body, white-tipped tail, silver and black checkered top surfaces, suddenly assumed a position on its back, and I noticed that the propeller was stopped. I flew close up to it, and to my horror, I saw the body of the pilot partially dangling out of the cockpit as if he were dead; in addition, the machine began to smoke badly."

Along with others, Van Ira was becoming concerned about the grim blood lust which was again coming to the surface of Mannock's feelings. It was not a desirable trait in an Allied pilot because it betokened a loss of control. Mannock risked his life several times when he followed crippled German planes down to shoot them to bits as they lay on the ground. He was believed to be callous, cold-blooded, and those who did not know him very well felt that he was exceeding the bounds. Caldwell, the CO of No. 74 Squadron, noted the following:

"Mannock and Dolan were up together, and on seeing British Archie bursting on our side of the lines, they chased along to see what could be done. They spotted a Hun two-seater beetling back toward the lines, and got down just in time to prevent this.

"The Hun crashed, but not badly, and most people would have been content with this—but not Mick Mannock, who dived half a dozen times at the machine, spraying bullets at the pilot and the observer, who were still showing signs of life. I witnessed this business, and flew alongside of Mick, yelling at the top of my voice (which was rather useless), and warning him to stop.

"On being questioned as to his wild behavior, after we had

landed, he heatedly replied: 'The swines are better dead—no prisoners for me!' "

While still quite approachable and talkative, Mannock was reserving the greater part of himself for the battles in which he was engaged. He was shooting down an average of one German every day, and often led his followers deep behind the German lines. The German attitude to aerial warfare had altered. No longer did the Hun aces flaunt themselves over the front line, tempting the Allied airmen to come out and duel. After great setbacks on the ground and the deaths of many of their best pilots, they could only hang about over their own flying fields, hoping for easy victories. These places were Mannock's chief objectives. It often meant having to fly more than twenty miles before any engagement could be made. Mannock forced every fight, generally managing to shoot down his unwilling opponents in flames. He let off steam by coming back to the mess and shouting at the top of his voice: "Sizzle, sizzle, sizzle, wonk, woof!" as a sign that he had shot down another one. It was this eternal urge to hunt which started to fray his nerves. He expected the Germans to be up there, watching for him and preparing for the next fight, but it was not working out like that at all. They were badgers in holes. He disliked having to do all the spadework. Sometimes, when he was so bored that he could not stand being on the ground any longer, he gave orders to the ground crews to have his machine fueled and the drums of ammunition clipped in position, then went out by himself to pick a fight. Doing this was strictly against his better judgment, but he suffered from boredom and it was the only way out. He repeatedly told younger pilots that it was stupid to fly alone over the front because any victories gained lacked the necessary confirmation. He had a complicated way of blooding members of his flight, and often guided two of them straight into the heart of a fight which he himself started. He then flew away to the sidelines to watch developments. Conscious of his critical eyes fixed upon them, the youngsters generally did very well.

Major Caldwell told of one of Mannock's victories when flying alone. "The only time I can remember Mannock got a Hun when alone, happened when he attacked a Fokker scout just east of Ypres one afternoon in June. He attacked at short range, did a climbing turn to keep height in case the Hun zoomed, and never saw the Hun again. When he landed on the airfield he told me that he thought he could not very well have missed from such close range. So I rang up the Archie battery near Ypres and asked for a description of any combats between 7,000 feet and 10,000 feet just east of Ypres between 3 P.M. and 4 P.M. The reply came straight back that an SE5 had shot down a Fokker in a vertical dive at the time Mannock reported."

On May 21 Mannock shot down four German scout planes and a two-seater. This incident is described by Van Ira.

"In his first fight, which commenced at 12,000 feet, there were six Pfalz scouts flying east from Kemmel Hill direction. One he shot to pieces after firing a long burst from directly behind and above; another he crashed; it spun into the ground after it had been hit by a deflection shot; the other, a silver bird, he had a fine set-to with, while his patrol watched the Master at work. It was a wonderful sight. First, they waltzed around one another like a couple of turkey cocks, Mick being tight on his adversary's tail. Then the Pfalz half-rolled and fell a few hundred feet beneath him. Mick followed, firing as soon as he got in position. The Hun then looped—Mick looped too, coming out behind and above his opponent and firing short bursts. The Pfalz then spun—Mick spun also, firing as he spun. This shooting appeared to me a waste of ammunition. The Hun eventually pulled out; Mick was fast on his tail—they were now down to 4,000 feet. The Pfalz now started twisting and turning, which was a sure sign of 'wind-up.' After a sharp burst close up, Mick administered the *coup de grâce,* and the poor old fellow went down headlong and crashed.

"This was a really remarkable exhibition of cruel, cool, calculating Hun-strafing. A marvelous show. I felt sorry for the poor Hun, for he put up a wonderful show of defensive fighting. His effort reminded me of mine on April 12. The only difference was, that he was miles over his own lines and had a slower machine. Had he only kept spinning down to the ground, I think he would have got away with it.

"I asked Mick after he landed why he fired during the spin. He replied, 'Just to intensify his wind-up.' And a very good answer, too! This was the first occasion that I have ever seen a machine loop during a fight. It was obvious to us, watching, that to loop under such circumstances is foolish. Mick managed, however, to keep behind him, and did not lose contact with him, although it was obvious by his maneuvers after he came out of the loop that the Pfalz pilot was all at sea, for he twisted and turned his machine in a series of erratic jerks, just as if he was a dog stung on his tail. Mick says he only looped as well for a bit of fun, as he felt his opponent was 'cold meat.' He says what he should have done instead of looping was to have made a zooming climbing turn as the Pfalz looped, then half-rolled and come back on his tail as he came out of the loop. By this means he would have been able to keep the Hun in sight all the time, while he would not have lost control of his machine as the Hun did while coming out of the loop.

"Mick's other Hun was a two-seater, which he shot down after a burst at right angles. The old boy crashed into a tree near La Couranne, south of Vieux.

"Four in one day! What is the secret? Undoubtedly the gift of accurate shooting, combined with the determination to get to close quarters before firing.

"It's an amazing gift, for no pilot in France goes nearer to a Hun before firing than the CO, but he only gets one down here and there, in spite of the fact that his tracer bullets appear to be going through his opponent's body! Mick, on the other hand, takes an angle shot and—Hun in flames."

Famous pilots were being just as well lionized as well-known authors and actors. Some fliers were outrageous in lapping up the extravagant praise. Only after some painful experiences did Mannock learn to take it in his stride. He was generally bluff and hearty, quite unlike his usual rather taciturn self seen at the airfield. When all the adulation was over and done with, he was able to revert to his other, more businesslike, nature, glad to get away from the sycophancy. He was, however, trapped into meeting General Plumer, one of the more admired members of the General Staff, who was going the rounds of the front and thought to call in on the squadron to see the aces for himself.

"This afternoon General Plumer, who commands the Second Army, came and gave us a surprise," wrote Van Ira. "He is a quaint little man to look at, but very charming to speak to. He is about five feet eight in height, corpulent, has a pudgy red face, white hair and mustache, a twinkle in his eye, wears a monocle, and stands like the grand soldier he is, very stiff and erect. He flattered us with his praises of our fighting efforts, but I have sus-picions that he did not approve of either the cleanliness or the mode of our dress. Naturally when off duty we are not particular about our dress, as we believe in being comfortable today, as to-morrow we may be dead.

"Mick, who had just landed, was the most disreputable of all. As he approached the group where the General stood, he was hat-less, without a collar, his tunic open, his hair ruffled; in fact, he looked a typical bush-ranger!

"The General said, 'Which is Mannock?' Mick was duly pointed out to him. When he set eyes on him, I really thought he was going to pass right out. By a masterly effort, however, he pulled himself together and literally seemed to stagger up to Mick with his arm outstretched. Mick's dirty paw clutched the gloved hand and squeezed it in his usual hearty manner. Plumer's face twitched, and for a second I thought he was going to give a shout. 'Mannock,' he stammered, 'let me congratulate you on your DSO.'

"This was the first intimation of Mick's well-deserved award which we've been expecting for some days. Later he said to Mick: 'Further, let me congratulate you on your first day's work.'

"Mick replied: 'We expected that, sir,' meaning that, having a lot of good fellows in his flight, he naturally thought they would shoot down some Huns. But, of course, it did not sound like this to General Plumer, and he departed with a puzzled expression in his face, no doubt wondering what sort of fellow Mick might be, and possibly thinking that he is spoiled by success. Quite wrong."

Mannock generally managed to mix well with the others, rising to new heights as an after-dinner speaker. He was always the one chosen to voice the sentiments, and he always earned his applause. There was, of course, another side to him. In the early morning, shortly before dawn, he slipped out of his camp bed and put on his flying overalls after a cold-water sponge-down to liven himself up. Going into the mess, he put the gramophone on. It was always the same sad lament of *The Londonderry Air* which he played as he stood at the window, watching the mechanics pushing his ma-chine into position. He never ate or drank anything and once said that he would like to die with an empty stomach if he had to die at all. As the song came to an end, he walked out to his plane, the last lingering notes sounding in his ear. An hour later he would be back after shooting down another German, sometimes more.

Often high-spirited, he liked to organize practical jokes and spoofs. He was responsible for an organized raid on No. 1 Squadron when a couple of hundred oranges were dropped as "bombs." Next day planes of No. 1 Squadron flew over in revenge and bombed Mannock's crowd with bananas, a fruit which seemed to make a more effective mess than the oranges. Peace was declared at a joint squadron dinner at Saint-Omer, where they converged on the George Robey café and drank together. That night Mannock was in great form.

Thoughts that he might become the victim of a violent roasting were never far from his mind. He was now having nightmares again about airplanes in flames, and was always saying to his close friends that he would blow his brains out rather than go down enveloped in fire. Evidence of the bad state of his nerves came when he somehow crashed two machines, one of them nose-diving into the earth, the other turning completely over on a bad run-in. That week other squadron pilots managed to write off seven of their own machines. One pilot smashed up as many British as he shot down German planes. Caldwell received a stiff note of reprimand from headquarters. Mannock felt angry that anybody had even noticed the write-offs at a time when a new phase of the war had to be fought and won, and he had an argument with Caldwell about it, but in the end conceded that he himself was probably in the wrong. Everybody knew that bad landings were usually the result of bad nerves. He was often in a state when he could hardly control the shaking of his arms and wrists after handling his machine in arduous combat. The immediate reaction to minutes of hectic warfare was too much for any nervous system, though he always insisted that it was his own frailty that was to blame. He promised to try and do better in future.

He now believed that the Germans were suffering from cold feet, and any similar trait in his own men sent him into spasms of anger. One young pilot who came up from a replacement pool did actually turn coward after Mannock had spent long hours instructing him in the kind of strategy which seemed best suited to squadron flying. He was so disgusted that he could not find any pity for the youngster. When the order came to send this man to a desk job in England he told his orderly to get hold of the pilot's jacket, rip off the wings and replace them with a scrap of yellow cloth. Certain officers viewed Mannock's attitude with distaste, but he insisted that his orders be carried out. While they were still shaking their heads over him he was cited in the *London Gazette* to receive a bar to his DSO. The citation said: "A fine example of marksmanship and determination to get to close quarters. As a patrol leader he is unequaled."

There was room for a man like Mannock to act as a morale booster, and he was selected to spend part of his time visiting various squadrons in the area. He tried to concentrate mainly on senior pilots, who would show an example to the younger members of the RFC. Although he was supposed to spend a lot of his time talking to them, he was in the habit of returning to his own flying field as soon as possible, so that he could get into the air. His machine was always kept at the ready. Once, when he came back too late to join the others, he went up with a seventeen-year-old fledgling, "Swazi" Howe, a South African and the youngest in the squadron. According to Van Ira it was an eventful flight.

"Mick came back in a furious temper from a patrol this morning. He had taken Swazi out on a private war to see if he could help him to get a Hun. At 11:20 A.M. he spotted half a dozen Albatroses flying in formation near Armentières and at the same time he noticed a flight of Camels patrolling near by, so he flew up to the leader and waggled his wings to attract his attention and to ask him to follow him, this being a recognized procedure. The Camels followed Mick while he maneuvered for position before attacking. Eventually he gave the signal to attack, and down he swooped on the completely surprised enemy. A dogfight immediately commenced, and when Mick had time to look around to sum up the situation he discovered that he and Swazi were alone and that some distance away was the Camel flight, flying away! Both Mick and Swazi eventually made a safe getaway after expending all their ammunition, but each of their machines much shot about, both the tires of Mick's machine were punctured, and as a result he turned a somersault on landing. He was so angered about the whole affair that he asked the CO to report the matter at once to Wing Headquarters. What apparently happened was, when the leader of the Camels commenced to dive with Mick, he saw another enemy formation approaching toward the fight from some distance away, so he thought he'd better go and intercept them. The result was that they sheered off and Mannock's fight was over before the Camels could return and join in the fray. They were, however, able to confirm that one of the Huns went down in flames. Mannock credited this victory to Howe."

On leave in England some time later Mannock was told that he had been promoted to major's rank and was being transferred to another squadron. On July 3, when returning to France and the front after a bad attack of influenza, he suddenly felt that he could not carry on much longer. He was stunned, remembering that he had told friends at the RFC Club in Bruton Street about pre-monitions of death in this, his third tour of duty. Even so, his new rank bucked him, though he did not want to leave No. 74 Squadron. He even cried over it in front of friends, who were embarrassed to see how low his spirits were sinking. They tried to cheer him up and he apologized for his weakness. Influenza left him debili-tated. He frankly admitted that he was not in a fit condition to do much operational flying at present. On reaching France his temperament changed. No longer did he feel impelled to carry on his relentless private war against the Germans. He was doubtful whether he could shoot a Hun in cold blood as he often had done in the past. He began living a new routine. He combed his hair with great concentration; he had his batman clean and press his uniform and stitch on the row of decorations. His boots were shined, and he somehow subjugated his passionate, often fierce manner. He went on telling people that he felt himself to be coming to the end, but did not know whether he was going to die fighting or not.

He was in the depths of this mood when he had tea with some VAD nurses from a nearby hospital. In the party was a man called Donald Inglis, a shy new fighter pilot, only recently arrived at the front. Mannock was stirring his tea when he caught Inglis' eye. "Have you got a Hun yet, Inglis?"

Inglis colored. Mannock was one of his private gods. "No, sir," he answered quietly.

Mannock put down his tea untouched. "Well, come on out and we will get one." To his hostesses he apologized: "Excuse us for a few minutes, please."

Something went wrong with Inglis' plane and he could not take off. Mannock flew on alone, returning two hours later to admit that he had seen nothing of the enemy. He was tired and his face was etched with fatigue. It was as much as he could do to walk into the mess and sit down, still wearing his flying overalls.

His personal interest in Inglis did not lessen. Once more the ace was teaching the beginner. Early one morning he made a determined effort to get Inglis initiated. Those who knew Mannock of old wakened to hear *The Londonderry Air* playing on the gramophone.

Mannock and Inglis strolled out to their warmed-up machines and the dawn was split by the roaring of their engines. It was an excellent morning for killing Germans.

There can be no better witness to what happened than Inglis himself.

"My instructions were to sit on Mick's tail, and that he would waggle his wings if he wanted me closer. I soon found that I didn't have much chance of looking around, as Mick would waggle, and the only thing I could do was to watch his tail and stick tight, as he was flying along the lines at about thirty to fifty feet up and not straight for more than thirty seconds, first up on one wing tip, then the other. Suddenly he turned toward home, full out and climbing. A Hun, thought I, but I'm damned if I could find one; then a quick turn and a dive, and there was Mick shooting up a Hun two-seater. He must have got the observer, as when he pulled up and I came in underneath him I didn't see the Hun shooting. I flushed the Hun's fuel tank and just missed ramming his tail as I came up, when the Hun's nose dropped. Falling in behind Mick again we did a couple of circles around the burning wreck and then made for home. I saw Mick start to kick his rudder and realized we were fairly low, then I saw a flame come out of the side of his machine; it grew bigger and bigger. Mick was no longer kicking his rudder; his nose dropped slightly and he went into a slow right-hand turn around about twice, and hit the ground in a burst of flame. I circled at about twenty feet but could not see him, and as things were getting pretty hot, made for home and managed to reach our outposts with a punctured fuel tank.

" 'Poor old Mick!' All I could say when I got into the trench was that the bloody bastards had shot my major down in flames."

Mannock died enveloped in flames, just as he feared he would. The man who shot down seventy-two Germans was no more. They never found his body. He had no known grave.

Death Before Twenty

There were many different aspects of the man, all of them personal.

He prayed ardently in the village church at Shenley, a Hertfordshire village close to London Colney, one of the RFC fighter squadron centers in World War I. He believed in an omnipotent God.

At the front he sold plots of English land to men who confessed that they were afraid of being killed, of being prevented from going home again. They bought the land because they wanted to provide security for wives and families.

And as a small boy he used pairs of pistols with uncanny accuracy, shooting at tin cans and knocking them down while his father, a knight, took a benevolent interest in his son, who turned out to be a crack shot before he was fourteen.

His Christian name was Albert, his surname Ball, and he was a popular hero before being killed before the age of twenty. Into his brief life was packed all the adventure experienced by a dozen wartime pilots. His death came in a larger-than-life tradition which set the warring nations agog for more details, though the news was never made public because nobody knew exactly what became of him.

Albert Ball was a romantic, a believer in a brand of patriotism just as fervent as that of Kipling. He came of a mold which England used to adore. He was conventionally religious ("the wicked shall be punished"), he liked music to the extent of playing a violin which he carried with him to the field of battle.

He was a bad student pilot, but practiced assiduously until able to duel with the most venomous German, even the great Richthofen, showing a familiarity which must have annoyed the indomitable Red Baron. It was only a routine fight: nothing much happened and for once Richthofen did not put in a victory claim. Even in the air some Germans were class-conscious. While Richthofen did not necessarily toe the Prussian line, he disliked the idea that he might, some day, be shot down by such a smooth-chinned youth as Albert Ball, who did not bother even to wear a flying helmet because he liked to feel the wind in his thatch of springy hair.

Like Edward Mannock, Albert Ball waged a one-man war, but not for the same reasons. Mannock hated the German race. His raging blood lust took him safely through every fight until the last one in which he was killed. Ball was patriotic and more phlegmatic generally. He said that there was nothing personal in the way he fought his war. It was only that he could not stand the thought of his England being overrun by Huns.

He thought he knew all about the forceful way in which the Germans would try to thrust their *Kultur* down English throats. Because he did not believe that the Germans would be "good" for England, he killed as many as possible in the time allotted to him. He was far from being the gloating butcher; on the other hand, he had none of the schoolboy gallantry which certain air fighters are supposed by certain writers to have demonstrated. He flew to kill and there was no end to his killing until he himself was killed. In his own time he did fight a war of consequence, one with such impact that it dented German self-esteem. He was probably one of the last great fighting pilots to do this. With his death came a firm British decision to put a new orderliness into the aerial war.

Scout machines now had to fly in groups of three. If one failed, the other two must escort it home without more ado. The greatest precautions were introduced to safeguard Allied pilots flying solo on hazardous missions. There must be no more of the single-machine dawn missions, when pilots were able to come back and announce that they had just shot down a Hun. The glamor was taken out of the air war in the shape of a few terse orders. Ball's life was the punctuation mark between one type of aerial warfare and the introduction of safety measures which must have seemed ludicrous to the daredevils. While it lasted, he fought hard and brilliantly, just as men like Voss, Schafer, Dormie, Lowenhardt, Guynemer and Harvey-Kelly had done.

Ball's instrument of German extinction was the sleek, fast Nieuport Scout, a French-designed plane with a 110-hp Le Rhone engine and such desirable characteristics as lightness of control ("like flying a feather," said one pilot), a better than usual visibility, which enabled the pilot to see exactly what was happening all about him. It had an eagle-like ability to climb quickly, 10,000 feet in ten and a half minutes. The armament was a Lewis gun fired straight over the top plane and operated by a Bowden cable which curled down to the pilot's hand. There was a certain initial strangeness about firing the gun. It meant that the pilot operated a release which could remain in his lap or in his fist while the burst of firing sounded just over and above his head. For all that, the gun was suited to the kind of marksmanship which Ball practiced from boyhood when he tried out some trick shots, holding a mirror over one shoulder and sighting the revolver through the glass. He liked the Nieuport for its speed. As soon as he got used to its few peculiarities, he threw it all over the sky in a series of aerobatics that frightened people watching below.

Albert Ball was not a great pilot, but he taught himself how to get the best out of his plane. In training he showed a clumsiness, and often seemed stupid to his instructors. He fluffed one or two landings and piled up a few training machines before acquiring the knack of bringing them in safely from his solo flights. Less than a year later he was classified as being a safe and cautious pilot who did not take to the air for idle amusement. He flew to achieve perfection. At the height of his career he used to spend more than four hours a day in the air, divided equally between the silver-painted Nieuport Scout and an SE5 always kept in reserve.

After four hours' flirtation with the clouds, looking for Germans to kill, he returned to base and rested in his own homemade hut. You could hear him practicing the violin if you listened. That was the reason for his billet being set apart, so that he should not disturb his fellow pilots. Sometimes, on warm evenings, he came out to stick a red magnesium flare in the ground and pace around it, playing a favorite air on the fiddle. It was a simple eccentric amusement for a boy who could fly like some airborne Mephistopheles and shoot like Buffalo Bill Cody. And all the time Albert Ball went on believing in God and country, that right would prevail in the end, that England would emerge triumphant and that the Germans would be taught a lesson they would never forget. Albert Ball was a simple man in the best sense of that word. Living in a frightened, bloodstained world, he still managed to remain more or less what he wanted to be.

He was born in 1896, the son of Sir Albert Ball, once alderman and mayor of Nottingham. The boy was eighteen when the war started and he enlisted under Kitchener's pointing finger, one of the first hundred thousand who felt the urgent appeal to be a genuine one betokening Britain's finest hour. He was posted to the Sherwood Foresters. In a fortnight they promoted him to sergeant in the 2/7th. He applied for a commission, which was granted. As a second lieutenant he was posted to the North Midland Cyclist Corps. He was still with his unit in the summer of 1915 when he became interested in learning to fly. He paid for his own lessons, given by M. Ami Bauman of the Ruffi-Bauman School, but had to get out of bed early enough in the morning to travel from Ealing to Hendon airfield on a motorcycle, take the lessons and then get back to his unit in time for parade at six o'clock. He learned quickly and, despite his poor landings, thought enough of his own progress to get himself sent to the RFC in January 1916, after gaining his pilot's certificate in October 1915. He was posted to No. 13 Squadron, flying BE2's.

It seemed dull work at first, but in France he managed to shoot down three Germans, no mean achievement in the heyday of the Fokker. His superior officers happened to hear him say that he was fed up with artillery cooperation and would like to finish with the BE2 machine. He was posted to No. 11 Squadron, equipped with Nieuport Scouts. That was on May 7; before the end of the month he shot down two more Germans.

There are several versions of Ball's career, and none of them is quite correct. Most of them idolize him, forgetting that he was only a young man and a very ebullient one at that. According to some records he shot down Germans practically every day, coming out of his fights unscratched, with nerves unruffled. Others claim that he shot down very few Germans; one author even suggests that Ball shot down only ten Germans in the whole of his career. Official communiqués are little use in this respect, because Ball did not bother to record half his successes.

It is not proposed to make a controversy out of this aspect of Albert Ball's life, but to confine these chapters to the relevant facts. It should be understood, however, that the forty or more victories attributed to him refer not only to the actual shooting down and destruction of German machines, but also to the forcing down of enemy machines behind the lines. Some of these were recovered and flew again.

No. 11 Squadron was a young unit. It had been transported to France in the summer of 1915, acquitting itself notably in pitched battles with the Fokker. Like other squadrons it operated on a distinctive operational principle, namely, that any enemy machine, once sighted, should be attacked and brought down regardless of personal risk.

On arrival at No. 11 Squadron, Ball was regarded as rather quiet and reserved. He did not join in any of the jokes organized by the pilots. Most of the time, while the other pilots were fooling about and trying to waste time in between flying, he could be found with the mechanics, asking searching questions about the Nieuports in for servicing. As soon as he could obtain permission, he took a Nieuport up and practiced shooting. When prevented from flying by bad weather, he had the guns lifted out of their mountings on the planes and laid down beyond the camp bounds where he could get used to handling them. Sitting alone on the grass, his pockets full of cake sent by his mother, he peered through the sights and took aim. His marksmanship amazed the others, but he himself insisted that there was nothing remarkable about it. He never considered himself perfect.

Apart from a few infantrymen who attempted to brighten up the battlefields by scattering flower seeds wherever they went, Albert Ball was probably the only man to set about the systematic growing of vegetables in the mud that surrounded the airfield. Soon after his arrival in France he wrote to his father, asking for

cucumber and pea seeds. Some of his spare time was spent cultivating the earth and making it into a suitable place to grow crops.
His first success created some amusement among the pilots. They
played jokes on him, saying that the cucumbers were suffering from
such diseases as "black rot" and "scab." In between shooting down
Germans, testing his Nieuport and giving himself some stiff target
practice, he did manage to raise a prize crop of vegetables which
he turned over to the cookhouse at a time when there was a shortage of fresh food.

Ball achieved his first prominence during 1918, the year after
the Somme holocaust. It had been a long and dangerous appren-
ticeship. Driving rain helped the German infantry to reinforce its
positions near and actually underneath the few houses which still
dotted a well-shelled landscape. While the Allies could not move
their bogged vehicles and heavy equipment, the Germans installed
themselves in quickly dug extensions of the house cellars, and
there they stayed in the vicinity of La Boiselle.

Flying overhead, Ball made out the snaking Albert-Bapaume
road. In the distance he could see German observation balloons,
each with its own lynx-eyed watcher on the lookout for any sign
of Allied operations. These balloons were one of the greatest barriers to any planned Allied movement. On June 25, Ball was
among those detailed to attack the twenty-three balloons. Before
taking off in his Nieuport, he sat and listened to objections voiced
by other pilots. Balloons were not popular targets. The Germans
often used them as decoys, and pilots had been tempted to their
deaths, flying straight into a heavy ground-to-air barrage of tracer
bullets and artillery. Nevertheless, the orders had been issued and
they must be obeyed. It turned out to be a short attack. Six balloons were sent down. Ball got one of them.

Returning to the airfield, he did not feel very happy. He should
have done much better. He obtained permission to fly over the
position again, and this time risked his neck in piercing a shower
of artillery shrapnel. One more balloon fluttered to the ground.
He was now eight miles from his own airfield and his battered
Nieuport was a dangerous projectile of metal and wood. Sitting
at the controls, he wondered whether to bale out and risk being
taken prisoner, but the landscape below did not look very inviting.
The Germans were known to take pot shots at parachuting air-

men. The Nieuport was a gallant machine, but it could not manage to maintain its usual turn of speed. Some of the shrapnel had broken the controls and fuel pipes. He had to use the last ounce of skill to keep it in the air.

From time to time the mainplane gave an alarming shudder, as though about to part company with the fuselage. He was on the verge of giving up all hope and trying for a crash landing, when he noticed that he was closer to his airfield than he believed. He could make out the boundary through the haze, yet it seemed that the Nieuport would carry him home without crashing. Juggling with the controls to stay on an even keel, he saw that he was now losing fuel pressure from a smashed pipe. He landed within a few feet of death.

Some time later he was awarded the Military Cross for his work. Members of the General Staff were very impressed with his tenacity and endurance. Inquiries were made about him. Confidential reports were received and studied. He suddenly achieved the same fame as Edward Mannock, though he did not realize how well known he was, and went on tending his cucumbers as though nothing else really mattered.

Ball had now been in France four and a half months. Like other artillery and observation pilots who were drawn into constant combat against crack German fliers, he felt so drugged and weary that it needed maximum will power to carry on from day to day. The Germans were counting on this cumulative battle fatigue. There was a chance of easy victory on July 1 when a major attack was envisaged. German intelligence knew that the British might attempt something of a large character. In the early hours they were able to mow down the advancing infantry with machine guns as the Tommies came striding through the muddy battlefield. It was nothing short of carnage. Hundreds of British bodies were thrown about in the awkward positions of death. The Allied attack was a failure.

With murder going on down below, the RFC quickly put 110 pilots into the sky, trying to prevent a German attempt at bombing and strafing. None came. In nine small fights only one German machine was shot down. The British now took the offensive in the air. Bapaume, Cambrai and Busigny were all heavily bombed. A German field headquarters was shattered by air-directed British artillery. Advancing German troops were halted in their tracks by British guns. As a day of strategy it was the most miserable failure imaginable and the British General Staff soon realized its enormous blunder. The Germans had been in a state of ready preparation. They had known exactly what to expect, and only the RFC saved the hour.

Ball flew throughout that day, and in the evening was stunned by the confirmed news that 80 per cent of his old regiment, the Sherwood Foresters, had been wiped out. He looked back on the afternoon's activity when he had shot down a German two-seater, converting it into a spinning piece of wreckage after filling it with the entire contents of his ammunition drum. He did not feel any of the zest common to other pilots when they gained their first official victory. This was not his first, but it was the first seen at close quarters.

One of his worries about the Nieuport was that it would not fly unaided; the pilot was indispensable. In Ball's view this was a hindrance, especially in moments of fast action when the pilot ought to be able to concentrate all his attention on marksmanship. While the Somme struggle continued, he hit upon a method of devoting more attention to his guns. The details involved an incredibly quick change of the ammunition drum while still airborne. Other planes had to return to base for new ammunition, but he reckoned on carrying a spare supply. Using this method, he was able to clock up a fast and efficient score.

Soon after the initial stages of the Somme battle were fought, he was flying on a mission on July 10 when he noticed three German machines moving above him. His spirits rose, a symptom common among pilots in those moments before combat. As he flew into a position from which he could probably shoot up into the belly of the enemy machine, his own engine began to stall at the last moment. He had to bank, sideslip, and then fly for his life. Returning to his airfield, he was nervous and angry at the same time. He berated his mechanics and later apologized for losing his temper.

About his victories he wrote: "Nothing makes me feel more rotten than to see them go down." He certainly did not hold any rancor against the individual German. Once he told his father that the Hun was a "good chap with very little guts, trying to do his best." Killing happened to be the job of the moment and Ball looked forward to the day when he could go home to Nottingham and start some kind of business. He took a keen interest in all his father's business ventures. News from home was the great panacea to the frustration he often felt while flying. His nerves were now frayed and he had to ask for a rest. The only reply was a posting to No. 8 Squadron, flying 90-hp BE2C's. It was the first squadron to join the expeditionary force armed completely with this type of machine. With No. 7 Squadron it was drafted to Colonel Brooke-Popham's Third Wing at Saint-Omer for duties in connection with special missions and strategic reconnaissance.

In a letter to his parents he said: "Oh, I am feeling in the dumps." He was out of patience with the RFC for sending him to a squadron as active as the one which he had just left. He disliked the BE2, preferring the Nieuport. Asked to flight-test a machine, he blurted out to General Trenchard that it was "a bloody awful machine."

They kept him with No. 8 Squadron long enough for him to put in some useful work as a "bus driver" to a number of different observers. One day, with Lieutenant H. E. Hervey as passenger, he flew a BE 1D toward the German observation balloons, deceptively easy targets. As they approached, Ball wetted his lips in anticipation of plunging into a ground barrage. When it did not come he began pumping bullets straight into the gas bag. The German observer immediately jumped for his life. Ball watched him as he floated down on the end of his parachute. Some British pilots would have followed him down, circling and shooting at the helpless man, but Ball was quite content to knock the balloon about. He could not take life so cold-bloodedly.

It was a hectic ride back. The Germans were in a bad temper and the machine suffered some damage from artillery. In the observer's seat Hervey had to hang on for dear life. A few moments before they touched down, Ball began singing at the top of his voice. Hervey thought him mad, especially when he got out and examined the damage to the machine. One wing tip was completely shot away by enemy fire. The main spar, key member of the mainplane structure, was barely hanging together. Ball gave it a cursory glance, then headed for the mess.

It was still a very dull life for Albert Ball. He wanted to vindi-

A group picture of the German aces which hung in many British mess
halls during World War I. Richthofen is in the middle.

March, 1913. Early military flying: American daredevil Bert Hall and his late model Blériot on a reconnaissance mission during the Turkish-Bulgarian War.

April, 1915. Lieutenant Oswald Boelcke in a Fokker E-1, using a synchronized machine gun which fires through the propeller for the first time, bags an Allied plane.

April, 1918. The last sortie of the "Red Knight," Baron Manfred von Richthofen, on his tail Captain A. R. Brown in a Sopwith Camel.

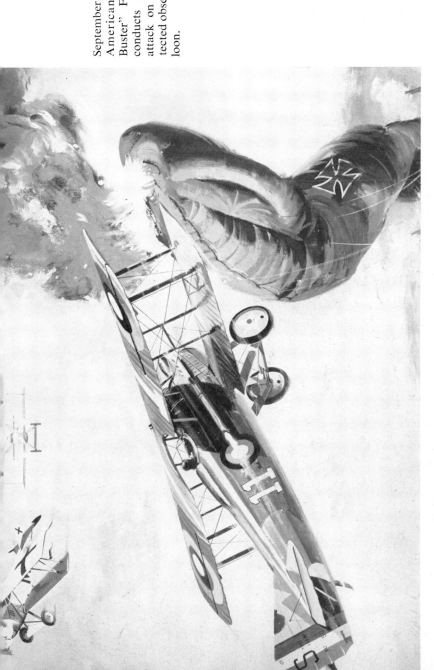

September, 1918. The American "Balloon Buster" Frank Luke conducts a low-level attack on a well-protected observation balloon.

April, 1914. Early psychological warfare: Max Immelmann drops a surrender note on Paris.

May, 1918. Major Edward "Mick" Mannock in an S.E. 5A outwits a flock of Germans by pretending to be hit.

August, 1918. German Ace Ernst Udet in a Fokker D-V11 accidentally collides with a Sopwith Camel.

May, 1918. Major William Barker in a Sopwith Snipe engages 50 to 60 German planes in an epic encounter.

May, 1918. Belgian Ace Willy Coppens lands on an enemy balloon and then safely takes off again.

September, 1917.
Werner Voss in his
Fokker triplane **DR1**
fights seven S.E. 5's.

June, 1915. British Navy pilot R. A. J. Warneford scores the first air victory over a Zeppelin.

July, 1915. Nungesser gains his initial victory in a Voisin bomber.

November, 1916. Richthofen in a D11 duels with the British ace Major L. G. Hawker.

1. Edward Mannock (*British*) 2. Georges Guynemer (*French*) 3. René Fonck (*French*) 4. Gerald C. Maxwell (*British*) 5. Hermann Goering (*German*) 6. R. A. J. Warneford (*British*) 7. Roual Lufberry (*American*) 8. Manfred von Richthofen (*German*) 9. Jean Navarre (*French*) 10. Lieutenant von Eschwege (*German*) 11. Albert Ball (*British*) 12. Billy Bishop (*Canadian*)

cate himself as far as No. 8 Squadron was concerned and then apply for a transfer back to a Nieuport squadron. The only way of doing it seemed to be by an extraordinary action which would bring him to the personal notice of those who anchored him down. It had to be something which would create immediate attention. . . .

He had his chance a few days later when he set himself up as "bus driver" to a spy called "M. Victor."

16

The Order of St. George

The British were anxious to deposit M. Victor, one of the most astute spies in the pay of the Allied powers, behind the lines in German territory as soon as possible. His true identity has never been revealed: he was probably a French or Belgian national attached to the RFC for the purpose of making special reports on enemy air power and plans direct to the British General Staff. Two or three landings had already been attempted, but each had failed, sometimes due to bungling, bad weather or indifferent planning. Hearing the sad history of M. Victor, Ball said that he would like to have a try at it. The result is told in a letter home. It was posted three days after the attempt, which took place on July 28.

"We got over the lines and after a few seconds three Fokkers came after us. We had no gun, for the machine could not carry his luggage, etc., and guns, so we had to dodge the beasts. At last it was so dark they would not see us, so they went down. The Archie guns started, also rockets were sent up to try and set us on fire. Oh! It was nice. I really did think that the end had come. The planes were lit up with the flashes. However, at last we found a landing place and we started down. Naturally everything had to be done quickly or we would have been caught. But we got down! Picture

my temper when we landed. The damned spy would not get out.
The Fokkers had frightened him and he would not risk it. There
was nothing to do but get off again before the Huns came along
and stopped us, so off we went. I went down three times again
after this, but the rotter refused to do his part. So we had to return."

Although Ball was in a foul temper over the spy's inability to
see things as he did, he had nonetheless done what he set out to do
and made the impression on his superior officers. His transfer back
to No. 11 Squadron was soon authorized, but fourteen days went
by before he arrived back on August 10. One of the first disap-
pointments was the loss of seniority. He found new pilots in the
mess, and felt rather strange when he realized that every one of
them represented a replacement for an old friend killed in his absence. On August 16 he wrote to his mother and father: "Dearest
People, Hello, I am back in my dear old hut. All is OK and my
garden is fine. You will be surprised to hear that I have started with
luck. I went up this morning and attacked five Hun machines. One
I got and two I forced down. After this I had to run, for all my
ammunition was used. However, I got back OK, with only two
hits on my machine."

As recompense for his promotion setback he was raised to the
rank of Acting Flight Commander. On August 22, 1916, he
showed that he was the human fighting machine the British were
looking for in their search for fiery talent among young pilots. This
is what happened. . . .

In the early afternoon the bad weather cleared up. Visibility
was better than it had been since dawn. Ball had been flying
through the rain and mist since the light was as good as it would
ever be, but without much success. At seven o'clock, after tea, he
went up with FE's of his own flight. Their job was to protect
bombers as they winged toward Warlencourt Valley on a surprise
raid.

The air was saturated and the airplane engines seemed to re-
verberate more thunderously than usual, but Ball was in good
form, joking with the mechanics as they prepared his machine. In
the air, circling the field waiting for the FE's, he was careful to
conserve his fuel, running his motor at a minimum so that his

machine seemed to hang on an invisible thread over the collection
of huts and service sheds.

Some time later the much-bombed rail center of Bapaume came
up as a well-known landmark. It was beginning to look like an
uneventful mission; there was no sign of the enemy. South of Bapaume, however, Ball sighted seven Roland machines with German markings. It would be foolish to start anything at this moment.
The sun was going down already. The interval between dusk and
total darkness made fighting a tricky business. Too many pilots
had been shot to bloody tatters, trying to score a final victory of
the day. Ball was tempted and in the end succumbed.

The Rolands were flying westward in a wedge-shaped formation, so he streaked away until he was able to work himself quietly
and without any fuss under the rear of the formation. This was his
fight. He did not want to drag the others into it. He was taking a
big chance in hoping that the Germans would not notice him. Had
an enemy pilot chosen to glance toward the back of the group he
would surely have seen the lone Nieuport and in an instant signaled to the rest to take up fighting positions. Ball's life would not
have been worth a nickel, and he was banking on the element of
surprise. It was vital that he pass unnoticed for the next few seconds.

Using some of Richthofen's tactics, with which he was familiar,
he elevated his gun until it marked down one of the rear Rolands.
At this close range he could not possibly miss. He pressed the
trigger. The deadly tattoo ran up into the Roland's guts in a red-hot
stream. Hearing the noise, the formation scattered, startled by the
unheralded attack. Keeping on after the wounded Roland, Ball
flew to within fifteen yards of it before the German pilot could
wrench the machine around, enabling his own observer to start firing. Only one stray bullet hit Ball's machine, and it caused no
damage.

A premonition told Ball that he must change the ammunition
drum if he was to survive the next ten minutes. Skipping the Nieuport into one of those oblique positions which made him an almost impossible target to hit for a matter of seconds, he pulled the
empty drum out of its well-oiled clip, and then reached down for
the other one, wedging the control stick with his feet to stabilize
the aircraft. The Nieuport flew on steadily. He thanked his stars

for patient hours of rehearsing himself against an emergency such as this.

With the new drum knocked into position, all ready to fire, he swept the machine up at top speed and straightaway expended half of the new ammunition, slamming it into the side fuselage of the German. After seeming to jolt, the enemy plane buckled and then began to crumple, like a paper bag. It landed close to a village west of Bapaume, a telescoped write-off.

Ball knew that the next stage of the fight must come sooner or later. After shooting down two of the Rolands, he was at the mercy of the rest, all massed against him and waiting. Dodging through the darkening sky, he was nearly clear of the old menace when a new one, comprising five more ominous-looking Rolands, became visible, flying at 7,000 feet southwest over Vaux. Unable to resist the chance of making a third kill, despite the frightful risk, he went for them, using the same tactics as before. He was directly beneath the rear machine, still unseen, when he discovered that he must put his Lewis gun into a near-vertical position to get in any useful action. He was actually shooting straight up at the German pilot, as near as he could estimate, but he felt vulnerable. After he had fired a dozen rounds upward, the Roland suddenly nose-dived to its death in a booming collapse of flashing fire as its fuel exploded.

Three of the Rolands banded together in an effort to exterminate Ball in a devilish crossfire. They came in at three different angles. The bullets swept over him, missing the Nieuport by several yards. Unperturbed by this torrid crossfire, he fired right back at them. Five rounds spat out to cripple one machine. It fell over a mile and a half and landed on top of a house.

Now more malevolent than ever, the remaining two Rolands zoomed after him. His only hope lay in a rapid loss of height. He let the Nieuport drop to 2,000 feet. Baffled, the Rolands let him go. He landed smoothly at No. 8 Squadron, shouted for a fresh supply of ammunition, and took off again with red-hot exhausts.

Dusk was now complete, but he stayed where he was, in the air, determined to have a crack at anything he could see. Between eight o'clock and eight-fifty he cruised over Vaux, then, picking up the returning bombers which he had originally set out to escort along with the FE's, he took up position, but not before yet another fast encounter with three Rolands. Nothing came of this and he reluctantly went back to his escort duty. Minutes later he was rooted out by some more keen-eyed Germans. A multiple formation of Rolands severed the sky in a Teutonic scimitar promising death without glory. Only his fast flying took him away from the edge of the grave. Twelve Rolands roared along after him, a calculated firing squad against which he could not fight because he was so heavily outnumbered. He dove down, almost to ground level, the wind trying to pull his head off his shoulders, then whipped around and up, scattering as many haphazard shots as he could among them. Shaken by his cornered-rat maneuver, they separated. He took advantage of the lull, and, pointing the nose of the plane toward home, pulled the last remaining bit of energy out of his engine.

This was his last operational flight with No. 11 Squadron. Twenty-four hours later, on August 23, he was posted to No. 60 Squadron, which arrived in France to be armed with Morane Bullets, Biplane and Parasol (the latter was later withdrawn), at Le Hameau, under 111 Brigade. In a letter to his parents about that last flight with No. 11 Squadron, he remarked that his Nieuport was not in very good shape after its battering punishment. In fact, the windscreen was smashed in four places, a spar of the left mainplane was shattered, the fuel supply was exhausted. The machine itself was hit a total of eleven times.

At No. 60 Squadron he met General Higgins, who joked that a big board with "Albert Ball" chalked on it was going to be erected in the trenches to frighten the Germans. He had been at odds with Higgins many times since coming to France, particularly when he asked for permission to rest, but it seemed that this officer now regarded him with something like bleak and distant affection. This was just what Ball wanted; it gave him carte blanche to act alone if necessary. He always had wanted to work as a lone scout pilot.

Under a new arrangement he was able to operate individually. In the next few weeks he disposed of many Germans, but seldom bothered to claim his credits. He did not want any false glory. All he demanded was the satisfaction of being able to fly at a moment's notice when the chances cropped up. He was influenced and in turn did influence an Irish eccentric named Smith-Barry, who was the first RFC casualty of the war.

Smith-Barry was at this time CO of No. 60 Squadron. He took the often obstinate view that his pilots were as individualistic as himself. There was as little red tape and restraint as possible on the squadron. Under such conditions Ball felt that he was in an ideal place. He went hunting for Germans practically every day, and was once forced down near Senlis. He slept the night under the machine, had it repaired the following morning, and got back to find a calm Smith-Barry waiting for him to inquire how the weather was. He had not been missed.

On August 28 he shot down a Roland and later the same day became involved in a hectic chase, once more with a Roland as his quarry at a time when he was supposed to be escorting bombers. Only shortage of gas forced him to go home. That same evening, when 111 Brigade was shelling Loupart Wood, he was in the upper air when three German machines lumbered into his field of vision. He came rushing down from 10,000 to 3,000 feet in one single straining swoop so that he was beneath them before they could do anything. He forced one down in a hail of Lewis gunfire, then turned steeply and at 7,000 feet nearly collided with a two-seater Roland. He fired the contents of one ammunition drum into its belly. It fell slowly and force-landed, leaving Ball free to head for an area east of Bapaume. Here he went straight into a thick formation of Albatros machines with a few LVG's and Rolands. Under the force of such a whirlwind attack as his, the Germans usually scattered to take up prearranged fighting positions. Ball was firing all the time, but for once most of his shots went wide because he was up against the heaviest odds. He half stood in his seat, holding the joystick with his knees and slapping at a jammed ammunition drum with his gloved hand, hoping to free it.

The Germans could have shot him at this moment, but none of them seemed to realize his plight. Petrified by the swift onrush of glacial wind, he slumped back in his seat again, concentrating on the job of getting away before it was too late. Simultaneously, the Germans lost interest in him. They took up formation once more and started disdainfully on their way in another direction. Ball glared up at the offending ammunition drum which had nearly been the cause of his death, and flew on in search of temporary sanctuary where the matter could be put right.

This was not the end of it. At the first Allied landing field, he commandeered five full drums of ammunition, had the tanks of the Nieuport filled up and then took to the sky again, a new exhilaration tingling in every vein. He reached the spot where the German formation was last seen, and at once encountered two Rolands and two LVG's, southeast of Adinfer Wood at about 9,000 feet. They were in loose formation, fanning out defensively when they saw him coming at them like a hornet. He shot down one, then went home.

He landed and had a meal. It had been an average day with several good moments, but he certainly did not care to look back over those periods of action when he had to fall back upon the resources of his own brain and instinct rather than depend upon what should have been an indomitable machine. The incident with the jammed gun still nagged at his mind. If that could happen once, it might happen again. He might not be in a position to escape next time.

He went home on leave to England early that September. For his work on August 26 he was awarded the DSO with a Bar for his two actions, one on August 28, the other on August 31.

Returning to France, he carried out a certain amount of colorful work with the deadly fire streaks called Le Prieur rockets. They were manufactured in bunches of six, wired to the plane struts and fired by a simple electrical system. He used them on balloon and aircraft alike, raising his score by leaps and bounds. The effect upon enemy pilots was totally unexpected. They usually turned tail and ran. Ball was quite elated with the rockets, but half-humorously complained that the Hun often ran too fast for him; it was all he could do to catch up and put half a drum from the Lewis gun into their backsides.

By this time the terrible pace of the Somme battle was beginning to tell on him, just as it was doing upon other fast-living pilots. He consulted Smith-Barry and the medical officers about "the shakes," but there was no cure for this kind of weariness. There was no cure except rest. Who, among the British, was getting any rest at this time? He felt sad about the loss of various friends shot down in battle, yet still failed to whip himself into a frenzy of hatred against the Germans for what they had done to those whom he

liked and admired. It was war, war unending, and that was all there
was to it. One must accept it or else turn coward. In one letter he
said: "I do so want to leave all this beastly killing for a while."
Somehow, he had to go on flying, fighting two battles at the same
time, one against the German planes, the other against his own
often tremulous nerves. He was at a dangerous stage when he did
not mind taking the worst kind of risks. Any pilot knew this attitude to be symptomatic of the breaking point. In some it sprouted
into a suicidal impulse. In Albert Ball it amounted to flying always straight into situations from which there was little chance of
escape.

He was using rockets and Lewis guns together, and his fighting
technique scared the wits out of the Germans as he headed for
them, a bat out of hell, spitting calculated venom. They would have
been surprised to meet the mild, quiet-mannered pilot behind all
that deadliness. Only on one occasion did he come near to meeting
a German on anything like social terms, and that was when he ran
out of ammunition at the same moment as his enemy. The two
planes flew side by side for a short distance, Ball grinning and
waving at his enemy, who reciprocated.

The day when he did shake hands with death and got away without being stung was the bright clear Sunday of September 23. He
had been up over Bapaume for some time when he found a collection of varicolored Albatros machines. They saw him at the same
moment and changed course. He was now looking straight into an
arrowhead of Germans as they began to fire in concert. Tracers
passed over and above him in a brilliant shower. He jiggled his
joystick about to baffle them, shooting back continuously. His ammunition was finished in a few moments. He was changing drums
when a spare one fell down into the rudder control. He was torn
between the instinctive desire to bend down and lift it away from
the wires and go on trying to fix the new drum in position. He felt
the Nieuport tilt downward. When the fuselage began to shudder
he knew that he was out of control. Every Albatros in the formation was on its way toward him, literally within yards of him, preparing for the kill. And what a kill it was going to be! He heaved
away at the recalcitrant ammunition drum. There was no time to
feel any gratification as it clicked into position. In less than a
second he gouged the other drum away from the rudder controls

and was screaming away from the approaching danger faster than any express train. The Germans could not keep up with his descent. They had to circle above, awaiting their chance. It was while they were idly swinging round and round that he came up in a climb to fire ninety rounds of tracer into the nearest machine. It burst into flames and tottered down toward the ground, a ragged tulip of destroying fire.

The action lasted for three-quarters of an hour, all turn and pursuit, a game played by experts. Ball was now out of ammunition. All he could do was make a dash for home. Landing at his own airfield, he saw that his machine was pitted with thirteen bullet holes, yet none of them had done much damage. Mechanics clustered around to have a look as he jumped out of the cockpit and walked away with his loping stride as though going for a stroll in the country.

On September 24 he was awarded the Order of St. George. It was given to him by the Russians, who had taken him up as a distant idol and now wished to honor his bravery. Albert Ball was as far removed from the Russian mentality and outlook as it was possible to get, but he felt so proud of the decoration that he sent a piece of the black and orange ribbon home to his parents. In the letter he said that he hoped the war would end soon. He was a captain now, a goal to which he had always aspired.

He was also just a little homesick.

17

The Last Patrol

It is sometimes very difficult to believe that Ball was perfectly sincere in the regret which he professed to feel for Germans shot down. Killing men has been a passionate business ever since the world began, and the killer must always experience a certain elation at the moment of slaying even if sick remorse does set in later. Albert Ball's letters indicate an almost parental attitude to the shooting down of German airplanes, an "it-hurts-me-more-than-it-hurts-you" frame of mind which cannot be reconciled with the way he went about his work. He once wrote to his parents: "I feel sorry for the chaps I have killed. Just imagine what their poor people must feel like. . . . However, it must be done, or they would kill me. . . ."

Albert Ball has long occupied a position of honorable gallantry in the annals of World War I aviation. Any hint of heresy has been quelled, but, in the light of all that has gone before, it is perfectly obvious that he was nowhere as great a fighter pilot as many of his opposite numbers in the German air force. Few Allied pilots ever were, granted; but it should now be asserted that Ball and his huge reputation have grown out of all proportion to deeds, especially in the beginning when the home-based blimps demanded something to worship. There was, too, a generation of young women who had to have a war hero to cherish.

There is no suggestion that Ball was not perfectly sincere in thought and action. He believed in God and the total destruction of the Germans. He was both hasty and fearless in combat, but he did not always utilize an immaculate technique in comparison with, say, Immelmann. Many of his "victories" were the natural outcome of a certain flying technique which was calculated to force his adversary to earth. In one summary of his career we see that he fought forty-nine combats, forced ten Germans to crash-land, edging twenty into forced landings. One German landed out of control. There were no less than eighteen indecisive and unconfirmed victories.

Why, then, was this man elevated to such a level that he vied with the superior Richthofen? At the time of Ball's growing confidence and the spate of early victories, British morale was low on the home front. There was very little confidence in the RFC and its work. Acting on suggestions from Whitehall, RFC Headquarters believed that a popular hero was the answer. The choice fell upon Albert Ball, in their belief a man who could keep his head under the emotional impact of popular worship and adulation. That, at least, is one of the explanations for Ball's prestige, but no documents exist, nor is there any proper proof. Rational thinkers will believe that RFC Headquarters made a good and worthy choice.

The press snatched up the idea of hailing Ball as one of the saviors of the war. The *Daily Mail* was first to discover articles about Ball which had been appearing in French magazines and newspapers, notably *Le Petit Parisien*. From then on Albert Ball was constantly in the public eye.

When he returned to France in April 1916 he had certain ideas about the design of a single-seater fighter machine which, he said, would be "heaps better than the Hun Fokker." He drew up the working plans and obtained permission to fly it if he could get one built. Back in England he searched for a likely backer and manufacturer. The Austin Motor Company accepted the contract on one condition, that the airplane be known as the Austin-Ball Scout. By the time the prototype was ready its designer was dead. The Austin-Ball Scout never did put in an appearance in France. Although flight-tested, it was never reported upon, but representatives of the Air Board, a body handling construction contracts and the supply of fighting machines for the front, granted it a superficial examination and reached the conclusion that it did not show any distinguishing or superior features which would warrant a wholesale cancellation of existing contracts.

Anxious to preserve their hero, the High Command in October 1916 decided that Ball must now become a tutor to the coming generation of pilots. He therefore went very reluctantly to No. 34 Reserve Squadron, stationed at Orfordness, and in the following month accepted the offer of a course at Hythe School of Aerial Gunnery. By the time this was half finished, he felt that he had had enough of what was now a long absence from the front. He began to make efforts at getting back.

His CO told him that the intention was to build him up as an aerial gunnery expert so that he could teach others. Like Edward Mannock, he rebelled against the idea of becoming a nonflying airman, in itself a misnomer. He did everything he could to correct the growing impression that he would not be returning to France, yet by the end of the year he was still being shuttled around, first to No. 25 Wing Headquarters on December 7, then on to the Austin works to study construction methods. Early in the new year, 1917, he found himself at No. 7 Wing, Eastern Counties, with the title "fighting instructor." Two days later, on January 4, his name appeared in the *London Gazette* as Mentioned in Dispatches. It did not give him much satisfaction, and he waged an agitated blitzkrieg on officialdom to get himself posted away to France. He addressed his first plea to General L. E. O. Charlton, Director of Air Organization, who replied that as soon as it was considered necessary Ball would certainly be sent back. There was only one hopeful sentence in the letter. ". . . I have my eye on you, and shall not forget you." Was this a sop to Charlton's own conscience?

Incensed by stonewall refusals, Ball started another bombardment, this time upon Mr. A. Duckham, an official of the Ministry of Munitions. Duckham refused point-blank to play any part in what he believed to be purely a military matter. Ball was rudely rebuffed. His next shout for a hearing went to Mr. Richardson, a Member of Parliament. Again a refusal. There followed a fast succession of letters to, and meetings with, a distant friend, the financier James White, and the newspaper proprietor Lord Northcliffe. Northcliffe did not have any luck with the War Office, though he certainly did try, conscious that his newspapers had been lauding Albert Ball as a modern hero.

While Ball was moving heaven and earth to get back to the fighting front, he was offered £1,000 by a group of directors on condition that he resigned from the RFC and accepted a position on the board of a new aircraft manufacturing company. Despite his irritated refusal, £1,000 was paid into his bank account as a retainer in order to secure his valuable services at the end of the war. He accepted, but never used the money.

In between protesting that he wanted to be sent on active service again, he happened to meet Brigadier General Brancker, Director of Air Organization, who was interested in the Austin-Ball Scout. Brancker suggested that Ball should have two of the new machines made. If they were any good after the usual testing, he would personally authorize an order for the construction of quantities for use at the front. Of course, this plan never came to anything because Ball's death did away with the idea. In any case, the plane did not come up to expectations.

On February 19, 1917, in the middle of his one-man campaign to leave England, his native city, Nottingham, pressed upon him the freedom of the city. In his short speech he could not resist saying that he hoped to be out in France again "very shortly."

His manner had become more abrupt than usual, because he was tired out after his efforts with various people who, he once believed, would help him to rejoin his squadron. Later, when invited to dine with a well-known newspaper owner in London, he curtly refused. He happened to be taking his mother to the theater and said that he did not want to disappoint her. He was fed up with the wiles of the great ones. He wanted a respite from fighting for his rights.

He was now posted to No. 56 Squadron at London Colney, near St. Albans, Hertfordshire. He accepted the posting with a premonition that this would probably be the last time he would go on active service. He told his father that no scout pilot who did "serious fighting" could hope to get through the war alive. Before leaving for London Colney he carefully put all his personal papers and belongings in order. A poignant last note of his life with his parents is provided by the fact that he badly wanted to say good-by to his mother while she was happy and enjoying herself. He took her to a movie on his last night at home and left when the film was only half finished.

London Colney was one of several centers for the training of pilots preparatory to going into action at the front. Albert Ball was almost a member of the older generation of the RFC, and he was soon face to face with youths who barely needed the use of a razor. But he liked the atmosphere of the place and fell straight into his role as teacher with tremendous zest. He also fell in love with a girl for the first time in his life. She was seventeen, and gave him an idyllic romance which sustained him by its unexpected beauty. He took her flying with him—to the horror of her parents, let it be said—and managed to see her every day. They took one another very seriously. When he flew his machine over her house, a London newspaper, the *Evening Standard,* was attracted by the story and published it with a few journalistic trimmings, calling him a "modern Romeo." He disliked intensely such a rude intrusion into his private life. He was determined to secure the girl for his own and in the end arranged to meet her in a nearby church at Shenley. There, quite alone except for the chirping of sparrows in the trees outside, the two young people went through their own solemn ceremony of plighting a troth. He gave her his identification disk and she brought a new one, especially engraved for him. She also gave him a volume of Robert Louis Stevenson's "Prayers." Later the same day she was heard singing to him. It was a ballad called "Thank God for a Garden." After that they said their farewells.

His heart was full of her; he knew that he must marry her as soon as he could get his first leave from France in about a month's time. She did not see him off on the Saturday morning, because she was afraid of crying and worrying him at a time when he must concentrate on the future. He often told her that he would like to win the VC for her. She protested: she did not want the VC for his sake or her own. She wanted only the man as her husband.

Her brother came to London Colney to shake Ball's hand and wish him well. Ball had written a letter to the girl. The brother said that he would deliver it. Ball turned away to face the distant gloom of the French battlefields.

No. 56 Squadron arrived in France on April 7, 1917. Ball lost no time in saying that he did not like the SE5 airplanes with which they were being equipped. He wanted to return to the Nieuport that was so familiar to him. He could not do any kind of efficient job with the SE5. He even went to the length of speaking to General Trenchard about it. Miraculously, his wish was granted. This sudden relaxation of rules and regulations surprised a number of people. Armed thus, Ball was now able to throw himself into a battle which was moving in spasmodic fits and starts over the advance areas.

On April 23, No. 56 Squadron was sent into battle and Ball was able to spend most of his waking hours in the air, near Arras. He was still using the same tactics, always coming up under the enemy and shooting straight into the belly of the machine. From time to time he had the chance of accepting delivery of the newer types of armament, but always remained faithful to his Lewis gun, though it frequently jammed in the heat of battle, endangering his life and safety. Some stubborn factor in his mentality prevented him from accepting the new and casting off the old. He said that the Lewis had proved its worth so many times that it would probably see him through to the end. If he was firm about guns, he was unexpectedly ambivalent about airplanes. He changed over to the SE5 when it saved his life on one occasion. He never did go back to the previously favored Nieuport.

No. 56 Squadron did not feature very heavily in the casualty lists for some time. At last the German warbirds made themselves felt when a total of thirty-nine pilots and observers were shot down over a period. Every time a man was posted missing or killed, Ball's determination to make amends increased, though he was quite unable to keep pace with German efficiency to the extent he so much desired. No Allied pilot ever could until the period just before the end of the war. Tension increased in Ball's mind until he was at a dangerous point. A pilot in this rash condition could easily be a deadly menace to those with whom he must fly. General Trenchard tried to talk Ball into taking fourteen days' leave in England. It was hopeless. Ball curtly told Trenchard that he felt quite fit; he did not want to be compulsorily rested at this important stage of the war.

That April it became apparent that the Germans might not be able to hold up their position of aerial supremacy. True, the Richthofen group seemed at its best, flying supremely well and taking a devastating toll of Allied planes. The cracks in the structure were not easy to see, but they were there every time a German pilot refused to accept a challenge. Sometimes, too, it was the German who broke off in the midst of combat. April was the month of indication for those who could read the signs.

On May 1 half a dozen Albatros two-seaters thundered through the sky over Cambrai. One thousand feet above them were some SE5's, among them Albert Ball, who cut away and went into an excellent position right above the foe. This was not his usual position, but he had to be content with it. He could not hope to get through to a lower altitude without being seen. He was now at an oblique angle, trying to get an Albatros into his gun sights. Abandoning all caution, he suddenly dived and fired a short burst at it. Only a matter of yards above the German, deciding whether to risk another few rounds, he saw the German plane slip away from him. Ball was now in great danger. Another Albatros moved in above him and was about to start firing when he threw his Lewis gun around and fired before the other could reach the trigger.

It was Ball's surprise victory. He planted his bullets in the best part of the machine, the engine, and followed it down, pumping a total of fifty rounds into the helpless carcass. It smashed up near the Marquion road. He then flashed away to find his patrol comrades, Lieutenant H. M. T. Lehmann and Lieutenant Knight. Both had suffered bad luck with jammed guns. Ball impatiently waved for them to follow him. Near Cambrai, their guns freed, they swept into another formation of Albatros aircraft. In a furious fight Knight was shot down, but survived a rough landing at Louvencourt. Ball and Lehmann flew on home to receive a telephone message from Knight, saying that he was quite safe and would be home very shortly.

Concentration of a fighting area bounded on three sides by Arras, Cambrai and Douai did away with the necessity of having to go out and find the enemy. In this triangular space many of the most exciting tourneys of the time were fought out. The area directly below was thickly littered with wreckage, a graveyard where the unidentified bodies of airmen moldered in the mud.

Allied policy was on the move now, and pilots were encouraged to go out on almost hourly patrols. This caused a heavy strain on both nervous system and body. Ball was among the first to experience a dragging languor. He could not stop yawning, he did not want to talk to people. Tempers did not improve after one engage-

ment in which three SE5's hunted a solitary Albatros only to have
their guns jam at the wrong moment.

On May 5, Ball had another narrow escape which shook him up.
He took off in the early evening and headed for Carvin, not far
from Douai, the much-bombed German air base. He managed to
reach a height of more than a thousand feet above two Albatros
machines, both mounting the latest quick-firing guns. In the climb
which the Germans started to make after him, Ball reckoned that
they must be separated by at least a quarter of a mile. It was an
ideal fighting situation. Selecting the nearest Hun, he went into a
screaming dive as it labored toward him, his guns blazing. He was
puzzled that the German did not shoot it out with him, but there
was no sign of resistance. He finished firing his second drum of
ammunition. Still there was no move. He could not understand it;
he suspected a trap. He was now so close that he could clearly
make out the brown and white markings, even see the pilot's white
face. Using both Vickers and Lewis guns, Ball was soon at the end
of his ammunition. Then, at the last moment, the Albatros fell
away in a death spin.

He turned away from the sight. It always made him feel physically sick to see pilot and plane in such a hapless plight.

Seeking revenge, the other Albatros came edging in at a fast clip.
He had to swing around violently to avoid being shot right out of
the sky. The two planes were now charging at one another. It had
all the makings of a head-on crash, not uncommon in fights of this
character. Reloading, Ball started to fire the Vickers, keenly watching the trail of tracer bullets as they penetrated the Albatros. The
German took terrific punishment, but still went on returning his
fire with interest. One of the bullets broke through Ball's oil line,
blinding him for the moment. In great pain, he closed his eyes,
hunched well forward. This was it! At any moment there would be
a tearing crash, he thought.

He was reconciled to death but that did not make him the less
afraid of dying. It seemed a long time coming. . . . At last, when
nothing happened, he wiped his face with the back of his glove,
feeling the cool sweep of the wind in his face. He opened his eyes,
automatically looking about him and righting the plane's nose dive.
As he was gaining height, he leaned over the side of the cockpit
and saw both Albatros aircraft on the ground, smashed to bits

within a few yards of one another. One of his bullets must have hit the German pilot a moment or two before he shut his eyes.

Ball barely got home, fighting against the lowered oil pressure all the way. Interrogated by T. B. Marson, the Squadron Recording Officer, he was hardly able to explain what had happened to him. He was badly shaken and insisted that God had looked after him. A few hours later he wrote home: ". . . I hate this game, but it is the only thing one must do just now."

On May 7 a special offensive patrol was arranged with Ball leading a flight. The plan, conceived by No. 9 Wing, was that six Spads, six Sopwith Scouts and six SE5's were to haunt the cloudy sky over Douai and Cambrai from six in the morning until ten-thirty, then from half past six in the evening until nightfall. The idea was to bring out the German aces, who seldom nowadays took the initiative.

Ball was in the air by half past five on the evening of May 7. Three flights of SE5's were airborne, one of them led by Ball himself, the other two headed by Captain C. M. Crowe and Captain H. Mientjes, a South African officer. They flew at three different levels through the drizzling rain. It had been a depressing, soggy kind of day. Morale was not at a particularly high level. Ball was flying at 7,000 feet and visibility was poor for him. Bourlon Wood, headquarters of General von Below, was approaching when Captain Crowe and his machines entered a towering cloud bank. At the same moment Captain Mientjes and his men, flying at 9,000 feet, found a lone German machine. They set upon it like ravening hounds, sending it to its doom in a matter of seconds, then resumed the patrol. The cloud bank ended abruptly, giving onto an amazing sight. Practically all the Richthofen circus was flying about in the open sky!

The fight started at a speed of one hundred miles an hour. The air was thick with the agitation of tracer bullets scattering in all directions. Mientjes was one of the first to be marked down by Richthofen's pilots. He desperately tried to get away, swooping down in a breakneck dive. The tolerance limit could never before have been reached in such a daring fashion. Mientjes had to hang on to his control stick for grim life. He was pulling out of one corkscrew dive when he saw two of the red enemy planes making short work of Lieutenant C. A. Lewis, a member of his own flight. Lewis went down in a widening plume of black smoke.

Albert Ball teamed up with another pilot, Knaggs. Together they went rushing headlong through the rolling, twisting circus of British and German planes, taking pot shots whenever they had the chance. Ball made a headlong dash at a German plane, then changed his mind at the last minute to swoop away like a frustrated hawk. Knaggs immediately took on the dismissed German, firing continuously after correcting a Lewis gun stoppage.

The fight, grimly scattered over an area of rain-washed sky, did not pause in the growing dusk. Pilots could hardly make out who was foe and who was friend. The birth of the night affected both sides equally. SE5's were scattered all over the area while the Germans were trying to get together for a new attack. Nothing remained but for the SE5's to do likewise and remuster at Arras, the place laid down in the master plan. Running fights continued to the stuttering accompaniment of restless guns.

Flying over Fresnoy, Crowe saw Ball's SE5 moving along steadily. He changed course to follow, hoping that Ball knew that he was actually heading for Lens. His assumption that all was well was broken when he saw that Ball was being dogged by a solitary German fighter. Ball could not have been entirely oblivious to the danger, because he fired a few shots at the German, though without result. Before Crowe could move in to help Ball, both planes were swallowed up in a huge cloud bank.

Albert Ball was never seen again.

Crowe later wrote: "The height was . . . 4,000 feet. As I knew that my fuel must be running low, I reluctantly made for our lines. . . ."

The Squadron Recording Officer, T. B. Marson, said that he once met a Captain Hunter, who was in a German hospital in the Lens district during May. Marson wrote: "On May 8 the German officer told [Hunter] that Ball had been killed. Hunter refused to credit it. On the following day the German brought Ball's identity disk and showed it to Hunter as proof of his story's truth. At the same time, he stated Ball was brought down by anti-aircraft fire, and that his machine was badly smashed up."

Albert Ball was only twenty years of age when he was killed. His decorations were the VC (posthumous), DSO (two bars), M.C., Croix de Chevalier, Légion d'Honneur, Russian Order of St. George.

18

Eschwege's Private War

Between 1914 and 1918 the war in the air was fought many thousands of times, often in unsuspected territories, but it was won as much by rebels as by those who toed the line of absolute discipline. The victors usually turned out to be men who insisted on following their own dictates without regard for consequences which might cost them the high price of life itself. Their battles with officialdom were just as fiery, but more prolonged than their daily duels with the enemy. The most brilliant of them won victories on both fronts.

In the middle of the twentieth century, when the tempo is faster than it ever has been in aviation, some of the most gifted rebels of the First World War would be the guiding brains behind the race to perfect supersonic planes, rockets and missiles. Some of them would have been fit enough to fly. Among them, probably at the controls of some high-speed fighter, would be a German called Eschwege. But, like practically all of them, he too is dead.

This man fought his war in the worst theater of all, at Drama, in Macedonia. It is an area fringed on one side by Greece, by Turkey on another, and with Crete at the far end, forming an amphitheater of huge proportions. Behind Eschwege stood the bastion of Bulgaria, with her German allies. Had he been less at-

213

tentive to the job of fighting his own fight, he might have felt depressed by the acres of denuded countryside, the bouts of malaria which he and most of the others suffered while they were there. Flying was more good luck than skilled judgment, and a new pilot had to discover for himself all the hazards created by the up-movement of layers of sun-heated air which haunted the airfield. The everlasting joke was that flying in France was better because French air was more solid.

A pilot at Drama had to resist such energy-sapping tortures as malaria. More than 50 per cent of one British squadron on the nearby island of Thasos was put out of action by the stinging mosquito. Drama was uncomfortably bounded on one side by the Struma marshes where the mosquito bred in its millions. It was said that no man could possibly live through a single night in that buzzing inferno. Another refined torture was the bedbug. Fledglings were sickened by the sight of hordes of them as they crossed the floor and scratched up and down the walls in search of blood to suck and flesh to bite. Eschwege was himself a mass of festering bites and at one stage could hardly bear to sit down in the cockpit of his Fokker.

But worst of all there was the temperature, usually well over 110 degrees in the shade only an hour after the sun shot up over the motionless waters of the Aegean Sea. It was difficult to know whether to wear many clothes or few. If you wore too many you stood a good chance of suffering heat stroke because the body must sweat and rid itself of waste. If you put on too little, the bugs and pests got at you, but they were entirely different from the mosquitoes and bedbugs of the nighttime. These were like small flying animals which clamped themselves onto the skin and would not let go.

The heat beat down all day, a menace to the delicately designed aircraft. Without benefit of oils blended especially for the tropics the viscosity of normal engine oil lessened and ran like water. Engines reduced speed, sometimes soon after a dawn take-off, and many youthful pilots lost their lives when their machines suddenly crashed without cause. In winter it was exactly the reverse. Freezing temperatures caused engines to seize up without warning. The bedbugs remained at their sabotage duties.

It was to this sickly, featureless place that Lieutenant Eschwege was posted. He was an ordinary-looking man with the exception of a pair of cold steel-blue eyes which missed very little. After seeing him fly, the Greek locals christened him "The Eagle of the Aegean," a title well earned from his many combats over that historic ocean.

His background was uncomplicated. After education at a military academy, he was sent to the mounted Jaeger regiment just after the war started. Half a year in the trenches gave him a lasting distaste for a war which had to be fought in mud and filth. He was fastidious, yearning to do something of a more noble nature. He also wanted to become an individual, and his opinions about the use of soldiers as so much cannon fodder did not bring him much popularity among the officer class. Because of his frank manner, he was dispatched from the Jaeger regiment to learn how to fly airplanes. Five months later he was no closer to proficiency than the day when he first saw an airplane. He crashed a large number of machines, muddled his navigation, often got lost, and, in general, made as persistent a nuisance of himself at the flying school as he had done in the trenches. He was never very popular, and his departure was accompanied by a collective sigh of relief from his instructors. They hardly expected him to last more than a few weeks at the front. Ten months later he was still flying two-seater planes on reconnaissance duties over France, chafing against discipline and the tediousness of the war. When things got too much for him, he applied for a posting to Greece. After some training in fighter strategy, he went to Drama.

Drama is eighty miles northeast of Salonika. Toward the end of the war it became the headquarters of German squadrons charged with patrolling the Struma sector. The mixture of opposition to German war aims was less clear cut here than in France, but the Allied army encircling the area consisted of a guerrilla mixture of English, Italian, Serb, French, Italian and Venizelist Greek troops. In the air the situation was dead set against the Germans. About fifty RFC machines were available to every six German planes. The Germans were using Fokkers, but a few of the heavier Halberstadt planes were to be had, too. The German air commander, Heydemarck, a man of some humor and quite unlike the popular conception of the Teuton soldier, allowed men like Eschwege free rein, but he had his work cut out, dealing with Allied opposition.

He told Eschwege that one of the drawbacks to flying in combat in this area was a difficulty in obtaining confirmation of every victory. Eschwege gravely undertook to shoot down twice as many Allied planes in order to make sure that *somebody* indentified them!

Eschwege seldom flew coolly. He handled his Fokker like a man possessed of an agitated devil, treating the machine like a huge power tool. He once said that he wished a designer would learn how to put a cannon into the air because a war plane should be nothing more than just that. He carried out many experiments in the humid heat, stripping his Fokker down to the essentials and increasing the armament. On one occasion he almost shot himself down when a breech block exploded in his face during a trial flight. On take-off he always gunned his engine to a roaring maximum so that the machine went off like a bullet out of a gun.

Watching the undisciplined antics of his new pilot, Heydemarck gloomily shook his head. He had seen far too many young pilots smash up their machines and bodies at the far end of the field when they were suddenly unable to manipulate their ailerons and gain enough purchase to lift the machines up into treacherous air that danced with reflected heat.

Eschwege spent most of his early days zooming about over the sea, trying out hundreds of runs on the many tiny islands of the Aegean, not looking for anything in particular, but learning exactly when the crucial point must come before he could lift the Fokker up to safety. He wanted to know how narrow the safety margin was in this heat.

One day, when he was sitting in some scant shade near the edge of the airfield, an Allied Farman appeared at about 5,000 feet directly overhead. It seemed to be following a course, he thought, but his attention was drawn to it once more when it tried to make a landing. The pilot must be mad!

Eschwege bounded to his own machine and took off. The Farman pilot saw him, took fright, and tried to sheer away. He did not want to follow it out to sea. It would be much harder to usher it back again once it got out there.

Eschwege's technique was superb. He lost all his usual clumsiness in the excitement of the situation, and, in a series of circling movements, lifted his Fokker until it was above the Farman. The Allied plane now began to buck about, first in one direction, then in another, but nothing the pilot did could shake Eschwege off. Recalling every trick he knew, Eschwege edged down until he was almost rubbing wing tips with the Farman.

Beaten, the Farman at last landed after a circling descent. When it came to rest, the guards were waiting for it. Eschwege celebrated his bloodless victory by throwing the Fokker about all over the sky. He landed, to find the Farman's crew, two Serbian NCO's, looking rather ashamed of themselves. For a moment he wondered whether to ignore them completely and walk straight past the scene, but their hesitant smiles impelled him to go and shake hands, then conduct them to the mess for a valedictory drink. Over their glasses he said that they must consider themselves his prisoners. He apologized for shooting one exuberant burst shortly before they landed. It had been quite accidental; he was not shooting at them. Before seeing them off to a prison-of-war camp, he gravely requested their permission to fly their Farman.

It was this cheerful carefree start to his "little war," which soon became as bloody as anything on the Western Front, that gave Eschwege more confidence. He was still finding his footing when a fellow pilot mentioned an Allied flier named G. W. M. Green.

Captain Green was the equivalent of a local ace, but few people had ever heard of him outside the radius of Drama. He often came skimming in from the sea, always timing his strafing raids to coincide with the moment when the German mess was full and the mechanics and ground crews were having a meal. He caught the Germans napping several times, but now that they were "Green-conscious" it was hoped that the pest of an Englishman would soon be shot down in flames.

Eschwege needed some honor. He wanted to establish himself as something more than a rash fool. If he got this man Green it would be as good as a wreath of laurels. Eschwege was vainer than most. Flaunting authority as he often did, he was still astute enough to realize that he must justify himself in the eyes of his commanding officer.

Green, he was told, sometimes flew about over Drama or patrolled the nearby sea area near the island of Thasos. Several German pilots had been startled out of their wits by the flashing speed of Green's machine as he came down on them from a tremendous height, guns firing all the time. Those who survived said that they were badly shaken by such surprise tactics. The rest were not alive to give an account of their emotions at the time.

What Eschwege needed most of all was a tempting bait. He could not ask any of his comrades to risk their necks on the off chance of getting Green. Even if one did accept the idea, there was no guarantee at all that he would get out of the ambush alive. Eschwege had the disadvantage of never having seen Green in the air, so he did not know what to expect except a flashy show of whirlwind flying. In the end he had to admit to himself that he, Eschwege, must be the bait, not one of the more seasoned pilots. He also hoped to become Green's executioner.

One morning, while the rest were still in bed, Eschwege walked out to his machine, serviced it without calling for a sleepy mechanic, and then filled up the tanks. The roaring engine could not be muffled for the take-off, so he headed for the sky at something like double his usual speed and was charging through the cumulus tufts before anybody found out what had happened.

The British always flew a high-altitude dawn patrol, looking for something to attack. Eschwege knew all about their habits from studying intelligence reports. As he eased the control column back between his knees he realized that he was doing something fool-hardy enough to kill him. But that seemed to be the penalty of being an individualist.

Green was also airborne, though some miles away from Eschwege. He had with him a man called Owen, flying a second machine. Green chewed a dry sandwich, while only a few hundred yards away Owen was struggling to unscrew a vacuum flask of hot coffee. Neither had had time for a proper breakfast.

Munching bread and meat, Green stuck the joystick between his knees and held it there while he stared without much interest down at the emerald sheen of the sea. Beyond stood the land; to the left, hidden in the early-morning mist, was Greece, a country with which he had always felt a certain affinity. Fighting a war in this part of the world was somewhat like reliving the ancient Greek sagas, and there did not seem to be much incongruity in the fact that airplanes were the arms of the modern heroes.

Owen carefully sipped his coffee, one hand wrapped around the mug. Green approached in a gentle climb, and the two men grinned a greeting.

The altimeter read something like 6,000 feet when Owen first saw the Fokker below him. There was plenty of time. He finished his coffee and signed to Green, who had by now also seen the enemy. Green made a twirling movement with one hand, which meant that he wanted to go down and attack. Owen acknowledged it by indicating that he would come too. Waiting for Green to make up his mind how he would tackle the Fokker, Owen tested his guns, firing a few rounds through the air, then prepared to follow. The Fokker pilot could not hear the guns. It was doubtful if he had seen either of the British planes yet. They had the prime advantage. Always attack from above, said some textbooks; this was one of those rare occasions when the situation measured up in every detail to those diagrams which puzzled trainee fliers so much.

The British planes keeled over, preparatory to the first dive. At the controls of his machine, Green exercised all the skill necessary to make a dive at a vertical angle. He thought that it would be better if Owen did the actual shooting and instructed his comrade by signs. Attacking in a dive like this was for the veterans. If the enemy was flying too low there was a good chance of going past and being unable to pull out in time. And at this speed the sea was far from soft!

Two hundred feet lower now, thought Green. It would not be long.

Whipped by the tumult of their own making, the British airmen still watched the Fokker, but it showed no sign of awareness.

The fight, a near farce, was over in seconds. Owen's guns jammed at the precise moment when he was about to shoot at point-blank range. Green was well away now; Eschwege had taken no notice of the decoy tactics. Before Owen could even think what to do next, Eschwege swung his Fokker around and, with deceptive ease, planted a burst straight in Owen's fuel tank. Owen barely managed to make a landing without piling up.

Although he had not shot Green down, Eschwege returned to Drama with a joyous heart. His ruse had worked. He had tempted Green out and would have shot him down but for the other machine. As a result of his victory over Owen, Eschwege's reputation reached places like Thasos, Monuhi, Badinal, where British pilots put his name down for early destruction.

Eschwege had not yet finished with Green, but in the absence of distinguishing marks on British machines he was at a loss how to spot the man. The only thing to do was shoot down as many Allied planes as possible in hopes of getting Green in the slaughtering process.

A few days later Eschwege was coming back from a desultory one-man patrol when he saw two British BE's bombing the German railway station at Angista. Selecting one of them, he went in with spitting guns. He did not know that the machine which he marked down was one selected to tempt him closer. The bombing raid was a legitimate one, but the British knew that Eschwege was somewhere in the vicinity and they had hopes of disposing of him. He had fallen right into the trap, he realized, when his Fokker was suddenly peppered with tracer bullets.

The decoy plane had taken advantage of height and now started tail-chasing after him in such a way that it was almost impossible to shake him off. In a bad temper now that he knew how easily he had been taken in, Eschwege jerked his control column back, sending the Fokker screaming up in a climb which made the mainplane vibrate dangerously. Glancing back, he had a full view of the length of the BE with the pilot looking up at him, grinning. To avoid a bad collision, the BE slipped over onto its right wing and fell into a side loop, a sickening, gut-pulling operation which could easily lead to a buckling of the fuselage.

Eschwege took advantage and made his Fokker fall like a leaf, throwing the British pilot off the scent. From above it looked as though the Fokker was about to pile up, but Eschwege knew what he was doing. A few hundred feet above the dun-colored earth he managed to level out, but there was now no sign of the enemy. Puzzled, he attended to his laboring engine, nursing it carefully. He had already flown a long distance before coming into this fight. Fuel was low and he knew that his tank might be punctured, the result of a stray shot a few minutes ago. Unless he made some decisive moves now, either toward home or into a renewed fight with the BE's, he might have to force-land. He was over his own territory. The irritating thought was that he would have to go home by car.

What had happened was that both British machines believed that Eschwege had crashed after that deceptively long fluttering fall. They were now miles away, returning to their own base at Monuhi to file a report that a German plane, believed to be piloted by Eschwege, had been eliminated. They could not have been more mistaken. Eschwege was still in the air, but having trouble with a stuttering, stalling, overheated engine. He vigorously banged on the hand pump that sucked gas into the engine. No response. There was an air lock which could not be broken without stripping the pump down. He moved over to the automatic pump. It, too, was out of action. He then tried to point the Fokker's nose toward the clouds, but the engine lacked power. He labored along for a time before the nose dipped, threatening to plunge him to disaster.

The only solution was to switch over to the emergency tank, his sole hope of keeping the engine running. He reached forward and knocked the switch over. The engine picked up and sang sweetly. There was thirty minutes' supply of fuel there, enough to get home on. He paused in his calculations. Why should he go straight home? Thirty minutes was in excess of the flying distance to Drama. He could easily catch up with the BE's and give them a thrashing, then still get back.

It was this kind of long shot—one which would have been taken by very few pilots—which distinguished Eschwege from all others. It took only a few minutes to catch up with the jubilant BE's. Reaching easy fighting distance, he sprayed their tails with bullets, then sat back to wait for the inevitable fight to develop.

No two more astonished British pilots existed at the moment when they swiveled around to find the "destroyed" German sizzling along after them, apparently in the best of condition. On the ground some Bulgarian gunners looked through their sights, ready to join in, but the whirling, turning jumble created by the three planes was so tightly packed that it was impossible to tell one from the other.

The British fought themselves into a frenzy while Eschwege sat in his cockpit, almost relaxed, watching their antics with amused contempt. Choosing his moment, he kept one eye on the emergency fuel-level indicator, the other on his foes. He got in some useful shots, but restrained himself from wasting vital ammunition. Bullets could easily be the deciding factor in a fight like this.

At last, and almost inexplicably, one of the BE's swooped away out of the fight, apparently heading for the British base at Monuhi.

This was Eschwege's moment, the one he had been waiting for.

He closed with the remaining machine and fired dozens of bullets straight into the engine. It was now a running fight, a twirling grapple for supremacy against a cloudless sky, with the wounded machine doing its best to egg Eschwege on toward Monuhi where help would probably be available. Eschwege knew quite well what the plan was, but believed that he could destroy the BE long before Monuhi came up.

He was about to slam in a series of death blows with his gun, when he was suddenly attacked from the rear. He had been stupid enough to believe that the first BE had left the fight when it banked away. He knew that the pilot must be Green, now his personal enemy. He recognized the distinctive way in which he flew, the long low sweep around to allay suspicion while the other BE occupied his, Eschwege's, attention.

Green was firing all the time now, trying for a quick kill. Eschwege's position was reversed. A moment ago he was the supreme master. Now he was the hunted. Unless he moved quickly he could lose his life.

They went on shooting at each other, those two giants of the air, but Eschwege barely kept his end up against Green, who was using every piece of strategy he could think of. While hope still remained, Eschwege decided to go home and fight Green some other day. He did not want to acknowledge the Englishman's triumph, but with barely enough fuel in his tank to take him to Drama, he had no choice unless he joined the suicide brigade and rammed the BE head-on.

He got back to his own airfield with two flesh wounds in the arm. When mechanics peered into the emergency fuel tank they found it bone dry. He had flown the last few yards literally on gas which was at that moment flowing into the engine through the feed pipes. No pilot could have judged it better.

Bandaged, Eschwege telephoned the various German observation posts for a report on Green's BE, discovering that one of his shots had brought it to a forced landing in a swamp not far from the village of Ahinos. Calling for maps, he saw that it was within easy flying distance. The doctor protested; with a stiffened arm in a sling, he could not possibly fly again for at least a week. The pilot impatiently brushed him aside to make some more telephone calls. The British, he heard, were trying to salvage the BE, but without much luck. It was still there, and seemed to be sinking into the morass, said the German watchers.

First thing next morning Eschwege had himself helped into a two-seater bomber. The volunteer observer was settling down when he received an abrupt order from Eschwege to pay more attention to the job. The machine was fully loaded with bombs which they would need very soon.

Eschwege found it hard to handle the heavy two-seater after his own light fast Fokker. His arm kept on getting in the way until at last he stripped off the bandage, rolled it into a ball and tossed it away into the slipstream. The wounds began to bleed, but he paid no attention to the mess of stickiness which filled his flying glove.

They sighted the BE as it lay half in and half out of the glutinous mud. Whistling to himself, Eschwege made a graceful circuit of the area. His long bombing run took minutes while the observer made certain that the target was going to be hit. Four gouts of mud were thrown up as the bombs exploded, one of them close to the stricken plane. It could not be salvaged now.

He flew back to Drama to argue with the doctor about his blood-soaked arm.

19

Balloon Fever

The Germans were proud of their ability to maintain and operate the tiny but important port of Kavalla, a tight-clustered huddle of near-white buildings which lay in an inlet directly opposite the island of Thasos. The British, on the other hand, were annoyed by German persistence in keeping Kavalla open despite aerial bombing raids and bombardments from the sea. Kavalla remained inviolate until the day when the British believed that a frontal attack from the sea might incapacitate the port, throwing the Hun supply route to the interior out of gear and generally dislocating the communications system. The British originally intended sending ten warships for the job, but eight sailed up the Aegean throughout the hours of the night, arriving a few hours before dawn and laying to until the agreed hour. Eight FE's escorted one Farman two-seater, the nerve center from which the sea shelling was guided. The FE was the ideal escort plane, very fast and agile in the hands of an experienced pilot. All eight pilots were hand-picked.

Eschwege was taken by surprise. Receiving a message which said that Kavalla was being bombarded and even now was burning fast, he scanned the words again. Could one man tackle eight battleships

224

and eight fast planes without aid of any kind? It seemed so doubtful that he halted in his tracks, wondering if headquarters had gone mad. He also had a mental picture of the heaving smoky holocaust which was once peaceful Kavalla, a place often visited on leave for the swimming. Two minutes with the squadron operations officer confirmed that there was no chance of obtaining fighter support for a raid on the British fleet. Eschwege was now quite sure that if he did not take this on singlehanded, Kavalla would soon be nothing but rubble and a network of felled iron girders.

His Albatros was already fueled and serviced. His shirt hanging out of his trousers, a pair of sandals on his feet, he hauled himself up onto the mainplane and dropped neatly into the cockpit. It seemed to take hours before the mechanic finished fastening down the cowling of the engine. Then the machine was airborne, a typical Eschwege take-off, nearly tearing the life out of the engine.

His first instinct was to head straight for Kavalla and fight it out with the British, but one moment of sensible thought showed that he would last less than five minutes. There would be nothing clever in it.

Above Drama on a second height-grasping circuit, he turned east toward the barren rotundities of the mountains. Foothills rose, then gave way to the taller peaks. From this altitude they looked deceptively low, but he had known many frightening instances of fliers being forced down to wander from valley to valley, stumbling to their eventual deaths from exposure. He knew the soft caressing treachery of the fluctuating air pockets into which the Albatros kept being tossed, but the engine regained strength to lift him to safety again. For some time he had to exercise every muscle in his arms and shoulders as he grasped the control column, fighting against maddening atmospheric conditions which tried to suck the Albatros down, then turn it over in savage gusts of wind which rose in the hills. Here and there, he saw when he had time, stood the peasant farmhouses, their whitewashed walls glistening like sheets of notepaper.

It was time to turn toward the sea. Halfway round the circuit he suddenly saw the dust and smoke cloud hanging over Kavalla. Some shells were still exploding; new plumes of destruction shot up, subsided and came up again to join the ominous cloud. A massacre was going on down there. He wondered whether one man could put a stop to it.

Where was the British fleet? He hovered, awaiting the next salvo, but it was practically impossible to distinguish anything against the grayness of the ocean toward the horizon where the marauders must be. He could see only about seven miles with any clarity; beyond that it was sheer conjecture.

He flew straight out over the inferno of Kavalla, estimating that he must be well above the trajectory of the shells. It was not long before he did spot the lined-up ships as they stood out to sea in a grim row, deadly monsters painted gray to match the sea's grayness, spitting tongues of fire, issuing a splintering death every few seconds.

After a right-hand bank he enlisted the aid of the rising sun. Shielded there in the growing golden light, he studied the situation through smoked glasses, a thousand thoughts racing through his perceptive brain. The air escort of FE's flew steadily over the scene below, but Eschwege was much higher and still unseen. There was no need for the RFC to go out and strafe Kavalla. Their task was to tend one machine which flew lowest in the formation, a Farman two-seater, the prime mover and nerve center of the bombardment as it radioed the results back to the flagship. Kavalla was visible to the Farman, but nobody in the ships could see anything of what was happening ashore.

Eschwege busied himself with his Albatros, raising its sleek nose higher and higher until the air lost every trace of early-morning warmth, making him shiver in his flimsy clothing. There had been no time to get into proper flying overalls. From where he sat he could watch the reflected rays on the polished cowling. Sunshine fractured on the propeller, making him blink. He did not want to be caught napping.

There was one objection to his quickly formulated plan of attack: he had to bring down the Farman at the end of the first dive. If he missed and tried a second time he would run straight into the escort planes. He would be at their mercy, seven against one.

At about 4,000 feet he leveled out and sighted the machine down on the speck which was the Farman. Carefully edging the control column forward, he waited for the first tilt which would precipitate him into a power dive, mounting to a speed of more than 120 miles an hour, a velocity which could not allow for any error of judgment.

And if he failed . . . what then?

He grimly comforted himself with the knowledge that he would go straight into the sea before the escort planes could get at him. There would be no mess, no blazing coffin of a plane. If he had to die, he would like to perish in the salty purity of the calm ocean.

The Albatros was picking up speed now. He could feel the drag on his feet increasing. Craning forward with an effort, he could see the battle fleet, still firing while the FE's idled above the all-important Farman. Soon they would be as big as eagles, then as big as the Albatros itself. Soon . . . in five seconds!

He pushed his right knee hard against the control stick and wrapped chilled fingers around the trigger of the gun upon which so much was going to depend. It would not jam, it must not! It was serviced and tested every day, every morning before he started flying.

He had a frightful thought. . . . This morning the ground crews had had no chance of going through their usual routine. He had only assumed that they had done so. The gun had not been tested at all. The ammunition supply consisted of a few rounds left over from yesterday's operations. Great God, this was suicide! There was only a few hundred feet left. In the remaining time he could not escape because they must have seen him already.

At a hundred yards, almost on top of the Farman, he desperately opened fire, a brief but devastating demonstration of accurate shooting which ripped through the Farman's fuselage, slaughtering pilot and observer.

It was all over in less than one minute, from the time he pressed the trigger to the stunned silence broken by the escort planes as they zoomed in all directions—startled beetles whose routine had been disturbed by an unheralded catastrophe out of the blue. The bombardment of Kavalla finished sooner than it had begun. The FE's made no attempt at chasing him home. The ships turned away, silenced.

Eschwege was the sudden hero of the Aegean. Even the British thought highly of him for his courage. When he heard that the pilot and observer of the Farman had been washed ashore, one with a bullet through the heart and the other with a bullet through the brain, he dutifully attended the military funeral organized by the German commander, but refused to look at the soggy corpses as they lay in their rough coffins. It was unlucky to look death in the face. It was a reminder of what could easily happen to him.

Not unnaturally, the British were still smarting under the blows lashed out by a human thunderbolt called Eschwege. Daring full-scale bomber attacks on Drama were the revenge, going on for whole nights without cessation. There was only one way to stop this, and in it Eschwege saw a new chance of shooting down Green, now his long-standing enemy.

He was in the air long before the British arrived, taking off before dawn and passing the tedious period until early light. He was unlucky. It seemed that Green was not leading the raids at all. Eschwege picked what fights he could, hoping to lure Green out. After shooting down a BE, flown by a friend of Green's, Eschwege learned that he had unwittingly touched the British ace on a raw spot. Green came over Drama to toss down a challenge, forcing the unreluctant Eschwege to meet him over Lake Takhino. The engagement was quite up to Eschwege's usual standard. Green barely escaped with his life when his gun jammed.

As one of the principal protectors of Drama, Eschwege grossly overworked himself, but still kept up a remarkably high standard of airmanship. He shot down a few more British planes, and once forced a Farman down into the sea. He patrolled the area until an Allied motorboat appeared. Under the impression that pilot and observer were safe, he was amazed to hear that the pilot had died in the water before the motorboat could reach the place. Such incidents as this made him feel gloomy. He came to believe that he himself might one day have to meet death in this sun-baked hell of mountain and uncompromising ocean. Sure enough, a day did dawn which put a brake on his impulsiveness.

Toward noon he was fighting four Sopwiths singlehanded, wriggling out of their way and shooting back whenever he had a chance. One Sopwith went down in a curling wreath of anguished flame under the punishment of his guns. A little time later he suddenly lost control of his own machine. The engine lost power while thick smoke plumed upward from the dying Sopwith, entering his lungs and making him choke. His eyes smarted and watered while he lunged forward in search of the emergency fuel pump.

His fingers were all thumbs; he could not find it. Was there no escape this time? Was this the prelude to death?

He was only 1,500 feet above the sea, dropping vertically all the time. There was no chance of gliding the four miles to the land, even if he could straighten out the shaking plane. His breath tore from his chest as he ripped his collar open, trying to collect his thoughts.

He took the one remaining chance. Forcing the control column as far forward as it would go, he put the plane into the steepest possible dive, believing that this *might* start the fuel flowing again through an air lock which must be starving the engine. He knew that long before the point of terminal velocity he would hit the sea. At this speed he did not stand a chance.

At 400 feet the engine was barely stammering; at 350 feet the propeller stopped turning. There was not a chance of getting out of this now. He was committed up to the hilt.

Less than 300 feet from the sea, the propeller still showed no sign of life. He wrathfully banged on the instrument panel, maddened by the inefficiency of the plane. He kicked the barrel of the emergency fuel pump, shouting aloud at the engine to start.

But it was no use.

At only 90 feet above the sea, when it seemed that the machine would dive headlong through the waves, the engine abruptly cleared itself and started up with a roar. Everything ran at full pitch. He had the advantage of flying at the high speed picked up in the dive. He flipped over on one wing, scarcely conscious of what he was doing, but knowing that he must get up into the thin clouds again or perish.

When he eventually landed at Drama he could hardly speak to the waiting mechanics and officers. It was more than an hour before he recovered from the shock of that dive.

The audacity of the British always baffled Eschwege. Time after time he proved that German air superiority was an accomplished fact, yet still the Allies flew over Drama airfield with their bombs, taking the most absurd chances and often killing themselves. Sometimes they tried to be very clever and appeared at dawn to strafe the living quarters and hangars. When they damaged a newly delivered Halberstadt intended for Eschwege's personal use, it so angered him that he immediately set off in a Rumpler with an observer named Konig to teach them a lesson. What irritated him was that he had taken weeks of troublesome negotiation to get hold of the Halberstadt. He had not even flown it and mechanics were still checking it when British bullets smashed it up.

On a breakneck flight he gave the British a taste of panic by setting their island base of Thasos on fire. This was one of the most heavily fortified British bases, he knew, but he managed to get through untouched. Konig, huddled in the rear cockpit, was scared stiff and only just managed to drop the incendiary bombs on the target when Eschwege pierced the artillery fire which came up in a steel curtain.

Next morning he was told that the prized Halberstadt was not too badly damaged after all. In fact, it was now repaired and could be flown at any time. Perhaps he had been taking a stupid risk in flying against Thasos, but it did not matter very much. The British needed to be taught a lesson.

The end of Eschwege, when it came, was the result of a British trick. Since they could not destroy this man in combat, they were forced to adopt a subterfuge.

For some time a campaign was waged against him. The idea was to encourage a new rashness in attacking and destroying British observation balloons in the Allied sector. They allowed him to shoot one or two down in the region of Orlyak without retaliating. Of course, he should have seen what they were up to, but the thrill of the chase was on him. He was suffering from an attack of "balloon fever," the malady which took many airmen on both sides to their deaths. He was sickened to see one observer jump to his death when a parachute did not open. A dispassionate war was good, but when it came to flesh and blood and suffering he preferred not to be too closely associated with it.

He was using quick-firing Spandau machine guns, essential equipment to the balloon hunter. They gave out a reliable spate of bullets which raked the silver sausages, creating a brilliant scarlet flash when the gas container exploded.

At no time did Eschwege guess that most of the balloons were deliberately planted in his path in preparation for a lethal finale planned by the British. True, now and then his plane was slightly damaged by artillery which went through the motions of opposition but meant nothing. When a comrade of his pointed out that it was almost too simple, knocking down the observation balloons, he scoffed at the idea.

Over Kalendra one day he was chased by a BE two-seater and a Sopwith Pup. They came out of the rain clouds to sit on his tail. A few shots were fired. He was an ideal target, he knew, and they could easily down him if he made a wrong move. There was no point in letting them get away with it. In a fight which swung from one quarter of the damp sky to the other, he shot down one Allied plane. When he banked, ready to blast the survivor, there was no sign of the plane. Amused, he scouted about for a few minutes, and saw it scuttling back to the British lines. The British had very little nerve and less spirit than the Germans. Two against one and still they failed to make a killing. Incredible! His confidence buoyed up, he wished they would stop putting their balloons in the sky, distracting him from his principal mission of combat and escort.

Only half a day later he was flying alone over Orlyak when he saw a balloon swinging languidly in the breeze. The observer, clearly visible, was standing in the basket, evidently dozing, for he made no attempt at climbing out and parachuting down to safety before Eschwege's Spandaus tore the gas bag to bits.

Eschwege went straight into the attack without preliminaries. The first shots had no effect whatsoever, so he had to come around again. As he closed with the balloon there was an explosion which could be heard over an area of miles. The balloon became a fireball with a backlash which caught hold of Eschwege's machine, wrenching the wings off and blowing the fuselage apart. The observer had no time to escape. He did not want to: he was only straw and old uniform.

The British trick was complete. Their balloon, studded with explosive charges fired by electricity from the ground, had served its use. Late the same day a solitary British plane winged over Drama to drop a message announcing the death of Eschwege. Three days later a parcel was dropped. It contained a few personal belongings and two rather indistinct photographs of a military funeral.

CHAPTER **20**

Captain Willy Coppens

Only one man ever actually landed on, and took off from, a German observation balloon when it was up in the air. His name was Willy Coppens, a young man with a large nose, an exasperating sense of humor and an apparently senseless evaluation of risks which took him all the way through the war and delivered him safely into the lap of peace minus only a leg.

Coppens came from Belgium; he was born at Boitsfort, a country place which later became citified. He was interested in land yachts. Between 1907 and 1913 he built seven of them, the majority with a sail surface of 150 square feet. He was riding his latest model along the beach at Westende when an airplane happened to pass overhead. He had a girl passenger with him, but the plane caught his attention and he forgot all about her. The land yacht careened round and round in a circle, turned over and threw the girl out, but he continued watching the airplane. From that day on he did not bother very much with girls. When he mentioned that he would like to learn to fly, his father went into a rage and threatened to throw him out of the house.

The war started; Belgium began to mobilize, and Coppens was drafted to the 2nd Grenadier Regiment. That November he saw the departure for Étampes, the chief French aeronautical training center and headquarters of the Farman School, of new friends like Carl Kervyn de Lettenhove, Jacques de Meeus and Edmond Desclée. Thinking that he, too, might be able to follow them, he wrote his application. Nothing came of it. He stayed where he was, an ordinary soldier with the Belgian Motor Machine Gun Corps.

In 1914 Belgium was in a far more embarrassing position than Britain as far as air power was concerned. All she could show in the way of a flying corps was a collection of twenty-four Farman pusher-type biplanes, fitted with the usual 80-hp engine. True, there was a government provision for six escadrilles (squadrons) consisting of four airplanes apiece. One year before the war, in the summer of 1913, only one squadron was available for exercises because so few pilots could be found. In fact, it was hard to find proficient pilots of any kind at that time.

Coppens went on pestering the authorities and sending postcards to his parents in the German-occupied city of Brussels, saying that he was organizing his own transfer and hoped to become a pilot any day now. In the end he won out. On September 6, 1915, he arrived at Beaumarais, near Calais. The position here was hardly conducive to good flying. Coppens inspected a fence which had just been erected around the flying field by order of the CO. Twenty-four hours later a pilot named Tyck piled his Nieuport up on the palings when attempting to land.

Coppens' first job was to dismantle the wreckage and salvage whatever he could. He was delighted with the task; it gave him a chance to see exactly how the Nieuport was built and find out what happened to it when it crashed. When that chore was completed he was transferred to a gang of amateur pilots, who were laying a cinder path between the huts. He felt proud to be in aviation circles. After a few days of trundling wheelbarrows about and crunching gritty cinders flat with a hand roller, he changed his mind about the glamor of the air service. He must make a definite move if he wanted to fly. This might be a very short war. He did not want to go home and admit that he had been making cinder paths, not flying at all.

In the end he wheedled an application for eight weeks' leave, then made his way to England where he had heard that it was possible to qualify quickly at one of the five private flying schools at

Hendon or the "nursery" at Bournemouth. He did not guess how little these schools taught. Fees were high and he never received any return for his investment from the Belgian government. He took a bed-sitting room and walked straight to Hendon airfield to complete the forms. He could not speak much English and felt flattered when a woman, who offered to do his washing, asked for his autograph. He later discovered that she wanted him to sign her laundry book as a steady customer.

He spent his first few days driving a machine called a Penguin up and down on the grass near the landing strip. The Penguin was actually an adapted flying machine with clipped wings and low-powered engine. It could not fly but it did show the pupil how to handle the controls. Most of the students thought it ludicrous, others quickly moved on to some other flying school where pilots actually took to the air.

These flying schools, many of them set up overnight on a get-rich-quick basis as soon as the war started, were the "sausage mills" of wartime flying talent. It is a wonder that they ever produced anything at all, yet in them young men like Albert Ball first learned how to handle airplanes. Coppens was more critical than the others of the slapdash system. His enthusiasm was tempered by a knowledge that he was now running out of money and must qualify soon or else fail completely. He finished his course as soon as he could, but later said: "When we left Hendon we did not even know that one had to land head to wind! And I remember a wretched Englishman being disembarked in a corner of the field, owing to the fact that safety belts were unknown at that center. With nothing to hold him in, he had been emptied out of his plane as the result of a miserable twopenny-halfpenny somersault. The Englishman died. . . ."

He did not think much of the two machines which were at the disposal of pupils. "The Lord alone knows how these aircraft held together. Neither of them had been subjected to any form of inspection during construction."

More than forty hopeful Belgians passed through one or other of the Hendon flying schools, including André de Meulemeester, who flew a Grahame-White biplane and hogged ground level because, he said, he felt dizzy if he went up to any great height; Charles Degrauw, who chased all the pretty English girls and

eventually married one. Another future ace was Jean Pauli, a man
who carried himself like a penitent priest and later fought the Germans like an inspired devil. The taunting tongue of Arsène de
Launoit, another fine pilot, got them all in trouble many times.
Adrien Richard and Florent Schollaert meanwhile risked their
necks in a rickety Wilbur Wright machine.

Many of these men were unpopular with the English instructors.
One of the ringleaders was Jean Stampe. Incensed that his training
was taking so long, he brought out a loaded revolver and made his
teacher provide additional lessons so that he might gain his certificate and get into the war. His friend Maurice Martin helped him
bully the director of the Beatty Flying School into submission, and
later threatened to shoot anybody who stood in his way.

Then there was the quick-witted humorist Lucien Hallet, a man
who did not believe in the aims of the war, but nevertheless wanted
to get out to the front to see for himself. He shot Germans down
like flies. George Medaets, an enthusiastic amateur cook, spent
most of his time in a corner of the hangar, getting together tasty
little snacks over a Primus stove. The senior member of the group,
and an accomplished practical joker, was Maurice Medaets, the
man they christened the "Flight Commander."

These, then, were some of the men who wanted to fly for Belgium. Most of them were killed within the first few months. Coppens was among the lucky ones. He came through the war more
or less in one piece. Despite the petty annoyances of Hendon he
finally gained his "ticket." "On December 5," he reports, "having
had some thirty lessons and put in a total of three hours, fifty-six
minutes (according to the calculations of the schools, who reckoned one minute for a flight in a straight line of 500 yards, half of
which was on the ground), I was given a machine and was allowed
to go up on my first solo; that is to say, do two 'straights,' or,
otherwise expressed, execute two 'leaps' of a couple of hundred
yards each.

"This was followed immediately by my being sent up for my
'ticket.' This involved describing two series of five figures-of-eight
and then landing within a given area in front of a point marked by
the little group comprising the instructor who, with solicitude written all over his face, and a mouth bulging with invective, stood
ready to bound forward at a moment's notice, and the rest of the

pupils anxiously expecting to see their one and only airplane destroyed."

The second part of the examination, which consisted of gliding with a dead engine from a height of 450 feet, could not be taken until December 9 because of fog. Nevertheless, he did pass and went straight over to Étampes in hopes of going to the front. In many respects this period was similar to the "phoney war" of 1939. Men and machines waited without receiving news of any movements. As a result, morale rotted while irritation rose. Of all the aviators, Coppens was the most hopeful. Just before his arrival at the Farman School he was unlucky enough to see the funeral of a pilot who had been killed in action, yet even this did not disturb him very much.

At Étampes he spent most of his time trying to avoid meeting the CO, Lieutenant de Caters, because he "had a tendency to confuse an airplane with a mowing machine." It was Caters who once had the future ace Edmond Thieffry thrown into prison for looping a training plane because he believed it to be dangerous. These were hard days; progress seemed so slow. Advanced pupils learned how to fly the "Maurice Farman 1913 Model (with forward stabilizer, known to us as the 'breadboard') and from that course we passed on to the 1914 model (which dispensed with the forward elevating device referred to." In both types the engine, a 70-hp air-cooled Renault, was behind the pilot, but in the "Longhorn," or 1913 pattern, the aviator was enclosed in the structure which supported the "breadboard."

Coppens actually enjoyed flying these clumsy machines. "[It] glided marvelously, and, what was more, landed with great ease. It could be put on the ground at a speed of 25 miles an hour, or even less, and could glide a distance of from eight to ten times its height." The only snag seemed to be that if the engine was stopped or throttled down at about 10,000 feet, the pilot could, theoretically at least, land at a spot some fifteen miles away. It did not work out like that at all. In a high head wind, the Farman often flew backward!

Who else was at Étampes with Coppens? Together they comprised a collection of men destined to lift the flying colors high over the skies of France, men such as Charles de Munck, Abel de Neef, Jean-Marie Lambert, Louis Van den Born, Max Orban, Charles

Ciselet. With the thirty or forty from Hendon, they made a formidable array. Spirits were very high, but sometimes, when a plane crashed in full view of the assembled pupils, good humor died. Coppens himself once described such a scene. "Just as I raised my eyes, a Farman, descending in an unexplained and almost vertical dive, found the speed too great for it and broke up. The structure literally burst, scattering planes, struts and other parts in all directions. I made out the tail-plane, the engine, and the pilot; the whole lot hurtled down and fell in front of us, 500 yards away in a field. It was the first fatal accident I had actually seen happening, and it was horrible. One must have heard that ghastly noise of wood being torn asunder, followed by that indescribable stillness, to appreciate any description. For the space of a second I found myself clinging to an insane hope; but it was all too obvious that the pilot was dead, and the only question requiring an answer was 'Who was it?' Some of us rushed across the field to find out, the others stayed behind, preferring not to see. I was one of the latter."

At Étampes it was the callous but cautionary custom to detail pilots to keep a night watch over the body of the pilot killed in an accident. One authority has called this a "shocking procedure," but it did serve to sober up the lighter-minded students.

Coppens had many arguments with the men who were to become his close friends. He was still conscious that the war was growing larger than anybody suspected. How could they go on hanging about at Étampes, wasting time? "The months went by, and very few of us, summoned one by one, had been sent up to the front. The turn had not yet come for any of those who had been with me at Hendon."

More tedium followed at Villesauvage when he arrived there with other nonflying pilots. The only relief lay in organizing practical jokes. They also gambled and lost money to one another, flirted with girls, and shredded the nerves of the high-strung CO, Captain Renard. When other diversions palled André de Meulemeester built a three-stringed instrument which he twanged hour after hour, playing the same three notes over and over again. The atmosphere of general lassitude in which these men were forced to live was one which led to the corruption of the spirit. It made the authorities complain to General Headquarters about the moral caliber of the pilots. Mass transfers took place to break up the clique. Coppens was left with one companion, Thieffry, but soon he too vanished into the jailhouse. Coppens ran into inevitable trouble when he forged a leave pass and went to Paris for a weekend. When he was caught and sent to the lockup he found himself in the same cell with the bubbling, good-humored Thieffry. "We whiled away the time," says Coppens, "in our imprisonment playing chess, reading, and listening to the yarns of our guards. In the morning, through the dormer window of our cell we jeered at our comrades as they fell in on parade in the half-light of the dawn. This done, we would retire to bed again! Lucien Hallet took a photograph of Thieffry and me at our window. Captain Renard seized the film and destroyed it. . . ."

Most of their time was spent polishing boots and field boots. Coppens was now absolutely desperate to escape the boring mockery of being in a camp where flying was actually discouraged. He was prepared to accept almost any offer of active service. "Chancing to meet a Russian colonel passing through on duty, I very nearly succeeded, in company with one or two others, in getting sent to Russia." Nothing came of the attempt. Some weeks later he was glad to take a posting to No. 6 Escadrille. "I did not dream of protesting against a decision that ignored my legitimate claim to be posted to a single-seater fighter squadron."

Despite the drab atmosphere at Villesauvage, Coppens had managed to learn something during his stay there. He made a total of 203 solo flights, occupying sixty-two hours, fifty-five minutes, and sixty-nine flights as a passenger, a further total of nine hours and ten minutes. He had been more or less instructed in flying Maurice Farmans, BE2C's, Henri Farmans, Nieuports and Voisins.

So the rebel was bound for the front at last. It seemed a belated start to his career. He meant to catch up with the others.

21

Bombing By Night

At Houthem Coppens shook his new comrades by flaunting a standing order and flying off alone in a heavy snowfall to see the front for himself. He had been at the airfield only an hour when he asked for a plane. Mechanics thought he was joking, but he eventually got his own way and flew off to look at the occupied country beyond the Yser River. Circling, he returned to Houthem, picked up an observer, and then flew to Ramscapelles where he came under fire for the first time. With shells bursting all around the machine, he was "thrilled and immensely proud." His observer did not share his feelings; he was far too busy, holding on for dear life.

"A battery at Westende was firing shells of 135 mm at us," reported Coppens. "I observed the flash of each shot, and counted the seconds, and then at the appointed instant a sack of coal appeared to burst into atoms quite close to us, with a report that drowned the noise of my engine. Soon the sky in the neighborhood was filled with smoke of innumerable shellbursts, giving the effect of a straggling bouquet of dark exotic flowers. Imagine my joy on landing at finding the trace of a shell splinter in my top plane!"

His machine was the British BE2C with a 90-hp engine. Cop-

pens did not like it very much. He considered the arc of fire "very
restricted," commanded by the pivot-pillar-mounted machine gun.
Attempts were made to improve the arrangement by transferring
the pilot into the front seat and the observer into the rear one.
The gun, also shifted back with the observer, was now placed on a
rotating turret, providing a normal field of fire. "Even transformed
in this way," Coppens said, "the machine was inadequate. Its ceiling, in particular, was too poor, being rarely more than 11,000
feet. In July 1917 it was replaced by the RE8, another airplane of
British design."

The RE8 was a two-seater tractor, fitted with a 150-hp air-
cooled engine. It was designed at the Royal Aircraft Factory at
Farnborough, becoming the standard British artillery airplane in
1917. It was used for short-distance day and night bombing. For
day bombing it carried four 20-pound Hales (25-pound Cooper)
bombs. For night work the bomb load was two 112-pound bombs.
The machine carried one fixed Vickers gun firing forward through
the airscrew, and one Lewis gun (or two, coupled) aft. At the time
of the Armistice fifteen RFC squadrons in the field had these
planes.

It was with a certain diffidence that Coppens joined No. 1
Squadron, for this was reputed to be one of the finest fighting units
in the entire air corps. The CO was Captain Jacquet, the first Belgian pilot to shoot down five Germans. Other members included
Coppens' old friend André de Meulemeester and Jan Olieslagers,
a born pilot who could do nearly anything with a plane.

Coppens was a man who had to tackle things for himself without
taking much notice of advice proffered by more seasoned hands.
Invited to lunch at No. 22 Squadron, he ignored the advice that he
should not try to fly in such a high wind as was blowing at the time.
"It is a wonderful sensation to feel the machine shaken bodily by
a strong wind, and to slow down the engine and feel the full
strength of the 'bumps'—without once letting the machine take
charge of one." Arriving at his luncheon rendezvous, he abruptly
discovered that the plane would not land. Shaken, he did everything in his power to get it down to the ground, painfully conscious
of groups of pilots and villagers watching him. But every time he
put the nose down, the wind rushed underneath it, lifting him up
again. It took half an hour to make that landing.

Houthem airfield was excellently situated . . . as an airfield.
When staff officers noticed the place, arrangements were made to
bring the General Headquarters over and settle there. Along with
the rest, Coppens foresaw a time in the not too distant future
when they would feel conscious of the big brass living next door.
There was no solution to it until the Germans learned the where-
abouts of General Headquarters and flew over on a mass bombing
raid. At the last moment the Hun deserted the center of operations
and tried to ruin the airfield instead. It was enough for the staff
officers. Unnerved, they packed up and left next day.

Although the Belgians wanted to do some night flying and bombing, British coordinators were always against it. Certain elements
of the RFC did not trust Belgian pilots to behave themselves in the
air. Coppens was among those who felt angry about the British attitude. In the end he did get his chance.

"The Belgian Flying Corps did very little flying by night and I
can only lay claim to five or six night flights. The first, of which I
remember witnessing the start, was on April 5, 1917. The village,
outwardly asleep in the pale light of the moon, was in reality agog,
for it was one of those ideal air-raid nights when hostile airplanes
might be expected at any moment. Those villagers who had not
sought refuge in the few isolated farms in the neighborhood, stood
in groups on their thresholds, ready to flee—the Lord knows
whither. In the Flying Corps mess, where dinner was cheerily
drawing to its close, an indefinable excitement was observable, as
pilot after pilot rose from the table, beckoned or called to his observer, and slipped out into the velvety shadow of the streets—a
velvet backed with silver, wherein human figures passed at once
into oblivion. On the airfield, other figures, ghostly figures these,
moved about among the motionless fleet of wings and struts standing outside the sheds. The *consigne* [blackout] had been absolute,
and not a single light could be seen anywhere; it was indeed an
ideal air-raid night. Ears strained to catch the slightest murmur
from the skies—the murmur of aircraft that one could not hope to
see, steady and monotonous, filling space with its rhythm, converting the moonlit heavens into a fount of sound.

"The bombs had been hooked on to their racks under the wings,
and the mechanics were swinging the propellers. One by one, as the
engines started, the exhaust pipes spat out long tongues of blue

flame, intermingled with red sparks that spun eddying into the darkness. Then, with a roar that grew, each machine lurched forward, gathered itself together and drove full tilt into the night, away and upward, a compact contrivance of all that was dangerous —an engine vomiting fire, tanks containing gallons of the most inflammable of any known liquid, and fabric-covered wings draped with explosives. . . ."

Those who were left behind, the riggers and mechanics, the odd-job men and administrative staff, returned to their billets to wait. Some entered the empty sheds for a surreptitious cigarette and mug of hot coffee and rum. It was a long wait. Some of the more gloomy elements believed that the entire bomber fleet would be caught and wiped out by German night fighters. They would not stand a chance with their bombs still aboard; they could not move quickly, they could not gain any more speed. The Germans would be on them in a matter of seconds and that would be the end of a Belgian squadron which had set out with such show and splendor earlier that night. And those left behind were conscious of the vulnerability of the airfield. Coppens once said: "Had they only known that we had no effective defense against such visitations, the Germans would have come and attacked our airfield at point-blank range, even by day!"

The bombers returned several hours later. This was the scene witnessed by Coppens: "As they returned from their expeditions, the machines fired a prearranged color light, calling for the landing ground to be lit up. An answering light fired from the ground was provided for, to warn pilots should it not be safe for them to land.

"On this night, Lieutenant Louis de Burlet had just signaled his return when Captain Gallez buckled a wheel of his airplane while landing in the center of the airfield. The following machine was therefore warned not to land. De Burlet had circled the airfield once or twice and had asked a second time to be allowed to land, when a third light signal of a different color attracted our attention. Strange though this unforeseen signal appeared, no precautions were taken, and a few seconds later we clearly made out the silhouette of a German machine diving toward us. It passed us not more than fifty feet away, with a machine gun spitting fire at us as it came and went. By a miracle no one was hit, and the majority of those of us present, taken completely by surprise, un-armed, turned and ran. It was too funny for words.

"Lieutenant de Burlet, who had landed just before this hap-pened, with commendable presence of mind climbed back into the nacelle of his Farman, and, getting hold of his machine gun, opened fire on the vanishing intruder, but without visible results."

On April 8, 1917, Coppens was promoted to First Class Ser-geant. He did not get much pleasure out of it. He wanted only to fly on operations and have the chance of actually fighting the enemy. One of his grudges was against squadrons of mixed na-tionalities. It came as a relief when, in 1918, his Squadron, C.74, was converted to one containing all-Belgian personnel. In the last few months there had been a subtle mockery in the interchange of decorations; the Belgians had large collections of French medals, the French had Belgian ones. This became a huge joke to Cop-pens, who believed that the aims of the war were being lost in a comic-opera atmosphere.

April 8, when he was elevated in rank, was a day of small but saddening disaster. A group of two-seaters and scouts flew toward Bruges on reconnaissance. The operation continued satisfactorily until the moment when the formation swung around to make its return, then a Hispano-Suiza BE belonging to No. 6 Squadron and piloted by Glibert with Lieutenant Callant as observer, was singled out behind German lines by German interceptor planes. What followed had a dreadful inevitability about it. The BE could hardly move out of the path of the killers; it was a slow-moving machine and already flying at ceiling height. The faster Germans closed in like ravening hounds, hammering out a vicious tattoo of bullets. The rest of the Belgian formation was now too far away to help; they could only wait for that moment when fire must spurt out of the BE on its last dive. Callant and Glibert were killed instantly.

It was not to be the end of a cycle of disasters which almost unnerved Coppens. Jean Pauli, a close friend of his from the days at Hendon and Étampes, was trapped while flying a Farman F.40 over enemy lines. The machine was itself obsolescent, but Pauli used it fondly because it was the squadron mascot and he wanted to prove that life remained in the old engine. With him on that last flight went Lieutenant de Bersac. The Farman was shot to bits. It fell out of the sky in a ragged shower. The bodies of the two men hurtled to destruction. Watching from an accompanying plane, a Belgian pilot said that he believed Jean Pauli was alive when he was thrown out of the wreckage.

About ten days later Willy Coppens was posted to No. 4 Squadron, an escadrille within No. 6 Group, commanded by Captain Paul Richard. Richard was intensely proud of the fact that his men had recently shot down and rebuilt a German twin-engined bomber of advanced design. As soon as it was airworthy, he flew it to Paris to hand over to the French for inspection and research.

No. 4 Squadron was equipped with Farman biplanes of the F.40 type, powered by 130-hp Renault engines. Coppens was as critical as usual after looking them over in the sheds. "These machines flew well and glided marvelously, but their speed was inadequate, and the observer, placed in front of the pilot, the wings, the engine, and the propeller, was unable to fire toward the rear. There was consequently no means of defense when the machine was attacked from behind, and its powers of maneuver were insufficient to enable it to break away from a determined enemy single-seater, once the latter had secured a position on its tail. It could not be dived steeply, owing to the danger of the structure collapsing under the strain—as had occurred in the case of one of our people, Michaux, at the Étampes school.

"Two-seaters of the 'pusher' pattern ought to have been discarded at the front as early as 1916, and yet we were still using them in 1918—French F.40's and F.60's, and the Belgian GN biplanes. . . ."

Despite the exposure of the crew to enemy action, Coppens soon came to like the machine, particularly for its extensive gliding powers. In gliding lay the salvation of many a pilot, particularly if he had incurred engine damage in a fight and must get home more or less intact.

Because he had been refused the chance of night flying with his previous squadron, Coppens renewed his plea to Captain Richard. On April 26 his wish was granted. He was to make his first real night flight. The operation was to bomb German billets at Zarren, making two separate journeys. What puzzled him was that the artillery could easily do the same job with much less risk, yet the entire squadron was briefed to make a most elaborate raid. No explanation was forthcoming.

"I was rather astonished to discover that, when flying at night, at a height of about 1,000 feet, visibility was quite good. The eye can only penetrate darkness, or for that matter, mist, at any angle very close to the vertical. It is therefore necessary to gain a certain height in order to command a sufficient area of the ground beneath one.

"Below, a few points of light could be seen coming from un-shuttered windows, betraying the homes of beings forever unidentified. Near the front, colored lights rose in curves, their momentary reflections visible in the flood waters. Other flares, attached to silken parachutes, threw patches of the sky into dazzling light, making the stars appear pale by contrast.

"Soon we entered the danger zone. As we droned our way across the lines, clusters of incendiary balls of fire came winding up to meet us for all the world like the bubbles breaking on the surface of a glass of champagne. Searchlight beams, giant's fingers groping sinisterly for us, cut the firmament into so many wedges of blackness, and, now and then, like a moth crossing in front of a headlight, an airplane would emerge into a beam from one of these wedges and turn into a thing of silver, while the giant's finger, trembling with excitement, essayed to hold it, and other beams converged to assist, and the guns below concentrated their fury on the target, filling the sky with detonating high explosive; until the airplane, diving and twisting this way and that, plunged back into the obscurity whence it had come.

"In the pattern of the carpet moving in beneath me, I could see our objective. As we drew near, the enemy's fire became fiercer and the fanlike glow from our bombs, bursting at the end of their unseen fall, added itself to the pyrotechnic display.

"I could visualize the stir being caused down there: the gunners and the machine-gun crews sweating at their weapons, and the [ambushed ones] fleeing for their lives and going to ground to the huge delight of the combatant troops present. That was what invariably happened on our side, and I could see no good reason for a similar comedy not being enacted here.

"The first time I released my load of bombs, I was astonished at the extremely slight movement imparted to my machine, which went on its way undisturbed. I had expected the sudden release of a hundredweight or more of cargo to have more effect on an airplane.

"On the homeward journey I switched on my instrument lights at intervals in order to read my compass, and in the calmer regions of our own lines my pistol rocket of prearranged color turned away our searchlights and quietened our anti-aircraft guns. The landing searchlight was lighted in answer to our request, and I went down into an artificial daylight, my shadow preceding me—running along over the grass of the airfield, growing longer and longer, until my engine stopped and my wheels kissed the ground. The next instant my machine was trundling toward the sheds under its own inertia, to the accompaniment of the hollow rumble of its undercarriage. A sharp turn, and the airplane pulled up in front of the hangars."

The excitement and the sheer perfection of it whetted Coppens' appetite for night flying. On May 3 he was one of those who attacked the German airfield at Ghistelles. Everything went well, although he nearly killed himself overtaking one of his own machines, which was faltering due to engine failure. His wheels missed the lower plane by inches.

The re-equipping of No. 4 Squadron with Sopwiths (the "one-and-a-half-strutter") became due. This was the tractor biplane with a 130-hp Clerget motor. The pilot was behind the mainplanes. The observer was in the rear seat and—horror!—the fuel tanks were sandwiched between the two men. Coppens made a great joke of this when he noticed it. The designer of the machine was obviously a German, who wanted to do away with British aviators!

The Sopwith was armed with a fixed machine gun which, fired by the pilot, shot between the propeller blades. "The interrupter gear was poor, giving a very slow rate of fire," Coppens observed. He was referring to the Scarff-Dibovsky gear. Scarff, a Royal Naval Air Service warrant officer, collaborated with a Russian engineer, Dibovsky, and produced this apparatus which was not, however, completely satisfactory. Many pilots reported that the Vickers gun, used in conjunction with the Scarff-Dibovsky, was slow in its rate of fire. It was vital to improve it as soon as possible, but little was done. Many pilots lost their lives because of this very factor. The

Sopwith observer had the use of a turret-mounted gun which could be fired in a field of 180 degrees.

The first Sopwith to be handed over to the squadron was smashed to matchwood within a few hours of delivery. Coppens had been counting on getting this one for himself, but a pilot named Orta, senior in rank and service, was the lucky man. Coppens subsequently had an argument with Orta, who claimed that Houthem field was no good for Sopwiths. It was far too small, and there was not enough landing space. Coppens thought this nonsense. He said that he could easily make a landing at Houthem with a dead engine. Orta tried to laugh it off, but Coppens insisted that he was right. Orta then wagered that Coppens would not do it three times in three different kinds of planes and still live.

It happened that Coppens was detailed for special duty involving the collection of illicit liquor from the base at Hondschoote. As part of his bet with Orta involved the use of a Farman, this seemed the ideal time to prove his point about landing at Houthem on a dead engine. Loaded with the precious liquor, he had to circle the area until all the pilots collected to watch him make his risky landing. Satisfied that he had a good audience, he calmly leaned forward, switched off the engine and let the plane fall in a dizzy twirling motion. A few hundred feet from the ground he leveled out, still on a dead engine, to make a perfect landing.

The first man to greet him was a breathless senior officer, obviously in search of an explanation. Behind him trotted Orta, making frantic signals and gestures. Coppens gravely apologized and lied that his engine really had cut out.

He still lacked the experience of using a plane in a fight. He had never been in a hand-to-hand fight of any account. On May 1, presented with a new Sopwith, he knew that his time had come— at last!

"We crossed the lines at Ypres, and steered obliquely for Langemarck. Over Houlhulst Forest we saw four German single-seater fighters climbing toward us. These we watched carefully, not to be taken by surprise; for, on the contrary, we wished to be the ones to open the ball. Suddenly we were attacked by four other black-crossed single-seaters whose approach had entirely escaped us. I heard the rat-tat-tat of a burst of machine-gun fire, and felt a violent blow on the side of my skull. A splinter from a bullet, split

open on one of my steel struts, had buried itself in my leather helmet, without, however, causing a wound. The burst had been well
aimed, and the Sopwith, in spite of all its good points rather slow
in maneuvering, was hit by close upon twenty bullets before I
could swing sharply right; for the smack had taken me on the left
side of my head. I did wisely; the burst had ripped along the left
side of the fuselage and engine cowling. Had I swung left, we
should have caught the full strength of the burst."

For a young man without very much previous experience Coppens already showed the experience of a veteran, due, in the main,
to a meeting he had with the French ace, Charles Nungesser. The
Frenchman, often wounded and always leaping out of the hospital
to rejoin his squadron even if he had to drag a plaster-encased limb
along with him, told Coppens some interesting things about the
art of fighting in the air. Coppens says: "Nungesser had pro-
pounded . . . this very sound argument: that a two-seater airplane,
when attacked over enemy territory by a single-seater possessed
of greater speed, must accept fight and turn steeply whenever the
single-seater dives upon it; the single-seater, in effect, can only fire
straight ahead, along its axis of flight; it follows that it cannot hold
a two-seater for long in its sights, if the two-seater twists and turns,
while the observer in the latter keeps the Scout under fire by means
of his movable gun."

Nungesser's words certainly saved the life of Coppens not once
but many times. Although this was strategy for the evader, the
tactics were immensely superior to the Immelmann turn, used for
attacking purposes.

"I remembered this piece of advice," says Coppens, "and kept
continuously turning—first one way and then the other—rarely
coming back for more than a second onto an even keel; for we
were subjected to repeated attacks from all four of our adversaries.

"At the first burst, hearing the crack of the bullets, I had the
impression that I was being sprayed with molten lead. Being under
fire is bad for the nervous system. I could do nothing by way of re-
taliation myself, having no machine gun, but my observer's fire,
maintained with the utmost calmness throughout, in short bursts,
was incredibly soothing."

Coppens and his observer, Captain Declerq, were both mentioned in dispatches for the cool way in which they fought the

enemy that day. The engagement lasted a total of four and a half minutes.

Among others who flew with Coppens, Thieffry was doing extraordinarily well for himself. In two months' flying with No. 5 Squadron, under the command of Captain Donis, he shot down ten Germans. It has been alleged that he was not as "finished" as certain other pilots, that he lacked a certain finesse, but he did get some amazing results. Sometimes this was because he lost his head at a crucial stage of the fight, adopting a bullish technique which literally knocked the German planes out of the sky.

He held an all-time record for crash landings, especially when flying two-seaters. Thinking to minimize his menace to observers, the authorities transferred him to single-seaters. Settling down to understand the peculiarities of the high-powered machine, he had a run of bad luck which brought his career almost to an end. He several times plummeted with his machine, splashing into the mud immediately in front of the trenches. Once, when he was being heavily shot up by enemy artillery, he sat in his machine, taking photographs of the flak and its effect on the plane. The prints achieved a wide viewing public; squadrons used them to deter younger pilots from being overenthusiastic.

Thieffry was twice shot down in flames. On the second occasion he was taken prisoner after a tigerish fight with German ground troops. In the stockade he tried to make a run for it three times and had to be watched day and night. The Germans admired him but treated him with the utmost caution. Like Coppens, he survived the war to become a pioneer in his particular field of long-distance flying. He lost his life in a typhoon over Lake Tanganyika. It happened some time after his headline-crashing air trip in which he sought to prove that it was possible to fly from Brussels to the Belgian Congo with a minimum of discomfort. His feat was the first signpost to a regular service which has endured to this day. But for Thieffry's daring approach to the possibilities of air travel, whole areas of the Congo would still be out of touch with the modern world.

Apart from Thieffry, whom he very much admired, Willy Coppens learned something of use from Pierre Braun of No. 5 Squadron. Braun was a man who treated a plane as though it was a trapeze. He could do practically anything with this structure of wood and wires. He originated many high-speed movements which other pilots copied and found useful in beating the Germans at their own game. Braun was only just starting his career as a fighter pilot, having two victories to his credit, when he crashed in the sea off La Panne and drowned before help could reach him.

Coppens' contemporaries were as colorful a group of young men as any to be found in the Allied air forces. Louis de Chestret, for instance, had amazing strength and perspicacity. Shot down and taken prisoner just after his second victory, he squirmed free of the prison-camp guards to turn up in Holland from where he made his way back to his squadron and flew again. Charles Ciselet, a tragic figure who lost three brothers, all pilots, fought his battles under terrible conditions, once conducting a singlehanded combat against five Fokkers while he himself streamed with blood from a deep chest wound. Teddy Franchomme, on the other hand, was a clown who wore riding breeches and massive horn-rimmed spectacles with plain glass lenses when on the ground. In the air he was a menace to the Germans. Jean-Marie Lambert, a man fated to have accidents throughout his career, suffered a peculiar mishap while still learning to fly at Étampes. Making an emergency landing in a field near the school, he jumped out of the cockpit and went forward to give the propeller a swing. The hot engine started up with a roar, pushing him over. He scrambled up in time to clutch hold of the tail assembly as it skidded past. He lost his grip and the machine soared up into the air without a pilot at the controls. It then nose-dived into the plowed soil, destroying itself noisily. Lambert trudged back to make light of his "accident." When this had been investigated, he faced a charge of negligence. His offer to pay for the airplane was accepted. Five louis a month was deducted from his pay. At the end of the war he was still paying. His final debt was never discharged.

There was a growing fashion of keeping dogs as pets. Most of the Allied soldiers, who were peacetime hound fanciers, had their mongrels, but the foreign air corps thought they would go one better. The Medaets were first, with two shaggy sheepdogs which they tended as prize animals, going to the most fantastic trouble to get meat for them. Once, when supplies were very short indeed, they borrowed a plane, landed behind German lines and raided an officer's mess for a joint of beef. Other animals were kept by Max

Orban, who had a bad-tempered fox terrier, and Edmond Desclée and Jacques de Meeus, who had sheepdogs. Another crack pilot, Roger d'Hendecourt, had an Airedale which he sometimes contrived to take along on air trips. But mainly the two men to introduce the idea of keeping dogs were the Medaet brothers. One day they discovered a muddy miserable collie wandering about on the battlefield. They took it back to the airfield, washed and fed it, then left it to rest. Two practical jokers, Robert de Leener and Maurice Siraut, crept up on it and paid off an old score against the Medaets by treating the collie to a classic poodle-cut.

These were great days for great men. Coppens knew that he was finally a part of a growing tradition. A romanticist at heart, he found a keen pleasure in seeing the machines take to the air.

"How well I remember those squadron departures," he says. "The machines are lined up, head to wind, on one side of the ground. One by one the engines are started by the mechanics, and one by one they are run full out for a few seconds to the accompaniment of a deafening din. They then subside into a leisurely purr, ticking over as regular as clockwork with that indescribable hollow cough now and then escaping from the twin exhaust pipes that run back along each side of the fat-bellied fuselage. The airscrews trace twinkling cockades in the air and flatten down the oil-soaked grass behind the machines in shining ripples.

"Fifteen airplanes are lined up there, fifteen rockets fitted with wings, all ready to take their departure. Fifteen pilots have lowered their goggles over their eyes and fifteen pairs of eyes—round eyes that stare fixedly—are focused upon infinity. The next instant, with a roar that sets the ground trembling, first one and then another of the line of machines lurches forward, gathers momentum and is gone. The whole sky slowly fills with their noise, as machine after machine leaves the ground and climbs upward. The first to leave circle while waiting for the remainder to take up station behind them and on either side, and almost before one has realized that the last has left, the whole formation is in v, heading for the lines and rapidly growing smaller and smaller, a compact, disciplined entity composed of specks, now being greeted with full military honors above the horizon. The sky becomes blotched with the dark clusters of shell smoke that spring up in front of and all around the invaders. Thirty machine guns aim their barrels into the depths of the enemy's lines, and before them the enemy's scouts disperse and dive—in the way that frogs around a pond plunge to safety on the approach of man.

"It is not such a very large step from this to a vision of the future. No very vivid imagination is needed to picture complete battalions at grips in the immensity of the heavens."

22

Alone Over Brussels

The Belgians always believed that they owed a considerable debt of gratitude to *Charles Nungesser,* the extrovert killer-pilot who fought the war for his native France, was wounded seventeen times but every day still managed to do some damage or other to German prestige, either by shooting down one or two Hun planes or crippling a few pilots. Flying with the *Stork Squadron,* he provided a dazzling example of just how fast a war could be fought and won in the air. Acknowledging how much they had learned from him, the Belgians eventually decided to give a banquet in his honor. *Coppens,* who was there, afterward wrote in his diary:

". . . the man . . . a square-set figure of medium build, very fair-haired, with eyes as blue as cornflowers—deep luminous eyes, whose glance impressed themselves upon the memory. His whole person expressed an indomitable energy, and in every way he was comparable to the heroes of medieval history whom we used to worship in our youth. Had he lived in those days he would have been canonized automatically."

Before the war Charles Nungesser was a well-known boxer. He therefore knew how to withstand punishment, staving off so much pain that even seventeen war wounds did not affect his career as a pilot. After his transfer to the air force from the Hussars he immediately smashed up a Morane and was taken to the hospital with two broken legs and a jaw that dangled loosely. He was out of bed in less than a month, using a pair of walking sticks to propel himself out to his plane. After that he shot down four Germans in less than four hours.

Nungesser was one of the few to meet and talk to the German spy *Mata Hari* when he was in Paris on leave. He saw her frequently, but openly scoffed at her clumsy probing questions. He knew quite well that she was a spy, double-dealing with both British and German intelligence services. He fed her some confusing information about the types of planes operating at the front. Mata Hari must have been a naïve kind of woman: she believed his story that the French had a new plane powered by eight supercharged engines!

While in Paris he also met such Americans as *Bert Hall, Bill Thaw, Raoul Lufbery, Jimmy McConnell,* later flying with many of them before returning to his own squadron. In this period he managed to shoot down a Fokker. The Americans were thrilled with him.

Now promoted to First Class Sergeant Major, Coppens "felt about as important as a country policeman," but he had cause to curse the Sopwith he was flying while awaiting a transfer to a fighter squadron. One day he was detailed to escort some photographic reconnaissance machines piloted by *Gaston de Mesmaeker, Louis de Burlet* and others.

"In one of these outings," he wrote, "the Orta-de Burlet machine, which should have left with the rest of us, was delayed in starting and followed on behind, intending to catch up with us. On its arrival at the lines, Louis de Burlet tapped *Orta* on the shoulder and signed to him to change direction slightly to the right. Orta next heard his observer's machine gun open fire and *de Burlet* then indicated to him with a wave of the hand a German airplane that was falling past, completely out of control. It was not the first occasion that de Burlet had shown proof of extraordinary coolness. The account I have set down is just as it was given to me when we landed, but I am afraid that, with the passing of the years, Orta's share in the proceedings may have assumed a greater importance.

"This success inspired me with a fierce longing to do likewise and bag my own enemy machine. *Captain Declerq* accepted my invitation to help me in this, and on July 7 we left together in search of adventure. Over Nieuport, I saw a two-seater bearing the telltale black crosses some 3,000 feet below us—at 9,000 feet. I dared not put my Sopwith into too steep a dive, and was therefore forced to go down in a broad spiral. Even so, at the speed the machine thus gathered, the wires screamed and the controls became terribly stiff. Assuredly, the *Sopwith* was no fighter plane."

With a cold shock Coppens found that he was accidentally on the tail of another German plane. He was quite unprepared, but then, one German was as good—or as bad—as another.

"So the dance began with my adversary streaking down in a wide spiral with me—seated as well as I could—on his tail. His observer opened fire on me, but none of his bullets reached their mark. Declerq confided to me afterward that, as he contemplated the scene from his cockpit behind me, unable to use his gun, it had seemed to him inevitable that one of the two machines would take the count—and more than probably ours! My machine got up a terrific speed, and I was compelled to switch off the engine, my propeller continuing to spin in the rush of air, windmill-fashion. The fire of my machine gun, which, being synchronized, depended upon my engine speed, slowed down considerably and the shooting appeared to me to occur at preposterously long intervals. In addition, the stiffness of the controls, unrelieved at the speed at which we were traveling, even with the engine off, prevented me from bringing my fixed gun to bear on its target as accurately as I should have liked, in spite of the fact that I was clutching the control lever with both hands. My goggles were of poor quality, and my eyes, inadequately protected by a ridiculously small windscreen, streamed with water. How long it lasted, I do not know. I suppose one, or possibly two minutes—I certainly did not count!

"Suddenly my quarry dived more steeply, and I found myself quite unable to follow. We were then at 4,500 feet over *Middel-kerque,* and it was time to think of going home. We returned without mishap."

From Coppens' description of the Sopwith in action, it is perfectly obvious that this must have been one of the most inadequate planes in use at the front. It also constituted a menace to pilots who liked to be masters of their own machines.

Posted to Les Moeres, Coppens at last became a member of the regular brigade of fighter pilots, flaunting their collective successes before the proud Germans. They were flying Nieuports with 120-hp Le Rhone engines, but Coppens found it practically impossible to get one of his own. He had to borrow a plane while conducting a personal campaign against the objections that no spare machines were available. When he did get into the air he practiced a series of daring new aerobatics, including a modification of the Immelmann turn, then becoming popular among the Allies.

"Looking back now," he said at the end of the war, "I realize too truly where I failed and the defects that prevented me from doing better than I did in air fighting." He was referring to the lack of facilities at Les Moeres, the slapdash method of allowing inexperienced pilots to find their own guiding stars. Perhaps he also remembered the day when he tried to loop a plane only to have it stall at the top of a wide circle, nearly throwing him out of the cockpit as empty cartridge cases and cockpit debris showered down all over him. No one told him that the Nieuport could be hard to handle.

Only half-prepared for combat, he met a German two-seater on July 21, 1917, attacked it with firm resolution, but achieved no result, though the German gave him the peppering of his young life. He cheered himself up by reflecting that he was in good company. Others did not even get away with such an experience.

His group now had neighbors. The *Cigogne* (Stork) squadrons of the French air force arrived to station themselves not far from Les Moeres. Commanded by Brocard, they included such men as Guynemer, Fonck, Auger, de la Tour, Heurtaux, Deullin and Raymond. The Storks started to scour the skies, knocking Germans down like ninepins, to the annoyance of the more sedate Belgians, who complained that they could not go out on a sweep without meeting their savage French counterparts somewhere in the sky. The French fought at about 120 mph, killing ruthlessly, and often getting wounded but still firing their defiant guns. It was a war to the death as far as they were concerned. They were by no means beginners at the job of slaughtering the Germans. From the first they treated Richthofen and his circus with disdain and abandon.

In the end they won through but the cost in French lives was too terrible to contemplate.

What really irritated Coppens was the regularity of promotion. The war, he thought, was in danger of becoming too complacent. Now that the novelty had worn off, he wanted only to fight and be fought against, rank or no rank. On August 19 he became a warrant officer. Yet while others of lesser rank were flying the newly arrived superior Spad—it was *the* fighting plane between 1917 and 1918—he was still trying to use a Baby Nieuport with its Le Rhone engine. De Meulemeester had a Nieuport, but on getting a Spad, he passed it on to Olieslagers. The machine was no favorite, so it ended up in the hands of Coppens.

This swapping about went on for several weeks until Coppens at last found a Hanriot for himself. It was not a very popular machine, but he felt grateful for anything. It had only one machine gun. He knew that the Italian ace, Captain Scaroni, had managed pretty well with it, while Baraca, another daring Italian pilot, had shot down thirty-six Germans from the cockpit of a Hanriot. On testing the armament, though, Coppens and his friends discovered just how erratic the gun could be. If it did not jam or seize up, it fired at the wrong moment, apparently selecting its own targets! A cow was killed, and a peasant complained that his spade handle had been split lengthwise by a stray bullet. Still, it was a gun and the only one available for the Hanriot.

Coppens was on leave at Delapre Abbey in Northampton, England, when tragic news reached him. Georges Guynemer was dead, killed somewhere near Poelcappelle a few days before, on September 10, 1917. Many men saw that the death roll was growing. Only a handful of pilots well versed in the wiles of the Germans remained to avenge those deaths. Coppens cut short his leave, determined to take his Hanriot in hand and convert it into a lethal instrument.

Arriving back at Les Moeres he was greeted with news of the death of two personal friends, Lieutenant Hanciau and Jules Goosens.

Things were now getting very bad, with every fatality list containing the name of some friend or other. The situation struck home when Olieslagers happened to be passing through the workshops one day and saw a mechanic French-polishing a newly finished grave cross. When he asked for whom it was intended, he received the answer: "The next." Not very long ago crosses were made only when an aviator was killed. They were now being mass-produced. An additional problem was presented by the women, wives of the pilots who somehow managed to smuggle themselves to the airfields, where they found billets in nearby villages so as to be close to their men.

Coppens, the aspiring avenger, was still far from fighting with the cold-blooded efficiency he desired. In October he had only six fights, most of them hit-and-run skirmishes. When he did shoot one plane down, his victory could not be confirmed. It galled him, especially as he was having trouble with his guns. On October 2, while patrolling with De Meulemeester, he attacked two single-seaters over Knocke, but chances of victory were lost when his guns would not fire at all. On October 10 they attacked five Albatros biplanes at 16,500 feet over Vladsloo. They were about to fire when the enemy turned tail and ran for it. It would have been a simple massacre had the Germans elected to fight. Coppens found that his guns were out of action again.

The war sometimes took a comical turn. On October 14 Coppens had a unique experience. He says: ". . . De Meulemeester and I sighted, flying in the neighborhood of Loo, at 14,400 feet, a group of twenty-five enemy machines that included ten large twin-engined biplanes of the Friedrichshafen type. We dived side by side, each picking out his nearest opponent. Going down almost vertically, my machine attained a terrific speed, and, after I had fired a burst from my machine gun at my quarry, I came, in my turn, under fire from a hostile single-seater that sought to interfere with my little game. Partly to avoid colliding with the twin-engined machine, and partly to escape from the dive of the single-seater, I pulled out from my dive rather sharply; and the tubular framework, supporting the seat I sat on, bowed to the onslaught of my person, and I found myself sitting on the bottom of the fuselage. In order to see outside, I had to hoist myself up with a struggle, only to find that my controls had jammed almost immovably under my weight. I had lost sight of De Meulemeester, and the only thing I could do was to fly home and land as best I might. The squadron greeted me with shouts of laughter; for they saw a machine come in and land, for all intents and purposes without a pilot."

When they were bored the pilots looked for diversions, the more daring the better. Some risked their necks to scare the enemy by using low-flying tactics. A few, like De Meulemeester, were content to curb their primitive instincts and have their planes painted various colors. De Meulemeester had his colored yellow. The "canary" became quite well-known, but not until the pilot suffered several narrow escapes from misguided artillery fire. Trying to familiarize gunners with the idea, he took his odd-looking machine on a "personal appearance" tour of the gun sites . . . and returned with a large selection of bottled beer and wine.

Believing that he, too, might acquire a similar haul, Coppens had his plane painted blue. "It was the ambition of every ace to have his plane painted a distinctive color. . . . My blue machine soon became known to the Germans, who were to nickname me 'The Blue Devil.' Even since our squadron had taken to having a white thistle uniformly painted on the fuselage of its airplanes, we had added distinctive markings near the tail to enable us to recognize one another. Pierre Dubois, a placid soul, chose a double 'broken' chevron in the form of lightning which earned him the sobriquet of 'Jupiter.'

"Our patrols of three airplanes each (Gallez, Dubois and De Meulemeester, Mevius and Kervyn de Lettenhove—and Olieslagers and his young pilots) were distinguished by the color of the engine cowls, which were painted white, yellow, green, etc., excepting my machine, which I insisted should remain blue throughout. The whims of a pilot after he had secured his fifth enemy machine met with nothing but approval—in time of war."

Contrary to popular belief, the battlefields of France were populated not only by soldiers but also by a variety of other people. Government officials, brass hats, the King and Queen of the Belgians, journalists—these and many more besides traveled from one sector to another in search of news and knowledge. Because the airplane had obviously become a useful war machine, airfields were always a favorite rendezvous of those with scientific minds. On November 15 Coppens' squadron suffered a unique experience. ". . . We received at Les Moeres," he wrote, "a party of American senators; I think they must have allotted us the Texas contingent, if appearances count for anything on the other side of the Atlantic. They wore enormous soft felt hats and generally looked like cowboys in their Sunday best. . . ."

Five days later tragedy laid a sudden shroud over Les Moeres airfield. Robert Ciselet, a promising young Belgian pilot, was on patrol over Caeskerke when five Albatros scouts suddenly thundered out of the clouds like a massive juggernaut, riddling his plane and body with bullets.

Gloom increased with the weather. The Germans could easily have taken the initiative. Coppens was just one of many who knew that at any single moment of the daylight hours a skillful enemy pilot might dive out of the low clouds and strafe Les Moeres, then make a swift turn and drop a few light-caliber bombs on the landing strip. If the Germans could do it, why could not the Allies? Coppens tried it out on three solo flights and failed. There was no sign of a target. The RFC, on the other hand, had better luck when Sergeant S. J. Clinch flew a Martynside by compass through blinding rain and mist to Ghent and Gontrode. It took several hours to find the airship sheds at Gontrode, but he finally took a chance and dropped two 112-pound bombs on the estimated points marked on his map. The Germans, needless to say, were furious.

Coppens was now possessed of an ambition which, on the face of it, was both risky and pointless. Quite simply, he wanted to fly over Brussels, an occupied, heavily defended city. His parents were there, but it was beyond hope that he would be able to see them from the air if he went through with the preposterous idea. There was opposition from senior officers, some of whom accidentally overheard him talking to his friends about the chances of hopping over one of the best-organized anti-aircraft emplacements in Europe and back again without being killed. Coppens did not think that the Germans would attempt to shoot down any plane while it was actually flying over the city. It could easily create massive damage, especially if it happened to be carrying a clutch of live bombs. On the other hand, the Hun might wait for the intruder to move toward the edge of Brussels, then attack with anti-aircraft guns and fast scout planes. Undeterred, Coppens went on conjecturing, estimating, but always believing that he must at least attempt the flight even if he failed. The night before he was due to take off, he trembled with excitement, but when the dawn came, after a sleepless night of turning over his chances in his mind, he felt calmer than he had ever been.

"Half an hour after leaving the ground, I was above Dixmude at 17,700 feet. Two French Spads were recrossing the lines, some distance below me, surrounded by German anti-aircraft shellbursts. I probably owed it to them that I was not greeted by the enemy's artillery, and passed across unnoticed.

"My lack of experience in flying over unknown country, and my fear of losing myself, made me describe a detour toward Bruges, whose red roofs I could see bathed in the sunlight. From there I followed the railway to Ghent and Brussels. While passing to the south of Ghent, over the Plain of Saint Denis, I suddenly sighted an airplane beneath me on my starboard quarter. I had been gradually going downhill and was at a height of 10,500 feet. My first impulse was to climb again as fast as I could, but I at once thought better of this, and, even as I caught sight of the black crosses, I dived upon my potential danger. At the same moment the enemy pilot saw me and went down at full speed. I had time to notice that the machine, a two-seater biplane, had no rear gun mounted. In all probability it was engaged in a test flight. At all events, it dived too steeply for me, and I realized that pursuit was hopeless; so I flattened out at about 9,000 feet and continued my journey.

"One has little idea of the thoughts that pass through the mind of a pilot venturing thus for the first time, alone, so far behind the enemy's lines, where he has only himself to count upon. I was pretty certain of my engine, and had not any very serious fear of a breakdown of the kind that would put a foolish stop to my flying career. In spite of this confidence, when I lost sight of the lines behind me, and the distant Yser, the lake of Blankaert, and the dim outline of Dixmude started to merge into the horizon, my sense of isolation so closed in upon me that I ceased to look back, preferring to keep my eyes fixed on my front at the risk of being surprised from behind. After all, my goal was Brussels, and nothing should turn me away from it. Had the German two-seater only deferred its appearance until I was over the capital, I should have gone after it to the bitter end. What a fight it would have been for all the town to witness! . . .

". . . Over Alost my height had fallen to 5,400 feet. I leaned forward in my seat and peered ahead, and there before me I saw the Palais de Justice of Brussels! At first I could hardly believe my eyes. It seemed scarcely possible that in a few minutes I should once again behold the streets and houses of my own town, that I should once again see my own house—and all those things, in fact, that I had not seen for close upon four years. . . . I was seized with emotion that literally hurt. Doubts assailed me: were my parents there? Should I see them? Certainly, I had had tidings from them— frequent tidings; the last card was dated from but a fortnight before. . . . And yet to us Brussels had appeared so far away, so inaccessible, during those long, weary months! The Germans were there, occupying the town in force, but I was going to snap my fingers at them. The thought gave me complete self-control, and I flew on with a smile on my lips until, my enthusiasm getting the upper hand, I burst into song; sang at the top of my voice. But I soon got out of breath, and, anyway, I could not hear myself.

". . . It was 9:52 A.M. when I arrived over the city, after making a detour toward the south to avoid flying over with the sun in my eyes. I passed over the Gare du Midi at a height of 2,400 feet, and dived suddenly, very nearly touching the roofs of the houses at the Porte de Hal, the outline of which, as I saw it then, will ever remain imprinted in my memory.

"The town appeared wonderfully white in the sunlight. . . . A succession of snapshots engraved themselves upon the retina of my eyes: the light-colored houses of the Avenue Louise where two streetcars were just passing each other; the green expanse of the city water reservoirs alongside the Parc Solvay, at Ixelles; and then the rue des Champs Élysées! A tall, white house with a red roof— *my* house! I dived still farther and flew past very low. I saw the shutters over the windows on the ground floor. Was the house oc- cupied? Immediately in front of the door, a man in a brown over- coat stood, motionless, his face toward me, turned up toward the airplane whose roar must have taken him by surprise. He must have seen the tricolor circles on my wings: the whole town must have seen them. Passing the house I banked over and turned sharply to the right. A window was open at the back—evidence of life. Still turning, I passed the house again, and saw the red reflection of the curtains of my study on the second floor: in there, hanging from the ceiling, was a model of an airplane that had hung thus ever since 1910—it was too far in for me to see it, but my thoughts flew to it!

"On the floor below, standing at the big window I knew so well, I saw the silhouettes of two women. It was quite impossible to recognize them; yet I was certain that one of them was my mother!

"Oh, that I could have stopped my machine and hovered motionless just to see more clearly! I went on turning.

". . . I again passed in front of my house, so low that I brushed the treetops in the Parc Solvay, and this time I saw, and *recognized,* my father, leaning from one of the windows in the roof, waving wildly to me. This time I went so close to him that I was even able to see the color of his tie. But I felt that his signs meant that I ought to go, and the thought was brought home to me that, if the Germans opened fire, they would not hit me but would injure the townspeople; for the shell splinters would fall back on the town. They would take advantage of that fact to fire all the harder, at random, on the houses, on the pretext of shooting at the airplane. Accordingly, I decided to leave. My heart was too full, in any case.

"I passed over the Palais Royal, and flew across the capital without a single gun having opened fire. My calculations had proved correct: owing to the fact that I had kept just clear of the roofs, I had only been visible to those immediately beneath me, and the fire-control posts had been unable to pick me up. If I did pass over any of these posts, I did so too quickly. Had I flown any higher, I should have given the enemy the time to locate me and take aim. . . ."

"My parents subsequently told me that half an hour after I had left, a German airplane began a lengthy patrol above the capital.

". . . I left Brussels at 10:05 A.M. . . . I was a speck low down in the distant sky. At first I struck too far north . . . thereafter I climbed slowly, and passed Ghent once more, whence I flew straight to Dixmude. . . . I slipped across the lines at Merckem at a height of 1,500 feet. I intended to wait there for a big German two-seater that I had seen a little while previously, leaving the ground, but it turned and went off toward Bruges, and it was quite hopeless to try and catch up with it. Feeling that I had done enough for one morning, I pointed my nose down, and glided into the airfield at Les Moeres, landing at 10:45 A.M., after a total time-in-air of no more than two hours and ten minutes."

He had breakfast, laughing almost hysterically from sheer reaction as his fellow pilots congratulated him on his feat, but his good humor and high spirits soon evaporated when he was given a note asking him to attend Colonel van Crombrugge's quarters as soon as possible. Shivering, he arrived—and walked out a few minutes later with the Colonel's congratulations sounding in his mind.

It is evident that very little operational coordination existed between the various Allied air powers which came together to defeat Germany. Up to a comparatively late period of the war, most of the air groups acted on their own initiative, but when confusion became embarrassing, an attempt was made at rationing out the air war. The CO of Coppens' group insisted that all pilots now fly in pairs, following the British method. Flights must be pre-notified and duly authorized. Under the revised regulations, every pilot had to carry out two patrols a day at specified hours. The only "optional extra" was a third patrol. Whether this was flown or not was left to the discretion of the pilot himself.

These rulings were discussed with the other squadrons in the area, and a mutual agreement arrived at. It was probably the best moment to revise procedure: a fresh generation of pilots had now arrived at the front and some of them came to Les Moeres. The Belgian aces each selected a new man in much the same way as Richthofen, Immelmann and Boelcke did right from the start. Jacquet, the CO, believed this to be the best time to weed out the undesirable ones and re-form the entire group. Not every new pilot was suited to this kind of life. Potential aces did not throng every airfield. The fighter pilot might not be temperamentally suited to scout patrols and vice versa. It was therefore economical to get the grading done.

Jacquet was a peculiar man; almost a recluse for long periods of time, coming out of his shell to do the irritating administrative work, throwing parties and flying on patrols with his men. He had a disconcerting personality and, unlike the rest, never expressed any firm opinion about the war. It was as though he was only a visitor to the front. His popularity did not increase when he decided to post Robert and Charles Gordinne and Alfred Mouton to other squadrons. They had not been with his group very long. From the start he made no secret of his dislike for their boyish spirits. Coppens was one of the few to agree with Jacquet. The Gordinnes and Mouton were not potential fighter pilots, but, as Coppens later remarked, "The Squadron lost a lot of its gaiety with the departure of the three . . . pilots."

No. 3 Squadron was formed under the command of Captain Hierneau, operating within the group, and pilots included Willy Heyvaert, Arsène de Launoit, Étienne Hage, Maurice Jamar and Victor Benoidt. Coppens was the man who demonstrated in practical terms to the fledglings that by far the best way of conducting an aerial war was to attack and go on attacking all the time. This, he said, applied especially to shooting down balloons. . . .

"No Belgian aviator had up to then shot down a kite balloon. Two or three had considered the possibility, but had not persevered with the idea. One of them had suggested using 'Le Prieur rockets' which the aviator had to light when in close proximity to the balloon. There were eight of these 'torpedoes'—four on either side, and they were fired by an electric switch; as soon as the switch was operated, the rockets lit up (literally enveloping the plane in flame), and then darted forward and set fire to the balloon—if the pilot had aimed correctly. The system had many drawbacks, and was superseded by incendiary bullets fired from machine guns. The best were of 11-mm caliber, but these could only be fired from the large-bore infantry-pattern Hotchkiss gun. One of our pilots had had a Hotchkiss mounted under his airplane, fixed to the undercarriage and arranged so as to fire outside the arc of the propeller. But all that was experimental and was never adopted. At the period of which I am writing, we only had incendiary ammunition of 7-mm caliber, suitable for our Vickers guns. Commandant Jacquet had conducted tests, as it happened, a few days before this, and these had shown that a number of incendiary bullets of this caliber had proved incapable of setting fire to a small balloon filled with hydrogen gas, even though they had successfully set fire to a tin of gasoline. On the other hand, in 1918, balloon attacks were considered highly dangerous on account of the anti-aircraft fire, which was very violent, and, so it was said, almost certain to hit one at the low height at which these balloons 'flew.' "

The day dawned when Coppens had a chance of proving his theories about destroying German balloons. One of them was a constant nuisance to the Allies generally. Known as the Bovekerke balloon, it directed enemy fire on two important points at Regersvliet, always forcing the Belgian Cavalry Division back at a time when progress was badly needed. Pressure from the Belgians on the ground to the Belgians in the air was tremendous. It was absolutely necessary to retake the positions; something must be done, and the only way to do it was by destroying the observation balloon. When Jacquet called for volunteers, Coppens and Charles de Motigny were first in the queue. Coppens did not know what he was letting himself in for.

"In order to reduce the length of time necessary to reach the balloon, which was flying at some 3,000 feet about four miles behind the German lines, I climbed to 7,500 feet, and from that height dived at full speed for the gasbag, which was immediately whipped down to the ground at the topmost speed of its motor winch, while the anti-aircraft guns in the vicinity let fly at me for all they were worth. More than a hundred shells were pumped into the balloon, while the Germans did their best to get in some ground fire at the invaders. They were using the vicious 20.10-mm-caliber ammunition with incendiary and luminous bullets of 2 inches in length."

He decided to try again.

"In a flash the balloon was in front of me, increasing in size at every second. When it appeared absolutely enormous, I let it have it, and at the same moment the two observers jumped out in their parachutes. I had opened fire at a range of about 600 feet, and continued firing until within 150 feet, when I pulled up my nose and passed over the balloon. Flying away, I banked around and came back again, again firing as I approached. I fired more than eighty rounds—all incendiary—but the balloon did not catch fire. . . ."

Ground fire forced him to take evasive action.

". . . I was at a bare 3,000 feet, but they did not hit my machine. Whereupon, carried away by my feelings, I let myself go and began to indulge in a series of loops to tantalize the enemy. . . ."

Montigny had no better luck but he certainly did have some closer shaves than Coppens. The balloon was hauled down, out of range of Montigny's mischief, and the Regersvliet position taken in a daylight raid.

The Germans valued their observation balloons at about $4,000 each.

Later in his career Coppens had the unsteadying experience of actually landing on top of a balloon and taking off from it without even scratching himself. He says: ". . . I attacked the Houthulst balloon at a height of 3,900 feet. . . . Although I fired three times at it at point-blank range, it did not catch fire. To make more certain, I slowed down, flying horizontally, and approached—firing at the last half-second. Then, as though relieved of a weight, it suddenly shot up and I collided with it. My wheels struck the gasbag, which gave under the shock, although it capsized my machine and my tail rose up into the air. My right wing also touched the envelope and for a second I pivoted on my nose, while the balloon sagged and sank under the weight. I had the presence of mind to switch the engine off with the control-lever switch, and my airscrew, which had been turning over slowly, stopped dead. At this moment, I said to myself (in the following actual words): 'That's the end! It is bound to happen to those who dare risk too much.'

"The next instant my machine began to slide across the spongy thing that gave way beneath me as we advanced, until it plunged under the 'side,' nose first, gathering speed as it fell. The propeller started spinning like the wings of a windmill in a puff of wind; I took my thumb off the button switch on the control lever, opened the throttle and—my machine scarcely any the worse for its experience—took to my heels for our lines, while the balloon, torn and leaking, fell to the ground, where it luckily burst into flames, to such good purpose that the conflagration was seen from our lines and the victory could be credited to me.

"The tale of my adventure left many people unconvinced. It was necessary for me to point to the traces of white 'down' from the side of the gasbag on my lower wing and the front right-hand interplane strut, as well as the marks on the wood of my propeller of the outline of a cord, struck by one blade, before I could convince the doubters, of whom the most obstinate was Olieslagers. Finally, the observer posts in the line sent in their reports confirming the destruction."

23

No Pilot Worth His Salt . . .

For some weeks Coppens acted as "delivery boy" to a boyhood friend of his serving in the army and now stationed at a desolate observation post not far from the airfield. Parcels, notes, were dropped, and several times Coppens even found time to stage an amusing one-man flying display for the bored soldiers. One day, after trying to understand why they were waving frantically at him, he saw, high overhead, one predatory German plane evidently waiting for him. A Belgian anti-aircraft gun took up the cudgels for him, putting up a modest barrage and trying to help De Meulemeester and a few others who were flying on escort duty. De Meulemeester had a narrow escape when he wriggled into an attacking position in front of the German. At that moment his gun gave out a useless clicking sound. He could only take evasive action until Coppens was able to climb up to help him. The German fought like a terrier, evading the Belgians and leading them away on a high-speed chase at treetop height over Allied and enemy lines.

Calling off the chase because their planes were hopelessly outclassed by the Hun, Coppens shot off at a steep tangent to start hunting the enemy in his own fashion. He was still rising, surveying the scene, when, without warning, his engine cut out. He was 9,000 feet above the ground, almost stationary in a silent world with only the muted sound of the wind as it roughly buffeted the fuselage. The coast was nearby. He decided to make for it and risk a crash landing while there was still time. In a long slow glide, he finally passed over the upturned faces of the anxious troops. He felt that there was something odd about the situation, something he could not quite explain.

A moment after the machine ground to a jerky halt in the coarse sand, he realized that he had mistakenly landed between the lines. The German field guns were leveling at him from a point about a mile and a half away. He stood a fair chance of being shot to pieces unless he ran before they started firing. He only had two minutes, less perhaps, to save his own life. He got out of the cockpit, calmly at first, but as panic seized him, he started to scramble toward the Allied lines. He had not taken more than ten steps when he heard the hideous express-train whistle of an approaching shell. German marksmanship was only fair that day. He looked over his shoulder to see the shells burst within a radius of fifty yards of the grounded plane. Sand was ripped up and showered over him as he went on toward the sheltering dunes on his hands and knees.

Locating the Belgian troops, he asked the men whether they would volunteer to recover the machine. It was too valuable to lose like this. They could not sit there and watch the Germans blow it up. He had a small group of volunteers around him when an officer protested. Coppens must be mad, thinking that he could get the machine out of such a situation with German guns covering it. Coppens went on arguing until nightfall. In the end he talked them into it, and, as soon as night fell, he took a group of infantrymen out toward the machine. It was quietly stripped down and the parts carried to a safe place, out of range of enemy guns. He believed that he would be able to repair the choked fuel system before dawn, then fly the plane home. He was counting on making a quick take-off while the Germans were having their breakfast.

There was nothing more he could do, so he went back to his squadron, arriving after midnight. After a couple of hours' sleep he drove back through the early morning mists to Coxyde where the plane was stranded. Full of misgivings about the next hours' work, he parked his motorcycle some distance away and walked the remaining distance. Then, as he struggled over the crumbling dunes, he was halted by the roar of an airplane engine—his own! The infantry had been tinkering with it throughout the night, though practically none of them knew anything about the intricacies of such engines. It was all ready for the air. He leapt into the cockpit, waved his gratitude, and was aloft within a few seconds, twirling about and mock-strafing the German emplacements along the coast.

Coppens was an odd man in some ways. He disliked being decorated. He was to receive many orders and decorations, always against his will. Some weeks after the beach incident he was amazed to hear that he had been awarded the Croix de Guerre merely because he had flown 200 hours over the lines. His bitter complaints that many other pilots had achieved much more galled the authorities. They told him to shut up and take what was being offered.

His fighting technique was now impeccable. He had taken part in thirty-six engagements, though not always with great success, as he himself often admitted. The German planes were tough; they could take severe punishment. There was only one course open to him. He would hold his fire until he was really close to them.

"As I raced toward the enemy group (of twenty-one planes) with my throttle wide open, followed by Captain Gallez, I saw an enemy single-seater leave the group and head back for the lines. This was the machine to be attacked, outclassed and overcome! I drove forward to cut it off, and, controlling my desire to open fire prematurely, waited until it shot across my bows. Then I gave it to him, good and plenty, and had to rear violently to avoid ramming him, so close were we. Immediately, I tried to run an attack again, but my cursed machine gun had jammed. The enemy machine was going down spectacularly in a succession of nose dives followed by rocket-like zooms and somersaults. I followed with difficulty, while I struggled with my machine gun—and my adversary struck the ground between Ramscapelle and Slype."

Squadron life was cheerful enough because of the new blood injected by an enthusiastic younger generation of fliers. Among them was Gusto de Mevius, a tough, hard fighter, who was to kill Germans like flies. His only sin was that he had the bad habit of whistling off key. There were many violent attempts to cure him, including a couple of water showers as he lay in bed. In desperation, when he remained uncured and whistled louder than ever, they awarded him the final insult of the "Paddington Cup," a chipped teacup "borrowed" from the famous London railway station. Still he whistled. The one thing that did eventually put a stop to it was marriage. He never whistled again.

Other pilots had their own interests. There was a bridge school which drove the card-game haters mad with its air of cozy seclusion and concentration. Those who owned dogs took their animals for sedate walks round and round the perimeter of the airfield. Olieslagers decided to start gardening. His allotment had to be walled around to keep the others out, and here he spent his afternoons, when flying was out of the question, tending his carrots, radishes and lettuces. Once, when it looked as though the advancing Germans might easily overrun the airfield, he ignored the others, who told him that he was wasting his time. He gravely assured them that they would soon be eating Olieslagers' salads, Germans or no Germans. Several months later they did sit down to eat produce gathered from the famous garden. He believed that working on the land brought an unusual tranquillity. He was probably right.

One of the great losses to No. 2 Squadron was Pageot, a daring young Breguet pilot who was shot down and taken prisoner. Like many of the others, he had a dog of his own, a ferocious mongrel crossbred terrier which always tried to fend for itself. The animal was inconsolable when Pageot failed to return. Day after day it waited on the edge of the airfield, seeing the Breguet XIV's safely in and watching for a familiar figure which never appeared. The dog was so intelligent that it never came out of its kennel to watch other aircraft.

Promoted to Second Lieutenant at the same time as De Meulemeester, Coppens knew only one fear, the cold horror of having his engine fail him when he was traveling at high speeds. After his flight over occupied Brussels—a flight which was now legend —he believed that he was capable of doing practically anything. Moreover, he had faith in his battered old Hanriot. Searching for the chance of doing away with his own doubts, he pleaded for the chance of undertaking a special mission, any flight which called for that extra something.

He was passed over time and again because the authorities considered him much too valuable a pilot to waste on such suicidal missions as landing spies behind enemy lines or dropping messages. It was the same old story of waiting and hanging about, trying to stave off the paralyzing boredom.

Of course, he could always go on fighting the balloons. He did this almost daily for the sake of being able to fly, but on one mission over Dixmude he "felt a tremendous jolt that shook the whole machine, and my engine stopped dead. This engine being a rotary one, this meant a mass of close upon 200 pounds turning at 1,200 revolutions per minute, with the propeller. A rocker-arm bracket had broken, and the rocker arm had cut through the cowl enclosing the engine throughout its circumference, and the cowl had crumpled up and become wedged between the muzzle of my machine gun and the engine. My machine almost turned over under the blow; thereafter, there was silence, and I glided down with a favoring wind at my back and landed at Les Moeres. My plane had no cowl, but was otherwise intact. The engine had to be changed, and the machine gun also."

While he was away on a leave granted by reason of his recent promotion, he received a sinister-looking "present" from a Captain de Briey of the French Aeronautical Supply Department. It was a modified Vickers machine gun of 11-mm caliber, using incendiary ammunition. Coppens thought it "marvelous" and more than twice as useful as the ordinary 7-mm caliber. He had it mounted on his Hanriot, then went straight out to meet any patrolling Germans. The result was chaotic. His gun chewed one Hun into pieces in mid-air.

He was still using the new gun while flying with five other Belgian fighter pilots when he was tossed into an experience which proved to be one of the most savage he had ever known.

"Six against six. De Meulemeester, Kervyn de Lettenhove, Kervyn de Meerendre, Maurice Jamar, a pilot of 11 Squadron (named, I believe, Lamarche), and I, against six German single-seaters, that we surprised over our lines (at last!) where they were obliged to stand and fight. Of course, the westerly wind, so often against us, caused us to drift too quickly toward the German lines, where the enemy dived away and disappeared, flying close to the ground. We certainly stuck to them as best we could, but the fight ended without result on either side. . . .

"There were one or two amusing situations while it lasted. I remember a German machine that I was pressing hard, looping over my head, while I, myself, was caught from behind and had to follow suit to avoid a determined assault."

It was a moral victory, not a physical one. A few nights later the Germans took their revenge by pattern-bombing the Belgian field. With the hangars blazing like furnaces, pajama-clad pilots and mechanics risked a scorching as they dashed through the thick smoke, trying to drag their prized machines to safety. It was a hopeless idea with the enemy still circling overhead, waiting for a chance to drop another load of bombs. Some of the hangars had to be abandoned. Six aircraft were totally destroyed, many more were damaged. As the drone of the German engines grew less and the smoke and flames lessened, De Meulemeester sat down at the piano in the mess and quietly fingered out a popular song. The others left him alone and crept back to their beds. He stayed where he was until dawn, when he was found slumped over the keyboard, fast asleep. It took five days for new planes to arrive. Meantime, while the mess of charred girders was cleared away, Coppens received a brand-new Hanriot, but it was badly camouflaged. He told the mechanics to paint it an over-all blue. De Meulemeester followed his usual whim by having his new machine painted a bright yellow.

A day or two later, trying to down a German observation balloon, Coppens flew straight into the center of an Anglo-German air war being fought at 4,500 feet. Uncertain of what was happening, he went past the British machines as they massed for a fresh attack. Within a few seconds he was passing under another formation, but could not see which side they belonged to. He waved at the pilots. They waved back at him. He was banking to move away out of the area when he looked again at the machines. They were Germans. He fled for home. Other people's wars were no concern of his.

Coppens was becoming a definite nuisance to the Germans. His blue plane had been recognized and identified, his name was known to the enemy. He was on the "wanted" list. The Germans plotted to stage his execution in the best Teutonic taste by putting an explosive balloon up over Zarren. He was bound to attack it. A man of his temperament could not resist it. Special precautions were taken to keep the plan secret. The balloon was a massive booby trap, loaded with explosives. One bullet would make it into an aerial bomb. The blast would engulf a plane.

Hearing about it through Allied intelligence channels, Coppens decided to take off without obtaining permission. He arrowed his way through the clouds to give the "bomb" a treat of incendiary bullets. He arrived when the balloon was only halfway up to its ceiling. It took about ten seconds to get it in his sights. He pressed his trigger and there was a huge explosion which filled the vicinity. The plane was snatched up and nearly torn apart while the balloon fell to the ground, a fireball in itself, killing and injuring a large number of German staff officers who had gathered to watch Coppens fly to his own destruction. It was one of the neatest, best-timed attacks of the war.

The price of Coppens' success—he was also involved in several fights which were publicized in the newspapers—was considerable. He was becoming well-known, famous even. He once met a soldier who claimed that Coppens—yes, the famous Coppens in person—had stood him many drinks. Some time later, while at La Panne having his hair trimmed, the barber related some bizarre stories about Willy Coppens. Coppens was not angry, just sad.

He was disturbed by the antics of the newly trained pilots now joining the group in strength. They seemed so irresponsible, especially regarding the care of their machines. He was beginning to feel old compared with these youngsters and only the well-meant suggestion proffered by Olieslagers that he, too, was once like the newcomers brought him to a point where he could smile at his own seriousness.

Flying accidents were due to carelessness these days. Arsène de Launoit, an experienced pilot, one day slithered his plane in from a raid, buckling the undercarriage. The rest, sunning themselves on some grass, got up and ran to see if he was hurt. He was found sitting in the fuselage as though it was a hip bath. The affair was treated as a joke until the harsh-mannered Commandant Dhanis arrived. To the discomfited De Launoit he shouted: "When one has been clumsy enough to smash up his machine, he stays by it to superintend its dismantling!"

Three days later the pilots were again sunbathing when a Sopwith of No. 3 Squadron tried to make a puttering, ineffective landing, failed and landed with all the clumsiness of De Launoit. Going out to the scene to see if the pilot was hurt, they found Commandant Dhanis sitting in the collapsed cockpit. His face was scarlet, he was quite speechless as he climbed out of the wreck and marched away, with Max Orban shouting after him: "Mon Commandant, I thought that in your squadron, when a pilot was clumsy enough to smash up his machine, he stayed by it to supervise its dismantling!"

Coppens now became involved in a dubious incident. He was approached by the Army Cinematograph Section to fly the key plane in an instructional film about aerial warfare. Investigating, he found that the film might easily leak out and perhaps be shown to the public as a record of a real battle. He told the others that he would not go in for this false morale boosting. The rest were dead set against the venture. Their mass refusal to cooperate caused a stir, especially when they threatened to talk to the newspapers about it. The authorities had no choice but to abandon the project.

Combat was now very infrequent, but on September 1 Coppens searched out a serried layer of German kite balloons. He zoomed along over them, waiting for the German artillery fire, suspecting a trap. The trap was not sprung. The Germans seemed to have fallen asleep. He glided down for a closer look at about 3,000 feet, conscious of a thick layer of concealing cloud just above him. If they did start firing, he would be able to climb straight into it and make his escape.

Next day he went back again to discover that the Germans had introduced a new device which he had never seen before. Strings of smaller balloons were hung all around their bigger counterparts, forming a barrage against attack. He decided to shoot his way through the "protective layer," then, on second thought, knew how foolhardy that would be. Only a single cable need become tangled with his airscrew and he would be brought to a dead stop. He was sickeningly familiar with the sight of a pilot being wrenched out of the cockpit without any hope. As soon as he arrived back at his own airfield, he asked to see all recent reports on German balloons. There were more of them about these days, and army reports showed that they were hampering Allied troop and supply movements, putting many of the important roads under constant shellfire. Casting about for an ally in the destructive task which must be undertaken, he spoke to Commandant Gallez, who jumped at the chance of flying with him. With penciled plans drawn by Coppens, whose memory of the balloon layout was still fresh after his two flights, the pilots planned their campaign. First, they would approach to within a mile and a half of the lines and then check the position of all the balloons. As soon as they felt satisfied with the situation, they would climb to a higher altitude well above the cloud layer. The objective would be within seven miles. The most hazardous part of the attack, in Coppens' estimation, would be the moment when they made a simultaneous dive through the clouds or found a gap giving some visibility of the scene below.

A few moments before they started their engines Gallez mentioned to Coppens that he had never taken part in a balloon raid before. He only hoped that he would be adequate. Taken aback, Coppens cross-examined him about his actual experience. The minutes ticked by. Gallez muttered that he had shot down one German plane. Coppens decided to risk it.

"Everything at first went according to plan," Coppens reported later. "We climbed above the clouds and went on our respective ways, Gallez steering southeast and I northeast. I kept him in sight, and as his machine stood out clearly against the blue sky, this was easy. But why did he not dive? Surely he must have reached a point, as I had done, just in front of the target. We were wasting time, and I began to fear that they would pull the balloons down; for the noise of our engines must have been audible beneath the clouds. Finally, he dived, and from then on I thought no more about him. I dived, too, and as, owing to my earlier preoccupation with the fortunes of my partner, I had not been able to watch my own course as carefully as I should have liked, I found myself, on emerging from the clouds over Stampkot, exactly above the balloon; that is to say, too literally above it—so much so that I had to dive absolutely vertically on it, and my speed became enormous. The balloon appeared to fly at my face, increasing in size at an extraordinary rate. I had time to fire one round and no more, and then had to pull out of my dive with a jerk, narrowly missing a collision. With my engine full on, I shot away to the north, toward my second balloon, followed by the shells, whose black bursts leaped into existence all around me, and the 20-mm 'flaming onions' with their snaking milky trails curving away behind them.

To my ears there came the intermittent crackling of the small-caliber machine guns, whose invisible bullets whistled about me, accompanied by the angry *woof!* of the shells. . . .

"Three minutes later, I set the second balloon on fire, over Wercken, and at once started home. But, chancing to look toward the south in search of Gallez, I saw my first balloon, and his, both intact!

"What could have happened? Gallez told me later that he had drifted and come out of the clouds too far from the balloon. As for me, I had come out too much on top of mine, and my solitary bullet, although an 11-mm one, fired vertically downward, had not succeeded in setting it on fire. Or, perhaps, in my anxiety to avoid colliding with the gasbag, I had pulled my machine out of its dive as I fired. In which case I had missed the balloon altogether. But it was not too late to retrace my steps and cover once more the five or six miles separating me from it, and 'roast' the wretched thing before they hauled it right down! I might even be able to set Gallez's balloon off!

"Without further deliberation, I swung around to the south, and suddenly saw a strange object, apparently bearing down upon me at high speed, which I almost immediately recognized as a kite covered in white silk. It was, of course, stationary, supported by the wind, and its apparent forward movement was due to the fact that I was approaching it at a speed of over 120 mph. I immediately pulled my nose around and up, and began a spiral climb to avoid the apron of steel cables that I guessed must be stretched between the kites surrounding the balloon I had just sent down in flames. The enemy must have been bitterly disappointed not to have caught me in this practically invisible snare, that a pilot, flying at full speed, could not hope to avoid or detect. I continued my spiral descent under fire—a most unpleasant experience! I thought no more about my first missed balloon, climbed into the clouds, and made my way home."

Some time later Coppens was sent for by General Headquarters and taken to the mansion at La Panne by staff car. He was more at home scorching along these same roads on his motor-cycle. It was a new experience to be transported in this grand style! On arrival he was saluted by a complete battalion of infantry, then invested with the Cross of the Legion of Honor and the French

Croix de Guerre in the presence of the King and Queen of the Belgians, the Royal Princes and Georges Clemenceau. During the ceremony he very typically had trouble with his badly fitting helmet which kept wobbling about on his head. As soon as the ritual was over he took it off and had a few words with various people, carrying his headgear by the strap, like a bucket. Of course, he naturally had a complaint to make: why was De Meulemeester being forgotten? He, too, should have some decorations. Thieffry, too, should be recognized. Thieffry was, of course, very busy at that moment trying to escape from a German prison camp. Since nobody could answer his questions, he made his way around to the stores and scrounged a gallon of salad oil for the squadron which had been deprived of that condiment for weeks. It made his journey worthwhile.

Granted leave—a perquisite when one was decorated—he threw a suitcase into his plane and decided to fly to Calais where he would park the machine and catch the Channel ferry to England. So fascinated was he by the flight over new territory that he went straight on, past Calais. Over Cap Gris-Nez his engine suddenly seized up. Swearing violently, he made a sweeping landing in the teeth of a young gale, keeping the nose of his plane down only with the greatest difficulty. After a tussle, he landed at breakneck speed in a pool of water which fortunately cushioned his fall. Recovering from the shaking up, he struggled out of the cockpit to find a group of British officers playing polo on the beach. Some of them had a knowledge of airplanes. They tried to patch the machine up, though without much luck, so he left them to it and trudged off to find the nearest airfield.

At Buc he walked into the airfield to find it littered with all kinds of new, interesting machines, including the Hanriot HD3 Fighter fitted with a 260-hp Salmson engine. There was also the HD1, built for the use of the Italian air force. After a few trial spins in the Hanriot, he felt so delighted with its capabilities that he tried to obtain a few for the use of his own squadron. He was, of course, unsuccessful. Hanging around, waiting for his own machine to be repaired, he noticed that a miniature "field gun" was being developed in one of the sheds. It had a short barrel designed to fire through the hub of the airscrew with a Bowden cable trigger release.

"It had to be loaded before one left the ground," he wrote in his diary, "and could fire one round only, and that a cartridge weighing just about a pound containing thirty-two spherical bullets —each (if my memory serves me) of a diameter of 16mm. The gun and its firing device weighed just under 10 pounds. I was immensely taken with this weapon. As it held but one round, it would be essential to fire at point-blank range, and the thirty-two bullets, covering as they would a sufficiently large area to be pretty certain of striking a vital part, would work havoc on an enemy machine. . . ."

As far as is known, the weapon was never put into general use.

From a taxi driver in Paris he learned that he had been awarded an American medal in recognition of his work at the front. Practically every newspaper in Paris carried the news. The honor was bestowed by the Aero Club of the United States of America. He felt that he was now being loaded with undeserved honors, and wished that people would stop recognizing him on the streets. Old ladies kept coming up to him to talk about his experiences at the front. The only places where he could find peace were his own hotel room and the lavatory. When the mechanics at Buc failed to prepare his plane for the rest of his flight, he decided to get out of Paris and stay with trusted friends at Prunoy, in the Yonne. To get to that area he had to forge a special leave pass for himself. "In time of war an ace could do pretty well anything; for he was a spoilt child. But let him beware, the moment hostilities cease," Coppens told his friends.

Throughout most of his career Coppens was a second lieutenant in the Special Reserve, but after returning from leave he was gazetted a second lieutenant in the regular army and promoted to lieutenant. This baffled him; he never did understand clerical connivings. It amused him so much that when he was asked to select a section of the army from which he could be officially seconded to the flying corps, which was neither service nor regiment, he looked through a long list which showed the various rates of pay. At last he found the best paid proposition and applied to be seconded from the Army Chaplain's section! This led to an uproar among senior administrators, who accused him of being irreligious. Trying to pacify them, he agreed to let himself be seconded from the 2nd Grenadiers, his original regiment. To his astonishment, he was told to wear regimental badges. He capitulated with poor grace. As soon as all the fuss died down, he took the badges off his tunic and became an ordinary pilot again.

He was not long in gaining his thirty-first victory when he shot a German down near Leffinghe. Two days later he bagged another one in exactly the same spot. It nearly cost him his life, for a patrolling British plane pounced on him and started shooting. He had been mistaken for a German several times, but this man meant business. He longed to send a few hot shots back at that lumbering old RE8. Only patriotism stopped him as he saw the "Allied" observer triumphantly swinging his gun around. Furious, he managed to get back to base where he sat down and wrote out a strong report which was sent by special courier to the British. In due course he received a cool apology. The observer in question was a beginner and not very well up on the shapes of airplanes. They promised that it would not happen again. In fact, it happened all the time. Some men were not quite as lucky as Willy Coppens.

The entire squadron mourned the loss of Commandant Donis when his Spad engine cut out on a trip back to the airfield. He had just fought a glorious action singlehanded, flying back with his head—metaphorically, at any rate—in the clouds, and he was unable to lengthen his gliding approach to the landing strip. The Spad hit the ground at about 100 mph. Donis was killed instantly.

Death was frequent, and not always due to misjudgment or poor flying. In many cases it was sheer bad luck. Coppens himself once landed on the water-strewn sands at La Panne. He was unhurt, and a fisherman with a horse and cart drove out and picked him up. He reached dry land without even wetting his flying boots. An hour later he returned with a group of grumbling mechanics. Together they managed to heave the plane out of the pool in which it had been sitting like a sad duck, but it fell straight into another one. Feeling more and more irritated, Coppens shouted at them for their inefficiency. He was in the middle of his tirade when he was struck by the peculiar expressions on their faces as they listened to him. His voice trailed away. Conscious that somebody was standing behind him, he slowly turned to find the King of the Belgians watching. The head of the nation smiled, listened to his apologies, and then made some practical suggestions for getting the machine out of the quicksand.

The balloon menace was as great as ever. Because he was now

classed as an expert, Coppens was selected to lead an attack on
kite balloons at Thourout. They were standing at about 1,800 feet
when he arrived. It was a swift attack. He placed four rounds in
a Praet-Bosch balloon, which shot up to 2,400 feet. There was
a great deal of ragged artillery fire which he did his best to evade.
He made a detour and went in to get at another balloon at about
900 feet when he "heard the vicious bark of the small-caliber
machine gun. I was about 450 feet away, when I felt a terrible
blow on the left leg. An incendiary bullet, after passing through
the thin planking of the floor, had struck my shinbone, smashing
everything in its passage and inflicting a wound all the more painful
for the fact that the bullet, being hollow, had flattened, becoming
in effect a dumdum bullet. The muscles were torn apart, the bone
shattered, and the artery was cut in half.

"So great was the pain that my right leg became rigid, stretched
out to its full extent with the result that my rudder bar was kicked
violently forward on that side (my left leg being without say in
the matter, limply inert) and my machine swung around and went
into a spin. Simultaneously, my hand clutched the trigger control
on the control lever (for I had been on the point of opening fire),
and for several seconds my gun spat bullets in every direction,
hose-fashion, until at last my grip relaxed. The first of these bullets,
at least, hit the balloon, which burst into flames; but that was a
thing I did not know at the time, and I did not claim as a
victory. . . .

"My only thought at the time was of how to get back to our
lines. I could have landed at once, in enemy territory, but that
was a thing no one worth his salt would have dreamt of doing. So
long as his airplane continued to fly, and his heart to beat, a pilot's
only thought in such a case was to get back—to recross the lines.

"My rudder bar was fitted with straps at each extremity, and
my feet passed under these straps. This prevented my left leg from
jamming the bar, and allowed me to work the rudder with the
right foot alone. I was in this way able to bring my machine out of
its spin after it had described two or three turns. . . .

"One inlet pipe on my engine had been perforated by another
bullet, and my revolutions had fallen slightly, but Houthulst Forest
was gradually drawing nearer. I still had five miles to cover before
reaching our lines—call it six, before I should be clear of the
enemy's fire. At the speed at which my engine was turning this

occupied three minutes, during which I could feel the severed artery beating furiously. A sweat on my forehead made me snatch down my goggles, so that they remained hanging around my neck, and pulled off my fur-lined cap, and nothing would have parted me from it; with an effort, I stuffed it under my coat. On the other hand, I tore off and shed my silk muffler protecting my face from the cold. I wanted air, ice-cold air, to bathe my face and keep me from fainting.

"I had the impression that I was a hunted animal, and longed for the firing, incessantly dinning in my ears, to end. I felt my strength forsaking me and fought against it desperately. I wanted at all cost to avoid falling into the hands of the enemy.

"At last the firing died out. I was home. . . . At the end of my strength, unable to go any further, I landed near Essen, to the east of Dixmude. I chose a small field by the side of the road, on which a fair amount of traffic told me that I should soon obtain help. The field, all too small, was hemmed in with hedges, and I had to put my machine down rather heavily in order to arrest its progress. My undercarriage, which had been badly weakened by the machine-gun fire, collapsed on contact with the ground. The machine had, indeed, been pretty badly shot about all over. I learned later that the pivot holding the rudder bar had been cut through . . .

"As soon as my machine came to rest, I saw stretcher-bearers forcing their way through the hedge, hurrying to my rescue. They at once started ripping open the fuselage of my airplane, which caused me some concern; the feelings of a pilot are very much those of a horseman toward his mount. They experienced some trouble in disengaging my left foot from the strap that held it to the rudder bar, and the pain was acute. I heard one man say that I had lost a tremendous amount of blood. Then they laid me on a stretcher. . . ."

While in hospital, following the amputation of one leg, he had plenty of callers. Even the King came to visit him when they transferred him to Brussels. Special facilities were arranged for his parents to come and see him. Thieffry, now free, also arrived, and brought a very special present for his old friend. It was a huge chocolate fish.

This marked the end of Coppens' war.

24

The Canadian Ace

There was a time, during the boredom of the war, that a Canadian pilot named Bishop painted a number of ducks red, white and blue, then tried to teach them how to waddle along in formation. When the experiment failed he captured a French sow and decorated it with Gothic crosses. He was, in general, a man of some broad humor.

Bishop devoted his war years to one thing, killing Germans, and he shot down more than forty enemy planes, running up a far greater score in less time than any other Allied airman. He based his technique as a marksman upon that of Albert Ball VC and Manfred von Richthofen, who often had raided Bishop's field with his dawn wolf pack. Bishop was the man who won the Victoria Cross in an action which lasted less than five minutes. Earlier, he qualified for the Military Cross in a fight that endured exactly two minutes. It will now be appreciated that he was fast and he was deadly in his purpose. He knew what he wanted and heaven help any man who stood in his path.

Fighting the Germans, he used a shattering technique of pointing the nose of his Nieuport straight at the approaching adversary and waiting until that last horrifying moment of possible collision before

283

sending a spurt of demoralizing bullets into the enemy's engine. In cold print this may sound simple enough; in point of fact it was the riskiest thing in the world to do at a time when aircraft were so unpredictable and guns jammed regularly. One second of bad or even mediocre judgment could easily lead into a head-on crash and explosion from which there was no escape, yet Bishop went on doing the same thing time and time again, trusting his keen eyes and keener shooting to take him out of the web of death which he himself was spinning at 100-120 mph.

It is possible to uncover many interesting facts about Bishop and his career as a pilot. One of them was the urge to fly. He would not take anything less than a pilot's rating, but when he was bitten by the urge to start flying, his judges at the selection board thought very little of his capabilities. They said that he lacked "go," because his nerves were in bad shape. His nerves certainly were bad at the time. He was fed up with fighting a war in the mud of the battlefields. He disliked grime and filth. He had a passion for washing his hands, but this was by no means as psychological as it sounds.

The war itself left a bad taste in his mind. It took a long time before he was able to relish the job of killing Germans. Death had no glamor for such a sensitive man; he never became hardened to it.

He joined the Canadian Militia in 1911. On the outbreak of war he was commissioned in the Canadian Cavalry. After some tough experiences in action he wrote: "A few more days of cavalry mud and I was convinced that to be an observer in the air was far better than commanding a division on the ground." His early application for a transfer to the RFC was accepted after several setbacks and point-blank refusals, and he was sent to Netheravon for training.

The next few weeks were spent sitting in an old "air bus" which shook and shuddered with effort as the pilot lifted it off the ground so that a green-gilled Bishop could go through the prescribed routine. He was supposed to be learning how to be an observer, yet it was not enough for his kind of mentality. He was soon pestering his officers for a chance of sitting in the forward cockpit. This marked the beginning of many interviews. No one considered him good enough to fly a plane.

In France again, this time in RFC uniform, he went through some unique experiences. Of course, he knew many of the battlefields all too well from his days with the Canadian Cavalry. From the air they took on a new aspect. "Leaving the border-guarding Archies far behind, you fly on until you pick up the four mounds that indicate the German battery position. You fly rather low to get a good look at it. The Huns generally know what your coming means and they prepare to take cover," he wrote.

From the other side of that war a German infantryman observed: "The air activity is very great. The English will soon be taking the very caps off our heads." Bishop always thought it "great fun to fly very low along the German trenches and give them a burst of machine-gun bullets as a greeting in the morning."

Flying on artillery cooperation duties, he reduced tactics to a fine art, first getting his pilot to make a wide sweep over the terrain in order to first size up his chances, then humming back over the British lines when he notified the range and the first signal to fire. "Then nothing seems to happen for an eternity," he once noted. In reality it was less than thirty seconds before the elevated gun barrels spouted points of flame and a trail of cordite smoke. Circling lazily, Bishop grinned to himself as he saw a piece of earth erupt in the distant German sector. At the end of the morning shoot he always felt that he had been right into the mouth of war and heard the steel teeth clash together. The experience invigorated him, yet there was something missing. He never stopped wanting to become a qualified pilot. The idea of remaining in the observer's seat made him squirm. Apart from guiding the artillery onto their targets, he had so little to do. Perhaps the only advantage of being an observer was an improvement in his marksmanship. He was better able to assess distance and time. The dull routine ground on more than four months until he became restless enough to demand again that he be trained as a pilot.

At his first interview he went to great lengths to explain that the general war effort should consist ideally of putting round pegs in round holes. It did not go down very well with the brass hats. The chairman of the board stared hard at the presumptuous Canadian. "I see, Bishop, yes, I do see your point. But how can you be so sure you are suitable to handle a plane?"

Bishop stared back in turn, feeling that he was having less success than ever. Giving up, he went out, noisily shutting the door of the hut behind him. A few days later he went away on leave, his

hopes of becoming a pilot practically dashed. When he returned
in June 1916 he was amazed to discover his name posted on
Orders to train as a pilot. Had his officers had second thoughts
after all? It was scarcely possible. In those days, though, it was a
matter of great importance to keep the lists of pilots in training as
lengthy as possible because the mortality rate was so high. Anything
was better than nothing, so long as that anything was able to lift
a plane off the ground and harry the Germans.

"Billy" Bishop had his big chance at last and he believed that
he was fully equipped for it. He knew the racy slang of the air.
He even knew the parts of the airplane—vaguely. In November
1916 he dumped his kitbag in his new billet at the School of Elementary Training. Next day he was shoved into "a steady type
called the Maurice Farman," but the exercise was a fiasco. The
dual-control Farman was hard to handle. It did not do as he
wanted. The strange thing was that it behaved itself very well for
the instructor. Realizing how very green he was after all, Bishop
was astonished to feel the dual-control column moving under his
own limp hands as they sailed through the wind-blown sky. When
he tried to put some strength into his fingers, it came at the wrong
time. The Farman lumbered on through the clouds with an anxious
instructor saying a prayer and a tight-lipped pupil doing his best
to keep the erratic fabric and wood construction on something
approaching an even keel.

"After that," Bishop confessed, "I would get what you might
call timid-handed and not hold the controls tightly enough. My
instructor and I both suffered tortures. So when suddenly one day
he told me I could go up alone, I had my doubts as to whether it
was confidence or desperation that dictated this decision. I didn't
worry very long as to which it was; I was willing to take the
chance."

Holding the bucking machine in check as it rose, his eyes took in
the suggestive sight of the ambulance moving into position near
the landing strip. On turns he did what no other pupil-pilot had
ever done, he actually skidded the Farman around in the air as
though the very atmosphere had turned to ice. His stomach revolted. He wanted to vomit over the edge of the cockpit, but the
sight of the earth, now all askew, put him off and he studied the
controls as the needles jumped about, apparently of their own

volition. The Farman could be a beast of a plane to those who wanted to master it.

His last and most monstrous error was made when he tried to land the machine while still forty feet in the air. At a second attempt he did exactly the same thing when only eight feet from the surface of the earth. He sat there sweating profusely, wondering if the ambulance crew was still watching him. The Farman plunked down on the grass in heavy protest.

The Farman was a machine with few instruments, so it was hard enough to tell how much fuel was left, let alone judge such minor things as altitude and air speed. On night flying duties Bishop could not tell whether he was upside down or right way up half the time. Only when he made a landing was he able to reassure himself that he had escaped one of the ghastly pile-ups which seemed to be more plentiful as pupils suffered a dangerous overconfidence and let their machines become the master.

After joining a unit stationed on the Thames Estuary he found solace in trying to hunt the Zeppelin, but no Zeppelin ever came his way. It was the closed season as far as the Germans were concerned. On March 7, 1917, he was sent back to France where he joined a squadron at Boulogne, ready for what he called his "second go" at the war.

Soon after leaving Boulogne, he was sent to the front and allotted a Nieuport. He gave the plane a close inspection. "The modern fighting scout . . . may have the power of 200 horses throbbing in its wonderful engine," he wrote. "Some of the machines are very slender of waist and almost transparent of wing. Airplanes do not thrust their warlike nature upon the casual observer. One has to look twice before definitely locating the gun or guns attached so unobstrusively to the framework, and synchronized, where necessary, to shoot through the whirring propeller in front. Such guns are connected to the engine itself by means of cams, and are so arranged that they can fire only when the propeller reaches a given position, thus allowing the bullets to pass safely between the blades. . . . The nacelle, or cockpit, of the modern machine, I have heard people say, suggests to them the pilot house of a palatial private yacht in miniature. They are generally finished in hardwood and there are polished nickel instruments all about you. . . . There are ingenious sights for the guns and rangefinders for bomb-dropping. When he is tucked away in the nacelle, a little well-like compartment about as big around as an ordinary barrel, only the pilot's head is visible above the freeboard of the body of the machine—the body being technically known as the fuselage. Directly in front of the pilot is a little glass windscreen, a sort of half-moon effect."

Throughout the years of peace, until his death on September 11, 1956, Bishop held on to a memento of the war, the windscreen of his own Nieuport. Through the middle of it was a bullet hole.

With the other initiates he felt very much the new boy while listening to tales of air fighting, hoping all the time that he might shortly be in a position to tell a tale or two about his own fights. When first it came, his mission was not a happy one. He was briefed to fly at the rear of a formation of half a dozen planes, standing guard throughout the operation, as it were. He had a devilish time of it, trying to keep the others in view. His Nieuport flew too fast or too slow, never at any pace to match that of the others. He ran into trouble when he tried to control it, feeling like an urchin in pursuit of bigger boys in an elaborate paper-chase. When the other six planes dived or climbed, it took him several minutes to grasp the general idea.

His plane was often the most vulnerable of the whole flight. He had to place his very life in jeopardy. The sky hunters of the German air force specialized in snapping up stragglers and shooting them down without mercy. He kept his head well up, knowing that the Germans always skimmed through the upper heights, awaiting a chance to fight. The Hun, he decided as he tried to penetrate the thick clouds with his eyes, was not very sportsmanlike.

Next day he had an experience which almost cost him his life. He was flying "tail-end Charlie" to the others as usual when the German anti-aircraft batteries saw him through their sights. "I felt the tail of my machine suddenly shoot up into the air, and I fell about 300 feet before I managed completely to recover control." This was the nearest he ever came to Archie fire; it was close enough.

The war, they say, was full of sportsmanship. "Never kick a man when he is down," states the leftover legend. In the air, mottoes like that were forgotten. The planes gathered over the trenches, often about twenty-five at a time from both sides, and fired at one another until the scarlet plumes denoted victory. Running dogfights went on all the time, especially in the period 1916-1917 when the Germans had air superiority and plenty of fast machines in commission.

Bishop saw that the war held its own humor. He was much amused by the incident of the "white pig," a certain German two-seater which hovered over part of the British sector on radio observation duties every day. Most of the pilots believed it to be flown by total amateurs. Coming back from their patrols, they always made a special point of dipping their wings to the pale-colored "pig" in sorry salute. One day some of the younger pilots went for it in mock battle, buzzing round and round it until the German pilot panicked. It swung round and round, trying to escape or at least enable the radio operator-gunner to take a few pot shots at the invaders. "The observer," Bishop said, "was a very bad shot and never succeeded in hitting any of our machines, so attacking this particular German was always regarded more as a joke than a serious part of warfare. The idea was only to frighten the 'pig,' but our patrol leader made such a determined dash at him the first day we went over that he never appeared again. For months the patrol leader was chided for playing such a nasty trick upon a harmless old man."

Even now Bishop did not have complete control of the Nieuport. Rather, he trusted to the machine's own instinct to carry him through if he happened to get mixed up in a fight. On March 25 he was blooded. The German army was in retreat, harried by the RFC. Flying conditions were fair, actual combats few.

"Those were very queer days," Bishop reported after his retirement. "For a time it seemed that both armies—German and British alike—had simply dissolved. Skirmishes were the order of the day on the ground and in the air. The grim, fixed lines of battle had vanished for the time being, and the Germans were falling back to their famous Hindenburg positions. The clouds had been hanging low as usual, but after we had gotten well in advance of our old lines and into what had so recently been Hunland, the weather suddenly cleared. So we began to climb to more comfortable altitudes, and finally reached about 9,000 feet."

Knowing that his fuel was lessening, he looked around for some Germans. Then three planes appeared to the east of his patrol.

What the devil was the matter with the British leader? Bishop asked himself. He was flying serenely on without a care in the world. Bishop gained speed to signal the presence of the enemy. He was thrashing every ounce of power out of his engine when it spluttered, nearly failing. He throttled back to give it a chance to pick up.

"Like nearly all other pilots who come face to face with the Hun in the air for the first time, I could hardly realize that these were real live, hostile machines. I was fascinated by them and wanted to circle about and have a good look at them. The German Albatros machines are perfect beauties to look upon. Their swept-back planes give them more of a birdlike appearance than any other machines flying on the Western front. Their splendid graceful lines lend to them an effect of power and flying ability far beyond what they really possess."

While he was studying the enemy with almost academic interest, the three Huns moved around and were in position right behind the British patrol before Bishop could do anything to distract their attention. They were now about 400 feet behind the British leader, who was now aware of what was going on. He suddenly swept his Nieuport around to face them. Bishop had never seen it done as neatly as this. Like the rest of the Allied pilots, he tried to follow his leader's example, and was immediately faced with the problem of handling what felt like a mass of machinery gone mad. For a moment he could have sworn that his Nieuport was falling to pieces under the strain.

"I flew straight at the attacking machine from a position where he could not see me and opened fire. My tracer bullets . . . began at once to hit the enemy machine. A moment later the Hun turned over on his back and seemed to fall out of control. This was just at the time when the Germans were doing some of their famous falling stunts. Their machines seemed to be built to stand extraordinary strains in that respect. They would go on spinning down from great heights, and just when you thought they were sure to crash, they would suddenly come under control, flatten out into correct flying position, and streak for the rear of their lines with every ounce of horsepower imprisoned in their engines."

Not taken in by the aerobatic display, he dropped down after the German, and, at 1,000 feet, saw the enemy plane flatten out in nick of time. In a fury, Bishop swooped down, wanting to smash up his clever opponent. "I had forgotten caution and everything else in my wild and overwhelming desire to destroy this thing that for the time being represented all Germany to me."

He was about forty yards away when he fired again. The German went into another dive. Was this just another trick? Bishop continued diving to see what would happen while the Nieuport's frame strained, threatening to break up as he achieved a velocity of about 200 mph.

Bishop still had about 1,500 feet to go when he saw the German plane collide with the ground and explode in a horror of flame and smoke. Satisfied, he pulled out of his own dive, using all his strength to pull the Nieuport back to a more normal speed. All sense of distance had gone; he was feeling ill from excitement. Over it all he knew that it was good to be alive at a time when you could so easily be dead.

Then his engine stopped. Suspended up there between an indifferent heaven and an uncompromising earth, Bishop had to do some fast thinking. All he could see below him was the ruinous outline of a shelled village. He could not recognize it but believed it to be behind the German lines. His career as a flier had only started; was it to end so soon?

The rattle of a machine gun brought him back to the ever vital present. The Germans were firing at him from their ground positions, their gun muzzles following the Nieuport's long descent. He did not possess sufficient fighting experience to console himself with the idea that he might have been in a much worse position. Other aviators sometimes tried to get their tattered travesties of airplanes back home through an unceasing hail of shellfire. Bishop was at least in one piece.

Hunting through the side pockets of the cockpit, his hand closed thankfully on the butt of a Very signal pistol. It might not be much use, but it was better than nothing. In a machine now fluttering about over the beaten deserted village, he rapidly checked to see that the fat cartridge was in place in the cumbersome pistol, then gave his full attention to helping the machine make a landing of sorts.

The Nieuport settled down with a grinding thump on a path between the ruins of cottages. He half-expected to be instantly surrounded by German soldiers, savage Huns who would wave their bayonets in his face, perhaps even fire at his legs to cripple him and prevent an escape attempt. After several moments, when nothing happened, he crawled out of the cockpit, Very pistol in one hand, prepared to shoot at the enemy. It was very quiet in that desolate avenue. Of course, they could be hiding in the broken houses, waiting to see if he was armed or not. That could be the reason for this deceptive calm, he thought, slithering into a damp ripple near a shell crater. It was better than nothing. He scarcely realized that if he were caught here he could be shot like a dog by any soldier who took care to approach from the other side of the shell hole.

"Then I saw some people crawling toward me," he wrote. "They were anxious moments, and I had to rub my eyes two or three times before finally convincing myself that the oncoming uniforms were muddy brown and homely, if you will, but to me that day, khaki was the most wonderful, the most inspiring, the most soul-satisfying color ever beheld by the eyes of man. . . ."

They turned out to be British Tommies and they told him that he was less than one hundred and fifty yards inside British lines. Their mission was not to rescue him, but to see if the plane could be shifted because it presented a new and tempting target to nearby German gunners. Bishop hovered around as they began to man-handle the wreckage toward the British sector, but no sooner had they lifted it than the German guns opened up. One shell fell two hundred yards away, giving Bishop a nasty turn as he fell on his face to avoid shrapnel. When he lifted his eyes, he found the soldiers still standing and looking at him with some curiosity. Two hundred yards was as good as ten miles to these veterans. A couple of minutes later another shell came hurtling over. Feeling much braver and remembering the previous example, Bishop stayed where he was, standing up, only to find that the soldiers had fallen on their bellies in the mud. The shell landed twenty yards away and failed to explode. Bishop felt foolish but brave.

They carted the plane to a place behind some trees and then tried to repair it. The airframe was not too badly damaged, but the engine was in poor shape. Bishop went back with them to their dugout for food and a place to sleep. Next morning, after getting the engine running again, he tried to taxi over the muddy ground and in so doing split the propeller in half. After that he had to give up for the time being. He sent messages to his squadron, explaining that he was stranded and temporarily attached to the British army until he could be transported back to the airfield.

Some weeks after this incident he was promoted to patrol leader, being given the job of leading the others into battle. It was not the best kind of job for a man who wanted to act independently and had already shown an ability to run headlong into trouble of all kinds.

"The patrol consisted of a flight of six machines," he wrote. "I led my companions up to 12,000 feet before heading across the trenches just south of Arras. Once over the lines, we turned to the north, not penetrating very far into Hunland because of the strong wind that was blowing about fifty miles an hour from the west. These westerly gales were one of the worst things we had to contend with at the front. They made it very easy for us to dash into enemy territory, but it was a very different story when we started for home and had to combat the tempest. If an airman ever wishes for a favoring wind, it is when he is streaking for home."

On a day such as the one described above, he squinted down through the murky air to find a German plane flying about half a mile below him. It was scudding about in the mobile air currents like a modern glider, clearly using the wind to conserve fuel. He dipped his nose as a signal that he intended going down and invited the rest to help in the slaughter. He was about three-quarters of the way down when he knew, with terrible finality, that he was probably leading his men into a clever ambush. The solitary Hun was not solitary at all; it could be a decoy! He was right. Out of the fringes of the dark clouds another machine with the Gothic cross came thundering. Then a third one appeared from nowhere, firing at Bishop.

Bishop was too busy trying to deal with the second machine to attack the third one. For once his shooting was off the mark. He was badly flustered by the speed whipped up by the fight itself. Try as he could, he failed to make any direct hits. The rest of his patrol had scattered about all over the patchy sky, apparently without any coordination. He could not expect immediate help from any of them while they were so divided. Swiveling his head from left to right, in desperate need of assistance, he was shaken when the third German machine fired several dozen rounds of incendiary bullets at him. By a sheer miracle they passed between the wings. He saw them all too clearly in their smoking trails. One plane tried to keep him occupied while another slipped in at a different angle, shooting at his engine.

What happened then saved his life. He shoved over the rudder bar and did extreme things with the other controls—things which he would not dream of doing in the normal course of events. With a whine, the Nieuport flipped over on its back, entering a dizzy half loop which took him out of range of the two Germans and evaded the third one. It had been a close shave, Bishop knew, but he thanked God he was now alone again. He still had to cover his tracks. They could easily follow him. He decided to make a run for it. It was all he could do. A more foolhardy pilot might have stayed where he was to fight it out, one against three, and perished in the Flanders mud, his blazing plane on top of him as a tombstone.

Wrapping his fist around the control stick, he hauled it back until the nose lifted steeply. The Nieuport climbed fast, taking him out of range and into the high safety zone where the Germans could not follow.

Looking down on the aerial battlefield of France that day, an observer would have seen several dogfights in progress. Bishop noticed one about a mile to the east of him and headed for it, feeling more confident.

When it did reach a fiery fruition, the fight had lasted about fifteen minutes, by which time Bishop found himself more than fifteen miles within the German lines at a height of 4,000 feet. As the combat petered out and the German fled for his life, he managed to round up his patrol again. Only four were left. Two were missing. In a tight, fast-moving formation they scudded from cloud to cloud, running straight through the artillery fire, risking a chance hit in their engines.

Later that night, after a day of epic flying, they heard that one of the two missing machines, piloted by a boy of only eighteen, had landed within the British lines. The pilot had been hit in the stomach with an explosive bullet. He summoned enough presence of mind to coax his faltering plane into remaining airborne until he was out of range of the German guns. Scarcely able to make out the ground through his failing senses, he brought his machine down in a field and fell out of the cockpit. First he crawled, then he pulled himself to his feet, hands clasped to the bloody wreckage of his abdomen. After walking a few steps he collapsed and was discovered by some medical orderlies who saw the plane coming down near their field hospital. He was rushed to a sick bay for immediate attention but died as dawn flushed the fields.

Those who were there never forgot that wretched winter. The Allies had to bide their time, waiting for a letup in conditions before making their assault on Vimy Ridge. The cold continued, delaying supplies, hindering everything in the way of progress, paralyzing both sides. Whenever the chance presented itself, the Germans took the initiative, doing their utmost to demoralize the British troops by shelling them. Bishop wrote: "During the long cold months of winter, the old Boche had been looking down on us, pelting the infantry in the trenches with all manner of bombs and trench-mortar shells, and making life generally uncomfortable."

The calculated irritability of the Germans did nothing to prevent the Allies from massing guns, ammunition and men in preparation for the tremendous attack on Vimy Ridge. Playing an important part, the RFC received orders to sweep the skies clear of the enemy so that German scouts stood no chance of seeing what was going on. For days the RFC was hard at it, harrying any German machines they could find, pushing them back until they had no alternative but to operate over their own lines.

The Germans then adopted the use of observation balloons. The Allies immediately started out after the new targets. Bishop's early attacks on them were incredibly risky because he lacked experience and did not know what to expect. He nearly lost his life when the protective ground-to-air fire of "flaming onions" came whistling up at the very moment when he was getting his sights on one gasbag. The missiles seemed to be fired from some kind of rocket-gun device and they came up at such a rate that it was almost impossible to get out of their way. British High Command orders brooked no argument, despite the hazards of the task. The Germans must at all costs be prevented from interfering with the plan for the Vimy attack by land forces.

When the attack did come, it started on Easter Monday. This was the best possible time, for it was a misty, cloudy day with plenty of cover. On the other hand, it was not very good flying weather. Bishop was among the first off the ground, heading his own formation. He eventually left them to their own devices after he had singled out a balloon. He dived down to see whether an observer was stationed in the basket. The weather so obscured his vision that he had to slow down and cruise round and round. On his third circuit the Germans opened fire from the ground. Alarmed, he revved his engine and whistled off into the sheltering clouds.

Next day he decided to fly alone, but found no opposition anywhere. It was exactly the same during the next twenty-four hours. The Germans were in no mood to risk men and planes at such a time as this when the British might attack at any moment. When Bishop did manage to pick a fight his marksmanship was so erratic that he flew back to base, disgusted with himself, to spend hours on the range. He could not afford to make mistakes in these anxious days. Ironically, when he did shoot down several Huns in the ensuing days, he found himself hampered by the British system of confirming victories. Flying on lone patrol seldom resulted in a confirmed win. He received his reward later when he was gazetted for the Military Cross for his part in the Vimy action.

Prior to the Battle of Arras he was hunting balloons. The Nieuport carried him on and on, more than five miles within the German lines, until he finally found what he wanted, a balloon that looked unguarded.

"But just then I heard the rattle of machine-guns," he reported, ". . . and saw bullet holes appear as if by magic in the wings of my machine. I pulled back as if to loop, sending the nose of my machine straight up in the air. As I did so the enemy scout shot by underneath me. I stood up on my tail for a moment or two, then let the machine drop back, put her nose down, and dived after the Hun, opening fire straight behind him at very close range. He continued to dive away with increasing speed, and later was reported to have crashed just under where the combat had taken place."

Annoyed that he had been caught napping like an amateur, he turned back to look at the balloon. Within a few seconds it was on its way to the ground, a sheet of flame. He then went down to shoot up the ground crew. While he was putting the plane through a series of tortuous movements, an isolated gun battery armed with a "flaming onions" device sent showers of blazing missiles at him, shooting almost at zero altitude in an effort to blow up the Nieuport before it turned on them, too.

With the artillery crew dispersed and the balloon no more than a pile of smoldering canvas, he was about to turn away for home when his engine suddenly oiled up, coughed and stopped. Determined to put up a fight of some kind, he glided down to within fifteen feet of the ground. He was about to steady himself for the crash which was only seconds away when the engine roared into life again. There was one serious drawback to his good luck; he could not gain much height. The plane was now moving at a hundred miles an hour. He dared not give it the increased responsibility of trying to lift itself into the clouds because it might stall again. He had to undergo the strange experience of crossing the German lines at twenty or thirty feet. Before him, laid out in meticulous order, stood the trenches with the sight of a German helmet here and there. He would have given anything to fire the guns. Again the engine must rule his actions. Within a few seconds he had flashed across the three lines of enemy fortifications and was home.

With all the ground troops fully engaged, the army of the air went farther afield to fight its own battles. Some days after his scurry across the German positions, Bishop was up at 10,000 feet when he came upon three enemy planes flying toward the British lines with an escort of two more moving along below them. "By quick thinking," he explained, "I estimated that I could make a running attack on the lower two before the upper three could get into the affair."

He was on to the first one when the second came in on his tail, giving him what he admitted to be "some of the most uncomfortable moments of my fighting career." One bullet even grazed his flying helmet while another hammered through the center of the windscreen, passing over his shoulder in the process.

In this position he only had to glance upward to see that the other three Germans were now diving down at him, all firing simultaneously. He had absolutely no other choice but to start climbing up into that hail of bullets. When he reached a suitable range he began to fight back, spraying first one then another. An enemy machine backed out of the melee, perhaps sensing that Bishop was in a killing mood. The other two went into lifesaving dives, out of his range. Soon he was all alone in the peace of the sky, one of the few aviators to have taken on five planes and vanquished them all. Home again, he wrote his report and waited while his CO went through it, an incredulous expression on his face.

"Well, Bishop, after that lot, I think you'd better have a rest."

"That's very good of you," said Bishop. A leave in London perhaps?

"Yes, you have a rest," said the CO. "Take the afternoon off."

That night Bishop slept deeply, oblivious to the thunder of guns.

The Battle of Arras became the signal for the RFC to start continuous low-level sweeps over all German emplacements, bullying the enemy back as far as possible, and at the same time dissuading enemy scout planes from flying over the area. Bishop discovered just how dangerous this could be, especially when he flew through a British barrage and had part of his wing tip shot away. At about five o'clock one morning the barrage, which had been continuous, died down to a whisper, paused for fifteen minutes and then started up again with renewed thunder. Ground conditions were terrible. A storm had been blowing all night, but this did not put off the Allies as they left their trenches to start the scramble forward, just behind a creeping barrage supplied by the artillery. It was one of the heaviest "shoots" of the war.

Bishop was still flying along with the best of them. From his cockpit he could see the long lines of guns spitting out their funeral threnody. Every few seconds his machine wildly tossed about as it was caught in the slipstream of a passing shell. "We had to endure it with the best spirit possible," he said optimistically. The panoramic picture of the battle showed hundreds of British troops as they straggled across a nondescript no man's land without any show of hurry. It was hard to believe that all this had been carefully planned.

Somewhat listless and bad-tempered because of loss of sleep since the offensive started, Bishop took his plane off into a snowstorm on the fourth day of the battle. He was amazed to see how fully the snow had obliterated all the mud and the craters, the untidy litter of dead soldiery. He could see nothing except the dazzling whiteness. He felt like the last man in the world.

Not quite sure what time the infantry was booked to start moving up, he idled about at about 500 feet, watching for signs of activity in the British trenches so that he could start his own support operation. Soon a line of khaki-clad figures came crawling out of the newly captured trenches and began to walk forward toward the silent German lines. Bishop cut his engine and glided down to watch war from an unusual angle, all the time feeling sorry for the "poor bloody infantry" who had to wade through a mush of snow and mud while he himself was able to sit up here, cold but dry enough.

He was about to swing away in search of any German scout aircraft when the infantry line was devastated by a concealed German machine-gun nest. The soldiers wavered and then fell back in retreat. If they could not see the machine gun, Bishop certainly could. The onus was upon himself. He put the plane into an almost vertical dive, engaging the startled snipers from the rear and firing all the time into the very core of the trouble. As he lifted the plane, eagle-like, he saw some of the British soldiers waving their gratitude to him. The advance started again as he flew away, confident that they would be able to enter the next position without further trouble.

Bishop averred that the RFC were the "air policemen." Nothing seemed simpler than maintaining a constant front-line patrol over the harried Germans throughout the battle. Many counterattacks were forestalled by the skilled use of the fast Nieuports. This made a lasting impression on his mind. It was coordination that counted, not haphazard scraps fought by lone aces.

He was a captain now. Celebrating his promotion, he had his machine painted blue, and his mechanics made a round nose for it to provide the distinction that it was flown by one of the new aces qualified by having shot down more than five enemy machines. Believing that he must fly with more dash, more *élan,* than before, he was in the air on April 20 when he managed to shoot another German down in flames. This was actually the first one he did shoot down in flames. It made a great impression on his mind. This is how he summed it up:

". . . to see an enemy going down in flames is a cause of great satisfaction. You know his destruction is absolutely certain. The moment you see the fire break out you know that nothing in the world can save the man, or men, in the doomed airplane. You know there is no 'camouflage' in this, and you have no fear that the enemy is trying any kind of flying trick in the hope that he will be left alone."

The same day he managed to discover a two-seater German flying without escort. It seemed so unusual, especially after the Battle of Arras which should have taught the enemy a lesson. Bishop had been cruising over a mounting layer of white cumulus cloud, playing tag with the flirtatious air waves and in general biding his time until something turned up. He had had his eyes on the German below him for about five minutes, but still made no move to intercept it. He unobtrusively glided down unseen to a point below the enemy machine. There was something highly exciting about being there, knowing that he had not yet been spotted. It must have been this excitement and the natural tenseness which deflected his first ten rounds, for none of them made a hit. The fight started with a series of rolls, dives and climbs, each machine jockeying for a position in which the guns could be best used. Bishop came down at a fast rate, shooting point-blank but without any success. The German was leading a charmed life for all his size. Now desperate, his excitement turned into a mood of murder. He slithered into a broadside position, a position from which it was impossible to miss!

For one moment it looked as though either machine might be the victor. The question was, which plane would shoot first? The German observer started shooting with fearful accuracy, raking Bishop's mainplane in a traversing fire, but the Canadian had the advantage of being able to look at a much larger and more obvious target while throwing his Nieuport about in a diverting zigzag motion. He kept his finger on the trigger until the closeness of the enemy showed that he must abandon the attempt. The German was much too close. Banking steeply, Bishop returned, prepared to pepper the two-seater with as much fire as his depleted ammunition supplies would allow. He passed over the German at a height of only five feet—from here he could look straight down into the cockpit. Leaning over to take in the sight, he noticed that the observer was slumped over his guns, obviously dead. He was about to turn about and meet the German head-on when he heard the decisive sound of a small explosion behind him. Black smoke was coming out of the enemy. It began its death plunge.

After such an odds-against engagement and the others that followed it, Bishop always thought the German two-seaters fair game, almost too easy despite their superior armament. He began to exceed his normal patrols by looking for his pet prey. Once, when he lost his quarry, he found another one and forced it to land. So enraged was he by the fact that it would not fight him that he followed it down and, as it landed, pointed his guns at it. The pilot and observer did not appear, so he shot it up.

Because of the failure of the German air force to hold the British back during the Battle of Arras, the High Command decided to shuffle some of their better pilots around in an effort to quell the new progress made by the RFC. The class of fighting increased on both sides. It was no longer quite so easy to shoot the Germans down.

One of the reasons for this was the arrival of Richthofen.

25

Attack at Dawn

Those who saw Richthofen in the air often referred to him either as a "typhoon" or a "cyclone." Those who found themselves pitted against his guns seldom had the chance of thinking up a descriptive word until later if they managed to get away alive. One man, Billy Bishop, did survive.

When Richthofen appeared he brought with him many of his own brilliant pilots, comprising the cream of German air fighters. British intelligence was slow on the uptake. Because the fighting front was so fluid, fluctuating from day to day, there was little or no chance to obtain information through spies. Only when some of the perceptive British fliers happened to see a red plane making individual sorties, displaying an unusual professionalism, did it occur to anybody that Richthofen might be in their midst.

It was only a matter of days before Bishop had his first, and only, fight with the Red Baron. It occurred one afternoon, after a morning of fierce fighting against aggressive patrols. Bishop had just finished his lunch and was standing near the landing strip, gazing up at the sky, trying to estimate what conditions would be like for the next three or four hours. Most of the other pilots had gone to their beds to snatch some rest before any new emergency called

302

them out to their refueled planes. Bishop was able to appreciate the quietness of the early afternoon. The Germans were risking very little these days. They seldom came out over a British airfield looking for the chance to fight. Bishop missed them and the chances which they always brought along with them. It now meant that he had to take his fighters far beyond the German lines in a time-wasting search for a fight.

Twenty minutes later, after cleaning his teeth, he thought that the weather was too good to be missed. He had six members of his flight roused. They gathered around him as he gave them their orders. They would fly toward the German sectors and supply points, the very places which might be patrolled by German planes. Nothing might come of it; that was a chance they must take. He agreed with one man who said that it was a waste of fuel. The war must go on. If they stayed where they were, nothing would happen. They did not want a peaceful life, did they? He looked from one face to another, smiling slightly, inviting them to argue. None did.

The Nieuports were well strung out behind him as they passed over the first line of enemy trenches. The war was always altering its complexion. Prior to recent offensive actions the German artillery would have been firing at them all the time. It was different now. The place was silent.

Bishop glanced at his watch. They had been airborne fifteen minutes. He shifted in his seat, seeing an empty sky before him. He gave the signal for the others to follow him, then moved off on a new course which arrowed straight toward the enemy forward areas.

Five Albatros scouts were flying to the south of Bishop's group. His pilots saw them first. They were better than nothing, so Bishop went into a gradual dive which would take him into an excellent firing position immediately behind them. The Nieuport tilted sharply under his touch. He was on his way, warmed by the anticipation of a spirited fight. After a couple of hundred feet something prompted him to stare hard over to the right. Four red-painted Albatroses were there. They looked far more promising than the others. He had a fleeting impression that this might be Richthofen. Banking to get out of his dive, he thought, By God, if this is Richthofen, it'll be some fight!

Followed by the others, he singled out the leader, whose style of flying showed that it must surely be the Red Baron himself. While his men challenged the rest, Bishop discovered that he was embroiled in a terrific fight. From the start the tempo of the conflict was faster than anything he had ever before experienced. Bullets flew everywhere, in every possible direction. Within the compass of a few dozen cubic feet all hell was being packed in one whirling mass of planes. There was no time to even think. Bishop was man enough to admit that he expected to be wiped out by the Germans at any moment.

Richthofen was waiting for him, perhaps recognizing his plane as being that of the flight commander. In a fashion almost medieval, the two giants got to grips, with Bishop saving his fire until he brushed wing tips with the calculating German. A stampede of wild beasts could not have been more frightening than having to face up to the enemy's number one fighter pilot. He realized his danger as he tailed Richthofen during one of the German's scintillating turns, which brought him back into the very center of the fight. He knew that Bishop was dogging him. In the meantime, he was content to play tag, encouraging him to exhaust himself and waste some of that good British ammunition.

Richthofen was in a clear area of sky, away from the main fight, so Bishop treated him to a few bursts to shake him up, but the German flew on, ignoring the bullets. Then, by a combination of circumstances which stemmed from the fight itself, Bishop saw that he would get within range of Richthofen in a matter of seconds. Steadying himself, he prepared to start firing with every skill he possessed. A chance like this came only once! He fingered the trigger as Richthofen loomed up in front of him. Nothing happened. His gun was jammed solid!

Richthofen did not bother firing back. He could have done so very easily and probably put an end to Bishop once and for all. There was a breathless pause while Bishop grappled helplessly with the gun, trying to correct the fault, and all the time keeping an eye on his men, who were still battling only a few yards away. With the gun mechanism cleared, he recovered speed and went after the Red Baron for the second time, firing all the time, looking for a chance to finish him off. He had the satisfaction of seeing a row of bullet holes appear in the fuselage, but there was very little hope of killing the master pilot, who outpaced him all the time. He flashed under the red plane and was about to skim around for a fresh try, when he saw four triplanes approaching. His heart jumped painfully. If they were Germans this fight would have to be abandoned—and just at a time when his men were getting into their stride.

Waiting a few more seconds to be sure of the position, he at last identified the new arrivals as belonging to an Allied naval air squadron. He was quite prepared to carry on with the combat, but when he turned to see what the Germans were doing, he found the sky empty except for British planes. The Germans were making a run for it. They, too, must have seen the triplanes. The odds were too great for them. They were accommodated by the clouds. Bishop collected his men and flew home. On landing, he inspected his Nieuport. Seven bullets had passed within an inch of his body. "It was a close shave," he admitted, "but a wonderful, soul-stirring fight."

Bishop was among the first to witness the sight of German Gothas flying over the British lines. To his mind they were too big and very clumsy besides, these three-seaters which might have created a turning point in Germany's air offensive. But as with so many other things, the Teuton was adept at manufacturing the means without visualizing the possible end. Certainly, the Gotha was very useful in its day. As a weapon of war it was, however, not in exact tune with the times.

In this new and final phase of the war Bishop did receive the unique chance of observing the flying of the Richthofen squadron, and wrote: "One day I had the distinction of engaging in three fights in half an hour with pilots of [Richthofen's] squadron. Their machines were painted a brilliant scarlet from nose to tail—immense red birds, they were, with the graceful wings of their type, Albatros scouts. They were all single-seaters, and flown by pilots of undeniable skill. There was quite a little spirit of sportsmanship in this squadron, too. . . ."

Bishop came to believe, lightheartedly perhaps, that the Germans had adopted an ancient Oriental manner of warding off evil spirits. They were painting their airplanes in a most bizarre way. Some were encircled with multicolored bands, others had a series of wavy lines painted across the underside of their mainplanes. More used to the conventional way of the RFC, Bishop scarcely

realized how extremely subtle could be the uses of aerial camouflage. He thought that the "spring fancies" of the German airmen
were running riot. He was wrong, of course. The camouflage—for
that is what it was—was done with a deadly purpose in mind, to
enable the Germans to make surprise attacks. It was one lesson
the British failed to learn.

British losses about this time were not very great or frequent.
For this reason Bishop, who had become rather complacent, was
badly affected by an incident in which a friend had his leg broken
by German machine-gun fire. Unable to control his machine, at
the mercy of two enemy aircraft, the boy was showered with gasoline when a stray bullet punctured the fuel tank. Then, when the
Germans sensed that the pilot was in a poor state and could not
fight back, they rushed after him, shooting away all his controls and
then setting the plane on fire with incendiary bullets. The plane
went into a dive, burrowing into the soft ground, trapping the pilot
in an inferno from which he could not escape, though he was still
alive and managed to scream for help. Some soldiers pulled him
out and rushed him to the hospital. One leg and an arm were
smashed, he was burned to a crisp, and bullets had passed through
his chest, splintering his ribs. He had been in France less than six
weeks. Bishop went to see him, feeling ill when he saw the terrible
ravages of fire and bullet on the young body. Despite every surgical
intervention, he died that night.

As Bishop walked away from the scene of the military funeral,
a resolve hardened in his heart. It was quite unlike him to seek
bloody revenge; he never held any rancor against the Germans.
This was different; he changed overnight.

A few days later, still fighting mad, he went through nine engagements in one hour and forty-five minutes, a whirlwind risking
everything in a bid for destruction. Those who saw him said that he
fought like a maniac. He used his trick of the bull-like charge,
introducing tactics which took him toward the enemy's nose at the
maximum speed. Had he suffered a collision he would have been
killed at a total combined speed of more than 200 mph. Altogether
Bishop made more than a hundred of these attempts to demoralize
and destroy his opponents. Some of the time he succeeded. The
Germans, to their credit, were not at all reluctant to take up the

challenge, risking their lives just to see how far this mad Canadian would go.

Bishop was awarded the DSO, his second decoration, after a particularly difficult day in the air war. After being mixed up in a massed fight over the trenches and outposts, he was angry with three German two-seaters that tried to get away to safety. He raced after them with the intention of dealing out what he termed a "justly deserved lesson."

"Catching up with the rear one," he said, "I saw that all three were firing at me from their back guns. I was so much faster than the Huns I could zigzag on my course—wondering as I did so if I resembled an ocean greyhound dodging a submarine. Finally, I closed to within twenty yards of the fleeing Germans and let go at them. The rear machine was my easiest target. Soon I saw my bullets going into the observer's body and I feel sure that some of them must have passed on from him to the pilot who was seated directly in front. The observer's face was white as a sheet, and out of pure terror, I think, he had ceased to fire at me. The pilot was now gazing back over his shoulder and was too frightened to maneuver his machine. He had turned into a sort of human rabbit, and was concerned only with running for his life. Fifteen rounds from my gun sufficed for that machine. Down it tumbled, a stricken and dying thing."

Bishop now made a bad mistake. He stayed where he was, almost gloating over the German plane as it hit the ground and buckled. His attention distracted, he was easy meat for the other two. They turned on him like wolves and moved into a place where he could not see them, directly underneath his plane, firing upward into the exposed belly of the Nieuport. Simultaneously, four German scouts shot out from the clouds to try and finish him off. After firing more than forty rounds back at them all, Bishop saw that he was hopelessly outnumbered. Finding a handy cloud, he buzzed into it, but in the excitement of not quite knowing whether the fight would go on, he lost control.

His plane fell about a mile before he could flatten it out. When he looked about him, the sky was completely empty. It seemed incredible that he had been through no less than four major fights in the last forty-five minutes, yet was still alive. He did not want to think too hard about the miracle. Introspection could lead to death.

It was more important to live from hour to hour, concentrating on the routine—routine such as the day when Bishop and his fellow pilots were sitting down to lunch. Headquarters telephoned to ask for pilots to go up and shift a couple of artillery-spotting Germans. It was worse than being a fireman, having to answer these emergency calls, Bishop remarked cheerfully. He stuffed a roll in his pocket and asked the mess waiter to keep the rest of his food hot in the oven.

Airborne, he noticed that several of the other pilots were following. They quickly found the artillery-cooperation planes and, in a fight which lasted less than five minutes, managed to wipe out one while the other dashed away home. Rubbing his empty stomach, Bishop signaled to the others to follow him. They landed and went back to the mess table. That was the meaning of routine. If every move were questioned, a pilot would be a wreck in more ways than one.

While action was freely available the average pilot went on flying and fighting without showing any reaction. During slack spells, however, certain symptoms did become evident. Bishop was himself no exception. When he and his friends raided a French farmyard, he painted some ducks red, white and blue, then seized upon a savage sow and painted her hide with Gothic crosses. Sent on leave, he kept protesting that he was quite fit and did not want to go. The medical officer could not agree with him. When Bishop reached England, he suffered the shakes so badly that he had to take a long quiet rest in the country without distractions of any kind. After a week of it he felt much better and went off to London to enjoy himself. Nevertheless, he was very glad to get back to his squadron. If not exactly refreshed—his leave was hardly long enough for that —he found that he was in far better condition than before. He was also able to look back on his week of total inactivity with some gratitude.

Apart from soothing his jangled nerves, it had given him the chance of assessing his feelings about killing German pilots.

"To me," he wrote, "it was not a business or a profession, but just a wonderful game. To bring down a machine did not seem to me to be killing a man; it was just like destroying a mechanical target, with no human being in it. Once or twice the idea that a live man had been piloting the machine would occur and recur to me, and it would worry me a bit. My sleep would be spoiled perhaps for a night. I did not relish the idea even of killing Germans, yet, when in combat in the air, it seemed more like any other kind of sport, and to shoot down a machine was very much the same as if one were shooting down clay pigeons. One had the great satisfaction of feeling that he had hit the target and brought it down; that one was victorious again."

A few weeks later, after being in the middle of a dogfight of twenty-five planes, he said that he had very little compunction about killing in either cold or hot blood. The actual idea of killing certainly went against the grain, for he was by nature a peaceful good-natured man, but he realized that every German shot down meant one less in the war. At a later stage of the war he said that he "felt none of the thrills which I used to feel at first. I was quite cool and collected, but probably did not enjoy it as much as I did in the days when a certain amount of anxiety and fear was felt just before the fight started. But the moment my machine gun commenced to fire, I felt the old feeling of exultation, and this has always remained with me throughout the whole of every fight I have ever had."

He scored his twentieth victory soon after eight o'clock one morning. He was flying alone when he sighted two machines flying low, south of his position. They were about to land as he went down after them. His first attempt, an attack at a range of fifty yards, failed. The second enemy machine turned on him, sideslipping out of range of his chattering gun. Up against it, Bishop knew that his opponent was highly experienced. Every time Bishop tried to get into a better position, he was beaten to it by the streaking German. Chance of victory emerged after a few more minutes when Bishop did get behind the other, but at an angle which could be dangerous if the fellow turned sharply. With no time to spare, he fired as well as he could. The German faltered, fell out of control and crashed.

Next day he went through several more fights, one after another. The air was becoming more densely populated with Germans than it had been for weeks. The influence of Richthofen's boldness and strategy on a failing front was obvious. There was a need to belabor the enemy on his home ground. Bishop decided to take a chance on it.

He rose at three o'clock in the morning, groping for his clothes in the pitch-darkness, trying not to make a noise that might rouse the others. This was one day which had been very carefully planned. The main idea was to surprise-attack a certain German field, the seat of many operations. Reconnaissance patrols reported that the enemy parked planes in one particular place. Bishop had seen all the enlargements of photographs taken by the high-flying British experts. It was a perfect target if he could get over it without being intercepted or detected.

He was well advanced in his flight by the time day dawned. Presently the airfield, part of a sleeping world, came into view. To his surprise there was no sign of any planes in the area marked in the reconnaissance pictures. Disgruntled, he flew on, hedge-hopping in search of something to attack, unwilling to waste his time, especially after getting out of bed at such an unearthly hour. He was angry that his one-man expedition should show signs of failure and he hated the idea of going home to tell his breakfast-table companions that he had accomplished precisely nothing.

He was now approaching another German airfield where the hangars stuck up in gray geometric patterns. For thirty seconds he was right over the landing strip at an altitude of 300 feet, taking in the sight of seven planes, some of them with mechanics standing around while the engines were run up in preparation for early patrols. It was fantastic luck. Gasping with excitement, he had another look at the scene. There were six single-seaters and one two-seater. He had to get down there before any of them had the chance of taking off.

"I pointed my nose toward the ground, and opened fire with my gun, scattering the bullets all around the machines and coming down to fifty feet in doing so. I do not know how many men I hit, or what damage was done, except that one man, at least, fell, and several others ran to pick him up. Then clearing off to one side, I watched the fun. I had forgotten by this time that they would, of course, have machine guns on the airfield, and as I was laughing to myself, as they tore around in every direction on the ground, like people going mad or rabbits scurrying about, I heard the old familiar rattle of the quick-firers on me. I did not dare go too far away, however, as then I would not be able to catch the machines as they left the ground, so turning quickly, and twisting about, I did my best to evade the fire from the ground."

His mainplane was punctured in several places as the guns followed him on his circuit, but there was no time to worry about that. One of the planes began to move, ready to take off and intercept Bishop. He went down after it in a steep dive. Firing fifteen rounds, he managed to halt its progress as it was about to lift off the ground. There was a resounding smash. He turned quickly, waiting to greet another one which had just taken off. Following, firing at it, he could see his bullets going wide. The pilot must have seen Bishop and understood his intentions. He might even have looked over his shoulder at the Nieuport as it approached him. In that moment he lost control, caught the tip of his wing in a clump of trees and turned turtle.

Elated, Bishop returned to the main landing strip to find two planes taking off at the same time. He could do very little except wait for them. It was quite impossible for one plane to attack both, especially while they were moving in different directions, well spaced out. Continuing to circle and bank to avoid the machine-gun fire, he waited until one of them was within fifty yards at a height of about fifty feet, then went into a rough fight. By good luck he was able to get in the first shots. The other machine went down helplessly, crashing near the airfield.

Many planes were now taking a chance of getting airborne. Some took off in one direction, others in another. It had all the appearance of chaos. Bishop was not long in realizing how neat was the trap he had made for himself. If he did not escape very soon he would be shot to shreds. His ammunition was nearly exhausted. Without a gun he was finished.

In the end he actually managed to slip away through a group of four flustered German scouts without being noticed by any of them. About a mile away from the scene, he experienced a natural reaction when his empty stomach revolted and he retched hard, still trying to control his Nieuport. All sense of victory was washed away for the moment. His work was cut out trying to escape detection by early-morning German patrols and keeping to the scanty cloud layer. But by the time he found his own landing ground he felt much better. He circled, firing Very lights to announce his success. When mechanics examined the fuselage they found it to be holed everywhere. Much too excited to sleep, he went out for a long country walk, to return to a handful of congratulatory telegrams sent by squadrons where his exploit was already known.

Despite all he had been through in the last few weeks, he was still able to enjoy the peace of nature and wrote: "In the June evenings the sky was a beautiful sight at sunset. If there was any wind blowing at all, the mist would be cleared away, and one could see almost to the end of the world. The ground was a riot of beautiful colors, and the dusty roads stretched away like long white ribbons." The weather was so warm that many of the pilots and observers began playing tennis in the evenings, after the day's flying. In the middle of a set late one afternoon, Bishop received an emergency call. He told the others and together they went flying in their white shirts and trousers, then landed to finish the game.

By the end of the summer Bishop ran up forty victories against German planes and two against observation balloons. No great believer in the mockery of decorations and the hollow panoply of war itself, he continued to fly regular patrols. Returning one day, he was both surprised and apprehensive to hear that a high officer of the RFC had been trying to get in touch with him all day. He wondered what the trouble could be, and it took some time before he could overcome his fear enough to put a call through to headquarters. The officer came to the point at once. He wanted to congratulate Bishop on being awarded the Victoria Cross.

The Germans soon heard about Bishop's decoration. His machine was now very easy to distinguish with its red, white and blue markings coupled with the highly individualistic way in which he flew it. They tried to trap him, using elaborate ruses. One German pilot taunted him to such an extent that he angrily gave chase to an obviously preselected spot. When Bishop looked around for the man who had led him all this way behind German lines, there was no sign of him. Just then his machine was thrown about in a tumult of artillery fire. He nearly perished in a riot of high explosive which erupted slightly to the left of him. No sooner had the barrage ceased than he was savagely set upon by a group of German scout planes. He evaded them by nose-diving as fast as his plane would move, then flattening out a few feet from the ground, a trick which he was copying from the Germans in the hope that they would appreciate the compliment. Still infuriated with the pilot who had led him into the ambush, he climbed back into the clouds, waiting for the scouts to disperse, which they did within a few minutes. Idling from cloud to cloud, looking down through the fleecy fissures, he at last found what he was looking for. It took only one dive, but he missed his enemy by feet. The faster German machine vanished completely; but that afternoon, after lunch, he turned up again to tempt Bishop into more foolhardiness. After a time the game was abandoned. Bishop refused to take the bait.

Conscious that his tour of duty might be coming to an end at a time when an Allied victory was reasonably certain, he concentrated on getting in as much action as he could while the going was good.

Due to leave for England in twenty-four hours, he decided to make his last flight. Coincidentally, he thought that it would be a good idea to witness the Canadian attack on Lens at the same time. Over the area he found a Hun two-seater flying above him, also watching the battle. He sized it up, deciding whether or not to shoot it down. In the struggle for supremacy, he exercised his favorite trick of charging the German head-on, then noticed that two others were alongside his original target. In a steep climb, he started firing at them for all he was worth. His sweeping hail of bullets caught two of the machines dead center. They began to break up. He could not be bothered following them down, for that might bring him within range of the German artillery beyond Lens. Seriously engaged though they might be at this moment, they would still take it into their heads to shoot him down because he was an easy target at such a low level. Turning, he saw that other German planes had now joined the original one and were building up an escape formation to head for Germany. He gave chase at three hundred yards, knowing that a strong following wind was carrying him deeper into Germany. It might be difficult to return to his own base if he continued at this pace. He coerced every scrap of power out of his already overheated engine until it brought him to within firing distance of the rear German plane, then started to shoot. The enemy hesitated and dipped. It was a fall of something like 13,000 feet, in which time the plane broke up.

Bishop's score was now forty-seven. It was enough, it was final. He turned and made for home.

His greatest embarrassment of the entire war happened not over the battlefields of France but within the walls of Buckingham Palace when he had to stand in the center of a crowded room and hear a full account of his exploits read out to a notable assembly. The King then pinned three medals on his breast. Bishop's foremost memory of that day was the fact that his new boots squeaked as he walked across the room, all the way past the generals and the admirals, the civilians holding their hats, the scattering of women who smiled at him.

And so out of the Palace to face the newspaper photographers.

CHAPTER **26**

The Eccentric Russians

For a country which was the first to mobilize among the great powers, Russia was the least progressive, depending for success upon weight of numbers rather than upon the reserves of science. Comparatively speaking, she did not put many planes into the sky after the declaration of war on August 1, 1914, but the few that did fly under her colors performed remarkable feats.

It is interesting to put that most modern contrivance of warfare, the airplane, against the background of one of the oldest fighting powers, Russia—the huge bovine matriarch of a continent who placidly stood her ground in the face of a constant herding toward war by the waspish Germany. More remarkable still is that Russia ever had any planes at all in a regime notorious for its corruption and incompetence, but she did, in fact, have machines—an entire fleet of them, even if she did lack pilots to the extent mustered by other nations. In the long run this was a country which suffered massively at every move of the war. A quarter of a million men were slaughtered in just two battles. Similarly, on the industrial front hundreds of pilotless planes were left to rot after they issued from the factories. Some were sold as surplus to other countries; mainly they rotted. For this and other more complex reasons which

315

are beyond the scope of this book, Russia, a country with a far greater potential than the enemy, was in 1914 no greater in comparison from an initial war-strength point of view than Germany itself. But had she been able to find pilots for all those unused planes —machines in all categories designed by some of the best brains in the developmental phase of aviation history—world trends would have followed quite different patterns.

To begin with, factions of the Czar's family disliked the use of science in warfare. In particular, they hated airplanes which were dangerous and noisy and could not help win a war. The younger generation, on the other hand, endorsed a policy of mass production of scouts and bombers.

Yet in the end it was the manpower situation which beat Russia, the lack of manpower to fly those machines. In a country where the officer caste system was rampant and more prohibitive than anything found among other nations, it was impossible to envisage, say, a Caucasian pilot. A flying man had to have the best possible blood in his veins. The Russian forces were full of Caucasians. They heavily outnumbered all other nationalities. Finding airmen was therefore a prolonged business.

But in 1914, before other nations were able to demonstrate their aerial strength, the Russian air fleet was used to survey Hindenburg's lines. It was a kind of mobilization within a mobilization, for most of the Russian air force had to be sent to the sector to take part in one of the most important reconnaissance jobs of the war, an operation carried out in an effort to ensure that the Interburg-Nordenburg-Frankenau line could be securely defended by the air force if the time did come. The Russians were able to accomplish it only because these were early days and casualties were light.

Harking back to the industry itself, a correspondent of the London *Morning Post* wrote: "I was accorded the exceptional privilege in wartime, even for an ally, of visiting one of the Russian great airplane factories. Several have been established to keep up the large supply required by the various armies in the field. The one I visited can turn out five planes per day, or thirty per week. Imagine a London railway terminus, considerably reduced in size and with a broad gallery running round halfway to the roof. That is the fitting department. The whole floor area is crowded with complete airplanes in the rough, some awaiting their engines and others certain other pieces of mechanism used in the active war in the air. Around this central hall and communicating with it are a series of buildings for the preparation of the various parts, for everything, including the engines, is entirely constructed on the spot. Construction has been standardized, and many are the ingenious contrivances for simplifying the various processes of manufacture. Except perhaps the building of a ship, which is a slow progress to grasp, I can imagine nothing more engrossing than the rapid assembling of these modern hawks by a few skilled workmen. When completed they are lowered down from the gallery to the floor of the great hall. Thence they proceed to the flying grounds for the testing of the engines, and they have to be passed by an inspector, a skilled aviator, before being dispatched to the army. As boxed for the railway the entire airplane is got into a solid packing case which might contain, say, a couple of grand pianos, but rather longer. Thus packed, they fear nothing in transit, and are easily and rapidly got to work when they arrive at their destination."

The minute *corps élite* of pilots worked to standards unmatched by other nations. Coupled with the stubborn courage which was to reappear in the Second World War at the siege of Stalingrad, it did much to impress the Germans that here was a most ferocious enemy. The case of Captain Nesteroff is almost typical but not entirely representative. Before the war he was one of the Czar's pets, a man who could do unique things, feats which no other man in the length and breadth of Russia could accomplish. Special flying machines were built for him and paid for out of the Czar's private purse. He flew long distances, he organized amazing flying displays for many royal occasions. When the war started he was immediately sent to the front because the military chiefs had to obey their ruler, who believed that Nesteroff could fight the air war practically singlehanded.

Nesteroff was one of the first to believe in the value of constant reconnaissance and a system of reports. He practiced with his cameras and binoculars while the war was young and the battlefields were yet green. He flew low, taking pictures of fortifications. He flew at high altitudes to obtain exciting panoramic pictures of the whole front. Several times he nearly perished with cold. He wrote to Russia, demanding warmer clothing, and at once received a bulky bearskin hunting suit which, it was said, the Czar once wore to shoot game. But this was never confirmed. There are reliable reports, however, of Nesteroff sitting erect in the cockpit of his machine, clad in furs and wearing a kind of bonnet with loose earlaps as he manipulated his camera.

The day Nesteroff lost his life he was wearing more conventional gear. He set off with the intention of doing some general scout and reconnaissance work. It was a morning like any other except for a spattering of hail which splashed bleakly against the windshield. He had not been in the air more than twenty minutes before he noticed an Austrian plane some distance below him. Dipping into a challenging dive, he brought his plane up almost in front of it, behaving like an angry dog baring its fangs. The Austrian plane calmly went on its way, weaving neatly around Nesteroff and infuriating the Russian with its nonchalance.

Nesteroff raced after him, aiming his gun at the tail of the enemy. No result. The Austrian flew on, then banked slightly so that the pilot could get a better view of what was happening.

Still firing his gun, Nesteroff did everything he could to plant as many destructive rounds as possible in the other's engine. It had no effect. It was absolutely uncanny how the fellow went on flying in no particular direction, apparently aimlessly. His plane was like a cow in a pasture, moving here and moving there but never doing anything even vaguely decisive. It could have been a ghost plane for all the effect Nesteroff's agitated gunfire had on it.

Up to this time Nesteroff had been through very few real fights. He concentrated more upon the science of reconnaissance, believing like many others that this was the proper use of the wartime airplane. He was now puzzled what to do next. A more hard-bitten air fighter would have left the plane alone without inviting trouble. Nesteroff did not believe in discretion at such a moment. He was like a terrier after a rat. Deciding to make one last attempt at shooting the Austrian down, he retreated to a fair distance before going into a dangerous dive. He was within a few yards of the enemy as he curled his finger on the trigger. Nothing happened. He tried again. The gun was jammed—or perhaps he had no ammunition left. His mind flashed back to all the bullets so uselessly expended on the first bout with his incredible opponent. Not once had the Austrian fired back at him.

There was a sudden cracking, splintering noise as the two planes collided. Locked together, they began to tumble to the ground more than half a mile through the quiet air. Not until they hit the soil did they part, then the engines bounced apart like rubber balls. In the twisted cockpit of each plane sat a dead mutilated body. Troops later discovered a bullet lodged in the spine of the Austrian aviator. Nesteroff must have achieved his purpose after all, never realizing that he had been fighting a dead man during those last few minutes of his life.

Nesteroff was supposed to have had no equal in any of the air services, according to official histories which Russian historians were commissioned to create as the war progressed. They certainly lost sight of Kusminsky, a pioneer of long-distance flying and, incidentally, one of the first to examine survival techniques. It was said that he could go on living while encased in a block of ice. Some of his adventures seem to indicate that he had wonderful self-control, based perhaps on his early study of yoga and Eastern mysticism.

Kusminsky was the man selected to take an influential member of the Russian Army General Staff on a high-altitude flight during the war. The officer was a graduate of the finest military academies and, Kusminsky soon decided, a snob. But whether the pilot acted with any sense of malice as he lifted the army representative into the coldest part of the great refrigerator of the sky is another matter.

At a height of 10,000 feet the cold was so intense that it was impossible to continue shouting to one another. Quite happy and satisfied with their progress despite the layer of glistening white rime on his face, Kusminsky concentrated on the job of keeping the plane up as high as possible and idling an engine which showed signs of freezing up. The main idea was to keep in view the main road which gave the pilot an indication of direction. The still air was crystal clear for miles and it was possible to see the land formations all the way to the horizon. Undaunted by the paralyzing cold of the journey, the staff officer focused a huge clumsy pair of field glasses, leaning perilously over the edge of the cockpit to examine distant enemy troop movements and supply dumps, making detailed diagrams which would be useful to the army when the troops advanced.

For the next installment of this tragi-comedy we can listen to Kusminsky himself.

"When not far from the Russian frontier, and still at a great height, we suddenly heard an explosion, and the whole apparatus quivered and leapt in the air. We found that the suction valve of the motor had burst. We were saved from destruction by the self-possession of my officer. He kept his head and did not move a muscle, so that I was able to shut off the fuel and open the contact. We began to descend in a glide, and to avoid capture by the enemy did our utmost to prolong our flight in the direction of the Russian lines.

"Although we had a very good map we could not tell precisely where we were. At last as we touched the ground we saw in the fields not far away a group of peasants. The officer at once shouted, 'Soak the apparatus with fuel and get matches ready, so that if they are Austrians we can set the whole thing on fire.' We had no need to do this, for they were Russians. We had come down about three miles within the Russian frontier, and soon a party of our own troops arrived and carried us back to their quarters."

Russian aviators were destined to have some strange adventures which were quite in keeping with the quixotic character of the race.

On July 20, 1915, for instance, a German two-seater happened to land by accident behind the Russian lines. Pilot and observer were immediately tied up and roped together, and rushed off to a prison camp for interrogation. The plane was left standing in a field where it was discovered by a Russian scientist who was visiting the front as a specialist observer and adviser on rationing. He hurried to the nearest airfield to find a pilot who had nothing to do. They returned together to look at the plane. It took some urging by the professor before the pilot agreed to get into the cockpit. He thought the machine was mined with booby traps. Watched by a crowd of a hundred curious peasants, the professor scrambled into the cockpit himself, then jumped out again to prove that the plane was quite safe.

A few minutes later the pair of them were on their way through the clouds. Hands clasped on his stomach, the professor watched approvingly as the pilot handled the unfamiliar controls. They had to gain height quickly, otherwise the Russians might take pot shots at the German aircraft. Likewise, the nearby German troops would certainly fire at a plane which had been identified as one stolen by the enemy.

The professor had an idea where German aviation headquarters lay. He somehow managed to plot a course which he thrust into the pilot's hand. The plane chugged on through low cloud and finally came down into the lower air. Directly below lay an airfield with great outcrops of wooden buildings. German HQ! Officers and men were passing from one block to another. The professor could not see them very well. He forced the unwilling pilot to go even lower. Their wheels almost skimmed the grass. Behaving like a predatory owl—but moving with less speed—the plane swept over the rooftops. Not one German paused to watch.

Still feeling dissatisfied, the professor demanded that the pilot go down yet again. He was making a plan of the layout so that Russian scouts would recognize it when they made their visit. He would have liked to land and look around. Mad with fear, the pilot reflected that his passenger was the usual kind of academic wizard, without any conception of what war meant.

Not a single shot had yet been fired! Were the Germans so stupid?

They were making a fourth circuit, even lower than the rest, totally ignoring the clumps of Germans now pointing at them. Without any warning, the guns opened up, firing at dangerously low angles in an effort to catch them as they came around again. One shell took the roof off a hut in an explosion of cordite and splintered timber.

It was an exciting moment when the wings of the plane lifted for the last time. Pulling hard for the outer perimeter of the encampment, the pilot suddenly remembered that he had not checked the fuel tank before they started. The engine might stall at any moment. He stayed as low as he could, skidding across the tops of the trees to avoid anti-aircraft fire.

Somehow they managed to reach the field from which they started. Nobody had even missed the plane. All the peasants had dispersed. Not a soul appeared as the pilot brought the machine down to a perfect landing. Without speaking, the professor quickly hopped out of the cockpit and trotted away to borrow a horse.

He wanted to reach Russian headquarters as soon as possible and present them with the vital plans.

A few days later a flock of Russian scout planes paid German air headquarters a visit and wiped it out in a flash of incendiary bullets and small-caliber bombs. This is only one example of Russian eccentricity. There are others.

The demand for bigger and bigger aircraft has always existed ever since man made his first pair of wings and jumped off a tower. Russian designers now had to obey the orders of the high command, a collection of officers who did not know a propeller from an aileron. Like the Americans, few of them had ever flown. Some had never seen an airplane at close quarters. But they wanted bigger and better planes. And this at a time when America, Germany and Britain were concentrating more upon the possibilities of smaller and faster and less vulnerable machines.

The Russian warlords wanted to think big, act big and put the biggest planes into the sky. This was one of the reasons for the Ilya Mourametz, nicknamed "Dreadnought." Its sudden appearance threw Igor Sikorsky, the acknowledged pioneer, into a rage. He recognized its lines all too well; he had designed it. It was obvious that somebody had tampered with the idea which, in the original conception, was more cautious and more experimental. Recalling that sets of the trial plans were stolen from his workshops about a year ago, he felt more suspicious than ever. They hushed it up, refused to go on with the investigation. Now, watching the trials of the Ilya Mourametz, he saw what had happened. It was downright piracy. In a sick, irritable mood, he went back to his own quarters, determined to make representations. But he never did anything about it. He was the unhappiest man in Russia for many months.

The Ilya Mourametz was believed to have a far greater endurance and climbing power than other planes, but Sikorsky never quite believed that it was even capable of getting off the ground. He had, of course, already seen it in the air, but that proved nothing. A plane of that size could fall out of the sky like an autumn leaf!

Sikorsky's prestige was dwindling now that other lesser designers were gaining facilities for experimental work. The only possible way of saving face was to have one of his own planes in action over the front. That would prove his superiority once and for all.

The Czar had been very insistent that Russia's most prominent designer visit the troops to instill confidence in air service support. It would also give him a chance to examine the situation as far as organization was concerned. The royal command did not, however, include permission to fly.

Sikorsky did not spend much time with his associates after the party arrived at the front. He left them to their own devices and went off on a whirlwind tour of airfields, looking for his own machines. He was missing for a time but turned up at an engineering base where he was teaching mechanics how to nurse the machines. He felt very happy to see that many Sikorsky planes were taking part in operations. Servicing and general maintenance were good, too. Operational results were not exceptional, but this was accounted for by the newness of the crews. They did not intend throwing their lives away without first knowing how to protect themselves. In the end the Russian air services failed through lack of co-operation between departments and between the high command and the forces in the field.

Still brooding over the Ilya Mourametz, which he steadfastly resented, Sikorsky tried to arrange to be a passenger in one of his own machines which was going on patrol. He was snugly aboard, sitting in the cockpit, when a fussy-mannered officer appeared, waving his arms in consternation. Sikorsky had to get out at once! The designer stood up, shouting abuse at the man. He had designed the plane! Why could he not fly in it? For answer the officer gave the age-old reply, that he had his orders. The Czar himself had decreed that Sikorsky must not fly.

The huge plane, very much in advance of its time, took off, leaving the designer sitting on a stool, eying it like a father and growling at the officer, who stood nearby, guarding him.

As it happened, this was the very day when the German air force was out to fight. The Sikorsky was quietly getting on with its scouting duties when it was suddenly surrounded by three German fighters. They poured a fusillade of shots into the length of the long thick fuselage while the pilot wrestled with the controls, wanting to sideslip out of trouble. It was hopeless; the bulk of the machine would not yield immediately to an order. Desperate, the pilot yelled to the gunner for a defensive action. One gun was already out of action. It had frozen and the stricken observer was staring straight up at the Germans, who were now massing, ready to make a fresh charge. The other gun was working, but it happened to be on the far side of the fuselage and the second observer could not move it across in time. There was only one thing to be done and the pilot did it. He managed to swing the plane around so that the fire side was facing the Germans, now whistling into a menacingly aggressive dive.

The next few moments were an inferno. With only one gun working, the observer did manage to shoot one enemy plane which came too near for its own good. The others sheered off, sensing the new danger. One whipped up underneath the Sikorsky to rake the unprotected part with fire. Sixteen holes punctured the fuel tanks. Their design prevented any danger of fire because they were partly encased in armor plate and double-skinned. But this did not prevent the precious fuel streaming away, vaporizing in the cold air. Mistaking the streams of white vapor for smoke from the engines, the Germans flew off, satisfied, leaving the Russian pilot to handle his charge as best he could. He was about to swing the long wings around and head for home when a lone German attacker came out of nowhere, firing continuously. One bullet went through the upper part of the pilot's arm. While he was trying to clamp a pad to the gaping wound to hold back the gushing blood, the interceptor came back to try and kill the observer, who was plugging up the holes in the fuel tank. Helpless, the observer did not dare move an inch. Spread-eagled on an outer surface, he looked down through two miles of emptiness at the earth below. He half-turned his head to witness the horrifying sight of the enemy plane leveling off some distance away in preparation for a new attack. It was all too easy to imagine the calculating eyes as they looked through the ring of the gunsight. In a frenzy, he tried to lift his hands off the surface of the tank. They would not move; they were frozen hard to the metal. He had to do one thing or the other. He did not relish being shot to bloody ribbons and falling from his perch. He held his breath and deliberately ripped his hands away from the metal. When he looked back, he saw the shape of his hands imprinted on the tank. Every scrap of skin had been torn off. His palms oozing blood and feeling as though they had been shot through with tiny needles, he slumped back into the cockpit just in time to hear the rattle of the German machine gun. He was unhurt, untouched. It was a miracle!

They passed slowly over Krasnostav in search of their airfield. As they landed they saw the lone figure sitting on the stool near the hangar. Sikorsky strolled over as the machine jerked to a halt. Not even he, the creator of this monster, could quite believe that it was capable of taking so much punishment and still survive.

Skyborne Executioners

The country which contributed so much to the development of the airplane as a weapon of war also chalked up the highest aggregate of victories—France.

In the prewar period France had a mushrooming of many industries vaguely akin to airplane building. When the war started the government took over hundreds of minor automobile concerns. Any tiny workshop capable of turning out engine parts was instantly called to the service of the nation. Any large space with a roof over it was commandeered and made into a place where airplanes could be assembled. Some of the film studios were taken in hand and the irate producers and directors evicted, just as Beaconsfield studios were snatched on an overnight ultimatum when the British government wanted somewhere to settle a magneto-making plant in 1939. In all quarters of Paris and throughout the outlying industrial belt the smallest workshops were at work, turning out parts which were, in turn, sent to assembly points. La Belle France tucked up her skirts and ignored the oil stains. Fashion was out. Utility was in. The war was on.

One of the results of this standardization of production was that France soon turned out two or three completed planes every week, and this before other warring nations shifted toward anything resembling an industrial drive.

In military affairs the advent of the airplane made rethinking necessary. On the advice of seasoned French pilots the entire conduct of an army in the field was radically altered to prevent German reconnaissance machines gaining important information about troop movements. While on the move all troops were ordered to remain hidden without firing at enemy planes which came looking for them. For its part the French air service now entered into a period of intensive reconnaissance duty. Between the beginning of the war and the end of January 1915, 10,000 flights were made, a total of 18,000 hours in the air. No other air service equaled these figures.

The great enemy of the day was the Taube, a fast, agile German machine. The French high command was determined to sweep these planes right out of the sky before they could do any more damage. Despite all the hard, hazardous work put in by French pilots, adverse criticisms began to appear in the press. Some papers tried to give the impression that aviators were playboys, wasting their time flying high and safe over enemy territory. It was far from the case. Unless the operation demanded it, no pilot ever went above 5,000 or 6,000 feet, risking his neck in the curtain of shrapnel thrown up by enemy artillery. Determined to bring the air service into the limelight it deserved, the French government issued a press release to all newspapers and magazines, emphasizing that wherever possible it should be printed in full. Here, in the terse words of officialdom, is all the excitement and drama which was enacted in the first phase of the war.

"September 3. In the course of a reconnaissance a French pilot was attacked by a German aviator. The latter was promptly pursued by a second French aviator, who, subjecting him to a violent rifle fusillade, forced him precipitately to descend.

"September 5. A French aviator struck a bivouac of a company of the Guards, with the result that eight men and eight horses fell, while thirty-two soldiers were wounded.

"September 12. A German noncommissioned officer showed his men a coat almost torn to tatters, which belonged to one of some sixty men wounded by a projectile that had just been hurled by one of our aviators.

"End of September. At Autry a bomb killed some thirty soldiers at the edge of the Seriut, another projectile killing or wounding twenty soldiers. A staff major installed there had to change his quarters in all haste.

"October 15. To the southeast of Lille a cavalry division which had been pursued and fired on during the whole of the day was at length prevented from carrying out its object by a bomb.

"November 1. A staff major at Thielt had a severe trial from the fire of our airplanes, which hurled thirty-two bombs or shells there."

Most of this information was extracted, significantly enough, from enemy notebooks and official documents captured or taken from bodies as the French forces advanced over the battlefield.

The Germans soon found that the French aviators were willing to match their own bloodthirsty daring. As one writer said: "They even seemed to develop some sort of apologetic admiration of their opponents' daring." Out of that admiration came the age of the aces.

The Germans feared many French fliers, but most of all they feared Senator Reymond, one of the first to really scare the Hun. The London *Daily Telegraph* published this report of his death on October 23, 1914: "While reconnoitering the enemy's lines he was struck by a Prussian bullet, but made a final effort to regain the French camp. His strength failing, the machine fell at an equal distance between the two opposing armies. The result was a fierce combat for the possession of the fallen airplane and fallen aviator, as the Germans were quick to recognize the value of the information he had obtained. In the struggle the French were finally successful, and Senator Reymond was carried back to the French lines, where he had still the strength to furnish to his superiors a detailed and precise report, which proved of the utmost value. Senator Reymond died a few hours later."

Many French pilots were firm adherents of the Biblical maxim "An eye for an eye." In this case it was to be a life for a life. No less a pair than Garros and Pegoud flew their own sorties day after day. Garros felt quietly angry over Reymond's premature death. They had been good friends for months, determined to go through the war together and emerge unscathed. Not even Garros, who later invented his own form of quick-firing gun mechanism, was to know how many of his friends would be shot down and killed in the years to come.

Garros was flying at 6,000 feet. He wanted one lone German to kill and then he would go home, satisfied that Reymond was avenged. A clear sky invited daring, presaged quick death for somebody. Without cloud cover a man must act quickly. Still thinking about his many conversations with Reymond—they argued about politics and often nearly came to blows—Garros was about to start the long climb "upstairs" into the brilliant blueness when he saw three German planes below, going on their way toward the French lines. They were inviting trouble, without any attempt at a proper formation, without rearguard or upper cover. Several French patrols were out that morning, just waiting for the chance of tearing Germans to bits.

He happened to be in such a position that the Germans were actually heading straight for him. The sun was at his back. They could not see him for the time being. He was confident that he was unseen. One German was slightly behind the rest now, a laggard who would pay for such casual slowness with his life.

Garros felt an unholy satisfaction as his plane went into the dive. Garros was always an unusual man; he could actually relax when the fighting was at its most violent. Taking off and landing made him like a coiled spring. He had bad nerves at the wrong times, no nerves at all at the right times.

He began firing when well within range. The sound of the gun was deafening in his own ears, but he managed to concentrate on the effect of the bullets. The German moved erratically first to the left and then to the right until Garros suddenly swirled around him, showing only the front of his machine and preventing the enemy from getting a broadside view of him. Judging by the Hun's behavior, he must be sweating now. It was so easy to recognize the telltale symptoms—the nervous twitching of the ailerons, the up-and-down moves, the hesitant stutter of unsure gunfire.

Garros was only waiting, now that he knew his man. Then, at last, he raced in to smash out the death blow, the *coup de grâce* which would avenge Reymond. He fired thirty-four bullets, some of them straight through the flimsy fuselage. A row of newly punctured holes were clearly visible, the commas of the disaster to come within seconds. Here and there new bullets ripped the fabric back, exposing parts of the bleached wooden spars and framework. It was like slaying an animal on the run. The damage was not to Garros' liking. He wanted to make more of it. His next shot crashed deep into the guts of the German engine. A wavering plume of thick oily smoke was caught in the slipstream and thrown straight back into the pilot's face. He tried to stand up, waving his arms about in a creeping panic. This was precisely what Garros had been waiting for. Flying in from his favorite forward position, he hammered bullet after bullet into the man's chest. It was all over in a few seconds. The pilot was thrown across the rim of the cockpit, blood streaming from multiple wounds. While Garros sat watching, enjoying his role of executioner in this solitary drama of the clear skies, the German machine heaved over on its side and began to fall as flames gutted the engine, licking at the wedged body.

Garros flew home, singing.

Jealous of his friend's success in this game of fast revenge, Pegoud felt impelled to do likewise or better. For some time he had been studying dozens of intelligence reports, scrutinizing photographs supplied by the high-flying reconnaissance squadrons. When some sheets detailing the position of an ammunition dump about twelve miles away came in, he had his plane armed with twice its usual load of bombs. Telling nobody what he intended doing, he taxied the machine down the runway and took off to head for the place. He had been in the air less than fifteen minutes when he nearly bumped into a pair of enemy Aviatiks on the prowl, looking for trouble. Shooting fast, he downed both of them within a few minutes. This was a fantastic feat: his own plane was so slow on the controls, hampered by the abnormal bomb load. He was not so sure that he would be able to get through any more fights at this rate.

The ammunition dump was well guarded. They saw him a moment before he saw them. He had the bombs ready, all nine of them prepared for a simultaneous drop. He went down as low as possible. Any withering cross fire would convert *him* into a bomb! The Germans held their fire, wondering, their fingers itching on their triggers in an anxiety of uncertainty. It was what he was counting on. Five seconds . . . four seconds . . . three . . . two . . . one!

Then he dropped them.

He heard only one explosion, that was all. Disappointed and bemused, he was about to go down through the funnel of smoke and shoot the place up with his gun, when, with a rending roar which shook not only the earth but also the blanket of air over acres of ground, the earth went up in a cascade of black fumes.

Pegoud did not feel satisfied. He wanted to do more than blow up ammunition dumps. Next day he went out and shot up an enemy balloon. Twenty-four hours later he was back again, inflicting telling punishment on a battery of big-caliber guns which were supposed to be protecting the rest of the balloons. One gun received a bomb on top of it, splitting the thick barrel open along its length. They gave Pegoud the Military Medal for that. He declined it. Later he was forced into it. He told journalists that he was flying for one reason, to erase the terrible memory of Reymond's death. Nobody would print this odd statement. Nobody really understood it. The thought was too gruesome for a public which liked its popular romantic heroes. He turned away from the cluster of journalists, sickened by their attitude toward the war.

When the time came to die Roland Garros elected to finish himself off in the devil-may-care way which had been demonstrated in so many of his fights against the Germans. One of Germany's biggest Zeppelins was seen approaching Nancy. There was no doubt that it presaged a bombing raid designed to demoralize the civilian population. The gauntlet was flung down to the fighter pilots. The British would not take it up. They hesitated, they said, because a bombing raid was by no means certain.

The ominous shape of the Zeppelin could now be seen from the outskirts of Nancy, a town of about 110,000 people which stood · beyond the fighting areas and the bloodshed of the war.

In the streets, particularly near the eighteenth-century cathedral in the Ville-Neuve, hundreds of frightened people stood about, waiting for the sign which would show them the way out. They wanted to run but they had nowhere to go. The shadow of the Zeppelin would soon strike across the Place Stanislas, then creep onto the Place Carrière.

What would the damage be like? Few in the street crowds knew. They had no experience of bombing. Would the prized triumphal arch erected by Stanislas in honor of Louis XV be broken down to a heap of pitted stones? Or would some of the bombs destroy the wool and cotton spinning sheds upon which so many depended for a living?

There was no panic, only foreboding of death. Every intelligence post was using the telephone, contacting airfields. Would *anybody* come and protect Nancy? Would just one plane come out of the clouds and show fight?

Nothing came. The air was filled not with the wasp-tone of fighter machines but the sibilant hissing of the Zeppelin, looking like an air mammoth as she nosed across the city at about thirty miles an hour. Nancy was an ideal target, undefended, unprotected. The bombs could be dropped at leisure.

Some of the streets were deserted now except for cats and dogs which wandered without concern among the café tables. Everybody who could move was below ground, trembling in the cellars where some clawed others out of the way to find more protected spots.

Nancy waited in the early morning, waited to be killed, her arteries ripped apart by high explosive.

Nobody aboard the Zeppelin noticed one lone airplane following course on that first exploratory traverse of the city. The Germans were too busy looking down at the victim which would shortly be covered in a pall of smoke and dust as building after building toppled and fell.

Roland Garros did not spend too much time thinking about the position in which he found himself. His airfield had received a warning about the Zeppelin. None of the others wanted to chase it. They said it would be hopeless. If the reports were true, more than one plane would be needed to drive the Zeppelin away. From past experience everybody knew that nothing deterred the commanders of these gigantic weapons. They would fly through all the fire in the world, destroy the target and then, as calmly, come back through the fire.

Cursing the attitude of his so-called comrades, Garros ran to his plane and took off within a few minutes. In his pocket he stuffed the last bearing and position of the Zeppelin. Incredibly, he had never seen one at close quarters. Good—it was better to work in ignorance in a matter like this. One thing he did know was that every Zeppelin carried enough guns for an armada. There was only one safe point, they said, and that was directly above the gasbag. You could not be seen there . . . but you could be heard.

He picked the Zeppelin up some distance away from Nancy and followed it, hugging the clouds as much as he dared. From where he was flying he could see the Zeppelin and the target. How long did he have? Ten minutes, no more than fifteen. In that time he had to make up his mind what to do.

Aboard the Zeppelin they prepared the bombs, dozens of them, all waiting for the moment of descent.

After one inspection of the layout of Nancy the Zeppelin commander turned about and made a return trip. He was crossing the outskirts when Garros hit him with all the weight of the fighter plane. The Zeppelin crumpled in the center. Affected by the strain, the girders began to buckle until the entire core of the craft was falling inward. The bulk ceased going forward and began to move downward, almost gracefully, but always downward.

Somewhere in the wreckage of the hole caused by the entrance of the fighter plane lay the broken body of Roland Garros, the man who saved Nancy.

28

American Privateers

When the United States entered World War I in April 1917 it was possible for a man to hold in one hand all the plans for building aircraft then in existence. Since 1914 few American statesmen even tried to foresee a time when the nation might be dragged into a conflict which was taking place several thousand miles away. The American government had not paid out a cent for aircraft research, and when a cost figure of $1,500 million was allocated for that purpose the production lines were soon in such a chaotic state that few fighting planes were ready to be shipped to France on schedule. Politics also played a dangerous part in fouling up production plans. The power game seemed to rule the drawing board of industry. Attempts to perfect an engine, ironically christened Liberty, failed. After the war it was too late, but the Liberty design did reach perfection and was installed in various aircraft.

It is not generally realized that America was in the war for some time before the official declaration was made. It was Norman Prince, an attorney from Massachusetts, who first thought of getting his fellow Americans together. Many of these Continental rovers and itinerants were amateur pilots. They said that they were

334

willing to fly any machines they could get and under the French flag, too, providing the French government did not object to such a scheme. Prince called them together but failed to inspire them. One of the biggest objections to his scheme was that anybody flying or serving in any capacity for any country other than the United States would have to take an oath of allegiance. Although these men were living outside their own country for a variety of reasons, they did not want to give their unswerving loyalty to any country other than their own.

Prince was willing to try anything. He knew that he had stepped off on the wrong foot with his touchy contemporaries. Using his own slim resources, he arranged to meet one of the most re-markable—and still unsung—men of the First World War, Dr. Edmund L. Gros, the driving force behind the American Ambulance Service. The service was noncombatant and deemed very successful. Gros was in a good position. He knew just what certain government departments could do when they stood on the hind legs of dignity, supposedly safeguarding their own interests. He and Prince had many long talks about Prince's plan for a corps of American pilots. Gros was doubtful whether it would work. He wondered what the American State Department would have to say.

Prince told him that Washington need not be notified until the corps became an accomplished fact and a recognized entity in the war machine. Gros stubbornly said that the displeasure of Uncle Sam was something to be reckoned with, especially in questions of material aid. They might need help later on. Infected by Prince's enthusiasm, however, Gros did take it upon himself to write to two friends, Robert W. Bliss and Robert Astor Chandler, and they, in turn, talked to a liberal-minded member of the French Air Ministry, Jarousse de Silac, selling him on the idea that France could use all the war help she could get at this moment.

Like Gros, Silac at first dismissed the idea of France getting Americans to serve under the tricolor. It might lead to trouble, to international friction. Bliss said that far greater trouble could re-sult if the Germans reached Paris. For the next few days Silac made his own inquiries, knowing that the Americans would not swear any allegiance to France. He had a bunch of promising volunteers on his hands, a group of young men who could help

France, given the chance. The problem looked so simple. Silac knew that easy problems were the hardest. The solution lay under his nose, but he did not notice it until somebody mentioned the parallel case of the French Foreign Legion in which more than a dozen Americans were currently serving. Members of the Legion took no oaths of allegiance at all; they merely agreed to obey orders and France worked on the assumption that the officer giving the orders would be a Frenchman and subject to conditions of allegiance.

Thus, the first American squadron to fly over the battlefield was tentatively formed. Gros meanwhile spent weeks interviewing Continental Americans on the loose, the rich and the poor, a few drawn from the Foreign Legion itself. He asked only two questions: "Can you fly an airplane?" and "Would you *like* to fly an airplane?" Strange things to ask men who were often little more than wandering artists, daredevils, internationally minded adventurers and playboys. Those engaged in certain enterprises were ingeniously disengaged from their commitments. The Foreign Legion men were taken out of their uniforms and presented with khaki, and told to consider themselves members of the French air service.

By April 17, 1916, one full year before America officially declared war on Germany, the United States had a squadron in France, thanks to Norman Prince. It was cloaked under the title *Escadrille Américaine* (American Squadron). One source says: "With America standing coldly aloof from the war, these one hundred young Americans had freely volunteered their services to aid France in her hour of supreme trial."

One of the men, William Thaw, suffered defective vision, bad hearing and had something wrong with his knee, while the others were technically incapacitated. Gros politely looked the other way and scribbled evasive notes on their military dossiers, realizing that if he became too particular the Escadrille Américaine would never become airborne at all. At this stage there were only seven qualified men in the group, Elliot Cowdin, James McConnell, Victor Chapman, William Thaw, Kiffin Rockwell, Bert Hall and the founder, Norman Prince. All could fly airplanes more or less, but none of them knew anything about fighting. Gros and Silac took the opti-

mistic view that practice must make perfect. They were also aware
that every one of the seven was a strong individualist. Their planes
were to be Nieuports, the fast-flying planes, then in good supply.
Nieuports were suited to conditions in an era when heavy bombing
and Germany's Gotha had not made any impression on the opposition.

It was finally decided to send the Americans to Luxeuil, a
Vosges town, where a mass of brand-new equipment had been
assembled in preparation. More than seventy ground staff personnel
were there for several weeks, operating a nonoperational squadron
while the militarists desperately searched for pilots. Two French
officers were in residence to welcome the Americans, Lieutenant
de Laage de Meux and Captain Thenault. They saw to it that a
mass of transport was always available for the new boys, that the
best hotel in Luxeuil was at their disposal.

On arrival the Americans also found a real pilot waiting for
them. This was Captain Haape, a pioneer of bombing techniques,
but at that moment recuperating after several exhausting missions
in which he lost some of his best men. His first assignment was to
take the Americans out on a tour of the surrounding countryside to
inspect possible emergency landing grounds, the places where a
limping, shot-up machine could be put down with a minimum of
risk. It was not a very auspicious start to the careers of the Americans.

Gros was still busy looking through the lists of pilots who were
flying with French squadrons. He discovered a few more Americans,
namely, Didier Masson, Paul Pavelka, Lawrence Rumsey, Clyde
Balsley, Dudley Hill, Chouteau Johnson and Raoul Lufbery. Hearing about the gathering at Luxeuil, they agreed to go over there
to form the main echelon. All were versed in flying techniques. The
seven of them were to form the backbone of Luxeuil for a short
time before their ranks were thinned by German bullets.

Captain Thenault, a Frenchman, was appointed CO. He was a
pilot of exquisite skill and with a wide international outlook. The
French took their time selecting a leader for the oddly assorted
squadron. A nationalist would have been out of the question. Only
because of Thenault's habit of talking about "one world" and "one

people" was the job offered to him at all. For once his garrulousness stood him in good stead.

Some prejudice was now beginning to grow. It started when the French people got to know about the Escadrille Américaine. Criticisms of "foreign pilots who live in the lap of luxury" made the authorities red in the face. Dr. Gros quickly suggested that the Americans be allowed to show their prowess in order to turn the critics' disapproval into other channels.

Nobody felt quite sure that Gros was right. If some of the pilots were good at their job, others were still inept and clumsy, and a number of ex-factory Nieuports had already been thrown on the scrapheap after crashes when rookie pilots tried to land while still fifty feet or more over the grass runway. Others nose-dived into the hangars. The accident rate mounted with the write-off rate.

Miraculously, no lives were lost, but this was only due to the efficient ambulance corps which patrolled the field whenever planes were flying. Prejudice went on spreading while the French government made no attempt at achieving a friendly liaison with Dr. Gros, who felt a personal responsibility. Working alone, he did his best with a hostile press. After all, he had virtually enlisted them in this madness. At a meeting of the heads of the French armed services, he said that after some study of the strategic position, he had reached the conclusion that the Escadrille Américaine could be better employed at Bar-le-Duc, near Verdun, where there was every indication that the Germans would attack. Even Gros, an astute man, was not aware that Verdun was to be one of the decisive areas of the entire war. He was, of course, correct in his broad contention. The Germans had already attached Fokkers, flown by such men as Boelcke and Immelmann, to the Fifth Army. So successful was their impact that two new air groups were quickly formed. They were called the Single-seater Fighter North and South Commands, and placed under the direct personal command of General von Hoeppner, who was also in charge of the German air service in 1916. The General believed that the only way to make any progress in the difficult Verdun sector was to have the sky full of German planes throughout the hours of daylight.

Back in 1915 General "Boom" Trenchard, for Britain, and Commandant du Peuty, for France, tried to reach agreement over the Verdun question, and they drew up an agreement embodying an idea for a strategic offensive in which the Escadrille Américaine was destined to be heavily involved.

Verdun was becoming the focal point of the French air service, especially in the field of photographic reconnaissance. When the battle did finally develop, a network of processing stations worked at top speed, making thousands of prints a day to enable the infantry to go on fighting to the best advantage. One station alone produced five thousand prints in a single day, many within one hour of exposure by pilots as they surveyed the turmoil of the forward areas. Another example was demonstrated when planes flew over General Mangin's attack on Fort Douaemont on May 22, took their pictures and returned to a developing station where prints were made at a fast rate, showing the progress of the fight. Key sets of these were carried by fast planes to be dropped on General Mangin's headquarters.

American Nieuports, distinguished by the head of an Indian chief painted on their fuselage, were quickly put into action. Just as quickly the casualty lists came into being. Thaw and Rockwell were among the first to be injured. A bullet slashed an artery in Thaw's arm. Covered in blood, he managed to get his machine back to Bar-le-Duc before collapsing. Rockwell had a worse experience when a bullet exploded on his windshield, ripping part of his face to shreds. Almost blinded by streaming blood, he managed to reach his own airfield. Realizing that his nerve might go unless he did something about it right away, he spoke persuasively to a disapproving medical officer and wheedled permission to fly again at once. His head wrapped in bandages, he was among the clouds next day, looking for a good fight.

Thaw and Rockwell were not the only ones to receive an early and painful initiation. Some days later Victor Chapman got mixed up with four savage German planes, who literally shot his machine to pieces. One bullet streaked across his scalp, giving him a thorough bloodbath. Try as he would, he was unable to staunch it. He put one hand on top of his head, clasping his handkerchief down on the wound, but it soon soaked through again. He hoped that the blood would coagulate, but the wound was too deep for that. It had more than parted his hair; there was a furrow through the skull bone. Controlling the plane was impossible, especially after one of the enemy pilots put a burst through the stabilizing wires. Listing steeply, the Nieuport landed at Bar-le-Duc. Chapman had to be helped out, washed in blood from head to toe. He was a frightening sight. The doctor came running out of his quarters to assist the pilot but was allowed only to bandage him. Chapman argued that he would be no use in bed in the sick bay. All he wanted was an emergency dressing for his head. The doctor knew enough about the crazy Americans not to argue about it.

One of the first things the American squadron had to discover for themselves was how to fly under battle conditions and extricate themselves from dogfights. Captain Thenault reckoned that the only method of obtaining the answer was to plunge straight into it, disastrous though this might be. One day he took Balsley, Rockwell, and Prince out on a voyage of discovery and they ran straight into no less than fourteen alert Huns. There was no reaching the enemy; they were firing at the longest effective range, encircling the Americans and dodging about whenever one of the Nieuports tried to make a charge. Thenault led one final dash, not attacking but trying desperately to get away.

All but one machine made it. Balsley was left behind, one man against fourteen experienced, highly trained Germans. Diving and weaving, he could not shake them off. They followed him everywhere, sometimes in a solid angry arrowhead with all guns spitting, more often in a loose formation which confused him. Bullets tore at his plane. One entered his leg, ripping at the flesh and nearly making him faint with pain. Hardly able to see where he was going, he tried to lift his machine out of harm's way.

Still the Germans came, their guns barking a warning. They were using the outlawed explosive bullets which did tremendous damage to a machine. For some minutes it looked as though Balsley was going to get away with it after all. Only a few German pursuers remained, dogging his trail through the sky, trying to finish him off. A few moments later Balsley was out of their reach as he bumped his plane down in a field. He then half rose out of the cockpit, blood still pouring down his leg from the gaping wound. He collapsed just as help reached him. In the hospital he recovered slightly, then showed signs of picking up properly.

There was not an American in the squadron who did not feel bad about Balsley. Thenault, the leader, never ceased to reproach himself. He could, he admitted, have stayed where he was in that circle of Germans and fought it out, but at the time it looked stupid to do anything but try and escape. He believed that the others, all close personal friends of Balsley, were putting the finger of guilt on him. It was not like that at all. In truth, they admired him for his leadership, the pluck and courage he showed when flying with them.

Balsley was recovering when Victor Chapman, Lufbery and Prince decided to fly over to the hospital with some fruit for him. En route they were suddenly set upon by a wolf pack of Fokkers. Chapman was shot down within seconds when he tried to draw the German fire while the others made their getaway. His plane fell fast, a torch which broke up into a thousand pieces before hitting the ground.

Victor Chapman was the first American pilot to meet his death at the hands of the Germans. This was no senseless slaughter. Apart from the heroic aspect of the sacrifice which he made for his fellow pilots, the event itself served to bring to a sober halt the speculations of bloodless glory in which many of the young Americans had been reveling.

What were the reactions of the high command to the activities of the Escadrille Américaine during the five months in which it operated at the front? Certainly, none of the brass hats who visited the squadron returned to headquarters with anything to say against the young aliens who had chosen to fight for France. On the other hand, a number of reports did contain such words as "inexperienced" and "brash." Weighing one opinion against the other, the High Command now decided to withdraw the Escadrille Américaine from the front for the time being and station it at the former base at Luxeuil. Few of the ebullient Americans realized why they were being sent back.

On arrival at Luxeuil they met pilots of the Royal Naval Air Service, which had fifty fliers and a total of one thousand mechanics and ground staff. Together they cemented a perfect *entente cordiale*. The Americans carried their own aura of carefree life about with them despite recent setbacks and the tragedy of Chapman's death, and when Lufbery, Thaw and Hill went to Paris on leave, they lent color to their growing legend by pooling together to buy a lion cub which was adopted by the squadron and christened Whiskey.

Trips to Paris were a steady feature of life with the Escadrille Américaine, and the men always paid a call on their benefactor, Dr. Gros. They also met such aces as Nungesser, who gave them some useful tips about fighting the enemy. Operationally speaking, few of the pilots were now lagging behind in the race for a deadly efficiency. Sorties were flown daily from Luxeuil, most of the pilots going out with the avowed intention of killing Germans to revenge Chapman, whose memory had now become a spur which would take them through the hell of war.

Rockwell, in particular, seemed keen to avenge Chapman, but was himself shot to pieces when he became separated from Lufbery with whom he was flying. A Fokker tempted him away from his companion, dived at him at a speed of a hundred miles an hour and shot him through like a sieve. When they found his body it was quite obvious that the Germans were still using explosive bullets, for his throat had been torn out. The Americans were enraged. Armed with this evidence and a bunch of photographs of Kiffin Rockwell's ravaged body, they quickly made representations to Geneva, hoping to create a final ban of explosive bullets.

Nothing came of it. Geneva could not act. It was obvious that the only war law was the law of steel and fire. Again the Americans, aided by the French and British, set out to score off the Germans for what they had perpetrated. The pace was becoming much too fast, in the opinion of the High Command. It was essential to conserve the Escadrille Américaine for other duties. The Americans were put on the job of escorting bombers. On one of these missions, Prince, homing in the darkness, misjudged his height and collided with a high-tension cable. His machine somersaulted with a splintering crash while he was tossed out of the cockpit. He shot through the air and landed on both feet in soft ground. Trying to get up, he could not stand. Believing that his feet were firmly embedded in the glutinous soil, he tried again, only to discover that both legs were fractured. There was a choking sensation deep in his stomach. He knew that he must have internal injuries. His intestines churned as he cried out for help. After three days of sweating helplessness in a field hospital, he died.

They all missed Prince, one of the major forces behind the formation of the Escadrille Américaine, but this was no time for mourning and weeping. The Somme battle was raging. In dire need of aerial reinforcements, the strategists decided to risk a wild gamble on the Americans.

Before anything could happen, though, there was something to be dealt with. Many high officers objected to the actual name of the squadron. It must be changed for policy reasons. The public was getting the wrong idea about it. In the end they called it the Escadrille Lafayette. When this was announced, Dr. Gros was showered with offers of help. He had to turn many of them down. His brain child was becoming an embarrassment. In one press interview he said that what France needed was men. In a matter of days he had fifty volunteers, some of whom had to be shuttled to the École Blériot to learn which end of an airplane was which. It was almost unbelievable that many of the volunteers had never sat in a cockpit. Some had never seen an airplane.

They were wonderful Fokker fodder, moaned the pessimists.

29

Hellbent for Hades

When America entered the war, France dictated certain terms. Premier Ribot informed the newcomers that 4,500 planes with qualified pilots and ground crews would be needed in time for the 1918 offensive. Before America had recovered from the shock of that heavy order (and possibly the exaggeration of it!), Ribot said that production plans should use as a target the manufacture of 200 planes and 4,000 engines a month. An immediate vote of $640 million had to be made. The American government took many years to recover from that appropriation. There was now a growing danger of confusion on the factory front until such key groups as L-W-F, Burgess, Boeing, Vought and Gallaudet could regear their plants.

One of the first steps was to organize the production, under license, of British DH-4 machines. A start was also made on the production of JN-4D training planes, which were likely to be in demand. Designers mobilized one of the biggest drives in industrial history. Drawn into it was Orville Wright, who acted as consultant engineer to the Dayton Wright Company, Jesse G. Vincent and J. G. Hall. Vincent and Hall brought out a V-8 engine which developed 300 horsepower. The militarists considered it too powerful and a menace to any pilot, no matter how skilled. The L-W-F Company modified its existing designs and went into assembly-line production.

One of the first mistakes in this huge campaign, now employing thousands of skilled and semiskilled men, was a limitation of horsepower. Few of the advisers knew what was wanted; they let themselves be dominated by the army. No sooner had the first prototypes been bench and air tested than protests from France said that greater horsepower was certainly needed. Already the German Fokker factories were bringing out big-capacity engines which would soon be in use. The Germans knew, of course, that the Allied offensive of 1918 was bound to come. They were intent upon being one step ahead in men and machines. When Allied intelligence reports revealed the staggering details of German productivity, a panic went through the American factories like a chill wind. As a result, very few American aircraft ever reached the field of battle.

One department responsible for a whole series of pitiful blunders was the Aviation Section of the Signal Corps, a body appointed to guide America's war destiny in the air. None of the bigwigs on any of the innumerable committees which surrounded the Aviation Section had ever done any flying, few of them understood the use of the wartime plane. They, in turn, were supervised by the General Staff where ignorance was even more widespread. It was becoming obvious that a strong man was needed to control this organization. The choice lighted upon Major General George O. Squier, a West Point graduate with a Johns Hopkins Ph.D. He certainly had an international outlook and knew what the face of war looked like, thanks to eighteen months as military attaché to the British Army.

As soon as he sat down to start the job of forming a competent flying corps, he looked beyond the military field and picked civilians who were acknowledged specialists in their own lines. One of his immediate headaches was caused by the selection of flying instructors. A nation-wide hunt for would-be teachers produced the strangest crop of humanity ever assembled at any flying field. Some were downright eccentric, as witness the former rancher turned pilot, who issued a strict order that cadets must not make any more rough landings! But mingling with the oddities were those with some sense, including Colonel Frank Lahm, General Foulois,

Colonel Billy Mitchell, all of whom were to play a big role in the war.

Flying training within America was obviously too skimpy to fit the men for combat, and the United States made arrangements for sending recruits across the Atlantic for advanced flying. It was here that the fun and games started. Most of the cadet pilots were tickled pink at the chance of going abroad. Snail-like progress was made. Some of them were hopeless.

"The first one to take off," wrote one cadet, "was a bit uneasy and the instructor had to taxi out for him. He ran all the way across the field, and it was a big one, and then pulled the stick right back into his stomach. . . . The next one did better. He got off and zigzagged a bit, but instead of making a circuit he went straight on. His instructor remarked that he would probably land in Scotland, because he didn't know how to turn.

"I got off in a Pup yesterday. Gosh, what a thrill! They are not so different, but they are so quick and sensitive that they will crash taking off or landing before you know what they are going to do. I didn't bust anything but I pancaked like the devil landing. . . .

"Flew a Spad today. Easy to fly but dangerous as hell. Just like flying the famous barn door . . . and it has the gliding angle of a brick. I've always laughed at the regulars wearing spurs to fly in but I needed a pair in this Spad. It bucked just like a bronco."

And finally, after months of training:

"France! Here's where we sober up and get down to real serious work."

Dr. Gros, already a veteran in all matters affecting Americans in the air, was now commissioned as a lieutenant colonel in the United States Air Service. His work was supposed to take in liaison duties between the Americans and the French. He was still very much a free agent, though, and had 267 men in the Escadrille Lafayette; of these, 180 had been in action while the main body from the States was still in training. Fifty-one were killed while attached to the French forces, nineteen were wounded, fifteen were prisoners of war and eleven died in crashes and other accidents. The score against Germany was 199. Armed with these figures and very little else except a personal friendship with many of the individuals concerned, Gros began the difficult job of getting them discharged from the French forces and admitted to the American air service.

The first snag was age. Looking through his lists, he found that veterans like Robert Rockwell, Kenneth Littauer, David McK. Peterson, Robert Soubiran, Phelps Collins, Raoul Lufbery, John Huffer, Kenneth Marr and Charles Biddle were all well over Washington's idea of an age limit. Gros got in touch with Billy Mitchell, giving the ages of the men, some of whom were over thirty. After an entanglement with the usual thickets of red tape, Mitchell referred him to General Pershing, who, surprisingly, agreed not to say a word while these men were inducted into the American air service from the French-controlled Escadrille Lafayette.

Every American remained an individualist. "Kepi" Littauer, for instance, is still remembered as one of the finest observation pilots of the war. Norman Hall, who flew with him, said: "By some miracle he manages to survive. As flight commander of the 88th Observation Squadron he invariably flies at low altitudes; he is always being pounced upon by enemy pursuit ships, and one day a bullet punctured his windshield right in the middle, the bullet missing his head by the thickness of a cigarette paper."

Littauer was one of the few men able to handle the uncertain, unpredictable Caudron two-seater. The air force could not do without him. Colonel H. E. Hartney, onetime commanding officer of the First Pursuit Group and a Littauer admirer, said that he was always a "source of encouragement and enthusiasm to his men."

The Americans were now settling down to the task of organization in the air, as witness this diary entry written by an unknown pilot:

"There are six machines in a flight. Nigger leads and McGregor and Cal are on his right, behind and a little above. Springs and I are on the left and Thompson is in the center in the space between Cal and me. We fly in the form of a triangle with the back corners high. McGregor is deputy flight commander and takes command in case anything happens to Nigger. We fly pretty close together and have a set of signals. If Nigger is going to turn sharp, he drops his wing on that side. If he is going to dive steep, he holds up his arm. If he wants us to come up close or wants to call our attention to something he shakes both wings. If it's a Hun, he shakes his wings and points and fires his guns. If he means 'yes,' he bobs his nose up and down and if he means 'no' he shakes his wings. If we see a Hun and he doesn't, we fire our guns and fly up in front and point. We fly at three-quarters throttle so we can always pull up. If he has trouble and wants us to go on, he fires a red light from his Very pistol. If he wants us to follow him out of a fight he fires a white light. If he wants to signal the other flights, he fires a green light."

Despite this kind of arrangement, there were many casualties. The Hun was in good form, finding the Americans easy to dispose of. Among the early dead was Captain Benbow. A friend of his sent a letter to base: "Dear Bill, You remember that big dog back at Hounslow? Well, he ain't got no master no more." Benbow was buried where he crashed, his flying boots still on his feet, his own propeller forming a cross over the mound.

"He went out the other day alone," wrote a contemporary, "and managed to get up in the sun above a flight of Hun scouts. He got on the tail of the rear one and would have gotten him but both guns jammed. Then the others turned back on him and chased him home. He was as mad as a hornet and spent the next day oiling and adjusting his guns. He went back to the same place at the same time and found the same Huns again. No one knows exactly what happened but Archie called up and said they saw him coming out of Hunland with five Huns on his tail. Just as he got to the lines two of them fired a burst and his plane dived into the ground on our side of the lines and he was killed. He was certainly a fine fellow."

Some of the Americans met the Richthofen circus with disastrous results. One, Randall, was attacked by a Hun pilot who showed an unintentional humor by shooting him in the backside. After that Randall had to sit down in a lopsided position. "Fine for sitting on stairs," joked the others.

Even if they did not have much seasoned skill, none of the Americans ever shirked the responsibility of patrolling the lines. Divining their intentions, the Germans came over in force, catching them napping. "I was up above the main formation to see that nothing was dropped out of the sun," wrote one U. S. pilot, "and a Pfalz dove on me. He came right out of the sun but I've learned to put my thumb up and close one eye and unless they are at a dead angle, I can see them. I saw this one in time and just as he opened fire, I turned quickly and threw his sights off. His tracer was going a hundred feet behind my tail. The Hun went by and half-rolled onto my tail. I kept turning to keep his sights off me and he followed. We turned around and around—each maneuvering to get into position to fire a burst at close range.

"But I had learned my lesson well at Ayr and I could do perfect vertical banks and I began gaining on him. I was getting in position to open up when he half-rolled to break away, I half-rolled after him and was on his tail like a hawk after a chicken. I let him have both guns at close range. My sights were dead on his cockpit and I must have got in about a hundred and fifty rounds. My Lewis jammed after fifty rounds but my Vickers kept going. The Hun started to turn, then he flopped over on his back and went straight down. He was last seen headed toward his future home and breaking all records—hellbent for Hades! I couldn't see him crash so I only got an 'out of control.' But I know I got him. At the speed he was diving he never could have pulled out. It was quite evident that one of us had to die but I was cool as a cucumber and when we were turning around each other I could almost hear Nigger through the earphones from the front of an Avro telling me, 'Little top rudder now. Easy. Keep your nose level. Pull your stick back. Take off a little aileron. Now cross your controls.' "

Who was responsible for coordinating efforts in these painful, raw times? Colonel Billy Mitchell mainly, for he had already spent some time with "Boom" Trenchard, who was firm in his very British contention that although the German air service had caused tremendous damage this nevertheless amounted to only four per cent of damage done by the British. Despite Trenchard's strong personality, which led to many disagreements, Mitchell returned to American headquarters with the intention of forming an entirely separate branch of the war effort. In his later meetings with Pershing, Mitchell advocated bolder measures all around. But Pershing, ironclad that he was, thought that the air service was only a branch of the army and should be run along the same lines. Mitchell did not hesitate to say that this was absolute nonsense. Pershing was still apparently good-humored. This was very deceptive, for it was not long after the meeting that Mitchell found himself demoted and replaced by General Benjamin Foulois.

Pershing's viciousness was so well known that no disgrace attached to Mitchell's downfall when he was appointed Chief of Air Service of the First Army Corps. In this letdown the man found some solace, for General Hunter Liggett, the man in command, was one of his supporters and always had been. Despite Pershing's sour notes, which sounded almost daily in a stream of letters and cables, the two men cheerfully pressed on with their own conception of war.

Two pilots have stolen most of the limelight as far as the American story is concerned, Eddie Rickenbacker and Frank Luke, both awarded the Congressional Medal of Honor and the only pilots to receive it.

Like many other Americans, Frank Luke liked to think that this was *his* war, but his personality was the kind which must always lead to rows and quarrels. He was a big-mouth, they said, and one without much ability at that. After many disputes, he took to flying with a German-American, Lieutenant Joseph Wehner, because nobody else would go with him, and together they hunted observation balloons. It was a strange but successful partnership with Wehner providing the overhead cover while Luke attacked the targets. Within a single week they had polished off nine balloons and four German planes.

The others were much impressed but Luke was still barred from the "family circle." They just could not tolerate his well-projected personality. It jarred on their nerves. In desperation, and because he was angry and bored, Luke talked Wehner into flying more intensive sorties with him.

One day, when they were out together, they were snapped up by some Fokkers which came down at them out of a blue sky. It was a race between the Fokkers and the Americans toward a group of balloons already earmarked for destruction by Luke. Quickly signing to Wehner to stay where he was on the outer perimeter, Luke went straight through a rising barrage of "flaming onions" to start pumping incendiary bullets into the first target. When the Germans saw that the onions were not reaching the invader, they turned on a thumping artillery barrage which filled the air with flying shrapnel.

Anxiously watching from a quarter of a mile away, Wehner had to divide his attention between the crackling holocaust created by Luke and the deceptive calm of the sky all around him. Sure enough, a Fokker appeared out of the clouds to see what was happening. There was a desperate duel. Wehner failed to keep the

Fokker in his gun sights. Within thirty seconds, his controls shot into a useless tangle of wires, it was obvious that he could not go on fighting. His plane was now losing height.

Glancing through the shrapnel hail, Luke was horrified to see his friend and guard go crashing down in flames. While the last balloons were descending, with clouds of smoke billowing out of their punctured bellies, he flew toward the place where Wehner had been on patrol. As he arrived, four Fokkers came along, bunched together, waiting for him. There was no purpose in conserving his fire. If he started shooting now he might get away with it. His first bullets hit one Fokker, then another. He barely escaped with his life.

After Wehner's death, which left him introspective and moody, Luke found another partner, Ivan A. Roberts, if anything a better pilot than Luke but still a cautious flier who knew how to treat a plane. He agreed to fly a few trial missions with Luke but promised nothing. When Roberts was shot down by five Fokkers flying in deadly formation, Luke started flying alone and, for a time, suffered from rash aberrations in which he would go for anything marked with a Gothic cross. His officers tried to control him but it was quite hopeless. He was beyond their brand of discipline and refused to take part in organized operations. They had to give him up. He was now a rogue pilot, flying whenever he wanted to, never speaking to the others. His comrades deserted him, yet their interest was aroused when he deliberately committed a series of outrages against German ground troops. Because of this the Germans put him on their blacklist.

On his last mission he caused suspense because he was long overdue. His name was finally placed on the "missing" list. The mystery of his disappearance was not cleared up until Auguste Garre, Mayor of Murvaux, swore the following affidavit:

The undersigned, living in Murvaux, Department of the Meuse, certify to have seen on 19 September 1918 toward evening an American aviator, followed by an escadrille of Germans in the direction of Liny, descend suddenly and vertically toward the earth, then straighten out close to the ground and fly in the direction of Briers Farm, where he found a German captive balloon which he burned. Then he flew toward Milly where he found another balloon which he also burned in spite of incessant fire directed toward his machine. He shot down a third balloon and two planes. Then he apparently was wounded by a shot from rapid-fire cannon. From there he came back over Murvaux and still with his guns killed six German soldiers and wounded as many more. Following this he landed and got out of his machine, undoubtedly to quench his thirst at the stream. He had gone fifty yards when, seeing the Germans come toward him, he still had the strength to draw his revolver to defend himself. A moment after, he fell dead following a serious wound he received in the chest. The undersigned themselves placed the body of the aviator on the wagon and conducted it to the cemetery.

Cortine Delbart
Voliner Nicholas

Seen for legalization of signatures placed above,
Murvaux, 15 January 1919.

The Mayor
Auguste Garre

(Seal of Murvaux)

Frank Luke's name was placed on the roll of heroes. Personality did not matter. His deeds spoke for themselves.

Eddie Rickenbacker was a man of different caliber. Long before the war he appreciated the value of teamwork in handling high-speed machines. As a professional racing driver, he had often fought another enemy, time itself. He was earning about $40,000 a year when he decided to give it all up and become an aviator. Like others, he was involved in the red-tape war when they tried to restrain him from joining a front-line combat unit. He was more valuable, they said, as an engine technician.

He was partly trained as a pilot and wanted only to finish his course, but they saw to it that he was loaded down with engineering problems. He was eventually transferred to General Pershing's staff as a chauffeur. This was the crowning blow. Pershing would not listen to reason. He actually enjoyed being driven by the famous Rickenbacker. In the end it was Pershing's old enemy, Billy Mitchell, who organized the transfer, and Rickenbacker was posted to the 94th Squadron, part of the First Pursuit Group, where he was partnered by Norman Hall. A few weeks later he was promoted to flight commander with several planes under his direct control. His rapid rise was due, in part, to the cult of hero worship, a factor which long before caused the Germans to publicize the name of Richthofen and, more recently, the British to take up Albert Ball as a superman.

Rickenbacker's method of flying and fighting was calculated, fast and very dangerous, reminiscent of the race track. In the early days he was accidentally mixed up in fights between the French and Germans, finding it hard to understand the tactics of either side. On several occasions he did not realize that he was heading for trouble until his plane was in the middle of it. After shooting one Fokker down almost by accident when he triggered his guns in a moment of excitement, he told his mechanics: "I learned that whenever you're over the lines you have to keep twisting your neck in all directions every minute, or you're sure to be surprised. I was surprised today because I forgot to look behind me."

Among his many interests was the growing legend of the aces. He could not help wondering whether these new heroes were the keen-nerved men they were reputed to be. Every pilot received about the same amount of training. The planes were much the same, so were the guns. Why should one man achieve more skill than his comrades? Some of his questions were answered out of painful experience and the frightful sights he witnessed as he flew through the next few months. Other questions were never answered at all, for he himself was soon tagged with the appellation "ace."

A man like the thoughtful Rickenbacker could not go unnoticed for long. He was still flying daily missions when Major Hartney picked him as commander of the 94th Squadron. There was some discontent about the idea, though this did not ferment among the fliers themselves. They were happy enough to have Eddie Rickenbacker as boss. The objections were voiced by the brass hats, secure in the upper echelons of command, who did not believe that Rickenbacker had seen enough flying experience to be able to cope not only with the duties of administration but flying as well. When it finally did get started, the Rickenbacker regime disproved them all.

It was more rigorous than anything to be found elsewhere in the American air service. He had all available men out at dawn every day, doing physical training. His inquisitive nose was pushed into every corner of every hangar. If he saw an engine part lying idle, he demanded a full explanation. Every plane under his command always had to be ready to take to the air at a moment's notice. Unless this was so, the war was lost, he said. Just to prove that he was not losing his own touch, he often flew lone missions to shoot down the enemy in whirling dogfights. If he could tempt his opponents over his own airfield, where his pilots could stand and watch, he was happy to give them a lesson in practical fighting technique.

A satisfied General Billy Mitchell once filed a report about his prodigy in which he said that the success of Eddie Rickenbacker with the 94th Squadron showed beyond all doubt that it was important to place practical-minded men in key positions. Rickenbacker, by virtue of his approach and example, was an inspiration to his men.

"A squadron commander who sits in his tent and gives orders and does not fly, though he may have the brains of Solomon, will never get the results that a man will, who, day in and day out, leads his patrols over the line and infuses in his pilots the *esprit de corps*, which is so necessary in aviation and which, so far, has been so lightly considered by the authorities."

Billy Mitchell could not resist having a dig at the top brass.

Rickenbacker, with his load of responsibility, still managed to shoot down twenty-six German aircraft in little more than five months. He was an ace in any man's language.

Bibliography

Archibald, Norman. *Heaven High, Hell Deep, 1917-1918*. London: Heinemann.

Arnold, Major-General H. H., and Eaker, Colonel Ira C. *Winged Warfare*. New York and London: Harper.

Ashmore, Major-General E. H. *Air Defence*. London: Longmans Green.

Barnett, Lieutenant Gilbert. *VC's of the Air*. London: Edited by J. Burrow and Co., Ltd.

Biddle, Major Charles J. *The Way of the Eagle*. New York: Scribner's.

Bingham, Hiram. *An Explorer in the Air Service*. London: Oxford University Press.

Bishop, Major William A. *Winged Warfare*. London: Hodder and Stoughton.

Black, Archibald. *The Story of Flying*. New York: McGraw-Hill.

Bond, A. Russell. *Inventions of the Great War*. London: Appleton.

Bordeaux, Henry. *Georges Guynemer, Knight of the Air*. Translated by Louise Morgan Sill. London: Chatto and Windus.

Briscoe, W., and Stannard, H. R. *Captain Ball V.C.* London: Herbert Jenkins.

Burlingame, Roger. *General Billy Mitchell*. New York: McGraw-Hill.

Capart, Captain G. P. *A Blue Devil of France*. Translated by J. C. Drouillard. New York: Watt.

Chapman, Victor. *Victor Chapman's Letters from France*. A memoir by John Jay Chapman. New York: Macmillan.

Cleveland, Reginald M. *America Fledges Wings*. New York: Pitman.

Codman, Charles. *Contact*. Boston: Little, Brown.

Coleman, Frederic. *From Mons to Ypres with General French*. New York: Dodd, Mead.

Coppens, Willy. *Days on the Wing*. Translated by A. J. Insall. London: Hamilton.

Cuneo, John R. *The Air Weapon, 1914-1916*. Harrisburg, Pennsylvania: Military Service Publishing Company.

Dorman, Geoffrey. *Fifty Years Fly Past*. London: Forbes Robertson.

Drake, Vivian. *Above the Battle*. London: Appleton.

Fokker, Anthony H. G., and Gould, Bruce. *Flying Dutchman—The Life of Anthony Fokker*. London: Routledge.

Freudenthal, Elspeth E. *Flight into History—The Wright Brothers and the Air Age*. Norman, Okla.: University of Oklahoma Press.

Gibbs-Smith, C. H. *A History of Flying*. London: Batsford.

Gibbons, Floyd. *The Red Knight of Germany*. London: Cassell.

Gowans, Adam L. (editor and translator). *A Month's German Newspapers*. London: Gowans and Gray.

Grey, C. G. *The Luftwaffe*. London: Faber and Faber.

Grinnell-Milne, Duncan. *Wind in the Wires*. London: Hurst and Blackett.

Hale, Richard W. (editor). *Letters of Warwick Greene, 1915-1928*. Boston and New York: Houghton Mifflin.

Hall, Lieutenant Bert. *En l'Air!* London: Hurst and Blackett.

Hall, Lieutenant Bert, and Niles, Lieutenant John J. *One Man's War*. London: Hamilton.

Hall, James Norman. *High Adventure*. London: Constable.

Hall, James Norman, and Nordhoff, Charles Bernard (editors). *The Lafayette Flying Corps*. Boston: Houghton Mifflin.

Hall, James Norman. *My Island Home*. Boston: Little, Brown.

Harper, Harry. *The Aeroplane in War*. London: Blackie.

Harrison, John B. *This Age of Global Strife*. Philadelphia: Lippincott.

Hart, B. H. Liddell. *Strategy, The Indirect Approach*. London: Faber and Faber.

Hartney, Lieut. Col. Harold E. *Up and At 'em*. London: Cassell.

Heinkell, Ernst. *He.1000, Memoirs of a Pioneer of the Air Age*. Jurgen Thorward (editor). London: Hutchinson.

Hemingway, Ernest. *Men at War*. New York: Crown.

Heydemarck, Hauptmann. *Double-Decker C.666*. Translated by Claud W. Sykes. London: Hamilton.

Holland, Maurice, with a preface by James Doolittle. *Architects of Aviation*. New York: Duell, Sloan & Pearce.

Johns, W. E. *Fighting Planes and Aces*. London: Hamilton.

Johnson, Owen. *The Spirit of France*. Boston: Little, Brown.

Jones, H. A. *The War in the Air*. (12 vols.) London: Oxford University Press.

Jones, Wing-Commander Ira. *King of the Air Fighters*. London: Nicholson and Watson.

Kiernan, R. H. *Captain Albert Ball*. London: Penguin.

Lewis, Cecil. *Sagittarius Rising*. London: Peter Davies.

Middleton, Edgar. *The Great War in the Air*. London: Waverley.

Raleigh, Walter. *The War in the Air*. Oxford: The Clarendon Press.

Reynolds, Quentin. *They Fought for the Sky*. London: Cassell.

Richthofen, Captain Manfred Freiherr von. *An Autobiography*. Translated by T. Ellis Barker. New York: McBride.

Rickenbacker, Captain Edward V. *Fighting the Fighting Circus*. New York: Stokes.

Roberts, Lieutenant E. M. *A Flying Fighter*. New York: Harper.

Robertson, Bruce. *Von Richthofen and the Flying Circus*. Harleyford.

Saunders, Hilliary St. George. *Per Ardua*. London: Oxford University Press.

Schroder, Hans. *An Airman Remembers*. Translated by Claud W. Sykes. London: The Aviation Book Club.

Sigaud, Louis A. *Douhet and Aerial Warfare*. New York: Putnam.

Stark, Rudolf. *Wings of War*. London: John Hamilton.

Strange, Lieutenant-Colonel L. A. *Recollections of an Airman*. London: Hamilton.

"Theta" ("A Pilot"). *War Flying*. Boston: Houghton Mifflin.

Thetford, O. G., and Riding, E. J. *Aircraft of the 1914-1918 War*. Harleyford.

Throm, Edward L., and Crenshaw, James S. *Popular Mechanics Aviation Album*. New York: Popular Mechanics.

Toulmin, H. A., Jr. *Air Service, A.E.F. 1918*. Princeton, N. J.: Van Nostrand.

Unknown. *War Birds, Diary of an Unknown Aviator*. London: Hamilton.

Veil, Charles (as told to Howard Marsh). *Adventure's a Wench*. London: Bles.

"Vigilant." *French War Birds*. London: Hamilton.

———. *German War Birds*. London: Hamilton.

———. *Richthofen, The Knight of the Air*. London: Hamilton.

"Wing Adjutant." *Plane Tales from the Skies*. London: Cassell.

———. *The Royal Flying Corps in the Air*. London: Cassell.

Winslow, Carroll Dana. *With the French Flying Corps*. London: Constable.

Wintringham, Tom. *The Story of Weapons and Tactics*. London: Faber and Faber.

Wortley, Rothesay Stuart. *Letters from a Flying Officer*. London: Oxford University Press.

APPENDIX ONE

SPECIFICATIONS OF BRITISH MACHINES
(excluding bombers) 1911—1918

TYPE	DATE	ENGINE	WEIGHT	DATA	PERFORMANCE
Maurice Farman "Longhorn" (two-seater recce/trainer)	1911	70 hp Renault / 100 hp Sunbeam	1280 lbs (empty) / 1887 lbs (loaded)	*Wing loading:* 3.2 lbs/sq. ft. *Span (upper):* 50 ft. 9 ins. *Length:* 39 ft. *Height:* II ft. 4 ins. *Wing Area:* 64 sq. Ft.	*Max. speed at sea level:* 59 mph *Armament:* none
Maurice Farman "Shorthorn"	1913	70 hp Renault	1441 lbs (empty)	*Wing loading:* 3.3 lbs/sq. Ft.	*Max. speed at sea level:* 66 mph

recce/trainer)			...lbs (loaded)	*Length:* 31 ft. *Height:* 10 ft. 4 ins. *Wing Area:* 561 sq. ft.	*Armament:* revolver, rifle or Lewis gun.
BE 2C (two-seater recce)	1914	90 hp R.A.F. 10 hp Curtis OX5 150 hp Hispano-Suiza	1370 lbs (empty) 2142 lbs (loaded)	*Wing Area:* 381 sq. ft. *Span:* 35 ft. 6 ins. *Length:* 27 ft. 3 ins. *Height:* 11 ft.	*Max. speed:* 72 mph at 6,500 ft *Ceiling:* 11,000 ft. *Rate of climb:* 200 ft./min. at 6,500 ft. *Endurance:* 3¼ hrs. *Armament:* One Lewis gun and small bomb racks.

TYPE	DATE	ENGINE	WEIGHT	DATA	PERFORMANCE
Avro 504 (two-seater trainer)	1914	80 hp Gnome	(80 hp Gnome) 1100 lbs (empty) 1800 lbs (loaded)	*Wing Area:* 330 sq. ft. *Span:* 36 ft.	*Max. speed at sea level:* 504—82 mph 504k (110 hp)—95 mph *Ceiling:* (100 hp) 13,000 ft.
		100 hp Gnome Monosoupape		*Length:* 29 ft. 5 ins.	*Rate of climb:* 504A to 6,500 ft. in 25 mins.
		100 hp Sunbeam Dyak	(130 hp Clerget) 1231 lbs (empty)	*Height:* 10 ft. 6 ins.	*Endurance:* 4 hrs. Gnome. 3 hrs Le Rhone or Mono-soupape.
		75 hp Rolls-Royce Hawk	1829 lbs (loaded)	*Wing Area:* 330 sq. ft.	*Armament:* none.
		110 hp Le Rhone			
		130 hp Clerget			
Bristol	1914	80 hp Gnome	(80 hp)	*Wing loading:*	

(100 hp) 104 mph

	100 hp Gnome Monosoupape		*Length:* 20 ft. 8 ins.	*Rate of climb:* 385 ft./min. at 6,500 ft.
				Endurance: 2½ hrs.
	110 hp Le Rhone		*Height:* 8 ft. 6 ins.	*Armament:* One fixed Vickers machine-gun on later models.

Vickers FB5 & FB 9 (two-seater fighter-recce)	FB 5 1914 FB9 1915	100 hp Gnome Monosoupape	*FB5* 1220 lbs (empty) 2050 lbs (loaded) *FB9* 1029 lbs (empty) 1892 lbs (loaded)	*Span:* FB5 36 ft. 6 ins. FB9 33 ft. 10 ins. *Length:* FB5 27 ft. 2 ins. FB9 27 ft. 10 ins. *Height:* 11 ft. *Wing Area:* 382 sq. ft. *Wing loading:* FB5 5.4 lb/sq. ft.	*Max. speed:* FB5: 70 mph at 5,000 ft. FB9: 70 mph at 5,000 ft. *Ceiling:* FB5: 9,000 ft. FB9: 11,000 ft. *Endurance:* FB5: 4 hrs. FB9: 5 hrs. *Armament:* FB5: Belt-fed Vickers gun on free mounting. FB9: Drum-fed Lewis gun on ring mounting.

361

TYPE	DATE	ENGINE	WEIGHT	DATA	PERFORMANCE
Nieuport Scout 17c & 28 c (single-seater scout)	1915	17c 110 hp Le Rhone 28c 160 hp Gnome	17c 825 lbs (empty) 1233 lbs (loaded)	*Wing Area:* 17c 158.8 sq. ft. *Length:* 17c 19 ft. 6 ins. 28c 20 ft. 3 ins. *Height:* 7 ft. (both) *Wing loading:* 17c 7.7 lb/sq. ft.	*Max. Speed:* 17c 107 mph at 6,500 ft. 28c 140 mph at sea level. *Rate of climb:* 17c 6 min. to 10,000 ft. *Endurance:* 2/2½ hrs.
FE 2B (two-seater fighter-recce)	1916	120 hp Beardmore 160 hp Beardmore	120 hp 2105 lbs (empty) 2827 lbs (loaded)	*Span:* 47 ft. 9 ins. *Length:* 32 ft. 3 ins.	*Max. speed:* 120 hp 75 mph at 6,500 ft. 160 hp 81 mph at 6,500 ft.

		Weight	Dimensions	Performance
		3037 lbs (loaded)	*Wing Area:* 494 ft. sq. *Wing loading:* 120 hp 5.7 lbs /sq. ft. 160 hp 6.1 lbs/sq. ft.	*Rate of climb:* 120 hp 240 ft/min. at 6,500 ft. 160 hp 210 ft/min. at 6,500 ft. *Endurance:* 3½—4 hrs. *Armament:* 4 Lewis guns (2 - observer 2 - pilot).
DH 2 (single-seater scout)	1916	100 hp Monosoupape	800 lbs (empty) 1320 lbs (loaded)	*Span:* 28 ft. *Length:* 25 ft. 3 ins. *Height:* 9 ft. 6 ins. *Wing Area:* 228 sq. ft. *Wing loading:* 5.8 lbs/sq. ft.	*Max. speed:* 93 mph at sea level *Ceiling:* 14,000 ft. *Rate of climb:* 880 ft/min. at 6,500 ft. *Endurance:* 2¾ hrs. *Armament:* Lewis gun

TYPE	DATE	ENGINE	WEIGHT	DATA	PERFORMANCE
Bristol Fighter F 2B (two-seater fighter-recce)	1916	200 hp Sunbeam Arab 200 hp Hispano-Suiza 275 hp Rolls-Royce Falcon III	*Falcon:* 1745 lbs (empty) 2590 lbs (loaded) *Others:* 1733 lbs (empty) 2630 lbs (loaded)	*Span:* 39 ft. 3 ins. *Length:* 26 ft. 2 ins. *Height:* 10 ft. 1 ins. *Wing Area:* 406 sq. ft. *Wing loading:* Falcon: 6.8 lbs/sq. ft. Others: 6.4 lbs/sq. ft.	*Max. speed:* Falcon: 125 mph at sea level *Ceiling:* Falcon: 22,000 ft. *Rate of climb:* Falcon: 830 ft/min. at 6,500 ft. *Endurance:* Falcon: 3 hrs. *Armament:* One Vickers gun firing through airscrew. One or two Lewis guns on Scarff ring in rear cockpit.
Sopwith 1½ Strutter (two-seater fighter-recce)	1916	130 hp Clerget	1305 lbs (empty) 2150 lbs (loaded)	*Span:* 33 ft. 6 ins. *Length:* 25 ft. 3 ins.	*Max. speed:* 100 mph at 6,500 ft. *Ceiling:* 15,500 ft.

			Wing Area: 346 sq. ft.	**Endurance:** 3¾ hrs.
			Wing loading: 6.2 lbs/sq. ft.	**Armament:** One Vickers gun fixed forward. 1 Lewis gun on Scarff ring in rear cockpit.
S.P.A.D. Scout (single-seater scout)	1916	150 hp Hispano (early 1917) 175 hp Hispano (late 1917) 205 hp Hispano	150 hp 1177 lbs (empty) 1632 lbs (loaded)	**Span:** 25 ft. 6 ins. **Length:** 20 ft. 3 ins. **Height:** 7 ft. **Wing Area:** 200 sq. ft. **Wing loading:** 8.1 lb/sq. ft.	**Max. speed:** 150 hp 119 mph at 6,500 ft. 205 hp 132 mph at sea level. **Rate of climb:** 150 hp 810 ft/min. initially **Endurance:** 150 hp—2½ hrs. **Armament:** Vickers gun fixed forward.

TYPE	DATE	ENGINE	WEIGHT	DATA	PERFORMANCE
Sopwith Pup (single-seater scout)	1916	80 hp Le Rhone Gnome Monosoupape 100 hp	*80 hp* 856 lbs (empty) 1297 lbs (loaded) *100 hp* 868 lbs (empty) 1313 lbs (loaded)	*Span:* 26 ft. 6 ins. *Length:* 19 ft. 4 ins. *Height:* 9 ft. 4 ins. *Wing Area:* 254 sq. ft. *Wing loading:* 4.8 lb/sq. ft.	*Max. speed:* 80 hp 106 mph at 6,500 ft. *Ceiling:* 80 hp—17,500 ft. *Rate of climb:* 650 ft/min. at 6,500 ft. *Endurance:* 3 hrs. *Armament:* One Vickers gun firing forward. RNAS version had light bomb racks and Lewis gun.
RE8 (two-seater recce)	1916	R.A.F. 4A 150 hp	1803 lbs (empty) 2869 lbs (loaded)	*Span:* 42 ft. 8 ins. (upper) 32 ft. 7½ ins. (lower)	*Max. speed:* 102 mph at 6,500 ft. *Ceiling:* 13,000 ft. *Rate of climb:* 340 ft. at 6,500 ft.

Armament:
Vickers gun fixed forward.
One or two Lewis guns on Scarff ring in rear cockpit.

Height: 10 ft. 10 ins.

Wing Area: 377 sq. ft.

Wing loading: 7.6 lb/sq. ft.

Sopwith Triplane

(single-seater scout)

1917

130 hp Clerget

993 lbs (empty)
1415 lbs (loaded)

Span: 26 ft. 6 ins.

Length: 19 ft.

Height: 10 ft. 6 ins.

Wing Area: 257 sq. ft.

Wing loading: 5.5. lb/sq. ft.

Max. speed: 116 mph at 6,500 ft.

Ceiling: 20,500 ft.

Rate of climb: 11 mins. to 10,000 ft.

Endurance: 2¾ hrs.

Armament:
Vickers gun fixed forward.

TYPE	DATE	ENGINE	WEIGHT	DATA	PERFORMANCE
SE5 & SE5A (single-seater scout)	1917	*SE5* 50 hp Hispano *SE5A* 200 hp Wolseley Viper 200, 220, 240 hp Hispano	*SE5* 1309 lbs (empty) 1930 lbs (loaded) *SE5A* 1531 lbs (empty) 2048 lbs (loaded)	*Span:* SE5 28 ft. SE5A 26 ft. 8 ins. *Wing Area:* SE5 249 sq. ft. SE5A 247 sq. ft. *Wing loading:* SE5 7.7 lb/sq. ft. SE5A 7.8 lb/sq. ft. *Height:* SE5 9 ft. 5 ins. SE5A 9 ft. 6 ins. *Length:* SE5 21 ft. 4 ins. SE5A	*Max. speed:* SE5: 119 mph at 6,500 ft. SE5A: 132 mph at 6,500 ft. *Ceiling:* SE5: 17,000 ft. SE5A: 20,000 ft. *Rate of climb:* SE5: 650 ft/min. SE5A: 765 ft/min. *Endurance:* 2½ hrs (both) *Armament:* Vickers gun fixed forward. Lewis gun fixed on top of centre section.

Sopwith Camel (single-seater scout)	1917	F.I. 110 hp Le Rhone. 130 hp Clerget. 2FI 150 hp Bentley. BRI 150 hp Gnome Monosoupape.	*110 hp* 889 lbs (empty) 1422 lbs (loaded) *130 hp* 929 lbs (empty) 1435 lbs (loaded) *150 hp* 962 lbs (empty) 1471 lbs (loaded)	*Span: 28 in* *Length:* 19 ft. 6 ins. *Height:* 9 ft. *Wing loading:* 110 hp 6.1 lb/sq. ft. 130 hp 6.4 lb/sq. ft. 150 hp 6.5 lb/sq. ft.	*Max. speed (mph):* 110 hp: 118½ mph at 6,500 ft. 130 hp: 113 mph at 6,500 ft. 150 hp: 121 mph at 6,500 ft. *Ceiling:* 130 hp—19,000 ft. *Rate of climb:* 110 hp—1,000 ft/min. initially. 130 hp—880 ft/min. initially. 150 hp—890 ft/min. initially. *Endurance:* 2¾–2½ hrs. *Armament:* Two Vickers guns fixed forward.
Sopwith Snipe (single seater scout)	1918	230 hp Bentley Rotary	1312 lbs (empty) 2020 lbs (loaded)	*Span:* 30 ft. 1 in. *Length:* 19 ft. 9 ins. *Height:* 8 ft. 9 ins. *Wing Area:* 270 sq. ft. *Wing loading:* 7.4 lb/sq. ft.	*Max. speed:* 121 mph at 10,000 ft. *Ceiling:* 20,000 ft. *Rate of climb:* 970 ft/min. initially. *Endurance:* 3 hrs. *Armament:* Two Vickers guns fixed forward.

APPENDIX TWO

SPECIFICATIONS OF GERMAN MACHINES
(excluding bombers) 1913—1918

TYPE	DATE	ENGINE	WEIGHT	DATA	PERFORMANCE
Rumpler Taube (single or two-seater scout)	1913	100 hp Daimler. 120 hp Austro-Daimler.	682 lbs (empty) 1323 lbs (loaded)	*Span:* 46 ft. *Length:* 27 ft. 3 ins. *Height:* 9ft. 9 ins. *Wing Area:* 301 sq. ft. *Wing Loading:* 4.3 lb/sq. ft.	*Max. speed:* 75 mph at sea level *Armament:* none
Aviatik C II. (two-seater recce-bomber)	1915		1863 lbs (empty) 2831 lbs (loaded)	*Span:* 40 ft. 8 ins. (upper) 37 ft. 5 ins. (lower)	*Max. speed:* 82 mph at sea level *Ceiling:* 11,500 ft. *Endurance:* 4½ hrs.

Albatros C. 1. General-purpose two-seater	1915	150 hp Benz. D. III. 16 Mercedes D. III.	1925 lb (empty) 639 lb (payload)	Fighter-reconnaissance. Artillery-observation. Photography. Bombing.	*Length:* 26 ft. *Height:* 10 ft. 5 ins. *Wing Area:* 430 sq. ft. *Wing Loading:* 6.6 lb/sq. ft.	*Rate of climb:* 22 mins to 6,000 ft. *Armament:* One fixed gun forward. One free gun for observer. *Max. speed:* 82½ mph. *Climb:* 3280 ft. in 9¾ mins. 9840 ft. in 58½ mins. *Ceiling:* 10,000 ft. *Fuel:* 150 litres — 2½ hrs. *Armament:* Parabellum machine-gun on rotating mount in rear cockpit. Bomb load between cockpits.

TYPE	DATE	ENGINE	WEIGHT	DUTIES	PERFORMANCE
Albatros C. III General-purpose two-seater	1915	160 hp Mercedes D. III. 150 hp Benz III.	1928 lbs (empty) 3055 lbs (loaded)	Artillery-observation. Reconnaissance. Photography. Bombing.	*Max. speed:* 85 mph. *Climb:* 3280 in 9 mins. 6560 in 22 mins. 9840 in 40 mins. *Ceiling:* 12,000 ft. *Fuel:* 57 galls — 4/4¾ hrs. *Armament:* Parabellum machine-gun on gun-ring in rear cockpit or one Spandau gun operated by pilot and located on starboard engine cowling. Bomb load in chutes in rear cockpit.
Fokker E. IV (Single-seater scout)	1915	Oberursel Rotary 100 hp	1233 lbs (gross)	General scouting	*Max. speed:* 90 mph. *Armament:* synchronised twin machine guns.

NB. There is a lack of information ...

372

Aircraft	Year	Engine	Weight	Role	Performance
Halberstadt D. II & D. III (single-seater scout)	1915		1145 lbs (empty) 1608 lbs (loaded)	General scouting	*Max. speed:* 95 mph. *Climb:* 3280 ft. in 4 mins. 9840 ft. in 15 mins. *Endurance:* 1½—2 hrs. *Armament:* single machine-gun fired through airscrew disc or fixed to starboard side of engine.
Albatros D. II (single-seater scout)	1916	160 hp Mercedes	1485 lbs (empty) 300 lbs (loaded)	General scouting	*Max. speed:* 105 mph. *Climb:* 3,280 ft. in 3½ mins. 6.560 ft. in 7¾ mins. 9,840 ft. in 12 mins. 13,120 ft. in 18¾ mins. *Armament:* standard twin synchronised Spandau machine-guns.

TYPE	DATE	ENGINE	WEIGHT	DUTIES	PERFORMANCE
Fokker D. III (single-seater scout)	1916	Oberursel 160 hp	995 lbs (empty) 1560 lbs (loaded)	General scouting	*Max. speed:* 100 mph. *Climb:* 3,280 ft. in 3 mins. 6,560 ft. in 7 mins. *Ceiling:* 15,000 ft. *Armament:* twin Spandau machine guns. *Fuel:* 1½ hrs. loaded flight.
Pfalz D. III (single-seater scout)	1917	Mercedes D. III 180 hp	1580 lbs (empty) 1861 lbs (loaded)	Fighter Scout	*Max. speed:* 102.5 mph. *Climb:* 10,000 ft. in 17½ mins. 15,000 ft. in 41¾ mins. *Ceiling:* 17,000 ft. *Capacity:* 21½ galls 4 galls oil. *Endurance:* 2 hrs. *Armament:* twin synchronised machine-guns, firing forward

Albatros DV/DVA (single-seater scout)	1917	180 hp Mercedes (raised compression ratio) 220 hp Mercedes 200 hp Benz	1460 lbs (empty) 2050 lbs (loaded)	General scouting	*Max. speed:* 130 mph (low altitude) 100 mph (high altitude) *Climb:* 2,000 ft. in 2 mins 3,280 ft. in 4 mins. 13,000 ft. in 21 mins. *Armament:* standard twin synchronised Spandau machine-guns.
Fokker Dr. I (single-seater scout)	1917	145 hp Oberursel UR III Goebel III Siemens-Halske III 160 hp (4-bladed propellor)	829 lbs (empty) 1259 lbs (loaded)	General scouting	*Max. speed:* 115 mph. *Climb:* 3,280 ft. in 1¾ mins. 6,560 ft. in 3¾ mins. 9,840 ft. in 6½ mins. 13,120 ft. in 10 mins. 16,400 ft. in 14 mins. *Ceiling:* 18—20,000 ft. *Fuel:* 16 galls, giving 2 hrs at 10,000 feet. *Armament:* twin synchronised Spandau machine-guns on port and starboard cowling.

TYPE	DATE	ENGINE	WEIGHT	DUTIES	PERFORMANCE
Fokker EV/D VIII (single-seater scout)	1918	Oberursel 140 hp	893 lbs (empty) 1384 lbs (loaded)	General scouting	*Max. speed:* 124 mph. *Climb:* 3,280 ft. in 2 mins. 6,560 ft. in 4½ mins. 9,840 ft. in 7½ mins. 13,120 ft. in 10¾ mins. *Ceiling:* 20,000 ft. *Fuel:* 1½ hours. *Armament:* twin synchronised Spandau machine-guns.
Fokker D. VII (single-seater scout)	1918	160 hp Mercedes D. IIIA 185 hp B.M.W. (in D. VIIIF)	1540 lbs (empty) 1986 lbs (loaded)	General scouting	*Max. speed:* 120 mph. (low altitude) 110 mph. (high altitude) *Climb:* 3,280 ft. in 4 mins. 9,840 ft. in 12 mins. 16,405 ft. in 31½ mins. 18,000 ft. in 44 mins. *Ceiling:* 18,000 ft. (with BMW performance figures somewhat better). *Armament:* twin synchronised Spandau machine guns on cowling.

THE ACES AND THEIR VICTORIES

BRITISH AND BRITISH EMPIRE

Major Edward Mannock	73	Capt. Robert A. Little	47
Col. William A. Bishop	72	Capt. Albert Ball	44
Major Raymond Collishaw	68	Capt. H. J. Larkin	41
Capt. James McCudden	58	Capt. F. T. Hazell	41
Capt. Donald McLaren	54	Capt. J. I. T. Jones	40
Capt. A. Beauchamp-Proctor	54	Major Roderic Dallas	39
Major Philip F. Fullard	53	Capt. W. G. Claxton	39
Major William G. Barker	52	Capt. F. R. McCall	39
Capt. G. E. H. McElroy	48	Capt. John Gilmore	37
Capt. Frank G. Quigley	34	Capt, Henry W. Wollett	35
Major G. Murlis-Green	32	Major Albert D. Carter	31
Capt. J. L. M. White	31	Capt. W. L. Jordan	31
Capt. M. B. Frew	30	Capt. C. E. Howell	30
Capt. S. M. Kinkead	30	Major A. E. McKeever	30
Capt. J. E. Gurden	29	Capt. H. G. Lunchford	29
Capt. T. R. C. Hoidge	27	Capt. Brumwin-Hales	27
Major G. J. C. Maxwell	27	Capt. James A. Slater	26
Capt. John Leacraft	25	Capt. W. M. Staton	25
Capt. W. E. Shields	24	Capt. A. H. Cobby	24
Capt. John Andrews	24	Capt. H. D. Barton	23
Major K. C. Patrick	23	Capt. A. H. Whistler	23
Major A. Coningham	23	Capt. W. C. Lambert	22
Lt. W. M. Thompson	22	Major H. G. Bowman	22
Lt. L. C. Venter	22	Capt. E. R. Tempest	22
Capt. A. G. Cooper	22	Capt. P. J. Clayson	21
Capt. G. E. Thompson	21	Capt. S. W. Rosevear	21
Ft/Comm. J. E. Sharman	21	Capt. W. MacLanachan	21
Capt. C. M. MacEwen	20	Capt. R. A. Mayberry	20
Capt. Warren Gillette	20	Capt. I. R. McDonald	20
Capt. Cecil King	20	Capt. W. L. Harrison	20
Lt. J. J. Malone	20	Major A. M. Wilkenson	20

NOTE: 125 aces shot down a total of between 10 and 19 planes, and as many as 363 pilots qualify for the designation 'ace' by having shot down between five and nine 'planes each.

FRANCE

Capt. Rene Fonck	75	Capt. Pinsard	27
Capt. Georges Guynemer	53	Lt. Guerin	23
Lt. Charles Nungesser	43	Lt. Dorme	23
Lt. Georges Madon	41	Lt. Haegelin	22
Lt. Maurice Boyau	35	Sgt. Marinovitch	22

| Lt. Coiffard | 34 | Capt. Hertaux | 21 |
| Lt. Boursade | 28 | Lt. Dullin | 20 |

NOTE: The remaining French aces number 146, each of these having shot down between five and nineteen planes. Among them are Lt. Navarre (twelve victories) and Lt. Legoud, the pioneer ace, with six victories.

BELGIUM

Capt. Willy Coppens	34
Lt. Thierry	10
Lt. de Meulemeester	10

NOTE: There are five other Belgian aces.

UNITED STATES OF AMERICA

Capt. Eddie V. Rickenbacker	26	Lt. David Putman	12
Lt. Frank Luke Junr	21	Capt. Elliott W. Springs	12
Major Raoul Lufbery	18	Capt. Field E. Kindley	12
Major G. A. Vaughn	13	Major Reed Landis	10
Sgt. Frank Baylies	12	Capt. J. N. Swaab	10

NOTE: There are 77 other American aces with victories credited to them of between five and nine 'planes.

ITALY

Lt-Col. Fransesco Baracca	36	Lt. Ferruccio Ranza	17
Lt. Silvio Scaroni	26	Sgt. Marziale Cerutti	17
Major Pier Ruggero Piccio	24	Lt. Luigi Olivari	12
Lt. Flavio Baracchini	21	Lt. Giovanni Ancillotto	11
Capt. Fulco di C. Ruffo	20	Sgt. Antonio Reali	11

NOTE: Thirty-one Italian aces scored victories of five upwards.

RUSSIA

Capt. Alexander Kazakov	17
Capt. Kroutenn	6
Lt. Pachtchenko	5

GERMANY

Manfred von Richthofen	80	Lt. Emil Thuy	32
Oberl. Ernst Udet	62	Lt. Paul Billik	31
Oberlt. Erich Lowenhardt	56	Lt. Gotthardt Sachsenburg	31
Lt. Werner Voss	48	Lt. Theo Osterkamp	31
Lt. Fritz Rumey	45	Lt. Karl Allmenroder	30
Hpt. Bruno Loerzer	45	Lt. Karl Degelow	30
Hpt. Rudolf Berthold	44	Lt. Heinrich Kroll	30
Lt. Paul Baumer	43	Lt. Josef Mai	30
Lt. Josef Jacobs	43	Lt. Ulrich Neckel	30
		Lt. Karl Schaefer	30

Hpt. Oswald Boelcke	40	Lt. Hermann Frommherz	29
Lt. Franz Buchner	40	Lt. Walter von Bulow	28
Obltnt. Lothar von Richt-hofen	40	Lt. Walter Blume	28
Lt. Karl Menckhoff	39	Oblt. Fritz Roth	28
Lt. Heinrich Gontermann	39	Oblt. Otto Bernert	27
Lt. Max Muller	36	Vzfw. Otto Fruhner	27
Lt. Karl Bolle	36	Lt. Hans Kirchstein	27
Lt. Julius Buckler	35	Lt. Karl Thom	27
Lt. Gustav Doerr	35	Hpt. Adolf von Tutscheck	27
Hpt. Eduard von Schleich	35	Lt. Hurt Wusthoff	27
Lt. Josef Veltjens	34	Oblt. Harald Auffahrt	26
Lt. Otto Koennecke	33	Oblt. Oskar von Boenigk	26
Oblt. Kurt Wolff	33	Oblt. Eduard Dostler	26
Ltn. Heinrich Bongartz	33	Lt. Arthur Laumann	26

NOTE: Five German aces shot down 25 'planes each. 117 aces shot down between ten and twenty-four planes including Hpt. Hermann Goring — 22; Lt. van Eschwege — 20; and Oblt. Max Immelmann — 15. A further 133 aces scored more than five victories each.

Index

Albatros airplanes, 29, 53, 63, 71-72, 92, 106, 121, 123, 141, 199, 201, 209, 290
Army Cinematograph Section, 275
Arras, 208, 209, 212, 298
Austin-Ball Scout airplane, 204, 206
Austin Motor Company, 204
Aviatik airplanes, 330
Ayr, 21-22
Ayr Fighting School, 174

Ball, Albert, 87-88, 174, 184-93, 194-202, 203-12, 234, 353
Ball, Sir Albert, 187
Balloons, observation, 230-31, 232, 265-67, 272, 273-74, 275-77, 280-81, 295-97
Balsley, Clyde, 337, 340-41
Bapaume, 190, 196, 201
Baraca, pilot, 257
Barnes, E. W., 80
Bartrap, Lt. von, 169
Barwell, F. L., 86, 156
Bauman, M. Ami, 187
Beatty Flying School, 235
Beaulieu, Werner von, 128
Belgian Flying Corps, 241
Bell, Gordon, 32-33
Benbow, Captain, 348
Benoidt, Victor, 265
Bettington, C. A., 20
BE2's, 187, 192, 238, 239
Bialowicza, 91

Biddle, Charles, 347
Bigsworth, A. W., 133
Bishop, Billy, 283-301, 302-14
Bismarck, Graf von, 110
Blaxland, pilot, 156
Blériot, Louis, 24, 97
Blériot monoplane, 24
Bliss, Robert W., 335
Boelcke, Oswald, 36, 37-38, 39-42, 43-50, 52, 118, 139, 171, 174, 338
Bond, pilot, 156
Boultbee, A. E., 70
Bovekerke, 265
Bovvett, Sergeant, 160
Brancker, Brig. General, 206
Braun, Pierre, 249-50
Bristol airplanes, 50, 88, 91, 145-47
Brocard, Captain, 256
Broke, Sir Philip, 19
Brooke-Popham, Colonel, 192
Brown, Roy, 91-92
Brussels, 97, 260, 262-63
Buchner, Hugo, 99, 100
Burke, C. J., 20-21
Butler, L., 81

Caldwell, Keith, 174, 175, 176
Callant, Lt., 243
Cambrai, 190, 209, 211
Camera planes, 62-63, 92
Cameron, J. G., 55-56
Campbell, C. D. M., 12
Carmichael, G. I., 20

380

Caudron airplanes, 347
Central Flying School, 14
Chandler, Robert Astor, 335
Chapman, Victor, 336, 339-40, 341
Charlton, L. E. O., 205
Charman, Captain, 22
Cholmondley, R., 20
Churchill, Winston, 13, 14
Ciselet, Charles, 236-37, 250, 260
Clemenceau, Georges, 278
Clinch, S. J., 260
Clutterbuck, L. C. F., 91
Collins, Phelps, 347
Constantinesco, 37
Coppens, Willy, 232-38, 239-52,
    253-67, 268-82
Cowdin, Elliot, 336
Cremer, Fritz, 95, 96, 102, 110
Crowe, C. M., 211, 212
Cruikshank, G. L., 44-47
Cunnell, D. C., 88-90
Curtiss, Glen, 98

Dallas, Major, 155
Dayton Wright Company, 344
De Bersac, Lt., 243
De Bricy, Captain, 272
De Burgh, pilot, 156, 162
De Burlet, Louis, 242, 243, 254
De Caters, Lt., 236
De Chestret, Louis, 250
Declerq, Captain, 248, 255
Degrauw, Charles, 234
De Havilland, Geoffrey, 120
De Havilland Scout aircraft, 120
De la Tour, pilot, 256
De Leener, Robert, 251
De Meeus, Jacques, 233, 251
De Mesmaeker, Gaston, 254
De Meulemeester, André, 234, 237,
    240, 257, 258, 259, 268, 271, 272,
    273, 278
De Munck, Charles, 236
Dendrino, S., 49
De Neef, Abel, 236
Desclée, Edmond, 233, 251
Deullin, pilot, 256
Dewey, Captain, 55
Dhanis, Commandant, 274, 275
D'Hendecourt, Roger, 251
DH2's, *see* De Havilland Scout
DH4 fighter-bombers, 88, 344
Dibovsky, 246
Dixie Engine Company, 103
Dixmude, 261, 272
Dolphin airplanes, 122
Donis, Commandant, 280
Dore, A. S., 172, 174
Dormie, pilot, 186

Douaemont, Fort, 339
Douai, 21, 77, 78-80, 88, 118, 161,
    209, 211
Downer, C. P., 20
Drama, 213, 214, 215, 224, 228
Dubois, Pierre, 259
Duckham, A., 205
Dunn, R., 76-77
Du Peuty, Commandant, 338

Ellis, pilot, 156
Escadrille Américaine, 336-43
Escadrille Lafayette, 343, 346-47
Eschwege, Lt., 213-23, 224-31
Étampes, 236-37

Farman, Henri, aircraft, 104, 216-
    17, 238
Farman, Maurice, biplanes, 15-16,
    25, 233, 238, 243, 244, 286-87
FE2B's, 120, 121
Fitzmaurice, R., 23
Fokker, Anthony, 13, 33, 36, 39,
    40, 41, 51-52, 94-102, 103-15,
    116-26
Fokker, Edouard, 107, 110
Fokker-Aeroplanbau, 105
Fokker airplanes, 33, 36, 92, 103-
    15, 119-26, 141, 215, 216, 338
Fokker's gun-firing mechanism, 37,
    113, 116-17
Fokker's punctureproof tire, 95-97
Follet, Lt., 83-85
Fonck, pilot, 256
Foulois, Benjamin, 345, 349
Franchomme, Teddy, 250
Francis Joseph, Emperor, 60
Frech, Fritz, 170
French Foreign Legion, 336

Gallez, Captain, 242, 259, 270, 276
Garre, Auguste, 351-52
Garros, Roland, 24, 116, 328-30,
    331-33
Geertz, Captain, 107-08
General Electric Company of Ger-
    many, 124
George V, King, 149
German Air Service, 25
Gilmore, Graham D., 24
Glibert, pilot, 243
Goosens, Jules, 257
Gordinne, Robert and Charles, 264
Gotha bombers, 138, 305, 337
Graffe, Winand, 48
Grahame-White biplane, 234
Green, G. W. M., 217-20, 222-23,
    228
Gregory, pilot, 156

Grey, Spenser D. A., 133
Grieg, O., 62-65
Grinnell-Milne, Duncan, 115
Gros, Edmund L., 335, 336, 337, 338, 342, 343, 346-47
Guynemer, Georges, 186, 256, 257
Gwilt, Lt., 157

Haape, Captain, 337
Hage, Étienne, 265
Haig, Douglas, 143
Halberstadt airplanes, 71-72, 121, 215, 229-30
Hall, Bert, 254, 336
Hall, J. G., 344
Hall, Norman, 347, 352
Hallet, Lucien, 235, 238
Hamel, Gustav, 24
Hamilton, Patrick, 20
Hampson, Lt., 157
Hanciau, Lt., 257
Hanriot airplanes, 278
Harrow-Bunn, Lt., 55
Hartney, H. E., 347, 353
Harvey-Kelly, pilot, 186
Hawkes, Major, 57-60
Hay, John, 61-62
Heagerty, Lt., 81, 82
Heath-Cantle, Lt., 82-83
Henderson, General, 172
Henin-Lietard, 68
Hervey, H. E., 192
Heurtaux, pilot, 256
Heydemarck, Commander, 215, 216
Hiddessen, Lt. von, 128
Hierneau, Captain, 265
Higgins, General, 198
Hill, Dudley, 337, 341
Horter, Wilhelm, 119
Hotchkiss, E., 20
Houthem, 239, 241, 247
Howe, "Swazi," 181
Howlett, F. A., 70-71
Huffer, John, 347
Hunter, Captain, 212
Hythe School of Aerial Gunnery, 205

Ilya Mourametz, 322, 323
Immelmann, Max Franz, 33-34, 35-39, 44, 51-52, 115, 118, 139, 338
Immelmann, pilot (cousin to Max Franz), 55, 66
"Immelmann turn," 36, 115
Inglis, Donald, 182-83
Install, A. J., 113
Ira, Van, 175, 177, 178, 181

Jacquet, Captain, 240, 264, 265

Jagdstaffel No. 2, Royal Prussian, 43, 50, 53
Jagdstaffel No. 11, Royal Prussian, 50, 61, 72, 77, 80, 87, 88
Jamar, Maurice, 265, 272
JN4D training planes, 344
Johannisthal, 102, 103, 108
Johnson, Chouteau, 337
Jones, Ira, 33-35, 172
Junkers, Hugo, 120

Kavalla, 224-26, 227
Keen, Captain, 156, 167, 170
Kirkham, F. J., 83-85
Kirmaier, Lt., 50
Knaggs, pilot, 212
Knight, G. F., 56, 209
Konig, observer, 230
Kusminsky, pilot, 319-20

Laage de Meux, Lt. de, 337
Lahm, Frank, 345
Lamarche, pilot, 272
Lambert, Jean-Marie, 236, 250
Landmann, Werner, 128
Launoit, Arsène de, 235, 265, 274
Lefroy, Captain, 23
Lehmann, H. M. T., 209
Le Prieur rockets, 200, 265
Les Moeres, 256, 257, 259-60, 264, 272
Lettenhove, Carl Kervyn de, 233, 259, 272
Lewis, C. A., 211
Lewis, Cecil Day, 144
Lewis, D. E., 91
Liggett, Hunter, 350
Littauer, Kenneth, 347
Lloyd, G. L., 165
London, 129-30, 131-32
Longcroft, Lt., 21
Loraine, Eustace Broke, 19
Lowenhardt, pilot, 186
Luebbe, Heinrich, 119
Lufbery, Raoul, 254, 337, 341, 347
Luke, Frank, 350-52
Luxeuil, 337, 341, 342
L-W-F Company, 344, 345

Machine gun, synchronized, 113, 116-17
MacLenan, J. E., 62-65
Mangin, General, 339
Mannock, Edward (Mick), 22-23, 148-54, 155-67, 168-83, 185
Marr, Kenneth, 347
Marson, T. B., 211, 212
Martin, Maurice, 235
Martinsyde airplanes, 48, 49

Masson, Didier, 337
Mata Hari, 254
Mathy, Commander, 129-32
May, Lt., 92
McConnell, James, 254, 336
McCudden, J. B., 153
McCudden, W. T. J., 20
McElroy, pilot, 156
Medaets, George and Maurice, 235, 251
Meerendre, Kervyn de, 272
Merrick, G. C., 20
Mevius, Gusto de, 259, 270
Mientjes, H., 211
Minter, Florence, 150
Mitchell, Billy, 346, 347, 349-50, 352, 354
Montigny, Charles de, 266
Moore-Brabazon, J. T. C., 12
Morane-Solnier airplanes, 48, 121, 134, 135
Mouton, Alfred, 264
Mulholland, pilot, 156
Müller, Max, 43

Nancy, 331-33
Nathan, pilot, 21
Naval Flying School, 14
Nesteroff, Captain, 317-19
Nieuport airplanes, 81, 121, 154, 186, 187, 190, 191, 233, 238, 283, 287, 337, 338, 339
Night bombing, 241-43, 244-46
Northcliffe, Lord, 205-06
No. 1 Squadron, British, 240
No. 7 Squadron, British, 192
No. 11 Squadron, British, 187, 188, 195
No. 34 Reserve Squadron, British, 205
No. 40 Squadron, British, 155
No. 56 Squadron, British, 206, 207-08
No. 60 Squadron, British, 198
No. 74 Squadron, British, 172
No. 94th Squadron, U.S., 352-54
No. 100 Squadron, British, 79-80, 81
No. 209 Squadron, British, 91
Nungesser, Charles, 248, 253-54, 342

Olieslagers, Jan, 240, 257, 259, 271, 274
Orban, Max, 236, 250-51, 275
Owen, pilot, 218-19

Pageot, pilot, 271
Pappe, Lt., 128
Paris, 128, 342, 343

Pauli, Jean, 235, 243, 244
Pavelka, Paul, 337
Pegoud, pilot, 24, 328, 330-31
Penguin airplane, 234
Pershing, General, 347, 349-50, 352
Peterson, David McK., 347
Platz, Reinhold, 119
Plumer, General, 178-79
Powell, Lt., 73
Prince, Norman, 334-35, 336, 340, 341, 342

Randall, pilot, 348
Raymond, pilot, 256
RE8's, 240
Rees, Colonel, 21
Reimann, pilot, 48
Renard, Captain, 237, 238
Reymond, Senator, 328
Ribot, Premier, 344
Richard, Adrien, 235, 244
Richards, A. R. M., 80
Richardson, Mr., 205
Richthofen, Lothar von, 72, 74, 85, 87, 88, 91
Richthofen, Manfred von, 25, 26-27, 36, 41, 42, 43, 50, 51-68, 69-86, 87-93, 125, 139, 147, 185, 256, 301, 302-05, 353
Rickenbacker, Eddie, 350, 352-54
Riezenstein, Baron von, 69
Robb, B., 81
Roberts, Ivan A., 351
Robinson, Leefe, 145-47
Rockwell, Kiffin, 336, 340, 342
Rockwell, Robert, 347
Roland biplane, 141, 196, 199
Rosenstein, Willy, 104
Royal Air Force, 143-45, 295
Royal Engineers, 23
Royal Flying Corps, 12, 13, 204
Rumpler airplanes, 106
Rumsey, Lawrence, 337

Salmond, W. G. H., 12
Saxe-Coburg Gotha, Grand Duke of, 57
Scarff, warrant officer, 246
Scaroni, Captain, 257
Schafer, pilot, 186
Schollaert, Florent, 235
Schultz, Felix, 108-09
Schwerin, 109-10, 119, 124
Seekatz, Wilhelm, 119
SE5's, 88, 186, 207, 208, 209, 211, 212
Signal Corps, U.S., Aviation Section, 345
Sikorsky, Igor, 105, 322-25

Silac, Jarousse de, 335, 337
Siraut, Maurice, 251
Smart, Lt., 157
Smith-Barry, 199, 200
Sopwith airplanes, 45, 46, 76, 77, 91, 92, 121, 211, 228, 246-47, 255
Soubiran, Robert, 347
Spad airplanes, 18, 121, 211, 257
Sparks, H. J., 91
Squier, George O., 345
Stead, G., 85
Stewart, Lt., 157
Stiefvater, Otto, 128
Stork Squadron, French, 253, 256

Taube airplane, 327
Thasos, 214, 217, 224, 230
Thaw, William, 254, 336, 341
Thenault, Captain, 337-38, 340-41
Thieffry, Edmond, 236, 238, 249, 278, 282
Thomas, Meredith, 153
Thomson, A. A. B., 27-32
Thornton-Pickard Manufacturing Company, 12
Todd, Captain, 156, 158
Treeby, H. F., 20
Trenchard, General, 192, 208, 338, 349
Trenchard plan, 143
Tyck, pilot, 233

Udet, pilot, 36
United States Air Service, 346

Van Crombrugge, Colonel, 264

Van den Born, Louis, 236
Victor, M., 193, 194
Vincent, Jesse G., 344
Vinson, Lt., 157
Voisin airplanes, 238
Von Below, General, 211
Von Daum, Lt., 100-02
Von Herringen, General, 117
Von Hindenburg, General, 87
Von Hoeppner, General, 140, 338
Voss, Werner, 36, 74, 75, 121, 174, 186
Vraucourt, 53, 56-57

Waal, Bernard de, 119
Warneford, R. A. J., 133, 134-38
Warren, Peter, 76-77
Watt, G. M., 70-71
White, James, 205
Wilhelm, Crown Prince, 117
Wilhelm II, Kaiser, 83, 86, 140
Wilhelmina, Queen, 102
Williams, C. P., 90
Wehner, Joseph, 350-51
Wolff, Lt., 78
Wood, O'Hara, 33-35
Woodbridge, A. E., 88-90
Wortley, Rothesay Stuart, 113-14
Wright, Orville, 344
Wright, Wilbur, 97
Wright airplanes, 235
Wyness-Stuart, A., 20

Zeppelins, 127-38, 141-42, 287, 331-33